THE TAO
OF HEALTH,
SEX
AND LONGEVITY

THE TAO
OF HEALTH,
SEX
AND LONGEVITY

A Modern Practical Approach
to the Ancient Way

DANIEL REID

POCKET
BOOKS

LONDON • SYDNEY • NEW YORK • TORONTO

Dedication

This book is dedicated
to
all spiritual descendants
of the Plain girl,
East and West,
and to
Taoists everywhere,
past and present.

Acknowledgements

We wish to thank to following for providing illustrations:
Huang Chao-Ming, Frances Langton-Lockton, Russel McClay, Chou Yun-yü

Author's and publisher's note: This book is not intended to replace the advice of a trained health professional. If you know, or suspect, that you have a health problem, you should consult a health professional.

First published in Great Britain by Simon & Schuster UK Ltd, 1989
This edition first published by Pocket Books, 2001
An imprint of Simon & Schuster UK Ltd
A CBS COMPANY

12

Simon & Schuster UK Ltd
1st Floor
222 Gray's Inn Road
London WC1X 8HB

www.simonandschuster.co.uk

Simon & Schuster Australia
Sydney

A CIP catalogue record for this book is available from the British Library

ISBN-13: 978-0-7434-0907-0

Printed and bound by CPI Group (UK) Ltd, Croydon, CR0 4YY

Contents

PART II
The Tao of Sex

PART III
The Tao of Longevity

ADDITIONAL RECOMMENDED READING

INDEX

Preface

Tao is the primal power that forges all phenonoma in the universe, from the infinite to the infinitesimal. Invisible yet ever-present, Tao permeates the world with the very breath of life, and those who learn how to harmonize themselves with Tao may harness that power to enhance and prolong their own lives.

Though the principles of Tao were first formulated in words and symbols by the sages of ancient China about 5,000 years ago, Tao predates human civilization and transcends all boundries of space and time, race and culture, for Tao is the universal and enduring Way of Nature. But thanks to the wisdom and insight of the ancient sages who gave birth to the world's oldest ongoing civilization, traditional Chinese culture evolved entirely around the fundamental framework of Tao, and today its principles still lie at the heart of all the classical Chinese arts, from philosophy to poetry, calligraphy to cooking, medicine to meditation.

Tao is more than just a philosophy of life. It's a whole *way* of life, and the only way to realize practical benefits from Tao is to cultivate and practice it. This was the goal of the ancient Chinese sages, and fortunately they left us abundant records charting their progress along the Way. Today, the most enlightened practitioners of modern Western science are also approaching the Tao, but from the opposite direction, and they are arriving at precisely the same conclusions. This is most apparent in the fields of physics and medicine, where the mutable relationship between matter and energy, body and mind, is beginning to emerge. Still, while the conclusions are essentially identical, the poetic imagery and earthy allusions with which the Chinese sages elucidated the Tao and its power are far easier for the average man and woman to grasp than the complex technical jargon favored by modern Western scientists, and therefore it's simpler to view the Tao through Chinese eyes.

This book focuses on three practical aspects of Tao which have always been of vital concern to men and women everywhere: health, sex and longevity. All three are intimately related, and together they form the foundation of human happiness in this world. The purpose of this book is to provide the reader with a lucid introduction to the basic principles of Tao, and to offer a practical program by which men and women everywhere may apply those principles and tap the power of Tao to enhance and prolong their lives.

Research for this book was done primarily from original Chinese sources, although certain English translations of various Chinese texts were also consulted. Except where otherwise indicated, translations from the Chinese are based upon my own interpretations of the materials. My rendering of passages from the TAO TEH CHING, however, closely follows the interpretation of the great English sinologist Arthur Waley, as recorded in his most excellent translation THE WAY AND ITS POWER. In addition, I wish to acknowledge the deep inspirations provided by the prolific writings of the late sinologist John Blofeld, as well as the pioneering work of R.H. van Gulik.

Supporting evidence from Western science was culled from various reference books, medical journals, health studies, magazines, and recent newspaper reports, most of which are cited in the text or listed among the Additional Recommended Reading provided in the Appendix. However, lest readers mistake this book for a mere recapitulation of existing materials East and West, I wish to attest that I have been practicing all the regimens introduced herein for many years and that this book is based as much on personal practical experience as scholarly research.

May this book provide all readers with abundant food for thought and sufficient fuel for practice on the Way to a long and healthy life!

DANIEL P. REID

Phoenix Mountain
Peitou, Taiwan
October, 1988

INTRODUCTION

The Tao

History of Taoism in China

> There was something formless yet complete
> That existed before heaven and earth;
> Without sound, without substance,
> Dependent on nothing, unchanging,
> All pervading, unfailing.
> One may think of it as the mother
> Of all things under heaven.
> Its true name I do not know;
> 'Tao' is the nickname I give it.

These mysterious words come from the beguiling, 5,000-word poem on Tao called *Tao Teh Ching*, written almost 2,500 years ago and traditionally attributed to Lao Tze, the 'Old Sage'. The incisive insights contained in the terse verse of this enchanting book form a living fountain of wisdom that has brought comfort, advice and enlightenment to millions of people throughout the world. No other book on earth has been translated as widely and as frequently as Lao Tze's *Tao Teh Ching*, and no book except the Bible has been translated as often into English. As of 1955, there were 100 different translations in print throughout the world, 90 in Western languages, 36 in English alone.

The actual date and authorship of the *Tao Teh Ching* remain, quite appropriately, obscure. However, it has been established with historical certainty, based on consistency of language and metrical structure, that it was composed sometime between the third and fifth centuries BC, and that it was the work of a single author. That a man named Lao Tze existed is also fairly certain, for there are records of such a man, also known as Lee Tan, Lao Tan and Lee Er, in charge of the Imperial Archives during that period. Disgusted by the political chaos and greed that marked his time,

1

he retired from public life at an advanced age and rode off into the western mountains on the back of a buffalo. When he reached the final pass that marked the boundary of the empire, the passkeeper recognized the famous sage and pleaded with him to leave some sort of record of his teachings for posterity. Reluctantly, spontaneously, and with a wily sense of irony, Lao Tze paused on his pilgrimage into oblivion and swiftly composed the *Tao Teh Ching* in 5,000 characters, with the following disclaimer in the first two lines:

> The way that can be spoken is not the real Way
> The name that can be named is not the real Name.

Then, without uttering another word, he rode off into the mountains and was never heard from again.

Tao means 'way', *teh* means 'power', and *ching* means 'book' in the sense of an historical classic. So the title translates fully as 'The Classic Book of the Way and Its Power'. This title was most likely added by later commentators, for Lao Tze had no more use for titles and names than he did for fame and fortune.

Lao Tze did not invent Taoism. Like Confucius, who gained access to the precious Imperial Archives through his meetings with Lao Tze, he simply claimed to recapitulate an ancient way of life that had prevailed in China 2,500 years before his own time, during the reign of the 'Yellow Emperor' (Huang Ti) China's founding father. Both Lao Tze and Confucius revered the Yellow Emperor as the progenitor of Chinese civilization and acknowledged him as the foremost practitioner of the Way.

The Yellow Emperor reigned over a loose confederation of Chinese tribes around 2700 BC. He is credited with having discovered the secret of immortality through the subtle blending of male and female essence during sexual intercourse and the transmutation of the resulting 'elixir' into pure energy and spirit. He kept a harem of 1,200 women with whom he coupled frequently according to the tenets of the 'Tao of Yin and Yang', and at the age of 111 he is said to have achieved immortality and ascended to heaven on the back of a dragon.

The Yellow Emperor learned the Tao of Yin and Yang through discourse with his three chief advisors on sexual matters: the Plain Girl (Su Nü), the Mysterious Girl (Hsüan Nü), and the Rainbow Girl (Tsai Nü). Significantly, all three were female. Their conversations are recorded in *The Classic of the Plain Girl (Su Nü Ching)*, a text that dates from the second or third century BC but records information that was already current in China for over 2,000 years. It provides a gold-mine of original material on ancient Taoist techniques in which sexual energy is skillfully utilized to bolster health and prolong life. This remarkably frank and factual book will be explored in detail in Chapter 6.

2

In addition to sexual yoga, the Yellow Emperor was an avid student of herbal medicine, a field dominated entirely by Taoists in ancient China. His conversations with his chief medical advisor Chi Po are recorded in *The Yellow Emperor's Classic of Internal Medicine (Huang Ti Nei Ching)*, which also dates from the third century BC. This book, which remains an indispensable text for students of traditional Chinese medicine, summarized all the medical knowledge handed down in China since the time of the Yellow Emperor and clearly defined the fundamental Taoist principles that lie at the root of Chinese medical arts. Like the Plain Girl, Chi Po frequently reminded the Yellow Emperor of the intimate relationship between health, sex and longevity, a unique and salient point that distinguishes Chinese medical theory from all others.

Huang Ti and Lao Tze were the only ancient sages to leave a record of Taoist thought prior to the era of intellectual ferment that followed Lao Tze's disappearance. Therefore, Chinese historians often refer to Taoism as *Huang Lao Tao*, the 'Way of the Yellow Emperor and the Old Sage'. But the simple word 'Tao' by itself suffices to conjure up in Chinese minds the entire edifice of natural philosophy that has guided Chinese civilization for 5,000 years.

Western scholars often refer to Taoism as one of the world's major religions, but this is not entirely correct. To be sure, an organized church complete with its own 'Taoist Pope' did branch out from the mainstream of Taoist philosophy about 500 years after Lao Tze, but this church has little to do with the original Tao. To paraphrase Lao Tze, 'the way that can be organized is not the real Way'. Indeed, the very idea of an organized church, frocked clergy and religious dogma runs completely contrary to Tao.

Tao is a way of life, not a god or religion. It literally means 'Way' or path – a trail on the journey through life which conforms to nature's own topography and time-tables. Any path but Tao is, by definition, artifice. Western ways, which attempt to conquer rather than commune with the forces of nature, lead inevitably to a schizophrenic split between man and nature. Tao views man as a tiny, vulnerable creature within the grand scheme of things and suggests that our best hope for survival is to live in harmony with the great natural forces that formed us as well as our environment. To go against Tao is like trying to swim upstream against a strong current – sooner or later you will exhaust your energy, grind to a halt and be swept away by the cosmic currents of Tao.

Taoists see the entire universe as suffused with *Tao teh* (power of Tao). This primordial cosmic power has been called 'Tai Hsü' (the Great Void), 'Tai Chi' (the Supreme Ultimate Source), and 'Tai Yi' (the Supreme Mover). It comprises the very 'stuff' of the cosmos, the immaterial material from which the entire universe emerged.

Tao gave birth to the One;
The One gave birth to two things,
Then to three things, then to ten thousand . . .

The One is the Supreme Ultimate Source. When the 'Big Bang' split Tai Chi to create the universe, Yin and Yang emerged as the positive and negative poles of a vast electromagnetic field, thereby setting in motion the ceaseless ebb and flow of forces and phenomena we call the 'universe'. The three things are the Three Treasures discussed below. From the one, two and three evolved all the myriad plants, animals and objects of the universe.

Western religions propose the notion of a supreme being who rules the universe from his throne in heaven, and they refer to him as 'God' with a capital 'G' to underline his omnipotence. The focus of all Western religions is the 'afterlife', and most believers manifest a morbid concern with the fate of their souls after death. As such, Western religions are idealistic rather than practical, more concerned with the next world than this one.

Taoists, on the other hand, speak not of a supreme being but of a supreme *state* of being – a sublime state that lies deeply locked within every human being and can be reached only through the greatest personal effort and self-discipline. This state of being, commonly referred to in English translation as 'enlightenment', is as revered in the East as notions of 'God' are in the West and forms part of every human being's innermost potential.

One of the most distinctive features of philosophical Taoism is what the great sinologist and translator Arthur Waley termed its 'lyrical acceptance of death'. Taoists regard birth and death as transitions from one realm of existence to another rather than as absolute beginnings or endings. As Lao Tze's greatest disciple Chuang Tze told his students, 'How do I know that in clinging to this life I'm not merely clinging to a dream and delaying my entry into the *real* world?' Although the Taoist sage tends to live a long and healthy life in this world precisely because he patterns himself on nature, he also faces death without fear or regret because death too is natural.

. Taoism is concerned primarily with life on earth. It unequivocally equates physical and mental health and insists that only a strong, healthy body can house a strong, healthy spirit, which is why Tao focuses so strongly on health and longevity.

According to Tao, we reap what we sow within our own lifetimes. Therefore, Tao provides the seeds of wisdom we need to cultivate health and longevity in the fertile garden of life, and those who till the soil of Tao

4

with daily practice and self-discipline will surely harvest these luscious fruits. Tao maps a path between heaven and earth, but man must walk it on his own power. Unlike Western religions, which offer salvation in exchange for faith alone, the gates of Tao open only to those who really work hard to cultivate the Way. Tao cannot be petitioned in prayer, but it can be utilized in practice, and those who learn to harness its power will find that 'it is inexaustible'. The prime importance in Taoism of practice over faith, experience over erudition, cannot be overstated. Halfway measures never suffice: one must go 'all the Way'.

Dualistic Western philosophy splits the spiritual and physical realms into two hostile and mutually exclusive spheres and attaches superior value to the former. Taoism regards the physical and spiritual as indivisible yet distinctly different aspects of the same reality, with the body serving as the root for the blossom of the mind. A plant can live without its blossoms but not without its roots, and so it is with people. A person who has 'lost his mind' can still live a long time, but if he loses his heart, lungs or liver he will die, regardless of how intelligent or spiritually enlightened he is.

The essential Taoist approach to life is captured in the phrase *ching-jing wu-wei*, literally 'sitting still doing nothing'. 'Doing nothing' doesn't mean sitting around all day like a lump on a log, but rather doing only those things that really need to be done and doing them in a way that does not run counter to the natural order of Tao and the patterned flow of cosmic forces. It means engaging only in spontaneous, unpremeditated activity, doing things purely for their own sake rather than for ulterior motives, and living in harmony with rather than trying to conquer nature. Perhaps most importantly, *wu-wei* means knowing when to stop rather than overdoing things and knowing when to refrain entirely from inappropriate action. As Lao Tze put the point:

> When your work is done, then withdraw!
> That is the Way of Heaven.

As for 'sitting still', this is the actual Chinese term for 'meditation'. The word 'meditation' confuses or scares many Westerners because it implies 'meditating' on some profound but perpetually obscure idea that is never quite defined to anyone's satisfaction. In Buddhist and Taoist tradition, however, the 'non-activity' of meditation involves a conscious effort to completely *empty* the mind, rather than fill it with intellectual profundities. This sort of meditation is both relaxing and highly invigorating, for it dredges from the mind the incessant internal chatter that burdens and belabors the spirit during normal activity. The resulting calm and mental clarity permit all sorts of spontaneous intuitive insights on Tao.

Taoism remains one of the richest and certainly the oldest ongoing philosophical tradition in the world. A colorful, eclectic philosophy chock full of wisdom and humor, its history is cast with a delightful assortment of eccentric characters. With its unique blend of physical and mental regimens and its equal emphasis on theory and practice, Taoism has come to include such diverse elements as alchemy, deep breathing, calisthenics, sexual disciplines, herbal medicine, diet, heliotherapy, and much more. These various disciplines are discussed in great detail in the various Taoist texts handed down from master to disciple over the ages, and all will be covered in this book. Indeed the Taoist 'bible', a massive tome called *Tao Tsang (Treasury of Tao)*, ranks among the world's lengthiest canons, comprising 1,120 volumes compiled over a period of 1,500 years, and it provides a treasure trove of esoteric information.

Still, when all is said and done about Tao, it all boils back down to the entrancing verse of the *Tao Teh Ching*, which, despite Lao Tze's own disclaimer, packs a lot of Tao into a mere 5,000 words and covers a lot of territory in a few pages. That's because every line can be taken on several different levels at once, and every point reflects the multi-faceted Tao like a jewel reflects light. The *Tao Teh Ching* transcends the relative human boundaries of history and culture, time and place. Therefore, before exploring the incredibly fertile garden which sprang from the potent seeds of Lao Tze's words, let's devote a bit of time and space to a brief review of this remarkably rich little book.

'The Way and its Power'

Here's how Lao Tze illustrates the functional utility of emptiness over form and the dependence of all 'things' on 'nothings':

> We put thirty spokes together and call it a wheel;
> But it is on the space where there is nothing that the usefulness
>   of the wheel depends.
> We turn clay to make a vessel;
> But it is on the space where there is nothing that the usefulness
>   of the vessel depends.
> We pierce doors and windows to make a house;
> But it is on the spaces where there is nothing that the
>   usefulness of the house depends.
> Therefore, just as we take advantage of what is, so we should
>   recognize the usefulness of what is not.

The inherent superiority of emptiness over form and stillness over activity, as well as their indivisible interdependence, is a salient point in many Oriental philosophies. Most Westerners, however, geared as they are to concrete form and activity, usually find this point difficult to grasp. But the way Lao Tze puts it, even a child could grasp it, for Lao Tze patterns his points on simple, solid observations, not on specious abstract arguments. Objective observation of nature has always been the primary method of Taoist discovery, and such observation clearly reveals that 'the whole picture' must always include 'what is not' as well as 'what is' and that the utility of anything springs from the union of opposites.

Water was one of Lao Tze's favorite images, and it remains the quintessential symbol of Tao. Like emptiness, water goes largely unnoticed, yet it possesses far more *teh* than its own opposite elements:

> Nothing under heaven is more yielding than water;
> But when it attacks things hard and resistant,
> There is not one of them that can prevail.
> That the yielding conquers the resistant
> And the soft conquers the hard
> Is a fact known by all men,
> But utilized by none.

Here's a fine example of the manifold meanings tucked into every line of the *Tao Teh Ching*. First, the passage represents a simple, natural statement of Taoist philosophy, identifying Tao with the softness, flexibility, and irresistible power of water. Second, it's a clear-cut lesson in sex, illustrating how woman conquers man by yielding to his passion, using her softness to overwhelm his hardness. Third, this passage is frequently quoted by Chinese martial artists, who use it to explain the superior virtues of traditional Chinese 'soft-style' forms such as Tai Chi Chuan over the 'hard-style' offshoots such as Korean Tai Kwan Do and Japanese Karate.

Another reason Lao Tze admired water is that water benefits all living things without taking credit for doing so. Indeed, after bestowing its life-giving benefits to field and stream, man and beast, water is perfectly content to puddle up and rest in the lowest, darkest, places on earth. It falls as rain from heaven and, when its work is done, it flows down into the deepest recesses of the earth:

> The highest good is like that of water.
> The goodness of water is that it benefits the ten thousand
>   creatures,
> Yet itself does not scramble for attention,
> But is content with places that men disdain.
> It is this that makes water so near to the Way.

By association, this passage also implies the superior virtue of all things symbolized by water, such as the female of the species, who bestows life to all creatures through birth and motherhood yet herself 'does not scramble for attention' in doing so.

Closely related to the image of water is the concept of 'softness' and all its implications:

> When he is born, man is soft and weak;
> In death, he becomes stiff and hard.
> The ten thousand creatures and all plants and trees
> Are supple and soft in life,
> But brittle and dry in death.
> Truly, to be stiff and hard is the way of death;
> To be soft and supple is the way of life.
> Therefore, the weapon that is too hard will be broken,
> And the tree with the hardest wood will be cut down first.
> Truly, the hard and strong are cast down,
> While the soft and weak rise to the top.

This is another favorite passage for practitioners of China's 'soft-style' martial arts. It extols the virtues of non-resistance, of bending with the wind, and the last two lines clearly echo the familiar ring of the popular Christian belief that 'the meek shall inherit the earth'.

Lao Tze lived during a long, chaotic chapter of Chinese history known as the Warring States Period. While dozens of petty princes schemed and vied for supremacy, kingdoms rose and fell like waves on the sea, with alliances forming overnight only to dissolve at dawn and warfare raging throughout the land. The latter part of this period of intellectual ferment was called the 'Hundred Schools Era' and it produced great philosophers such as Confucius, who roamed from state to state trying in vain to persuade the warring princes to adopt his own pacifist philosophy as state policy.

As Confucius' contemporary, Lao Tze naturally had some things to say about politics as well, though he couched his concepts within his usual clever metaphors. Throughout the *Tao Teh Ching* he ridicules such lofty human ideals as benevolence, piety, loyalty and morality, condemning as wholesale artifice all social conventions and scoffing at the notion that people can be ruled by ideology. He points out that the very need for rule by law and threat of punishment indicates that society has already reached an advanced stage of decay. People everywhere are the same, Lao Tze said. When happy and healthy, they naturally treat each other with kindness and respect. When hungry and oppressed, they naturally become cruel and unruly. Since most rulers keep their subjects more or less in a state of perpetual hunger and oppression, they find it necessary to impose from above the unnatural fetters of law and punishment in order to stay on top. Even more ludicrous, in order to justify their privileged positions, they pose themselves to the public as morally superior persons.

The true sage rules the people 'by rearing them and feeding them but not laying claim to them', and by eliminating the *sources* of strife rather than punishing the *consequences*:

> If we stop looking for persons of superior morality to rule
> There will be no more jealousies among the people.
> If we cease to place value on products that are difficult to obtain
> There will be no more thieves.

Thus the enlightened leader rules his people 'by emptying their hearts and filling their bellies'. Most commentators and translators have misinterpreted this line as simply meaning that the best way to rule people is to keep them well fed but ignorant. That's true, but there's much more to it than that. To 'empty the mind' is an old Chinese term that refers to a traditional technique used in Taoist meditation to accomplish the goal of completely clearing the mind of all discursive thoughts, so that intuitive understanding of Tao may rise spontaneously. A cluttered mind obscures Tao, whereas an 'empty mind' reflects Tao like a mirror. Therefore, the sage ruler endeavors to keep his subjects' minds as empty as possible of artificial ideas and desires, for these serve only to confuse people, create conflicts and distract attention from Tao.

To rule people by 'filling their bellies' not only eliminates the major source of strife, it also stresses the primacy of nutrition over ideology, diet over dogma. Last but not least, 'fill their bellies' also refers to Taoist breathing regimens, whereby the breath is pushed deep down into the abdomen with diaphragmic pressure, a technique that requires adepts to 'empty their minds' in order to concentrate on 'filling their bellies' with breath. Such manifold meanings and linguistic versatility run throughout the *Tao Teh Ching*.

One of the most charming and incisive political commentaries in the entire book deals with relations between large kingdoms, what we call 'superpowers' today:

> A large kingdom must be like the low ground toward which all
> streams flow.
> It must be a point towards which all things under heaven
> converge.
> It must play the role of female in its dealings with all things
> under Heaven.

The female by quiescence conquers the male;
By quiescence she gets underneath.

This of course was the cornerstone of China's foreign policy for thousands of years prior to the twentieth century. Conquered several times by Tartar, Mongol and Manchu invaders, China simply lay down and 'got underneath' them, seducing these vigorous barbarian aggressors with the irresistible charms of Chinese food and dress, painting and poetry, music and dance, and, not least of all, Chinese women. Instead of fighting fire with fire, China fought fire with water and won, reducing her rock-hard conquerors to a heap of sand. In the long run, China survived and thrived while her various 'conquerors' passed forever from the stage of history. Such are the benefits of playing the part of the female in foreign relations.

Although the *Tao Teh Ching* was written several centuries before Christ and in a cultural milieu completely different from the West, it bears striking similarities to the spirit of the New Testament, and perhaps this accounts for its enduring popular appeal throughout the Western world. For example, Luke 6:27 advises, 'Do good to them who hate you', while Chapter 63 of the *Tao* suggests, 'Requite hatred with virtue'. In Matthew 26:52 we find the observation, 'They who take the sword shall perish by the sword', which agrees well with Lao Tze's line in Chapter 42, 'The violent man shall die a violent death'.

Conflict can only occur by establishing arbitrary rigid boundaries between opposites and then defending them: boundaries between man and woman, nation and nation, good and evil. By erasing boundaries so that opposing forces may meet and meld and yield to one another, the two blend together and strike a natural balance, automatically eliminating the source of conflict. As we shall see while exploring the various aspects of Taoism in subsequent chapters, balance and harmony among opposites form the philosophical key to all mysteries and the practical foundation of all avenues to health and longevity. Before exploring these mysterious avenues, however, let's complete our historical survey of Taoism in China.

The Parting of the Way

The greatest proponent of pure philosophical Taoism after Lao Tze was Chuang Tze, who lived around 300 to 350 BC. Chuang Tze was by far the best writer among the great Taoist sages of antiquity, and he was especially renowned for his ironic sense of humor. It was he who remarked to his students upon waking from a nap in which he dreamt he was a butterfly that he could not tell for sure whether he were a man who had just dreamt he was a butterfly, or a butterfly who was now dreaming that it was a man.

Chuang Tze was one of Taoism's strongest advocates of *wu-wei*, which he defined as 'getting things done by doing nothing'. In a discourse with his students he said, 'Is there such a thing as true joy? For me, the perfect freedom of doing absolutely nothing is true joy, but ordinary people consider this a waste.' As the *Tao Teh Ching* puts it:

> Tao never does;
> Yet through it
> All things are done.

The sage who patterns himself on Tao also gets things done by doing nothing.

Contentment and humility were the twin pillars of Chuang Tze's life. His sense of humility did not include the Western notion of meekness or self-denial but simply the frank admission that man knows very little about the great mysteries of the universe and occupies only a tiny, insignificant niche within the great scheme of things. As for contentment, he believed that it is a state of mind achieved by simply 'being content', not a process of material acquisition.

After Chuang Tze passed from the scene, the Way began to branch off into various byways, each focusing on a unique aspect of Tao while still growing from the same seeds planted by Lao and Chuang.

Soon after Buddhism began to take root in China during the second and third centuries AD, Taoist philosophy began to exert a powerful influence on the direction Buddhism took as it evolved there. Called *Chan* in Chinese, this sinified form of Buddhism was borrowed first by Korea and then by Japan, where it's known as *Zen*. Such familiar elements of Zen as irreverence toward ritual, non-verbal teaching, instant personal enlightenment (*satori*), philosophical riddles (*koan*), silence and ironic humor all bear the stamps of Chinese Taoism.

There followed in Chuang Tze's wake a series of eccentric Taoist sages the likes of whom the world has not seen since. These were true adepts of the real Tao, not clergymen or charlatans, and they dabbled in everything from alchemy and medicine to diet, deep breathing and sexual yoga. They wrote prolifically, recording their findings in lengthy tomes couched in secret terminology that made sense only to fellow adepts. Some of their ideas and achievements were indeed quite remarkable, if somewhat eccentric, and they merit close attention.

One of the earliest Taoist characters was Yang Chu, who lived around the fourth century BC. He gave rise to the hedonist tradition in Taoism, in

THE TAO OF HEALTH, SEX AND LONGEVITY

which gratification of the senses was regarded as a form of devotion to Tao. Some of his followers and successors indulged in unbridled debauchery, claiming thereby to find the same direct perception of Tao that others did by 'sitting still doing nothing'.

Among the most famous Taoist eccentrics of all time were the crazy characters known as the 'Seven Sages of the Bamboo Grove', who lived during the third century AD, a time when charlatans were corrupting the Tao in order to establish an organized church to compete with Buddhism. They were proponents of the 'Pure Conversation' (ching-tan) school of Taoism, and their goal was to revive the pure philosophical Taoism of Lao and Chuang. They also believed that Taoists should live within the world of men and women, not as hermits isolated from the world in mountain caves. They generally gathered in a bamboo grove near the villa in Honan of the poet Chi Kang (223–262). After an afternoon of 'pure conversation' they would stroll over to a nearby tavern for a night of serious drinking, which they continued until they were all drunk and at one with Tao. All of them were highly talented men who scorned social convention and preferred to devote their genius to Tao. They, like other Taoists through the ages, were renowned as prodigious drinkers with the 'capacity of the sea' for wine. For example, the famous poet and tippler Liu Ling (221–300) wrote all his poems under the influence and in praise of wine. Wherever he went, his servant followed him with a jug of wine in one hand and a shovel in the other, the latter to dig his grave on the spot should he happen to drop dead during a binge. Another famous drinking Taoist of that era was the alchemist Ko Hsüan, who cultivated Taoist deep-breathing techniques by holding his breath under water.

The term used to describe the lifestyles of the Seven Sages and others like them is *feng-liu*, literally 'flowing with the wind', a poetic way of saying 'to fly in the face of convention'. These adepts followed their own internal impulses throughout life, and they relished nothing more than the opportunity to ruffle Confucian feathers with their eccentric behavior. They were highly sensitive to the beauties of nature, and they believed that wine brought them closer to Tao. However, the pure conversationalists were not much interested in alchemy, diet, sexual yoga and other life-prolonging disciplines, because, like Chuang Tze, they regarded death as a transition, leading perhaps to an even better life. They were pure philosophers, and in their writings they preserved for posterity the original pristine spirit of Lao and Chuang.

One of the greatest all-round Taoist adepts in Chinese history was Ko Hung, who lived during the third and fourth centuries AD. A dabbler in philosophy, alchemy, diet, breathing, sex and every other branch of Taoism, Ko Hung wrote 116 volumes on Tao during his lifetime.

Ko Hung's contributions to Taoism were enormous. He wrote astutely on medicine, breath control, hygiene, exercise and sex. He concocted special herbal formulas to help sustain recluses living alone in remote mountain caves. He experimented scientifically in alchemy, and even tried to compound the elusive 'elixir of immortality' from various herbal, mineral and animal extracts. To his credit, he confessed failure in formulating the elixir, although he attributed that primarily to an acute lack of funds needed to purchase the more expensive ingredients and equipment.

Ko Hung represents the apex in the evolution of pure Taoism in China, culminating a 3,000-year tradition that began with the Yellow Emperor around 2700 BC. From Ko Hung's time until the present, the pure branches of Taoism continued to develop with only minor variations and offshoots, closely following the traditions established and recorded by Taoist sages during the 600 years between Lao Tze and Ko Hung. Ko Hung's most devoted disciple, T'ao Hung-Ching, rigorously cultivated the various disciplines recorded in his master's voluminous writings, and he too wrote many essays on the subject. It is said that at the age of 85 he still looked like a man of 35. He too attracted many followers who, in turn, continued the tradition, and so the Way came down to us today.

Taoism is the only major world philosophy that stresses the importance of disciplined sexual relations as an absolute prerequisite for health and longevity. The sexual school of Taoism began to blossom during the second to fourth centuries AD, although the *Classic of the Plain Girl* on which it is based first appeared about 400 years earlier and contained information handed down for at least 2,000 years prior to that. When practiced in private by individual adepts, sexual yoga had never caused much concern to Confucian authorities, who themselves practiced Tao in the boudoir. But when sects arose that practiced sexual yoga *en masse* in Taoist temples, they aroused stern repression and sexual pogroms by government authorities.

The sexual sects of Taoism continued to crop up from time to time right down to the present day. Commenting on their practices, the Buddhist monk Tao An (292–363) wrote 'These Taoists wantonly practice obscene disciplines from the Yellow Book [a secret sex manual], whereby men and women indulge in promiscuous sexual intercourse like birds and beasts in order to avert disaster and death.' Offended Confucian authorities stepped in to suppress these movements. The communist regime which came to power in China in 1949 has proven to be just as relentless and ruthless as its conservative Confucian predecessors. In an article dated 2 November 1950, the communist newspaper *Glorious Daily News* reported that 'shamelessly lustful leaders' held 'beauty contests' for

13

female adepts and 'forced' them to engage in licentious sexual behavior in order to gain health and longevity.

Another major branch of Taoism that began to blossom profusely in China soon after Lao Tze and Chuang Tze was alchemy. The earliest case of alchemy ever recorded East or West dates from 133 BC, when the Taoist alchemist Lee Shao–chün recorded an experiment he performed to transmute cinnabar into gold. The resulting compound was not ingested but rather fashioned into an eating vessel which conferred longevity to whoever ate from it. Lee also practiced deep breathing, diet, herbology and other Taoist disciplines, and he was one of the first Taoist adepts to organize the various regimens into a single coherent system of health and longevity.

Lee Shao–chün also introduced Taoism's first deity. In conducting his alchemical experiments, he required a good stove and intense heat, so he invoked the favor of Tsao Chün, the God of the Stove in Chinese folklore. Later, Tsao Chün became better known as the Kitchen God, and to this day almost every Chinese household throughout the world keeps a shrine to him over the stoves in their kitchens. As 'Director of Destinies', one of Tsao Chün's annual duties is to report the behavior of each family member to Heaven at Chinese New Year, which explains why Chinese families are so careful to curry his favor.

In AD 150, the Taoist adept Wei Po-yang produced the most complete text on Taoist alchemy ever written. Called the *Tsan Tung Chi* (*The Union of Triple Equation*), it discussed the alchemy of the 'External Elixir' (*wai-dan*), which involved refining pills from minerals and metals, as well as the 'Internal Elixir' (*nei-dan*), which involved the inner alchemy of breathing and sexual yoga. Although in the introduction to his tome Wei issues words of warning to dilettantes and charlatans, he also repeats the ancient Taoist view that Tao can be found and cultivated by anyone who is sincerely willing to study and practice its methods.

It was during this same period of intellectual ferment that Chinese medical theory was first formally codified from the vast accumulation of information already collected in China for thousands of years by Taoist adepts. *The Yellow Emperor's Classic of Internal Medicine* and the *Classic of the Plain Girl* were both compiled by this period, which also produced two very important Taoist physicians: Chang Chung-ching and Hua To.

Chang Chung-ching's book *Discussion of Fevers* (*Shang-Han-Lun*), written about 200 BC, remains one of the most important medical texts ever in China. It contains 113 medical prescriptions using 100 varieties of herbal, animal and mineral drugs, including his famous and still popular fever remedy 'Cinnamon Sap Soup', made from cinnamon, ginger, licorice, peony and jujubes. Dr Chang also developed a detailed system of diagnosis based on the Taoist principles of Yin and Yang, the Five Elemental Activities of Earth, Water, Fire, Metal and Wood, and the Three Treasures of essence, energy and spirit (see pages 32–43).

The physician Hua To, who lived around AD 200, specialized in an ancient breathing and exercise therapy called *dao-yin* ('induce and guide'). It is a method for inducing vital energy to enter the body, then guiding it to the various organs and limbs with rhythmic movements. He prescribed it for respiratory and circulatory ailments, constipation, arthritis and rheumatism, fatigue, and depression, and he prescribed it along with herbal formulas and dietary therapy. Hua To also made great strides in surgery and herbal medicine. He developed China's first topical anesthetic from datura, rhododendron and aconite and used it to perform major surgery. Chinese surgery, however, begins and ends with him. Soon thereafter Confucian authorities imposed a strict taboo on cutting open the human body, dead or alive, for they regarded the body as a precious gift from one's parents and ancestors. Cutting open the flesh for surgery or autopsies was thus a grave offence against one's ancestors and, by extension, against oneself.

The next great period of Taoist development occurred during the Tang Dynasty (618–907), universally acknowledged to be China's 'Golden Age' of culture, somewhat similar in spirit to the Renaissance in Europe. Taoism reached its apex of political and social influence during the Tang, not least because the family who founded the dynasty carried the surname Lee, same as Lao Tze, and therefore could claim the great Sage as their imperial ancestor. The Emperor Hsüan Tzung (712–756) declared the works of Lao and Chuang to be official classics on a par with the works of Confucius, and this honor gave Taoism in general a tremendous boost in China. That good image was somewhat tarnished in 820, however, when the Emperor Hsien Tzung died after ingesting an 'external elixir' pill prepared for him from toxic minerals and metals by his Taoist alchemist Liu Pi.

The Tang saw great leaps forward in all three major fields of Taoist research: alchemy, medicine and breathing. After the emperor's untimely death in 820, alchemy moved decisively away from External Elixirs made from toxic minerals and focused instead on Internal Elixirs compounded of human essence and energy. The term *dan-tien* first appeared during the Tang: it literally means 'Elixir Field' and refers to the region two inches below the navel and midway between the abdominal wall and spine where vital energy concentrates and the Internal Elixir is formed. Adepts 'refine' this elixir with breathing, meditation and sexual yoga in order to cultivate a strong spirit-body in which to achieve immortality. This internal alchemy became and still remains the most profound and mysterious of all Taoist disciplines. It is still taught today by a small handful of masters in Taiwan, Hong Kong and a few other Chinese communities outside the mainland. It cannot be mastered without the guidance of a qualified teacher and many decades of disciplined practice.

Medicine made even greater progress than alchemy in Tang China. One of the first decrees issued by the founding emperor of Tang was that all medical knowledge throughout the empire should be gathered and brought to the capital, where in 629 he established China's first medical academy. That was a full 200 years before Europe's first medical school appeared in Salerno, Italy.

Over 1,000 years had already elapsed since Lao Tze rode off into the mountains on his buffalo, and during the subsequent centuries Taoist adepts and recluses had combed the mountains and forests of China collecting and experimenting with various plants, animals and minerals in their quest to develop an elixir of immortality. In the process, they compiled an enormous pharmacopeia in which the chemical and therapeutic natures of all these items were recorded in detail. It is important to realize that Taoist adepts were truly the scientists of ancient China: they conducted their experiments objectively and in full accordance with the scientific methods used today. They recorded all their findings, and their discoveries led to momentous developments in medicine, porcelain, metallic alloys and dyes, and gave birth to important inventions such as the compass and gunpowder. The British sinologist Dr Joseph Needham has catalogued and analyzed the many Taoist contributions to the mainstream of world science in his massive, definitive series *Science and Civilization in China*. You'd be surprised how many things that we take for granted today were invented by the Taoist alchemists of ancient China.

The foremost physician of Tang, and perhaps in all Chinese history, was the Taoist adept Sun Ssu-mo (590–692). Dr Sun cultivated all the traditional Taoist paths to health and longevity, but his favorite approach in treating disease was nutritional therapy. For example, he observed that people living in remote, land-locked mountain regions were highly prone to goiter, an enlargement of the thyroid glands which we now know is due to iodine deficiency. So he prescribed a diet of seaweed and extracts of deer and lamb thyroid, thereby isolating the cause and providing an entirely nutritional cure for this troublesome disease over 1,000 years before it was discovered in the West. He also provided a nutritional cure for beriberi (a vitamin deficiency disease) by prescribing calves and lambs liver, wheat-germ porridge and vitamin-rich herbs such as almond and wild peppers. European physicians didn't figure out beriberi until 1642, again lagging behind Taoist physicians by 1,000 years.

Sun Ssu-mo wrote two editions of his famous book *Precious Recipes* (*Chien-Chin-Fang*), which forms a gold mine of information on traditional Taoist medical theory and practice. In this book are two passages – one on diet and one on sex – that succinctly summarize two of the most basic Taoist approaches to health and longevity. Regarding nutritional therapy he wrote:

> A truly good physician first finds out the cause of the illness, and having found that, he first tries to cure it by food. Only when food fails does he prescribe medication.

And in the section entitled 'Healthy Sex Life', he strongly states the Taoist case for male sexual discipline as a prerequisite for health and longevity:

> A man must not engage in sexual intercourse merely to satisfy his lust. He must strive to control his sexual desire so as to be able to nurture his vital essence. He must not force his body to sexual extravagance in order to enjoy carnal pleasure, giving free rein to his passion. On the contrary, a man must think of how the act will benefit his health and thus keep himself free from disease. This is a subtle secret of the art of the bed-chamber.

These subjects are explored in full detail in the chapters on diet and sex (Chapters 1 and 6–8). The important point to note here is that food and sex, which are nature's two strongest drives and the only two instincts any species requires for survival and propagation, are the two keys that unlock the gates to health and longevity. Conversely, when these two natural instincts are abused purely for pleasure, they pave the quickest way to the grave. Apparently Dr Sun practiced what he preached, for he lived in robust health until the ripe old age of 101.

Another important Taoist advance during Tang times was the development of *chee-gung*, which means 'breathing practice' as well as 'energy control'. *Chee-gung* became the most important method in the alchemy of the Internal Elixir, and it was practiced with great enthusiasm during the Tang era. Formerly, the practice was to retain the breath for up to an hour or more, like the Sage of the Bamboo Grove who liked to cool off by sitting at the bottom of his pond all afternoon. But this method, which often produces interesting visions owing to carbon dioxide intoxication, can only be practiced by a handful of highly advanced adepts and is not particularly beneficial to physical health. *Chee-gung*, on the other hand, was meant for ordinary as well as advanced adepts and focused primarily on controlling and balancing energy rather than mystical goals.

The switch to rhythmic breathing began during the fifth century AD, when the Buddhist monk Bodhidharma (Ta Mo) brought *pranayama* (breathing yoga) from India to China. He combined it with indigenous Chinese *dao-yin* exercises derived from animal movements, and the resulting blend became a fundamental practice and common denominator in Chinese meditative, medicinal and martial arts. The new method stressed respiratory regularity, rhythmic timing, deep diaphragmic breathing, moderate retention of the breath, and the conscious internal circulation of vital energy extracted from air. These breathing methods still form the technical core of Buddhist and Taoist meditation as well as the Chinese martial arts, and they will be discussed in detail in the chapter on breathing (Chapter 3).

Taoism enjoyed its greatest influence in China during Tang, but by the end of the ensuing Sung Dynasty (916–1279) it was already on the wane as a unified national force. During Tang, the higher teachings of Taoism strongly influenced and were gradually absorbed into Chan Buddhism, precursor of Zen, and this influence gave Chinese Buddhism broad popular appeal among common people as well as intellectuals. During the Sung Dynasty, the Confucian scholar Chu Hsi, in a concerted effort to revive and enliven Confucian philosophy as a national ethos, further borrowed many basic tenets of philosophical Taoism to formulate what became known as 'Neo-Confucianism'. Thus, with the higher teachings of Tao well absorbed into Chan Buddhism and Neo-Confucianism, only the vulgar, superstitious elements of the Taoist Church remained as an organized social institution.

It was at this point in Chinese history that true adepts of Tao (*dao-jia*) went 'underground' and retired to remote hermitages deep in the mountains, leaving the Taoist Church (*dao-jiao*) to deal with society.

Taoist hermitages sprouted like mushrooms on China's misty mountains, with small communities of like-minded recluses dedicated to cultivating the 'internal elixir'. The hermits came from all walks of life – scholars and poets disgusted with the 'world of dust', retired generals and magistrates, merchants and mendicants. Unlike Buddhist monasteries, there were few rules and little regimentation, which followed Lao Tze's maxim, 'With no rules, there are no rules to break'. Each adept pursued his own program at his own pace. When not practicing spiritual disciplines, they would read, write, paint, play music and practice martial arts to keep in shape. They welcomed wanderers to spend a night or two, and their main source of income came from pilgrims who flocked there on important religious holidays to participate in festivals – functions that the adepts themselves rarely observed but performed for the benefit of commoners, who left generous offerings of food and money. All in all, as long as one was willing to forgo the comforts and conveniences of urban civilization, life in a Taoist hermitage was about as relaxed as life could possibly be. Many of the hermits lived to be well over 100 years old.

During the Ming Dynasty (1368–1644), Taoist influence at court continued to wane, though the popular Taoist Church with its gaudy temples continued to thrive among the people.

The Manchus, who supplanted the Ming, were even greater prudes than Chinese Confucians, and they took a stern stand against the sexual cults that sprang from Taoism. As a result, genuine Taoism was driven even further underground, and few great Taoist adepts appeared during the Manchu Ch'ing Dynasty (1644–1911), which strictly enforced a highly conservative brand of Confucian classicism until it fell in 1911.

The Appendix at the end of this chapter provides a chronological 'Cast of Taoist Characters' from the Yellow Emperor to the present day, including some sages you haven't met yet.

The Tao Today

There are no organized Taoist sects in China today, though it's possible that a few individuals still practice the Way in private. When the communists suppressed the popular I-Kuan-Tao sect in 1950, they served notice that the Tao was no longer welcome in China. Many masters fled to Taiwan, Hong Kong, Japan and the United States, where they continue to practice their esoteric ways but keep low profiles.

While it is possible to seek out and contact some of these aging Taoist masters, it is not at all easy to be accepted as their students. You may have to spend years serving the master by sweeping his house and performing other mundane chores simply to establish your sincerity – long before he considers teaching you even the most fundamental practices. This has always been the Chinese way. And if you apprentice yourself to a master in Taiwan or Hong Kong, you most certainly will have to learn the Chinese language, although in the West there are a few masters who teach in English. Still, for those who truly wish to cultivate the Way, no effort is too great, no wait too long, no search too arduous.

Indeed, you may well discover an accomplished Taoist master living in your city or neighbourhood simply by broaching the subject with your Chinese laundry-man, chatting up a waiter at your favorite Chinese restaurant, or hanging around parks, markets, herb shops, tea houses and temples in any Chinatown in the world. They often earn their living as physicians and herbalists, astrologers and martial artists, calligraphers and painters, even as cooks and fruit vendors. They generally practice their Taoist disciplines in private at odd hours of the day or night. If you look hard enough, you are bound to find a teacher – or perhaps he'll find you. In any case, a teacher is required only for the higher teachings, especially those dealing with spiritual development. The basics you can learn from this book.

One of the basic benefits of studying Taoism, apart from obtaining health and longevity, is that it unlocks the 'inscrutable' mysteries of the Chinese character and culture.

The Tao runs like a golden thread throughout the fabric of Chinese culture. The basic principles of Chinese cuisine, for example, were all formulated by Taoist physicians and herbalists – not by cooks and gourmets – which explains why Chinese food digests so well in the stomach that you 'feel hungry again an hour later'. In Chinese painting, Taoists established nature as the primary theme of art, and they pioneered the technique of using empty space as a part of the picture. Chinese poets also found much of their inspiration in Tao, and they often emulated Taoist recluses by retiring to mountain hermitages for long periods to cultivate Tao. The arts of Chinese medicine and martial arts were entirely developed by Taoists, as were some of the world's most important scientific inventions, such as gunpowder, porcelain and metal alloys. The key principles of all Chinese arts, such as simplicity and restraint, balance and harmony, and the prime importance of creative spontaneity, all spring from Tao. In fact, so deeply ingrained is the Tao in the Chinese soul that even the communist regime felt obliged to deal with Lao Tze's thoughts by reinterpreting certain passages in the *Tao Teh Ching* to justify their own ideology. For example, the communist version of one key passage reads, 'In antiquity the people did not know private property'; in another passage, 'the mysterious leveling' that occurs when unnecessary desires are eliminated through Tao has been revamped by communist ideologists as a call to dissolve feudal class distinctions.

Lao Tze had no axe to grind, no personal ambitions to realize, no gods to appease, and no time for nonsense. What he endeavored so successfully to convey in the charming verse of the *Tao Teh Ching* was 'dependent on nothing, unchanging, all pervading, unfailing'. The rich tradition of scientific and spiritual inquiry which sprang from his words provides ample testimony to the power of the Way.

The Way is still there, as it always was long before Lao Tze and always will be long after us, and its power is readily available to whoever makes the required effort to discover and cultivate it. As we shall see below, Western science today is slowly but surely – and sometimes reluctantly – coming to many conclusions that confirm the ancient truths of the Tao.

Yin and Yang

The One gave birth to two things . . .

[*Tao Teh Ching*]

The original meaning of the Chinese ideogram for 'Yin' is 'the shady side of a hill'. It represents darkness and passivity, and is associated with the qualities of yielding, softness and contraction. It moves downward and inward, and its primary symbols are woman, water and earth. 'Yang' means 'the sunny side of the hill', represents light and activity, is associated with resistance, hardness and expansion, moves naturally upward and outward, and is symbolized by man, fire and heaven.

Yin and Yang are mutually interdependent, constantly interactive, and potentially interchangeable forces. Despite their polarity, each contains the embryonic seed of the other within itself, as illustrated by the familiar Yin/Yang circle. The circle itself represents the Supreme Source, half Yin and half Yang, each with a dot of its own opposite growing inside it. The S-shaped boundary between the two indicates that their borders are never fixed. Whenever the constant waxing and waning of polar energies leads to a critical excess of one or the other, it spontaneously transmutes into its own opposite. A good example of this transformation is when water (Yin) absorbs so much heat (Yang) that it transmutes into vapor (Yang) and rises upwards (Yang direction). Taoists thus perceive change to be cyclic rather than linear, and therefore predictable. The 3,000-year-old book *Book of Changes* (*I-Ching*) predicts events based on the cosmic interplay of Yin and Yang.

Yin is stronger and more abundant than Yang, but Yang is more obvious and active. There is more water on earth than fire, for example, but fire phenomena such as lightning are more exciting and attract more attention. Still, ever since the term Yin/Yang first appeared in China, the word 'Yin' has always preceded the word 'Yang', and in Chinese this indicates a position of Yin superiority that long antedates the advent of patriarchy in Chinese society.

The cosmology of Yin and Yang goes way back to the misty beginnings of Chinese civilization, long before Lao Tze's time. The earliest written reference to the term appears in the *I-Ching*, written around 1250 BC, in which it states, 'The ceaseless intermingling of Heaven [Yang] and Earth [Yin] gives form to all things. The sexual union of male and female gives life to all things'. The sexual union of male and female is thus regarded as the essential earthly manifestation of the great cosmic dance of Yin and Yang.

A commentary in the *Book of Changes* states, 'The interaction of Yin and

Yang is called Tao, and the resulting generative process is called "change".' Therefore the Way may be found in the interaction of Yin and Yang, in the union of opposites, not in one extreme or the other. Because of the ceaseless flux of Yin and Yang, the primary attribute of the Way is constant change, not stasis.

In the *Book of Changes*, the hexagram which symbolizes sexual union is the 63rd, called 'Completion'. It consists of the trigram for 'water/woman/clouds' placed over the trigram for 'fire/man/light'. This not only places Yin on top of Yang, it also suggests the image of a cauldron of water slowly coming to a boil over a fire. This is the quintessential Taoist image for human sexual intercourse, concisely symbolizing the essential differences between men and woman in the sexual act. In order to last long enough to bring that cauldron of water to a rolling boil, the man must ration his fuel and carefully control his fire. If he burns his fuel too fast, his fire expires prematurely, leaving the water only luke-warm. But if he conserves his fire long enough to bring the water to a boil, then even the smallest flame suffices to keep it hot for a long time.

'Completion' represents the fundamental relationship between Yin and Yang and clearly distinguishes Tao from the dualism of Western philosophy. According to the *Tao Teh Ching*, any force, object or idea is incomplete and meaningless without reference to its own essential opposite:

> Difficult and easy complete one another.
> Long and short compare one another.
> High and low determine one another.

Good has no meaning without evil to define it, beauty is invisible without ugliness to contrast it. In traditional Western thought, opposites are split into two mutually exclusive domains, with value attached only to the good, the beautiful and the true. The evil, ugly and false aspects of life are either deliberately (and vainly) suppressed or simply avoided as 'bad'. The Taoist way is to recognize and balance the opposing forces underlying all situations and phenomena, but no illusions are harbored about 'defeating' any cosmic force, positive or negative.

Newtonian physics, the hallmark of Western scientific thought until only a few decades ago, perceives the universe as a scattered collection of static, unrelated objects, each of which has value and behaves according to absolute laws. By contrast, Taoism sees the universe as a living ocean of flowing forces in a state of constant flux, like waves on the sea, with everything interrelated, interactive and dependent for existence on its own opposite quality.

Complements of Yin and Yang

Complementary couplings of Yin and Yang pervade the entire universe, and their elemental opposition provides the dynamic tension required for all movement and change.

In Chinese medicine, for example, the ten vital organs are divided into five pairs, each consisting of one 'solid' Yin organ and one 'hollow' Yang organ. The Yin organs are more vital than the Yangs, and dysfunctions of Yin organs cause the greatest health problems. The organs are not arbitrarily paired. They are linked by concrete functional and anatomical connections:

Heart Called the 'Chief of the Vital Organs', the heart regulates other organs by controlling circulation of blood. It houses spirit and governs moods and mental clarity. The condition of heart-energy is reflected in the color of the face and tongue: dark red indicates excess, pale grey indicates deficiency. The heart is paired with the small intestine, which separates the pure from the impure by-products of digestion, controls the ratio of liquids to solid wastes, and absorbs nutrients, which it then sends to the heart for circulation throughout the body.

Liver The liver stores and enriches blood and regulates the amount released into the blood stream for general circulation. 'When man moves, blood moves; when man is still, blood returns to the liver,' states the *Yellow Emperor's Classic*. This statement accords precisely with the established medical fact that during periods of rest, especially in cold weather, 30–50 per cent of the body's blood supply collects in the liver and pancreas. During sleep, blood is fortified in the liver for use by the rest of the body during activity. The liver houses the human soul (*hun*), as reflected in the Chinese term *hsin-gan* ('heart and liver'), which means 'sweetheart' or 'dear'. The heart and liver house our most distinctly human attributes.

The liver is the body's metabolic headquarters, and therefore it is most directly responsible for a person's overall sense of well-being and vitality. Liver conditions are reflected in the eyes, fingernails, toenails and muscles. The liver's Yang partner is the gallbladder, whose intimate functional relationship with the liver is well recognized by Western medicine.

Pancreas The pancreas controls production of vital enzymes needed for digestion and metabolism. This function links it directly with its paired Yang partner, the stomach. If the pancreas fails to produce sufficient enzymes, digestion in the stomach stagnates, causing food to ferment and putrefy instead of digest. The pancreas controls the human attribute of rational thought. Its dysfunction is reflected by emaciation of the skin, flesh and limbs, poor muscle tone, chronic fatigue, stagnant digestion and inability to concentrate.

Lungs 'Lungs control *chee*', state Chinese medical texts. Since *chee* means 'breath' as well as 'energy', the lungs govern both breathing and energy circulation. When breath is deficient, so is energy. The Yin lungs are associated with the Yang large intestine. Lung conditions are reflected in the skin, a fact well known to Western medicine, for the skin itself is a respiratory organ, and both the lungs and the large intestine are actually internal extensions of the skin, one pushed down from the top and the other up from the bottom. Pneumonia and other severe respiratory ailments are generally accompanied by constipation, and constipation usually causes distension and discomfort in the chest.

Kidneys 'The kidneys control water'. Excess water and waste fluids are sent to the kidneys and converted into urine, then passed down to the bladder for excretion. Thus the bladder is functionally linked to the kidneys as their hollow Yang partner. The kidneys are called the 'Gate of Life' because they control the overall balance of vital fluids in the body, which in turn directly influences energy level and balance. The kidneys are the major balancers of Yin and Yang in the human system. They house the human attribute of will-power and control the marrow, loins, lumbar and sacral regions. Their dysfunction is often indicated by lower back pains and the inability to straighten the spine. They are closely connected with the adrenal cortex (suprarenal glands), which straddle them and secrete cortisone, adrenaline and vital sex hormones into the blood stream. The kidneys and their related glands thus control sexual functions and potency.

Yin and Yang manifest themselves in every conceivable contrast, large-scale and small. In the human body, Yin controls internal surfaces, lower regions and front parts, both on the body as a whole and on each individual organ, while Yang governs external surfaces, upper regions and back parts. Yin controls blood, Yang governs energy. Innate instincts belong to Yin, acquired skills to Yang. Yin descends, Yang ascends. Eating is a nourishing Yin activity, while drinking alcohol is a depleting Yang activity. In breathing, inhalation is Yin, exhalation is Yang. In the turn of seasons, cool Autumn and cold Winter belong to Yin, warm spring and hot summer to Yang. The list of complements is endless, but the point always remains the same: nothing exists or functions except in direct conjunction with its own essential opposite, and all abnormal phenomena, from disease to thunderstorms, are caused by a critical imbalance between these two primordial forces.

Common symptoms of 'Yang-excess' include red complexion, high body temperature, dryness, hyperactivity, constipation and rapid pulse. 'Yin-excess' is reflected in a pale complexion, chills, dampness in the joints, lethargy, loose bowels and slow pulse. At this point, the Chinese physician steps in and performs an extraordinary balancing act to restore harmony among the body's various energies. Using powerful herbs, acupuncture, massage, diet and other traditional methods, he 'tonifies' deficient energy, 'suppresses' excess, 'cools' heat energy, 'warms' cold energy, 'dries' dampness, 'moistens' dryness, 'drives out' evil energy, and 'cultivates' nourishing energy.

The principles of Yin and Yang apply to everything from the movement of stars and planets to the most minute cellular functions of the body. Taoist dietary laws are based on the Yin/Yang balance of 'hot' and 'cold' foods, 'hot' and 'cold' referring to neither temperature nor flavor but to the sort of energy released when the food is digested. Chinese herbalists concoct and prescribe formulas based on Yin/Yang theory, blending 'warming' formulas for 'cold' conditions, 'cooling' formulas for 'hot' ailments, 'drying' blends for 'dampness', and so forth. In Taoist sexual Yoga, the abundant and powerful Yin element of woman is carefully balanced with the limited and vulnerable Yang energy of man.

Another extension of Yin and Yang is found in Chinese geomancy, known as *feng-shui*, literally 'wind and water'. The science of geomancy is based on both the cosmic and geological aspects of Yin and Yang. Its purpose is to determine the most advantageous position for erecting human dwellings so that occupants derive maximum benefits from the natural flow of cosmic forces in the area. The positions and angles of mountains, valleys, trees, rocks and bodies of water relative to the structure to be erected are carefully calculated to insure that no part of the building interferes in any way with the invisible 'dragon veins' that conduct Yang energy down from heaven and Yin energy up from earth. Temples and hermitages in China have always been built according to *feng-shui*, which perhaps explains why they seem to 'fit' so well into their natural surroundings.

The five elemental activities

The theory of the Five Elemental Activities (*wu-hsing*) further explains the cosmological associations between man and universe. Unlike the five elements in traditional Western philosophy, the Five Elemental Activities of Taoism refer to active forces, not inert elements, although they use similar symbols. *The Yellow Emperor's Classic* states, 'The Five Elemental Activities of Wood, Fire, Earth, Metal and Water encompass all phenomena of nature. It is a symbolism that applies equally to man.'

These five primordial cosmic forces function according to patterned relationships based on their relative characteristics. Each force is generated ('given birth') by one of the other forces and suppressed ('conquered') by a different one, as follows:

Generative (Mother/Son) cycle:

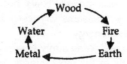

Suppressive (Victor/Vanquished) cycle:

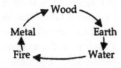

A literal look at the symbols explains their relationships. Wood burns to generate fire. Fire produces ash, which generates Earth. Earth generates and yields forth Metal. When heated, Metal becomes molten, generating the Water element. Water promotes plant growth, thereby generating Wood. Following the suppressive cycle, Wood depletes soil of nutrients, thereby suppressing Earth. Earth soils and channels Water, thereby 'conquering' it. Water suppresses fire by extinguishing it. Fire suppresses Metal by melting it, and Metal suppresses Wood by cutting it. The generative cycle is called the 'Mother/Son' relationship, and the suppressive cycle is the 'Victor/Vanquished' relationship. Their constant interactions produce the myriad phenomena of the universe.

The Five Elemental Activities manifest themselves in the human body through their association with the five sets of paired organs, primarily the solid Yin organs. The heart is ruled by Fire, the liver by Wood, the kidneys by Water, the pancreas by Earth, and the lungs by Metal. For example, there exists a generative Mother/Son relationship between the Wood-energy of the liver and the Fire-energy of the heart, but a suppressive Victor/Vanquished relation between the Wood of the liver and the Earth of the pancreas. Excess Water-energy in the kidneys suppresses the Fire-energy of the heart, sufficient Earth-energy must be generated by the pancreas/stomach organs in order to sustain the Metal-energy of lungs/ large intestine, and so forth.

The Five Elemental Activities have other primal associations as well. There are the Five Elemental Flavors, the Five Seasons, Five Sounds, Five Climates, and others. The charts opposite illustrate the important cosmic

Charts illustrating the Five Elemental Activities and their cosmic associations

Example I:

Element	Wood	Fire	Earth	Metal	Water
Yin organ	Liver	Heart	Spleen	Lungs	Kidney
Yang organ	Gall bladder	Small intestine	Stomach	Large intestine	Bladder
Sense commanded	Sight	Words	Taste	Smell	Hearing
Nourishes the	Muscles	Blood vessels	Fat	Skin	Bones
Expands into the	Nails	Color	Lips	Body hair	Hair on head
Liquid emitted	Tears	Sweat	Saliva	Mucus	Urine
Bodily smell	Rancid	Scorched	Fragrant	Fleshy	Putrid
Associated temperament	Depressed	Emotions up & down	Obsession	Anguish	Fear
	Anger	Joy	Sympathy	Grief	
Flavor*	Sour	Bitter	Sweet	Pungent	Salt
Sound	Shout	Laugh	Sing	Weep	Groan
Dangerous type of weather	Wind	Heat	Humidity	Dryness	Cold
Season	Spring	Summer	Mid-summer	Autumn	Winter
Color	Green	Red	Yellow	White	Black
Direction	East	South	Centre	West	North
Development	Birth	Growth	Transformation	Harvest	Store
Beneficial cereal	Wheat	Millet	Rye	Rice	Beans
Beneficial meat	Chicken	Mutton	Beef	Horse	Pork
Musical note	chio	chih	kung	shang	yu

* Sour like vinegar, bitter like bitter lemon, sweet like sugar, pungent like ginger, salt like common salt.

Example II: *Wu-hsing correspondences*

Activity	wood	fire	earth	metal	water
Direction	east	south	centre	west	north
Color	blue/green	red	yellow	white	black
Numbers	8 and 3	2 and 7	10 and 5	4 and 9	6 and 1
Climate	windy	hot	wet	dry	cold
Planet	Jupiter	Mars	Saturn	Venus	Mercury
Sound	shouting	laughing	singing	weeping	groaning
Virtue	benevolence	propriety	faith	rectitude	wisdom
Emotion	anger	joy	sympathy	grief	fear
Hour	3–7 a.m.	9 a.m.–1 p.m.	1–3, 7–9 a.m. 1–3, 7–9 p.m.	3–7 p.m.	9 p.m.–1 a.m.
Animal	dragon	phoenix	ox	tiger	snake, tortoise
Celestial Stem:					
(yin)	i	ting	chi	hsin	kuei
(yang)	chia	ping	wu	kéng	jén
Terrestial Branches:	yin, mao	ssû, wu	ch'ou, wei, ch'ên, hsü	shén, yu	tzû, hai
Zodiac	Gemini, Cancer	Virgo, Libra	Taurus, Leo, Scorpio, Aquarius	Sagittarius, Capricorn	Aires, Pisces

associations and systematic relationships of the Five Elemental Activities in convenient form.

Chinese physicians use a combination of Yin/Yang and the Five Elemental Activities to diagnose the cause and chart the course of disease and debility, as well as to prescribe appropriate remedies. It is a basic tenet of Taoism that the same primordial principles that govern the universe at large also run through each and every part of it according to the same patterns. This is also the conclusion of modern quantum physics, which regards the entire universe as a giant macrocosmic atom, and the atom as a mini-universe. Chinese doctors view the human body as a microcosm of the universe, and they make no distinctions between 'nature' and 'human nature', as in Western dualism, which isolates man from his roots in nature. Following are a few simple examples of how the Five Elemental Activities come into play in traditional Chinese diagnosis and treatment:

A person with a volatile temper who suffers from blurry vision and frequently shouts at people would be diagnosed as suffering from liver inflammation because, according to our chart, liver conditions are reflected in the eyes and associated with the emotion of anger and the sound of shouting. When the Wood-energy of an inflamed liver burns out of control, it causes over-excitation of Fire-energy in the heart, according to the generative relation of Wood to Fire. The doctor might take one or two approaches to re-balance the affected energies: either sedate the liver in order to suppress its inflammatory effects on the heart; or else tonify the kidneys to enhance their Water-energy, which is doubly effective because Water-energy nourishes the Wood of the agitated liver while at the same time suppressing the excess Fire fanned in the heart by the over-active Wood-energy of the liver.

A child who suffers from chronic fear (Water emotion) tends to wet his bed (a Water function), and therefore he probably suffers from a deficiency of kidney-energy (a Water organ). Comforting words and stern warnings can never 'talk' a child out of this condition. Instead, the Chinese approach would be to tonify the child's kidneys with appropriate diet, herbs, and acupuncture therapy, thereby enhancing kidney-energy to the point that the emotion of fear associated with kidney deficiency disappears along with the associated symptom of incontinence.

A person with a very red complexion (Fire color), who tends to laugh a lot (Fire sound) and is exceedingly jovial (Fire emotion) probably has an over-active heart (Fire organ). Here again there are two avenues of approach to quelling the Fire: one is to sedate heart energy with cooling Yin herbs; the other is to tonify the kidneys, as in the first example, thereby enhancing Water-energy sufficiently to suppress excess Fire-energy in the heart through the Victor/Vanquished relation of Water to Fire.

[Reid, *Chinese Herbal Medicine*]

The permutations and combinations of this system are complex and infinite, and the Chinese physician must learn to juggle all factors, internal and external, in making his diagnosis. Then he applies the same system of complementary forces in reverse to effect a cure. This requires a lot of practical clinical experience, what the Chinese call *lin-chuang* or 'bedside experience'. As in all the Taoist arts, the key to success in medicine is practice, not theory, and the measure of that success lies in practical results, not abstract deductions.

The Chinese medical system takes into account many vital health factors that are largely ignored or misunderstood in Western medicine. For example, when certain climatic conditions become extreme, such as wind or heat or dampness, specific internal organs are directly affected through the system of associated energies. Therefore, the Chinese always adjust their diets according to the weather and the season, in order to balance internal and external energy conditions. In highly humid climates and seasons, Chinese menus strongly favor ginger, garlic, peppers and other pungent Fire-energy flavors because they balance and 'dry out' excess dampness accumulated in the body from the climate and expel it in the form of perspiration. In winter, 'warming' foods and herbs are used to combat external cold, and in summer 'cooling' foods protect the vital organs from damage by external heat. Today, modern refrigeration and rapid transport systems have made all types of foods available all year round in most Western countries, which has only served to drive Western diets even further from the seasonal patterns intended by nature.

Sudden shifts in emotion and mood can trigger a chain-reaction of energy imbalance throughout the body, and these reactions are just as strong as those caused by wind and heat, diet and drugs. It is a well-known fact even in Western medicine that a person suffering from extreme personal grief, such as the death of a spouse, becomes highly vulnerable to all sorts of disease and debility, and if the grief is prolonged the damage can become irreversible. Fear, as we have seen, is a symptom of temporary kidney dysfunction, but prolonged chronic fear can cause permanent kidney damage. Frequent fits of anger reflect liver problems, but a person who is by nature angry all the time will damage an otherwise

29

healthy liver, which then generates even more anger in a vicious psycho-somatic circle. In Chinese medicine, physiological and psychological factors are as inseparable as Yin and Yang. The idea of treating patients suffering from serious mental and emotional disturbances by lying them down on a psychiatrist's couch and talking about it strikes Chinese physicians as a method more appropriate for spiritual exorcism in temple ceremonies but entirely useless from a medical viewpoint. As we shall see, recent research in nutritional therapy has confirmed the invisible links between physical and mental health, a fact of life known and recorded by Taoists thousands of years ago.

The dynamic duo today

Yin and Yang, perhaps the most ancient Chinese idea on record, remain intricately involved in the daily life of Chinese people today. Chinese architects consult Taoist geomancers prior to constructing modern sky-scrapers, Chinese doctors apply the system in diagnosing and treating patients, Chinese chefs balance ingredients and harmonize flavors according to their natural affinities, and so forth. Perhaps one reason that Chinese students today excel so remarkably in modern quantum theory and nuclear physics is that they already possess an inherent understanding of Yin and Yang, which is precisely the direction modern physics is taking today.

While most Western scientists continue to ignore the ancient Chinese theory of Yin and Yang, the few with sufficient imagination to explore the field with unbiased objectivity have been consistently amazed by its accuracy. Soulie de Morant, the French Consul in Shanghai who introduced Chinese acupuncture to Europe, wrote in 1919:

> The Chinese call the positive energy Yang and attribute its origin to the sun and stars; the negative energy is called Yin and they attribute its origin to earth. . . .
>
> How could the ancient Chinese (for these are ideas reproduced from works that date from the 28th century BC) have perceived these forces and under the name 'Yang energy' distinguished positive atmospheric electricity, and under the name 'Yin energy' the negative charge of earth?

The secret of course is that, proceeding from the fundamental Taoist premise that the human body is a microcosm of the universe. Taoist adepts gained deep understanding of universal cosmic forces by observing and feeling the effects within their own organs and energy networks. While Western science had to wait until the development of equipment sufficiently sensitive to observe, measure and record light waves, electric pulses and atomic particles, Taoists simply 'sat still and did nothing' long enough to awaken their own inner reflections of the universe.

Fortunately for Western philosophy, Western science has finally broken through the barrier of dualism and is now beginning to confirm the traditional Taoist concepts of matter and energy. For example, Einstein's famous equation $E=mc^2$ establishes as scientific fact the ancient Taoist premise that matter and energy (what Taoists call 'essence and energy') are interchangeable. Magnetic fields function in complete accordance with Yin/Yang theory, and no electric current could flow through any conductor without the Yin/Yang polarity of positive and negative charges. In nuclear physics, we find Yin and Yang at work on the molecular level, for it is the push and pull of opposite forces that literally 'glues' atomic particles together to form matter. But when those molecules are further taken apart, we suddenly discover that they cease to exist altogether as matter. Instead, they become vibrating bundles of pure energy organized in certain patterns that give the illusion of solidity when viewed from a distance. This fact takes some of the mystery out of the ancient Taoist (and Buddhist) tenet 'Form is Void and Void is Form', for we see that, as Einstein said, it's all relative to the observer's viewpoint: when Form is taken down to its ultimate constituents we find nothing but Void, and when the pure energy of Void is closely organized in rhythmic patterns it begins to appear and function as Form.

Yin and Yang are ever present in modern life, but we usually fail to recognize them. The airplane you ride across continents and oceans moves forward due to the principle of jet propulsion: 'For every action, there is an equal and opposite reaction.' Thus the forward motion is nothing more than a relative by-product of the combustive thrust coming out the back of the engines. Modern nutritional science speaks of the vital importance of a 'balanced' diet and of the biochemical reactions of certain food combinations in the stomach, such as acid/alkaline, protein/carbohydrate, sodium/phosphorus, etc. This is nothing more than Yin and Yang in modern dress, the same principles the Chinese have been using to unlock the secrets of the universe ever since the heyday of the Yellow Emperor 5,000 years ago.

The Chinese have a remarkable capacity for adopting and adapting foreign ways and adjusting themselves successfully to modern times, but they never do so at the expense of their own deep-seated Taoist beliefs. They regard their ancient traditions as complementary, not contradictory, to science and technology. This attitude is itself a complement of Yin and Yang, with traditional Taoist philosophy providing the intuitive Yin element and modern Western science providing the rational

Yang. Together, Yin and Yang form the 'whole picture', and each prevents the other from distorting things in its own particular light.

This complementary blend of traditional culture and modern science has been the key factor in the incredibly rapid and efficient modernization of East Asia over the past forty years. If the Western world were only able to absorb Eastern philosophy as readily as the Eastern world has absorbed Western technology, it would work wonders for the many modern malaises of contemporary urban lifestyles in industrialized Western societies.

Though the terms of modern science and traditional Taoism may be different, the conclusions are absolutely the same, and since, as Lao Tze said, 'the name which can be named is not the real Name', we need not fuss about names and will focus instead on the forces and relationships to which they refer.

The Three Treasures

The One gave birth to two things,
Then to three things . . .

[Tao Teh Ching]

The Three Treasures of life are: *jing* (essence), *chee* (energy) and *shen* (spirit). Like Yin and Yang, the Three Treasures are distinctly different yet entirely interdependent elements. Unlike the energies of Yin and Yang, which permeate both the inanimate and animate worlds, essence, energy and spirit are associated with life, especially human life. They comprise the three fundamental levels of existence for all living beings: physical, energetic and mental. The Three Treasures are regarded as precious gifts from Tao, the natural legacy of life conferred upon all living beings at birth, and it is their relative strength and balance that determine human health and longevity. In light of their central role in philosophical as well as practical Taoism, we may refer to the Three Treasures as the 'Taoist Trinity'. Along with Yin and Yang and the Five Elemental Activities, they form the theoretical framework for Chinese medical diagnosis and therapy, as well as Chinese martial arts and meditation.

Jing: the essence of life

There are three basic forms of *jing* manufactured within the body. The first is blood-essence, which includes all the various vital elements carried in the bloodstream, such as red and white blood cells and the nutrients absorbed from digested food in the small intestine. The second is hormone-essence, which comes in two forms: life-essence and semen-essence. Life-essence includes all the vital hormones secreted by various glands throughout the body's endocrine system, and which serve as master regulators for growth, metabolism, sexuality, immunity, aging, and so forth. Semen-essence refers to sperm and related male hormones in men, ova and related female hormones in women. The third form of essence includes the heavy fluids such as lymph and the lubricants surrounding joints and other connective tissue (synovial fluid), as well as tears, perspiration and urine. The latter are primarily involved in excretion of waste products and dissipation of stagnant energy. These three forms of essence, along with *chee*, are called the 'Four Vital Bodily Humors'.

Essence and energy are intimately related: '*Chee* is the general of the blood; if *chee* moves, then blood moves.' Since blood follows breath, it stands to reason that correct breathing controls and enhances circulation, and this indeed is a basic goal of Taoist breathing exercise.

According to traditional Chinese medicine, natural immunity factors and resistance to disease are found primarily in the body's vital essence. Here we see another clear-cut case in which Chinese medicine beat Western medicine to the punch by over 2,000 years. In *Time* magazine's cover story of 31 March 1980, there appeared a detailed report on the incredibly effective disease-fighting powers of the newly discovered immunilogical factor 'interferon'. Interferon is not a synthetic product, as most Western remedies are. As such, it confirms the basic premise of Chinese medicine that immunity and resistance are natural factors manufactured within the body in the form of highly refined 'essence'. Even more remarkable is the scientifically established fact that interferon is produced in the body by only three types of cells, cells which correspond precisely to the three forms of 'essence' which Chinese physicians have said all along provide the key factors of immunity.

The first source of interferon is leukocytes, or white blood cells. This corresponds to the 'blood-essence'. The second sort of cell that has been proven to produce interferon is fibroblasts, which are special cells associated with connective tissue. This corresponds with the fluids associated with joints and connective tissue that Chinese theory cites as the second source of immunity factors. The third source of interferon is a type of cell called T-lymphocytes, which produce a variety of interferon that works directly with the DNA master-molecules in transcribing genetic messages and is therefore associated with sexual fluids. The Chinese cite 'hormone-essence', especially sexual hormones, as the third major source of immunity factors. If ever there were an undeniable example of modern Western science confirming the findings of ancient Taoist adepts, this is it.

Chee: the energy of life

A basic premise of traditional Chinese medicine derived directly from Taoist philosophy is that all forms of life in the universe are animated by an essential life force called *chee*. *Chee* literally means 'breath' and 'air' as well as 'energy' and is the exact equivalent to the term *prana* in Indian yoga. Like Tao itself, *chee* is invisible, silent, formless – yet it permeates everything.

Chee takes many different forms within the human system. The most basic form is called *yüan-chee*, literally 'primordial energy'. This refers to the original burst of pure energy that occurs at conception and breathes life into the foetus in the womb. *Yüan-chee* may be compared to the potential energy stored in a battery. It begins to dissipate from the moment of birth, and the rate of dissipation determines one's lifespan. One reason that children are so much more active and energetic than adults is that they have not yet polluted and dissipated their original primordial energy to the degree that adults have. That's also why children don't show as severe symptoms of poor diet and breathing as adults do: they are still protected by strong primordial batteries. But by drawing on these batteries to compensate for poor diet and other bad habits they accelerate the rate of energy dissipation and sow the seeds of chronic debility in adulthood. *Yüan-chee* may be tonified and enhanced through diet, herbs, proper breathing, regulated sex and other Taoist disciplines aimed at recharging primordial batteries, retarding the rate of dissipation and thereby prolonging life.

Another form of *chee* is called *yang-chee*, which refers to vital energy in its volatile, kinetic, active form. It is the sort of energy that builds in the body during the excitement of sexual intercourse and is released in a burst during orgasm. It is associated with warmth, light and motion. *Yang-chee* is like the energy drawn from a battery in the form of electric current. It is absorbed directly from the atmosphere when breathing.

The body produces two distinct forms of *chee* directly from the essential nutrients extracted by digestion from food and water. One is called *ying-chee* or 'nourishing energy', which is extracted from the purest elements of digestion and energizes organs, glands, nerves, bones and all vital tissues. The other type is *wei-chee*, or 'protective energy', which is produced from the coarser by-products of digestion. It circulates across the surface of the body, just below the skin, protecting the entire organism from invasion by extremes of environmental energy such as heat, cold, dryness, wind, etc. When it moves, it feels somewhat like warm water spreading over the surface of the body.

When the *chee* of earth extracted from food and water meets with the *chee* of heaven absorbed from air, they blend in the bloodstream to form the unique variety of vital energy that gives life to the human system. That's why diet and breathing are fundamental and complementary approaches in cultivating health and longevity: they are our primary sources of vital energy. According to the *Yellow Emperor's Classic*. 'The myriad ailments all begin with energy. The moment there is energy imbalance, any ailment might occur.'

Despite its central role in the Taoist Trinity of essence, energy and spirit, *chee* remains the biggest stumbling block for Western students of traditional Chinese medicine. Although Western scientists have no trouble dealing with radar, radio, and gamma rays, ultraviolet light, electricity and other invisible forms of energy, they buck like wild horses when told that similar cosmic currents flow through and control the human system.

In order to bring this crucial point into clear focus for Western minds, we must devote a few pages here to a thorough exploration of the subject of *chee* from a Western scientific viewpoint. Since there exists no equivalent term in English for *chee* or *prana*, we shall refer to it as 'bionic' or 'bioelectric' energy. This combines the idea of living energy uniquely associated with living organisms (bio-) with that of electricity (-electric) and negatively charged ions (-ionic), which as we shall see below comprise the essential nature of *chee*.

Chee with a capital 'C' refers to the sum total of all energy in the cosmos, including gravity, magnetism, electricity, solar energy, radio waves, and so forth. When we speak of it with a small 'c', we refer specifically to the bionic energy that fuels living organisms. *Chee* is to the living organism what electricity is to a computer. Without it, the whole complex mechanism grinds to a halt. In the case of living organisms, the polarity of Yin and Yang establishes the dynamic force field required to move *chee*, much as positive and negative polarity cause electric currents to move. The dynamics of Yin and Yang keep *chee* in constant motion, both in the external environment and within the human system. When the level of bionic energy in the body is diminished, the entire organism loses vitality and becomes vulnerable to disease, debility and premature death.

In DeHufeland's *The Art of Prolonging the Life of Man*, published in France in 1838, we find *chee* described as follows:

> A careful study of the phenomena of the vital force in the organized world leads us to recognize in it the following properties and laws: the vital force is the most subtle, most penetrating, most invisible agent we have known until now in nature; in this respect it surpasses even light, electricity and magnetism, with which in other respects it seems to have the greatest

analogy . . . We find a striking analogy between the vital force and magnetism. The life force can exist in a free or latent state, and in this respect has a close analogy to heat and electricity.

The French, it seems, have a particular affinity for the notion of *chee*. Consider, for example, this statement by Dr J. Belot:

When we consider organic life in the light of biophysics, we find that electric phenomena are at the root of all cellular life and we conclude that the end of everything is an electric charge.

Dr Rene Allendy came to similar conclusions:

In the past, medicine and biology saw life as a simple chemical reaction, that is to say a completely mechanical exchange of atoms and molecules. Though this is still true, we can today interpret it more exactly for we now understand that these exchanges depend on an electric potential so that the essence of this phenomenon is moved from the atom to the electron.

This of course is precisely what Taoist adepts have been saying for 3,000 years – that all life ultimately depends on *chee* (bionic energy) and that all vital functions ultimately depend on *chee* in the vital organs, joints, nerves, blood, and all bodily tissues. The way to retard aging and prevent disease is to regularly 'recharge' the bodily tissues with fresh supplies of pure *chee* derived from fresh food, fresh water, fresh air, and a healthy sex life. While *biochemical* processes are important for health, they in turn rely entirely on sufficient levels of *bioelectric* energy to spark and fuel their functions.

The human energy system is strongly influenced by the various types of environmental energy, especially weather conditions, which the Chinese aptly call *tien-chee*, 'celestial energy'. Man and all other living things stand between the positive Yang pole of Heaven and the negative Yin pole of Earth, and the 'celestial energy' of weather passes through the human energy system just as electricity moves through a conductor. The Chinese have recognized the intimate relationship between atmospheric conditions and human health for millennia, but Western science is only beginning to unravel this mystery.

This brings us to the key issue of air pollution. In March 1968, the French newspaper *Le Monde* reported that the presence of negative ions in the air we breathe facilitates the absorption of oxygen and elimination of carbon dioxide in the alveoli of the lungs, whereas positive ions have the reverse effect. Toxic gases, dust, chemical fumes, and so forth all take the form of positive ions when released into the atmosphere, and these big, spongy ions trap and absorb the light little negative ions, leaving the air virtually devoid of vitality. Pure country air contains an average ratio of two or three negative ions for every positive ion. In cities, the ratio drops drastically to one negative ion for every 300–600 positive ions! Negative ions, or chee, are thus the vital difference between pure and polluted air, not oxygen. A healthy body can purge itself of airborne toxins, but it can do absolutely nothing to compensate for a critical lack of chee in the air it breathes.

In order to function, chee requires a strong electric field to propel it. In Taoist terms it requires the dynamic tension of Yin and Yang. The prime importance to human health and vitality of strong electric fields in the atmosphere is just beginning to be understood by Western science, although Oriental mystics have realized it for thousands of years. Recent research in the United States provides strong scientific evidence to confirm the powerful influence of electric currents and electric fields on human health. The results of this research are reported in detail by Andre van Lysebeth in his excellent book on breathing entitled *Pranayama: The Yoga of Breathing*:

> The importance of this principle and its application to vast fields become evident when we consider the latest discoveries of Professor Warburg of Germany regarding cancer cells. When healthy cells are put into a position where it becomes impossible for them to breathe normally [cellular respiration], they pass into a state of 'fermentation' and then become true cancer cells.
>
> The energy necessary for assimilation by digestion is obtained through the intermediary of the air of the atmosphere by means of an extremely complex electrical process. During this process, adenosine triphosphate (ATP), which is particularly rich in energy, seems to be the carrier of this energy. In nature the electrostatic field exercises an important influence on the 'respiration-phosphorization' chain during which the oxygen of air becomes 'active' to a corresponding degree.
>
> The absence of an electric current is *always* a disadvantage and *always* has negative effects on the vitality of the human being and can even dangerously influence his fertility. *The longevity of civilized man depends to a very high degree on the continual presence of a sufficiently powerful electric field*. The most important physiological functions – cardiac activity, respiration, digestion, metabolism, etc. – are favorably influenced and stimulated by this electric field. *A great many so-called 'modern illnesses' can be traced to the absence or considerable reduction in intensity of the natural electric fields in big towns*. Human beings who are forced to live in

buildings or rooms with metal frames and which therefore have the physical properties of a Faraday cage, from which any electric field is excluded, tire and are exhausted quickly.

Furthermore, modern urban lifestyles have strayed so far from the ways of nature that an actual 'negative field' surrounds urban organisms. The journal *Product Engineering*, published in the USA, defined such devitalizing negative fields (13 February 1967):

> Negative fields: certain spaces formed of plastic, like car bodies, can even produce negative electric fields (fields which reject negative ions and attract positive ions). Plastic furniture as well as plastic seat and wall coverings accelerate mental fatigue in the occupants of the room or the vehicle. Objects and coverings in polyethylene, for example, produce negative electric fields from 5,000 to 10,000 volts/meter: in a space completely enclosed by polyethylene the negative field may reach 100,000 volts/meter.

An article published in the January 1964 issue of *Aerospace Medicine* comes to the same conclusion:

> Clothes are important for the same reason. Certain synthetic materials produce enough electrostatic negative charges to repel the negative ions from the person wearing the clothing.

So, even if you're standing on an alpine mountain breathing the best air on earth, you won't fully benefit from the *chee* if you're wearing a polyester, nylon or orlon shirt and rubber shoes.

If *chee* energy travels by virtue of electrical fields, then how does it move within the body? It moves just as electricity moves through a computer – along well-defined 'circuits'. In Chinese medicine these circuits are called 'meridians', and they form a weblike network of invisible channels that carry *chee* to every tissue in the body. There are twelve major meridians, each associated with a major vital organ or vital function, plus numerous minor and 'exotic' meridians. Acupuncture therapy manipulates vital energy via the body's meridian network, achieving two basic therapeutic effects: *bu* (tonification) or *san* (dispersal). Tonification is caused by inducing energy to flow toward and concentrate in an area or organ where energy is deficient, while dispersal causes energy to move away from areas where energy is blocked and stagnant. Stimulation is achieved by inserting fine needles at appropriate vital points along the energy meridians, by burning moxa (artemisia) sticks over the points, or by using deep finger pressure to stimulate the points.

Most Western physicians, however, continue to insist that meridians are identical with nerve networks or blood vessels, although this is flatly refuted by Chinese doctors. The technique speaks for itself: when a needle is properly inserted at the correct point, not a drop of blood is drawn, nor does the patient feel any acute pain. If you were to stick a sharp needle into a blood vessel or a nerve, you would immediately draw blood or wince with pain, so the conventional Western view of acupuncture simply doesn't hold water. Dr E. Biancini, an avid enthusiast of Chinese acupuncture, explains the electrical nature of acupuncture therapy as follows:

> Some years ago, together with the late Dr. Dimier, a renowned electrologist, we carried out some investigations into the extent of human electricity. A highly sensitive galvonometer enabled us to perceive this electricity and we found that the Chinese acupuncture points had a particularly strong transmitting power. It was even possible, by linking with a copper wire the two San-li points on the leg of the same person, and by amplifying the wave, to note the presence of a continuing current between the two sides of the body. Numerous observations were made which showed that with persons in good health the electric charge averaged eight micro-amperes; the figure for tired people was barely one or two micro-amperes, while for over-excited or tense people it rose to fifteen.
>
> It is fair to suppose that what we call 'life force' [*chee*] is above all this electrical potential, and that when we feel weary and say 'my batteries are flat' the expression can be taken almost literally. Without seeking to reduce them to electricity, *vitality and health show their presence by an abundant bioelectrical charge, by ion exchanges, and by the tension of the electrical potential* and the harmony of all functions. That is to say, good health depends more on the distribution and harmonious diffusion of these 'currents' than is generally believed. The figure of fifteen micro-amperes found in over-excited persons shows that they really live in a state of perpetual 'short-circuit', 'bursting their batteries'.

Here we see that the 'life force' of *chee* is not a static *substance* like blood or neurochemicals but an active *force* in the form of negative ions that is moved by the polar potential of electric fields, i.e. by virtue of the dynamics of Yin and Yang.

The identity of the vital force of *chee* with electric energy opens up exciting possibilities in diagnostic and therapeutic medicine. The Acupuncture Department of the Veterans General Hospital in Taipei,

Taiwan, has recently developed a technique to detect diseases in various organs and tissues long before they become acute by measuring changes in electric currents on the cellular level. Blending the traditional Chinese theories of *chee* and acupuncture with modern electronic technology, the hospital has achieved an 80 per cent success rate in diagnosing the onset of a wide range of diseases before any physiological symptoms detectable by conventional Western methods such as blood tests, stethoscopes, X-rays, etc., appear. The tremendous therapeutic advantage of such early diagnosis is obvious. Appropriately, the hospital decided to name the basic unit for measuring human bioelectric energy the 'chee'.

Wilhelm Reich, the controversial medical scientist, who referred to bioenergy as 'orgone', made a lot of progress in his studies of health and bioelectric energy before the American medical establishment silenced him in the mid-1950s. Regarding bioelectric energy and mental health he wrote:

> We now look at neuroses in a totally different way from the psychoanalysts. They are not only the result of unresolved psychic conflicts or childhood fixations. Rather, these fixations and conflicts cause fundamental disturbances of the bioelectric system and so get anchored somatically. *That is why we think it is impossible to separate the psychic from the somatic process.*

This statement accords well with the ancient Taoist view. The *Yellow Emperor's Classic* describes the connection between emotions and energy as follows:

> Anger causes *chee* to rise, joy causes *chee* to slow down, grief causes *chee* to dissipate, fear causes *chee* to descend, surprise causes *chee* to scatter, exhaustion causes *chee* to waste away, thought causes *chee* to concentrate.

The next logical question is, if *chee* is like electricity and the body acts like a conductor, then how does the body store the *chee* it accumulates from the atmosphere? Here the analogy to a battery is very apt, for, just like a battery, the body stores energy in the electrolytes of its vital fluids. Electrolytes are non-metallic conductors of electricity, such as certain fluids, in which currents are carried by ions instead of electrons. Like battery fluid, the body's electrolytes accumulate and store electric charges as electric potential, then release them upon demand as active energy currents. Here again we see the scientific validity of the ancient Taoist view that essence, energy and spirit are intimately connected and transmutable. Essence (fluids) stores potential energy (electric potential) and releases it again as active energy currents when the spirit (mind) commands it.

To sum up, *chee* is a form of bioelectric energy uniquely associated with living things, while Yin and Yang are the two opposite poles that make *chee* move. The body stores *chee* in the electrolytes contained in vital bodily fluids (essence) and transports it through a complex network of invisible channels called meridians. When *chee* is 'full', the entire organism flourishes. When *chee* is 'empty', vital functions grind to a halt and the organism begins to wither.

Shen: the spirit of life

Shen encompasses all of our mental faculties, including rational thought, intuition, spirit, attention, will and ego. Traditional Chinese thought distinguishes four major aspects of spirit: *hun*, the human soul, associated with Yang and Heaven; *bo*, the animal soul, associated with Yin and Earth; *yi*, thought and awareness; *jir*, intent and will-power.

Unlike Western dualism, which sanctifies the spirit as an independent entity above and beyond the body, Taoism regards the spirit as the flowering blossom of the Taoist Trinity, with essence (body) serving as the roots and energy (*chee*) as the connecting stem. Only well-nourished roots planted in fertile soil generate strong stems and beautiful blossoms. Weak, undernourished roots and dry, brittle stems produce weak withered flowers.

In the most esoteric schools of Taoism, adepts transmute essence and energy into pure spirit during prolonged meditation and breathing exercises. Followers of this path cultivate the Three Treasures entirely through internal methods, refining their own inner essence, and eventually forming a 'mysterious pearl' which grows with practice and confers health and longevity to the adept. This pearl forms the 'embryo' of a spirit-body. The spirit-body corresponds roughly in size and shape to the physical body, but it has no material substance, though it does emit an aura of energy that is perceptible to highly trained adepts and can be measured by modern technology. Such adepts fast frequently, strictly control their diets, maintain celibacy, live in complete solitude, and spend entire days and nights rapt in the deep trance instilled by 'sitting still doing nothing', thus strengthening the spirit-body, just as a weight-lifter strengthens his body with physical exercise. At the moment of death, the adept enters his spirit-body, thereby avoiding the dissolution of consciousness and attaining spiritual immortality. This path is suitable only for monks and recluses, for it takes decades of disciplined devotion, great courage and dedication, and a qualified teacher. The latter is most difficult to find these days.

For the ordinary layperson, however, a different path for cultivating spirit by nurturing essence and energy is suggested. Called the 'parallel practice' or 'dual cultivation' because it involves two partners – a man and a woman – this is the path to health and longevity via Taoist sexual yoga. This method involves the mutual stimulation and exchange of sexual essence and energy between man and woman during properly disciplined intercourse. This path does not lead to the highest goal of forging an immortal spirit-body in which to house the soul at death, but it is a highly effective means of cultivating a strong spirit and a long life in this world. 'Dual cultivation' may be readily learned and practiced without the guidance of a teacher by following the guidelines given in this book in Part II.

The bridge of energy

Western medical science divides body (essence) and mind (spirit) into two separate domains and either ignores or is completely confused by the role of energy. This dualistic division of body and mind, which runs throughout Western thought, is highly irrational and unscientific and is based more on religious dogma than on scientific fact. You don't need to be a scientist or doctor to realize that the strength and integrity of the spirit are directly dependent upon sufficient nutrition and abundant energy, while 'poor spirits' have a directly depressing effect on vital organs and energy. Energy serves as messenger between mind and body and forms a two-way bridge between essence and spirit. The 2,000-year-old Taoist medical text *Classification of Therapies* states, 'Spirit is sustained by energy, the energy is derived from the transformation of essence. Essence transforms into energy and energy transforms into spirit.'

While spirit is a treasure which provides the body's guiding light and essence forms its basic building blocks, energy is the key functional element that links them all in the great 'triple equation'. In the ordinary course of life, there occurs a gradual but ceaseless process of depletion of the life force known as 'primordial' *chee* and when this energy reaches a critical level of deficiency, death follows quickly. The goal of Taoist health regimens is to keep our 'bionic batteries' fully charged at all times, so that both body and mind may draw energy from them as required and optimum health and vitality are constantly maintained.

Practitioners of the Way endeavour to store more energy than they burn by cultivating such disciplines as diet, breathing, exercise and sexual yoga. In the ancient Taoist text on alchemy called *The Union of the Triple Equation*, this process of reversal is called 'returning to the original', which means restoring essence, energy and spirit to their original primordial state of purity and sufficiency. Thus, the mysterious 'Union of the Triple

Equation' refers to the internal harmony of essence, energy and spirit, as well as the union of the positive and negative electrical energies of Heaven and Earth (Yin and Yang) with the bioelectric energy of man.

So much for theory. The rest of this book is devoted to practice. The various programs, regimens and exercises introduced in the following chapters have been successfully used by Taoist adepts for thousands of years to maintain health and vitality, prevent disease and debility, and prolong life. A brief glimpse of the higher spiritual goals of Taoism is presented in the last chapter, but otherwise we will focus primarily on the practical earthly disciplines involved in achieving health and longevity in this life, here and now. What you do with your extra years of life is a matter of personal choice that lies beyond the scope of this book to suggest. Tao offers a practical and powerful way of life, not religious dogma centered around mortality and the 'afterlife'.

In order to make these materials and methods appear less alien and more intelligible to Western readers, abundant evidence from Western science is woven into the traditional Chinese materials presented. That evidence is given primarily to help convince you of the profundity and universal validity of Tao, not to distract you with more theory or incite running debates between Western dualists and Chinese Taoists. Oriental adepts rarely demand rational explanations from their teachers for these practices, for they proceed with their practice on faith, intuitively realizing the validity of the teachings from the concrete results. By contrast, Western people hesitate to take a blind plunge into unfamiliar waters until they first 'test the water' scientifically to make sure it's 'safe'. Therefore, skeptical Western readers may use the scientific evidence presented herein to run a sort of mental 'litmus test' on the original Chinese materials, after which you should place theory on the back burners to stew and jump directly into the fires of practice, which comprise the main thrust of this book. You'll never reach the goal just by thinking about it. As one sage put it, 'An ounce of practice is worth a ton of theory!'

APPENDIX:
Cast of Taoist Characters

Huang Ti (Yellow Emperor): Founding father of Chinese civilization and the first Taoist sage; ruled over a confederation of Chinese tribes around 2700 BC; practiced Tao of Yin and Yang and herbal medicine and is said to have achieved spiritual immortality at age of 111.

Peng Tze: A legendary Taoist adept known as the 'Chinese Methuselah', he is said to have achieved a lifespan of over 800 years; a contemporary of the Yellow Emperor, he appears frequently in Taoist texts on longevity.

Chi Po: The Yellow Emperor's chief advisor on medical matters; their dialogues appear in the *Yellow Emperor's Classic of Internal Medicine*.

Su Nü (Plain Girl): The Yellow Emperor's chief advisor on sexual matters; their dialogues appear in the *Classic of the Plain Girl*.

Hsüan Nü (Mysterious Girl): The Yellow Emperor's second advisor on sexual matters.

Tsai Nü (Rainbow Girl): The Yellow Emperor's third advisor on sexual matters.

Yang Chu: Founder of the Hedonist School of Taoism, he lived during the 4th–5th centuries BC and advocated total self-gratification of the senses as a path to Tao.

Lao Tze: 'The Old Sage', also known as Lee Tan, Lee Er and Lao Tan, he was curator of the Imperial Archives during 4th–5th centuries BC; regarded as the patron saint of Taoism, he wrote the beguiling *Tao Teh Ching* in 5,000 characters before riding off into the mountains on a buffalo, never to be seen again.

Chuang Tze: Lao Tze's spiritual heir and Taoism's greatest writer, he lived during the 3rd–4th centuries BC and was renowned for his unconventional behavior and ironic sense of humor.

Lee Shao-chün: Personal Taoist alchemist to the Han Emperor Wu Ti; in 133 BC he fashioned a golden eating vessel for the emperor from cinnabar, lead and other ingredients, in the world's first recorded instance of alchemy.

Liu An: Nephew of the Han Emperor Ching Ti and author of several important texts on Taoist philosophy and alchemy; died in 122 BC.

Wu Hsien: A Han Dynasty Taoist adept who wrote extensively on the Tao of Yin and Yang as a path to health and longevity.

Liu Hsiang: Alchemist to the Han Emperor Hsüan Ti, he spent the years 60–56 BC trying in vain to concoct an external Elixir of Immortality for the emperor. Later, he wrote and annotated many Taoist texts on alchemy.

Liu Ching: A Han Dynasty Taoist adept who for 130 years took an external Elixir of Immortality in which mica was the main ingredient; according to dynastic records, he was still alive and practicing Tao at the court of the King Wu of the Wei Kingdom, long after the fall of Han, which would make him over 300 years old.

Wei Po-yang: In AD 140, he compiled the *Tsan Tung Chi (Union of Triple Equation)*, which remains the oldest surviving text on alchemy, East or West. Couched in cryptic terms, this text is densely packed with esoteric information on alchemy, hygiene, diet and sexual yoga.

Chang Tao-ling: Started a Taoist health cult during the mid-2nd century AD and later proclaimed himself to be the 'Celestial Teacher' of Taoism; claimed power to reincarnate himself in his own offspring; his descendants officially became the hereditary 'Taoist Popes' of China's popular Taoist Church until the communists expelled them in 1950; he died about AD 175, at the age of 123.

Hua To: One of China's greatest physicians and a highly accomplished adept of Tao, Hua To developed China's first anesthetic and pioneered surgery; developed rhythmic *dao-yin* exercises based on animal forms; he was executed in AD 220, shortly before his 100th birthday.

Wang Pi: One of the Seven Sages of the Bamboo Grove, he wrote the most important commentary on the *Tao Teh Ching* and is regarded as the founder of the 'Pure Conversation' school of philosophical Taoism during the mid-3rd century AD.

Chi Kang: Another eccentric Sage of the Bamboo Grove, he was a great scholar and a poet and wrote essays on the lute and on the Tao of Nurturing Life.

Liu Ling: A renowned 'Drunken Dragon' and the most celebrated drinker among the Seven Sages, he wrote verse in praise of wine and Tao and often greeted visitors to his home stark naked; lived about AD 221–300.

Ko Hsüan: An alchemist and member of the Seven Sages, he practiced breath retention by sitting submerged for hours under water in the pond behind his house.

Ko Hung: Author of *Pao Pu Tze* (He Who Embraces the Uncarved Block), and one of Taoism's greatest alchemists and most prolific writers, Ko Hung was an avid practitioner of Taoist health, sex and longevity regimens during the 4th century AD; he began his life as a Confucian scholar but turned to Tao in mid-life.

Tao Hung-ching: Taoist physician and hygienist who codified Taoist pantheon of deities around AD 500.

Sun Ssu-mo: One of China's greatest physicians and most accomplished masters of Tao, he is author of *Precious Recipes*; Dr Sun lived from AD 590 till 692 and served four emperors; advocated nutritional therapy, rhythmic exercises and sexual yoga.

Lee Tung-hsüan: Director of the School of Medicine during the mid-17th century AD at the Tang capital of Chang-an; author of *Tüng Hsuan-tze* (Mysterious Master of the Cave), a classical Taoist text on sexual yoga, hygiene and herbal medicine.

Lee Po: China's most beloved poet, personal friend of Tang Dynasty emperors during the early 8th century AD, and devoted adept of Tao; he was renowned as a 'Drunken Dragon' and nick-named the 'Wine Immortal'; martial artist, lover of women and occasional recluse, he is said to have died when he fell overboard drunk one evening while trying to embrace the image of the moon in the water from a boat.

Su Tung-po: A great poet and painter of the Sung Dynasty, Su lived from AD 1036 till 1101 and took up Taoist deep breathing and other health regimens in mid-life; he also dabbled in external alchemy.

Chang Chün: The greatest living adept of Tao when Genghis Khan conquered China; the Great Khan summoned him to his field head-quarters in Afghanistan in AD 1219 and was so pleased with his discourse that he appointed him head of all religious life in China.

Chao Pi-chen: 19th century AD Taoist adept of spiritual immortality and author of *Taoist Yoga*, one of the most authentic and detailed guides to the internal alchemy of spiritual immortality ever written.

Lee Ching-yuen: Master herbalist and Taoist adept from Szechuan, born in 1677, died in 1936, at age of 256; advocated ginseng, garlic and pennywort (Hydrocotyle Asiatica minor) for health and longevity; mentor to General Yang Sen.

Yang Sen: Chinese Army general who met and studied under Lee Ching-yuen in Szechuan during 1920s and 1930s, before he joined Nationalist Chinese exodus to Taiwan in 1949; practiced sexual yoga, used 'Spring Wine', and followed other traditional Taoist regimens until his death in Taipei at age 98, due to cancer.

Jolan Chang: Contemporary Taoist living in Sweden; author of *Tao of Love and Sex* and *Tao of the Loving Couple*; follower of Sun Ssu-mo's methods; currently into his late 70s and still going strong.

Huang Hsi-yi: Traditional Taoist physician and adept of internal-energy school of practice, living in Taiwan. A master practitioner of healing the body directly through the energy system of *chee*, he is the author's personal physician and mentor.

"water" ☵

"fire" ☲

"Completion" ䷾

PART I

The Tao of Health

CHAPTER 1:

_____ ◯ _____

Diet and Nutrition

> Food and drink are relied upon to nurture life. But if one does not know that the natures of substances may be opposed to each other, and one consumes them altogether indiscriminately, the vital organs will be thrown out of harmony and disastrous consequences will soon arise. Therefore, those who wish to nurture their lives must carefully avoid doing such damage to themselves.
>
> [Chia Ming, *Essential Knowledge for Eating and Drinking*, 1368]

One of the great advantages of learning Tao is that the same basic principles apply to everything from the macrocosmic to the microscopic. In the case of diet, the overriding Taoist principle of balance between Yin and Yang is established by harmonizing the Four Energies and Five Flavors in foods.

The Four Energies in food are hot, warm, cool and cold. These categories define the nature and the intensity of energy released in the human system when food is digested. Hot and warm foods belong to Yang; cool and cold foods belong to Yin. The former are stimulating and generate heat, while the latter are calming and cool the organs.

The Five Flavors are more subtle distinctions based on the Five Elemental Activities: sweet (earth), bitter (fire), sour (wood), pungent (metal) and salty (water). Each of the Five Flavors has a 'natural affinity' (*gui-jing*) for one of the five 'solid' Yin organs and its Yang counterpart: sweet influences pancreas/stomach; bitter moves to the heart/small intestine; sour has affinity for the liver/gallbladder; pungent affects the lungs/ large intestine; and salty associates with the kidneys/bladder.

The therapeutic effects of the Four Energies and Five Flavors are as follows:

- Cool and cold Yin foods calm the vital organs and are recommended for summer menus, as well as for combating 'hot' Yang diseases such as fever and hypertension. Yin foods include soy beans, bamboo shoots, watermelon, white turnips, cabbage, pears, squash and lemons.

- Warm and hot Yang foods stimulate the vital organs, generate body heat and are recommended for winter consumption, as well as palliatives for 'cold' Yin diseases such as anemia, chills and fatigue. Yang foods include beef, mutton, chicken, alcohol, mango and chilies.
- Sweet 'earth' foods disperse stagnant energy, promote circulation, nourish vital energy and harmonize the stomach. Corn, peas, dates, ginseng and licorice are examples of sweet foods.
- Bitter 'fire' foods such as rhubarb and bitter melon tend to dry the system, balance excess dampness, and purge the bowels.
- Sour 'wood' foods such as olives and pomegranate are astringent, tend to solidify the contents of the digestive tract, stop diarrhea and remedy prolapse of the colon.
- Salty 'water' foods such as kelp soften and moisten tissues and facilitate bowel movements.
- Pungent 'metal' goods such as ginger, garlic and chili neutralize and disperse accumulated toxins in the body.

Taoists balance their diets according to favorable combinations of energies and flavors and strictly avoid combinations that conflict. They also avoid excessive consumption of any single variety of food-energy. For example, frequent excessive consumption of 'hot' fatty Yang foods can cause fevers, heartburn, congestion, chest stagnation and other unpleasant effects of 'heat-energy excess'. As this excess 'evil heat' seeks escape from the body, carbuncles and abseses may develop. Too much pungent food can cause gastro-intestinal distress, upset the stomach and result in hemorrhoids. Even the freshest, most wholesome foods are rendered nutritionally useless if consumed in combinations that interfere with digestion, cause putrefaction and fermentation, block assimilation and cause internal energy conflicts.

Mother Nature's Menu

When formulating personal dietary guidelines, it is helpful first to determine your own basic metabolic type, of which there are three: vegetarian, carnivore and balanced. The vegetarian and carnivorous types each represent about 25 per cent of the general population, with the remaining 50 per cent falling into the balanced category. These human metabolic types stem from the prehistoric switch by some segments of the human species from a fruit and nut based diet to a meat diet.

Vegetarian metabolisms are 'slow oxidizers', which means that they burn sugars and carbohydrates slowly. Because the body must burn sugar in order to provide sufficient energy to digest meat and fat, slow oxidizers have trouble burning sugar fast enough to efficiently digest large quantities of meat, eggs, fish and other concentrated animal proteins. Consequently, large doses of protein foods tend to make vegetarian types feel tired and sluggish after meals. An easy test for metabolic type is to eat a large steak or a whole chicken and see how you feel afterward. If it leaves you feeling 'wiped out', mentally depressed and lethargic, then you probably tend towards a slow-oxidizing vegetarian metabolism, in which case you should restrict protein and fat consumption and favor vegetables, fruits and carbohydrates in your diet. If a large intake of concentrated animal protein leaves you feeling strong, vital and mentally alert, then you probably lean towards a fast-oxidizing carnivorous metabolism.

Since carnivorous metabolisms burn sugar and carbohydrates very rapidly, excess consumption of sugar or starch tends to make them excessively nervous and agitated due to overstimulation of the nervous system. Fast oxidizers derive energy by digesting large quantities of animal fats and proteins, which are sent to the liver for conversion into glycogen. The liver then dispenses the glycogen into the bloodstream in the form of glucose – the only form of fuel the body can burn – in gradual measured doses, as needed. That's why fast oxidizers require a steady supply of protein and fat in their diets and should restrict intake of sugars and starches.

Fortunately, most of us have balanced metabolisms that can handle both varieties of food when properly combined. Although our digestive *tracts* were originally designed by nature for a diet of fruit and vegetables, our digestive *systems* have evolved the capacity to produce the gastric juices required to digest the meat that became part of the human diet 50,000–100,000 years ago. If large quantities of animal protein don't leave you feeling depleted, and if large doses of sugar and starch don't make you nervous, then you are probably a balanced metabolizer who needs only worry about selecting wholesome foods from both categories and combining them properly for consumption. In the Tao of diet, however, these are just the first steps in regulating diet. Season and climate, for example, must also be considered in order to ensure that the extreme external cold winter is balanced by the extra internal heat of Yang-foods, hot summer weather is complemented by cooling Yin-foods, dry climates are compensated with extra moisturizing foods, and so forth. Foods consumed out of harmony with season and climate can cause all sorts of problems, including skin eruptions, constipation, gas, fatigue and bad breath.

Taoists tend to favor local produce because it is far more likely to be fresh and brimming with the vitality of its own *chee*. Today, the modern food-processing industry, in conjunction with high-speed transport, has made it possible to eat Florida oranges in Alaska, frozen prawns in the middle of the desert and all sorts of processed packaged 'junk food' any time of day or night, anywhere on earth. As a result, modern diets are completely out of synchrony with the natural prevailing conditions of geography, season and unseen cosmic forces.

Taoists also make a point of eating foods with natural affinities for their weakest organs and related energy systems. Taoist diets aim at strengthening four major systems in the body: digestive, excretory, respiratory and circulatory. When these four functional systems are properly nourished, harmonized and healthy, the health and vitality of the entire organism are assured.

A major goal of Taoist diets is to enhance sexual potency by stimulating sexual glands and strengthening sexual organs. The purpose here is not to increase sexual pleasure – though that is a definite side benefit – but rather to increase the body's store of hormones, semen and other forms of 'vital essence' required for optimum vitality and immunity. Sexual essence provides our greatest internal source of *chee*, and sexual potency is a major indicator of good health.

Since meat forms such a large part of Western diets, a few Taoist guidelines on meat consumption should be helpful. The great Tang physician Sun Ssu-mo and other Taoist dieticians have always warned against the long-range ill effects of eating large quantities of domestic animal meats, such as beef and pork. The only domestic meat they regarded as safe and healthy for the human system was dog, and that was recommended only for its potent warming effects during the intense cold of mid-winter. The reason that domestic animals are such a poor source of human nutrition is that their own diets consist mainly of kitchen slops, garbage and dried straw. Today, the situation is further aggravated by all the synthetic hormones, antibiotics and other drugs routinely fed to livestock.

Taoists have always recommended wild game as the most nutritionally beneficial type of meat for man. Venison is especially good, primarily because deer feed on all sorts of wild nuts, leaves, berries, barks and other herbs which appear in the Chinese pharmocopeia as remedies for man. The benefits of a wild deer's herbal diet are naturally transmitted to your own system when you eat its meat, just as all the chemical drugs injected into livestock today are transferred to your system when you eat a hamburger or fried chicken.

Note, however, that you will gain very little nutritional benefit from even the freshest wild game if you cook it 'to death'. Any meat that is suitable for human consumption should be eaten as rare as possible, preferably raw or at least partly raw. Steak tartare and Carpaccio are good examples of raw beef dishes that are brimming with their own natural enzymes and are delicious as well. Japanese *sashimi* (raw fish) is even better; indeed *sashimi* is arguably the most nutritionally potent, enzyme-rich, naturally digestible form of animal protein on Mother Nature's entire menu, a fact reflected by the longevity of the Japanese people. Taoists always recommend wild fish from seas and rivers over domestic fish raised in stagnant ponds and fed on 'fish chow'.

The same principle applies to chicken. Chinese physicians today still recommend that their patients consume only *tu-ji* ('earth chickens') and avoid *yang-ji* ('cultivated chickens'). Earth chickens are those left to roam about fields and forests to forage for themselves, rather than being fed the artificial, denatured diets of domestic fowl.

In order to prevent putrefaction, promote digestion and facilitate rapid elimination of wastes, all meals in which cooked meats form the major element should be supplemented with a dose of active proteolytic ('protein-digesting') enzymes, which are readily available at health and food stores today.

You may assist rather than interfere with Mother Nature's digestive principles by observing the following basic Taoist dietary guidelines:

- Eat sparingly, and you will live a long and healthy life. The basic Taoist measure is to eat till you are 70–80 per cent full. Mother Nature invariably punishes gluttons with all sorts of misery. The human body simply cannot utilize the enormous quantities and complex combinations of food with which civilized, sedentary man tends to gorge himself daily.
- Chew food thoroughly before swallowing it. This applies especially to carbohydrates, which require initial digestion by the alkaline ptyalin enzyme in the saliva of the mouth. Gandhi's advice on this subject rings with the wisdom of Tao: 'Drink your food and chew your beverages', which means that solid foods should be chewed to liquid form before swallowing, and liquids should be swallowed as slowly as solid food.
- Avoid extreme hot and cold temperatures in foods and beverages. Excessively hot soup, for example, irritates the tender lining of the

mouth and esophagus, which impairs salivation and peristalsis. One of the worst digestive offenses is to drink ice water or other freezing cold fluids with meals. Such freezing infusions on a stomach full of food freeze shut the tiny ducts which secrete gastric juices in the stomach, thereby halting digestion and permitting putrefaction and fermentation to occur instead. By the time the temperature of the stomach returns to normal, it is too late for proper digestion to commence. In fact, any beverage taken in large quantities together with food dilutes the gastric medium and impairs digestion. Wine and beer, however, are exceptions because they are fermented (i.e. pre-digested) and thus they actually assist digestion when taken in moderate quantities. Even the Bible advises one to 'take a little wine for the stomach's sake'.

The Human Dietary Devolution

Modern man bristles with pride on his 'evolution' from cave man to space traveler and looks upon his primitive past with disdain. When it comes to diet, however, the human species has experienced a severe 'devolution' in eating habits, a devolution sparked by the much ballyhooed advent of civilization, an event that has driven a permanent wedge between man and nature.

For millions of years prior to the tiny drop in the bucket of time which we call 'history', humans and other primates lived entirely on diets of coarse, fibrous foods gathered in nature and consumed raw. Throughout the realm of nature, animals that rely on diets with a high ratio of indigestible fibrous bulk and low concentrations of protein have evolved relatively long digestive tracts, whereas carnivores such as lions and tigers evolved short tracts. The human alimentary canal, which winds its way from mouth to anus with 40 feet of tubing, is one of the longest digestive tracts relative to body weight in all of nature.

Man's dietary devolution took a serious turn for the worse when he 'advanced' to become a hunter of animals and adopted meat as his major dietary staple. This occurred primarily in the northern hemisphere, where flesh became the only viable source of food in winter. Those human populations that switched to meat developed digestive juices and metabolisms capable of extracting nutrients from animal fats and proteins, even though their digestive tracts remained forever fixed in the vegetarian mold. This development is the source of the two basic metabolic types in man, one geared towards a bulky diet of fresh fruits and vegetables, the other to a fiberless diet of flesh.

Agriculture triggered the final stage of human dietary degeneration. When grain became the main staple of the human diet, a new element was introduced into the digestive tract, an element not at all intended by nature as food for man. That culprit is starch. The fact that grains are the only items in the entire human diet that cannot be eaten and digested in the raw state is sufficient proof that these items were not meant for human consumption. Grains became the world's first 'processed foods.'

Evidence indicates that precivilized man knew better than to consume grains as food. It seems that humans first began gathering and later cultivating grains not for food but rather to feed domestic animals and ferment beer. It was only after population pressure made wild plants and animals insufficient to feed the species that man turned to grains for sustenance.

Grains have been the mainstay of the human diet for only 6,000 or 7,000 years, and thus the Taoist sages of ancient China recognized them as relative newcomers to the human diet with deleterious effects on human health and longevity. Throughout the ancient Taoist literature on health and longevity we find the term *bi-gu* ('avoid grains') cropping up over and over. This agrees completely with the findings of such great contemporary nutritional scientists as Arnold Ehret, Dr Herbert Shelton, Dr Marsh Morrison, Dr Norman Walker and V.E. Irons, whose theories we'll look at in more detail later. The fact that for the past several thousand years the traditional Chinese diet has consisted of 80–90 per cent grains simply reflects the requirements of over-population. Taoists who 'avoid grains' live much healthier and longer lives than the general populace, but at least the traditional Chinese diet combines grains much more harmoniously than modern Western diets.

Thanks to the dietary devolution fostered by civilization, the human diet today, especially in the Western world, consists primarily of refined, denatured, overcooked food indiscriminately combined. Some of the consequences people suffer by eliminating coarse fibrous foods from their diets and relying instead on concentrated animal protein and concentrated refined starches are described here by Dr Robert Jackson:

> The removal of this waste matter [fiber] also removes from our foods the natural stimulus to the muscular activity of the bowel wall . . . This means a slowing up of the intestinal current. Slowing up the intestinal current means the decomposition of the protein contents and a fermentation beyond what is normal of the carbohydrate contents, the former resulting in evolution of very depressing poisons and the latter of irritants to the tube lining . . . Thus a vicious cycle is set up, leading to a chronic state

of body poisoning from the food canal, for slowing up not only adds to the fermentation and decomposition, it also allows more time for the absorption into the blood of the poisonous products produced.

About ten years ago, an interesting study was conducted to compare the average daily bowel movements of people in India and America. The results at first baffled researchers: although the average American consumed over three times as many calories every day as the average Indian, the latter produced daily bowel movements that weighed more than double the American average. India's diet, based primarily on vegetables and whole grains, provides a high ratio of fibrous bulk to propel wastes through the alimentary canal, while the typical American diet, rich in processed calories but poor in natural bulk, moves through the digestive tract so slowly that much of it putrefies and ferments rather than digests, and the resulting toxic wastes are retained for days, or even weeks, resulting in a chronic state of toxemia (a form of autointoxification of the blood caused by the constant presence of toxins in the stomach, colon, liver and other tissues). This condition is responsible for a host of chronic ailments rarely found in primitive societies, including arthritis, constipation, gastritis, fatigue, infertility, impotence and lack of immunity to infectious disease.

Master faster and colonic specialist V.E. Irons describes the modern American dietary disaster as follows:

> In many cases, food can stay in a person for months or even years. This food will rot and decay and will get buried in the crevices and folds of the colon . . . Most people's colons, instead of being fast-moving sewer systems, have become stagnant cesspools.

Trophology: The Science of Food Combining

Compared to Taoist concepts of balance, the Western notion of a 'balanced diet' is simplistic and superficial. Western physicians advise everyone to take 'a little of everything at every meal,' jumbling together such disparate ingredients as meat, milk, starch, fat and sugar. Such indiscriminate consumption of food is no different than pouring a combination of gas, oil, alcohol and sugar into the gas tank of a car. These blends will not burn efficiently, will provide little power and will quickly clog up the engine so badly that the entire system grinds to a halt. The advice given in the quote at the beginning of this chapter, from a book presented to the founding emperor of the Ming Dynasty on the occasion of the author's 100th birthday, clearly reflects the fact that the ancient Chinese were well aware of the importance of the science of food combining. This wisdom was once known to the West as well, as evidenced by Moses' strict regulation that meat and milk must never be consumed at the same meal.

In plain English, the Yin and Yang of diet boils down to 'trophology', a term which you and no doubt your doctor have probably never heard before. Modern medical training in the West, especially in America, is notoriously deficient in nutritional science, although there are a few enlightened nutritional scientists in America and Europe today who, despite sneers from their peers in the medical establishment, are making great medical strides through the science of trophology.

The Western scientific equivalent of Yin/Yang balance in food combinations is something we all learned in elementary high school chemistry: acid/alkaline balance, or 'pH'. We all know that if we did add a measure of alkaline to an equal measure of acid, the resulting chemical solution is as neutral as plain water. That's the principle behind reaching for bicarbonate (a strong alkaline) to relieve 'acid indigestion'.

It is an established scientific fact in Western medicine that, in order to initiate efficient digestion of any concentrated animal protein, the stomach must secrete pepsin. But it is also a well-known fact that pepsin can function only in a highly acidic medium, which must be maintained for several hours for complete digestion of proteins. It is an equally well-established fact of science that when we chew a piece of bread or potato or any other carbohydrate/starch, ptyalin and other alkaline juices are immediately secreted into the food by the saliva in the mouth. When swallowed, the alkalized starches require an alkaline medium in the stomach in order to complete their digestion.

Anyone should be able to figure out what therefore happens when you ingest protein and starch together. Acid and alkaline juices are secreted simultaneously in response to the incoming protein and starch, promptly neutralizing one another and leaving a weak, watery solution in the stomach that digests neither protein nor starch properly. Instead, the proteins putrefy and the starches ferment owing to the constant presence of bacteria in the digestive tract.

This putrefaction and fermentation are the primary cause of all sorts of digestive distress, including gas, heartburn, cramps, bloating, constipation, foul stools, bleeding piles, colitis, and so forth. Many so-called 'allergies' are also the direct result of improper food combinations: the bloodstream picks up toxins from the putrefied, fermented mess as it passes slowly through the intestines, and these toxins in turn cause rashes, hives, headaches, nausea and other symptoms commonly branded as 'allergies'. The same foods that cause allergic reactions when improperly combined often have no ill side-effects whatsoever when consumed according to the rules of trophology. The final fact of the matter is this: when you immobilize your stomach and impair digestive functions by consuming foods in indiscriminate combinations, the bacteria in your alimentary canal have a field day. They get all the nutrients and thrive, while you get all the wastes and suffer.

According to a recent survey in America, the average American male today carries about 5 pounds of undigested, putrefied red meat in his gut. Leave 5 pounds of meat in a dark, warm, moist place for a few days and see for yourself the results of putrefaction. The severely septic condition of the human intestinal tract is unique in nature, yet Western physicians take it for granted and even insist that it is harmless to the rest of the system.

In fact, however, in order to protect itself from the chronic toxic irritation of improperly combined meals, the colon secretes large quantities of mucus to entrap toxic particles before they damage the colon's sensitive lining. When this occurs at every meal, every day, every week, throughout the year – as is quite typical in modern Western diets – the colon ends up secreting a constant stream of mucus, which accumulates and gets impacted in the folds of the colon. This results in a narrowing of the passage through the colon and a constant seeping of toxins into the bloodstream by osmosis. When the impacting of toxic mucus in the colon reaches a critical pressure, it causes a pocket to balloon outward through the colon lining, causing a condition called diverticulosis. Colitis and cancer are the next stages of colon deterioration caused by these conditions.

Having correlated the Tao of diet with Western scientific terminology, let's take a close look at the practical side of trophology with some concrete examples of food combining. The following categories of food combinations cover most of the 'culinary crimes' against nature committed daily throughout the world today. This list is based mainly on the work of Dr Herbert M. Shelton, one of America's most distinguished nutritional therapists and author of the 'bible' of correct culinary combinations, *Food Combining Made Easy*:

- *Protein and starch*. This is the worst possible combination of foods to mix together at a single meal, and yet it is the mainstay of modern Western diets: meat and potatoes, hamburgers and fries, eggs and toast, etc. When one consumes protein and starch together, the alkaline enzyme ptyalin pours into the food as it's chewed in the mouth. When the masticated food reaches the stomach, digestion of starch by alkaline enzymes continues unabated, thereby preventing the digestion of protein by pepsin and other acid secretions. The ever-present bacteria in the stomach are thus permitted to attack the protein and putrefaction commences, rendering nutrients in the protein food largely useless to you and producing toxic wastes and foul gases, including such poisons as indol, skatol, phenol, hydrogen sulphide, phenylpropionic acid, and others.

If that is the case, you may well wonder, then why does the stomach have no trouble handling foods that naturally contain both protein and starch, such as whole grains? As Dr Shelton points out, 'There is a great difference between the digestion of a *food*, however complex its composition, and the digestion of a *mixture of different foods*. To a single article of food that is a starch–protein combination, the body can easily adjust its juices, both as to strength and timing, to the digestive requirements of the food. But when two foods are eaten with different, even opposite, digestive needs, this precise adjustment of juices to requirements becomes impossible.'

Rule: Eat concentrated proteins such as meat, fish, eggs and cheese *separately* from concentrated starches such as bread, potatoes and rice. For example, eat toast *or* eggs for breakfast, the hamburger patty *or* the bun for lunch, meat *or* potatoes for dinner.

- *Protein and Protein*. Different proteins have different digestive requirements. For example the strongest enzymatic action on milk occurs during the last hour of digestion, whereas on meat it occurs during the first hour and on eggs somewhere in between. It is instructive to recall the ancient dietary law which Moses imposed on his people, forbidding the simultaneous consumption of milk and flesh.

Two similar meats such as beef and lamb, or two types of fish such as salmon and shrimp, are not sufficiently different in nature to cause digestive conflict in the stomach and may thus be consumed together.

Rule: Eat only one major type of protein at a single meal. Avoid combinations such as meat and eggs, meat and milk, fish and cheese. Insure the assimilation of the full range of vital amino acids by varying the types of concentrated proteins taken at different meals.

- *Starch and acid*. Any acid food taken together with starch suspends secretion of ptyalin, a biochemical fact of life upon which all physicians agree. Therefore, if you consume oranges, lemons and other acid fruits, or acids such as vinegar, along with starch, no ptyalin is secreted in the mouth to initiate the first stage of starch digestion.

Consequently, the starch hits the stomach without the vital alkaline juices it needs to digest properly, permitting bacteria to ferment it instead. A single teaspoon of vinegar, or its equivalent in other acids, is all it takes entirely to suspend salivary digestion of starch in the mouth.

Rule: Eat starches and acids at separate meals. For example, if you eat toast or cereal for breakfast, skip the orange juice as well as eggs. If you're eating a starch-based meal of noodles or rice, avoid vinegar as well as concentrated protein.

- *Protein and acid*. Since protein requires an acid medium for proper digestion, you'd think that acid foods would facilitate protein digestion, but that's not the case. When acid foods enter the stomach, they inhibit the secretion of hydrochloric acid, and the protein-digesting enzyme pepsin can work *only* in the presence of hydrochloric acid, not just any acid. Therefore, orange juice inhibits the proper digestion of eggs, and a strong vinegar dressing on salad inhibits the digestion of a steak.

  Rule: Avoid combining concentrated proteins and acids at the same meal.

- *Protein and fat*. In McLeod's *Physiology in Modern Medicine*, we find a fact accepted by all physicians: 'Fat has been shown to exert a distinct inhibiting influence on the secretion of gastric juice.' For two to three hours after the ingestion of fat, the concentration of hydrochloric acid and pepsin in the stomach is sharply decreased. This delays digestion of any proteins taken together with the fat, which gives bacteria ample opportunity to putrefy the protein. That is why fatty meats such as bacon and 'marbled' steaks, or lean meats fried in fat, sit so heavily in the stomach for hours after eating them.

  Rule: Eat concentrated proteins and fats at separate meals. When you cannot avoid mixing them, eat plenty of raw vegetables to assist their digestion and passage.

- *Protein and sugar*. All sugars, without exception, inhibit the secretion of gastric juices in the stomach. That's because sugars are digested neither in the mouth nor in the stomach. Instead, they pass directly into the small intestine for digestion and assimilation. When consumed in combination with protein, such as cake after steak, not only do the sugars inhibit digestion of proteins by suppressing gastric secretions, the sugars themselves get trapped in the stomach instead of moving swiftly to the small intestine, and this delay permits bacteria to ferment the sugars, releasing noxious toxins and gases which further impair digestion.

  Rule: Avoid consuming sugars and proteins at the same meal.

- *Starch and sugar*. It has been established that, when sugar enters the mouth along with starch, the saliva secreted during mastication contains no ptyalin, thereby sabatoging starch digestion before it reaches the stomach. Furthermore, such a combination blocks passage of sugar through the stomach until the starch is digested, causing it to ferment. The by-products of sugar fermentation are acidic, which in turn further inhibits digestion of starches, which require alkaline mediums for digestion. Bread (starch) and butter (fat) is a perfectly compatible combination, but when you spread a spoonful of honey or jam over it, you introduce sugars to the blend, which interfere with the digestion of the starch in bread. The same principle applies to breakfast cereal sprinkled with sugar, heavily frosted cakes, sweet pies, and so forth.

Rule. Eat starches and sugars separately.

- *Melons*. Melons are such a perfect food for humans that they require no digestion whatsoever in the stomach. Instead, they pass quickly through the stomach and move into the small intestine for digestion and assimilation. But this can happen only when the stomach is empty and melons are eaten alone, or in combination only with other fresh raw fruits. When consumed with or after other foods that require complex digestion in the stomach, melons cannot pass into the small intestine until the digestion of other foods in the stomach is complete. So they sit and stagnate instead, quickly fermenting and causing all sorts of gastric distress.

Rule: Eat melons alone or leave them alone.

- *Milk*. Now we come to one of the most controversial and misunderstood items in the Western diet. Orientals and Africans have traditionally avoided milk – except as a purgative. But in the Western world, people are told to drink milk every day throughout their lives.

If we look at nature, we see that the young feed exclusively on milk until weaned away from it with other foods. The natural disappearance of the milk-digesting enzyme lactase from the human system upon reaching maturity proves that adult humans have no more nutritional need for milk than adult tigers or chimpanzees. Though milk is a complete protein food when consumed raw, it also contains fat, which means that it combines poorly with any other food except itself. Yet adults today routinely 'wash down' other foods with cold milk. Milk curdles immediately upon entering the stomach, so if there is other food present the curds coagulate around other food particles and insulate them from exposure to gastric juices, delaying digestion long enough to permit the onset of putrefaction. Therefore, the first and foremost rule of milk consumption is, 'Drink it alone or leave it alone.'

Today, milk is made even more indigestible by the universal

practice of pasteurization, which destroys its natural enzymes and alters its delicate proteins. Raw milk contains the active enzymes lactase and lipase, which permit raw milk to digest itself. Pasteurized milk, which is devitalized of lactase and other active enzymes, simply cannot be properly digested by adult stomachs, and even infants have trouble with it, as evidenced by cholic, rashes, respiratory ailments, gas and other common ailments of bottle-fed babies. The lack of enzymes and alteration of vital proteins also renders the calcium and other mineral elements in milk largely unassimilable.

During the 1930s, Dr Francis M. Pottenger conducted a 10-year study on the relative effects of pasteurized and raw milk diets on 900 cats. One group received nothing but raw whole milk, while the other was fed nothing but pasteurized whole milk from the same source. The raw milk group thrived, remaining healthy, active and alert throughout their lives, but the group fed on pasteurized milk soon became listless, confused and highly vulnerable to a host of chronic degenerative ailments normally associated with humans, including heart disease, kidney failure, thyroid disfunction, respiratory ailments, loss of teeth, brittle bones, liver inflammation, etc. But what caught Dr Potter's attention most was what happened to the second and third generations. The first offspring of the pasteurized milk group were all born with poor teeth and small, weak bones – a clear-cut sign of calcium deficiency, which indicated lack of calcium absorption from pasteurized milk. The offspring of the raw milk group remained as healthy as their parents. Many of the kittens in third generation of the pasteurized group were stillborn, while those that survived were all sterile and unable to reproduce. The experiment had to end there because there was no fourth generation of cats fed on pasteurized milk, although the raw milk group continued to breed and thrive indefinitely. If that is insufficient proof of the ill effects of pasteurized milk, take note of the fact that even newborn calves fed on pasteurized milk taken from their own mother cows usually *die* within six months, a fact which the commercial dairy industry is loathe to admit.

Despite such scientific evidence in favor of raw milk and against pasteurized milk, and despite the fact that until the early twentieth century the human species thrived on raw milk, it is actually illegal to sell raw milk to consumers in all but a few states in America today. It is far more *profitable* to the dairy industry to pasteurize milk to extend its shelf-life, though such denatured milk does nothing whatsoever to extend human life. Furthermore, pasteurization renders milk from sick cows in unsanitary dairies relatively 'harmless' by killing some, but not all, dangerous germs, and this too cuts costs for the dairy industry.

It required only three generations for Dr Pottenger's pasteurized milk fed cats to become sterile and enfeebled. That's about how many generations of Americans and Europeans have fed on pasteurized milk. Today, infertility has become a major problem for young American couples, while calcium deficiency has become so rampant that over 90 per cent of all American children suffer chronic tooth decay. To make things worse, milk is now routinely 'homogenized' to prevent the cream from separating from the milk. This involves the fragmentation and pulverization of the fat molecules to the point that they will not separate from the rest of the milk. But it also permits these tiny fragments of milk fat to easily pass through the villae of the small intestine, greatly increasing the amount of denatured fat and cholesterol absorbed by the body. In fact, you absorb more milk-fat from homogenized milk than you do from pure cream!

Women worried about osteoporosis should take note of these facts about pasteurized milk products. That such denatured milk does not deliver sufficient calcium to prevent this condition is abundantly evident from the fact that American women, who consume great quantities of various pasteurized milk products, suffer the world's highest incidence of osteoporosis. Raw cabbage, for example, supplies far more assimilable calcium than any quantity of pasteurized milk, yogurt, cottage cheese, or any other denatured dairy product.

Recent studies at the Human Research Center in Grand Forks, North Dakota, indicates that the element boron is also an essential factor in absorbing calcium from food and utilizing it to build bones. Even more noteworthy, the level of estrogen in the blood of women given sufficient quantities of boron more than doubled, eliminating the need for estrogen replacement therapy, which is a common stopgap measure against osteoporosis in the West. And where do we find boron? In fresh fruits and vegetables, especially apples, pears, grapes, nuts, cabbage, and other leafy vegetables, where we also find calcium. Nature has already provided abundant sources of all the vital nutrients we need in synergistic form, but man insists on cooking and processing them to death, and then wonders why his diet doesn't 'work.'

Adults should seriously reconsider milk as a constituent of their daily diets, unless they are able to obtain raw certified milk, which is an excellent food. To stuff children with pasteurized milk in order to make them grow 'strong and healthy' is sheer folly, because they simply cannot assimilate the nutrients. Indeed men, women, and children alike should eliminate all pasteurized dairy products from their diets, for these denatured dairy products only gum up the intestines with layer upon layer of slimy sludge that interferes with the absorption of organic nutrients.

Rule: Eliminate pasteurized and homogenized milk entirely from your diet. If raw certified milk is available, consume it as a whole food in itself, not in combination with other foods.

• *Desserts*. One should avoid any sort of sweet dessert after a big meal, for this type of food combines poorly with everything. Even fresh fruit should be avoided right after a big meal, because it will back up in the stomach and ferment instead of digest. If you really have a 'sweet tooth' and crave cakes, pies and pastries, indulge your habit occasionally by making a whole meal of them. They are still not good for you, but at least taken alone they will not cause as much gastric distresss and toxic by-products as when taken after meals.

Rule: Avoid sweet starchy desserts, as well as fruits, after large meals of protein or carbohydrates.

Correctly combining foods makes all the difference in the world to proper digestion and metabolism. Without complete digestion, the nutrients in even the most wholesome food cannot be fully extracted and assimilated by the body. Moreover, incomplete digestion and inefficient metabolism are prime causes of fat and cholesterol accumulation in the body. A low-calorie diet of overcooked, processed and improperly combined foods will still make you fat and leave sticky deposits in your arteries, just as the wrong mix of fuels will leave carbon deposits on the spark plugs of an engine, clog the pistons, and create foul gaseous exhaust. On the other hand, if foods are properly combined for consumption, then regardless of how many calories or how much cholesterol they contain they will not make you fat or clog up your veins and organs, especially if at least half your daily food intake is taken raw.

If one follows the rules of trophology, there is no need to be a fanatic about controlling one's diet, no need to count calories, and no need to worry about cholesterol. Note also that there is no such thing as a food that is 100 per cent protein or 100 per cent carbohydrate. What counts is whether protein or carbohydrate is the major nutritional element in any particular food. Generally speaking, if a food item contains 15 per cent or more protein, then it's categorized as a 'protein food', while 20 per cent or more carbohydrate makes it a 'carbohydrate food'. When combining different types of food in a single meal, it doesn't matter much if a little bit of protein is added to a basically carbohydrate meal or vice versa, especially if plenty of raw vegetables are included to provide active enzymes and fibrous bulk. Appendix I at the end of this chapter lists a wide range of foods according to the categories of protein, starch, fats, fruits and vegetables. As this list clearly shows, there are plenty of wholesome foods from which to construct a healthy meal, without resorting to artificially refined, processed foods. Appendix II provides sample menus for a week.

Ideally, one should consume only one variety of food at a single sitting. A glance at nature proves this point. Carnivorous animals never consume starchy items with their meat, but they do supplement digestion and occasionally purge their bowels by chewing on wild weeds that have medicinal properties. It has also been observed by birdwatchers for centuries that birds eat bugs and worms at one time of day, seeds and berries at another, but never both together. What makes modern man think that his digestive tract is so different from all other species in nature?

Even though the traditional Chinese diet relies heavily on rice, a closer look at Chinese eating habits shows that, up until the mid-twentieth century, the rice was consumed according to the rules of trophology. For example, when Chinese families eat at home, their meals are usually heavy in fresh vegetables and beancurd products and very light in meats. When Chinese go out for a big banquet in a restaurant, rice is generally not served at all, specifically so that it does not interfere with the enjoyment and digestion of all the meat, fish and fowl that always appear on banquet menus. Today, however, modern lifestyles have eroded these healthy eating habits among urban Chinese, much to the detriment of their health and longevity.

Back in the 1920s, before the modern world had much impact on Chinese lifestyles, an extensive study was conducted in China by Western nutritional scientists to compare the typical eating habits of Chinese and Americans. The regions surveyed were located in central and coastal China, in rural areas where traditional lifestyles and eating habits had not changed much for many centuries, but where relative peace and prosperity gave local households the full range of choice in foods. The study revealed that the average Chinese derived over 90 per cent of their food energy from grains and grain products, with only 1 per cent coming from animal products and all the rest from fresh vegetable sources. A blend of 90 per cent carbohydrate and 1 per cent protein, supplemented with the enzymes and roughage of fresh fruits and vegetables, is about as close to a perfectly combined diet as is practically possible.

The same study then turned towards the eating habits of typical Americans, with most revealing results: 39 per cent of the average American's food energy came from grains, 38 per cent from animal products, and most of the remaining 23 per cent came from refined sugars. Vegetables and fruits accounted for a miniscule portion of the American diet. One could hardly concoct a more poorly balanced diet from the point of view of trophology! According to the results of Dr Pottenger's experiments with cats, the damage from such denatured diets can be transmitted to the next generation.

Let's take a close trophological look at the 'Great American Meal', which is rapidly spreading digestive and metabolic malaise throughout the world via huge corporate fast-food chains. That all-American meal consists of a cheeseburger with French fries, washed down with a milk shake or sweet cola. A cheeseburger combines two different varieties of concentrated protein – meat and cheese. On top of that goes a big, fluffy bun of highly refined white flour – pure starch. Next comes a big bag of deep fried potatoes, thereby adding more concentrated starch, further fattened by deep-frying in stale oil, to the meal. Finally, this mess is washed down with a big frozen milk shake, adding pasteurized milk to the meat and the starch and the fat, plus several spoons of refined white sugar to thoroughly gum up the works. Breaking one or two rules of trophology at any given meal is bad enough, but the Great American Meal breaks at least six. Small wonder that in a recent nationwide health survey in America, reported in an Associated Press bulletin in July 1986, 49 per cent of the population reported chronic, daily stomach pain, gastro-intestinal distress, constipation, and other ailments of the digestive tract.

The dietary situation in the Western world is far more serious than any government health authorities care to admit. This is largely because the food industry has become one of the largest, most powerful businesses in the Western world, especially in America, where the processed food industry is represented by one of the most powerful lobbies in Washington. The Food and Drug Administration (FDA), which decides what foods may be sold in the market, is staffed primarily by professional bureaucrats, not nutritional scientists, and it conducts no scientific tests whatsoever. Instead, it relies on tests and reports submitted by the very corporations which want to get a new food product onto the market! Raw certified milk has become illegal in most states, and gone are the days when people could go down to a local open-air market to purchase fresh produce, as is still the custom in Asia and much of Europe. And so Americans continue to suffer among the world's highest incidence of heart disease, cancer, digestive disorders and other deadly ailments.

Facts are facts, so have a look at the following startling facts about diet and malnutrition in America, compiled by American medical scientists and published in the March/April 1958 edition of the *American Journal of Clinical Nutrition*. A careful comparative examination of the diets and health of beggars in India and apparently healthy young American teenagers revealed that in India the average daily calorie intake of the typical beggar amounted to less than half that of the typical American. Yet only 6.25 per cent of the beggars showed any signs of nutritional deficiency, while a staggering 75 per cent of the American teenagers showed signs of severe malnutrition. Only 1.25 per cent of the Indian beggars suffered dental cavities, compared with over 90 per cent of the young Americans. Conclusion: the typical beggar in India derives greater health from his meager diet than the average American teenager does from his 'rich' diet.

A similar study in Mexico found similar results. The September 1951 issue of *Harper's Magazine* reports the results of a long-term study of the dietary habits of Mexican peasants, conducted by MIT's Dr Robert Harris. States the report,

> To the surprise of investigators, these poverty-stricken Mexicans showed less evidence of malnutrition deficiencies than did Michigan school children . . .
> Analysis of all their foods by Dr. Harris' group showed that the Otomis (Indians dwelling in the arid Mesquital Valley north of Mexico City), like the slum dwellers of Mexico City, were obtaining nearly adequate quantities of all nutrients except riboflavin. In fact, their nutrition was definitely superior to that of the average person living in the Boston and New York areas of the United States.

Enzymes: The Culinary Spark of Life

Another important principle in the Tao of diet is to select foods that are fresh rather than stale, 'living' rather than 'dead', and, as far as practically possible, to consume them either raw or lightly cooked.

The best working definition of 'live food' was made by Dr McCullum of Johns Hopkins University over 50 years ago: 'Eat nothing unless it will spoil or rot, but eat it before it does!' Refined white flour, for example, will not spoil, while freshly ground whole grains will. Indeed, rats fed on diets of refined white flour soon die of starvation. In America, food wholesalers are now adopting the heinous practice of extending the shelf-life of fresh produce by radiating it with powerful doses of gamma rays. Bugs and bacteria will not attack an apple or head of cabbage that has been radiated because such food is not fit for consumption, but the food industry knows that humans will eat almost anything due to ignorance of basic nutrition.

The distinguishing feature between live and dead foods is the presence of active enzymes in the fresh product. Taoist physicians refer to this active living factor in foods as *chee*, and enzyme-*chee* constitutes by far the most vital element for health in food. Western science knows perfectly well that enzymes are fragile compounds that are easily destroyed by exposure to high heat, excess moisture, oxygen, radiation, and synthetic chemicals, all of which occur during cooking, canning, refining, preserving and pasteurising food. All enzymes are effectively 'killed' at temperatures exceeding 130°F, which is far below the boiling point of water (212°F) and less than pasteurization (140°F).

Traditional East Asian diets are rich in two types of enzyme-active foods: fresh raw foods such as fruits and vegetables and, in the case of Japan, raw fish; and foods prepared for consumption by treatment with aspergillus plant enzymes, which provide all the enzymes required for the digestion of proteins, carbohydrates and fats.

Aspergillus plants, which have been used to prepare foods for centuries in Asia, are exceedingly rich in vital enzymes and are used to prepare such nutritious and therapeutically active foods as *tofu* (beancurd), *yuba* (beancurd skin), *nado* (fermented soy sprouts), *miso* (fermented porridge of barley, rice or soybean) and other traditional foods. By adding active aspergillus enzymes to cooked grains and beans, the enzymes destroyed in the cooking process are replaced, and the food is consumed without further cooking. Every bite of *tofu*, *nado* or *miso* provides the body with potent infusions of enzymes, the vital culinary spark of life.

The term 'natural food' has become a much-abused label on commercial food products these days, appearing on everything from pasteurized yoghurt to sweet starchy candy bars. For our purposes, we define a food as 'natural' only if all the natural enzymes, vitamins, minerals, and other vital nutritional factors are still intact, which eliminates almost everything labeled as 'natural' in modern markets. On the other hand, there are plenty of good natural foods to be found in any supermarket without being specifically labeled so, such as raw fruits and vegetables, raw meat and fish, molasses, and unblanched, unroasted nuts and seeds. Even certain dehydrated foods, such as prunes, raisins and dates, retain their vital enzymes in dormant state if they are sun-dried rather than sulphur-preserved, and these enzymes are activated by the warmth and moisture of the mouth and stomach.

A careful look at how enzymes act reveals why they are so important for proper digestion, efficient metabolism and overall physical health.

Enzymes are biochemical catalysts secreted by the pancreas and other glands and organs. Some are used for digestion, others enter the bloodstream to scavenge for dangerous microbes, dead and damaged cells, and toxins. In the stomach, there are about 5 million microscopic glands which secrete various enzymes required for digestion, such as pepsin. All enzymes are specific in their actions, fitting the biochemical reactions for which they are designed as precisely as a key fits a lock. When incompatible enzymes are secreted together, owing to conflicting signals sent by incompatible food combinations, their actions are impaired or neutralized.

But enzymes are far more than mere catalysts in the conventional chemical sense of the word. One of America's leading authorities on enzymes, Dr Edward Howell, supported by over 50 years of clinical experience in the field, wrote in a 1979 issue of *Healthview Newsletter*,

> Catalysts are only inert substances. They possess none of the life energy we find in enzymes. For instance, enzymes give off a kind of radiation when they work. This is not true of catalysts.

Asked about Dr Howell's observations on enzymes, a Taoist physician in Taipei replied,

> That's *chee* at work. *Chee* manifests itself in this world as a sort of radiation that is invisible to the ordinary eye but can be clearly seen by advanced adepts who have cultivated this ability. *Chee* can also be detected and measured by sophisticated technology. The radiation you speak of in these 'enzymes' is their *chee* being released as they work in your system.

Here we see a remarkable conformity between the views of an enlightened Western physician and a traditional Taoist practitioner.

Since 'civilized' diets consist almost entirely of cooked, processed, artificially refined foods, they are completely devoid of their own original enzymes. Consequently, the body must produce the enzymes it requires to digest the huge quantities of stale, dead foods modern man consumes every day. Most of those enzymes must be provided by the pancreas, an organ so overworked and swollen in the human species today that humans now have the largest pancreases relative to body weight of any species on earth. 'In proportion to body weight,' notes Dr Howell, 'the human pancreas is more than twice as heavy as that of a cow.'

One's capacity for enzyme production is limited. 'When it gets to the point that you cannot make certain enzymes, then your life ends,' writes Dr Howell in his book *Enzyme Nutrition*. This accords well with the Taoist tenet that when your body can no longer produce semen, hormones and other forms of *jing* ('vital essence', which includes enzymes), then you die. Enzymes contain a spark of *chee*, and therefore it requires the input of *chee* to produce them. Every organism's store of living *chee* is limited: the faster one uses it up, the sooner one's life ends. Diets of denatured, overcooked foods put tremendous demands on the body's enzyme capacity, and Dr Howell believes that this unnecessary, unnatural and unabated depletion of the body's enzyme capacity is 'one of the paramount causes of premature aging and early death' and the 'underlying cause of almost all degenerative disease'.

In order to service the mass of enzymeless food in the stomach, other parts of the body – such as the brain, muscles, joints and nerves – are chronically deprived of the vital enzymes they require to function normally, and all sorts of ailments occur. For example, fossil evidence indicates that Neanderthal man, who ate mostly the charred carcasses of dead animals roasted over fires in his cave, suffered crippling arthritis 50,000 years ago. But Eskimos, who traditionally ate a diet that consisted almost entirely of raw meat, raw fat and raw fish, had never been known to suffer arthritis, heart disease or any other chronic ailment until they started eating the packaged processed foods introduced to them by their 'civilized' brethren from America. The Eskimos were the only tribe in all of North and South America that never developed the tradition of a tribal 'medicine man' because they virtually never got sick. Indeed, the word 'Eskimo' comes from an old Indian term which means 'he who eats it raw', and therein lies the secret to their former health and longevity.

Enzymeless diets aggravate the very core of our bodies' 'vital essence' network, which is the endocrine system. According to Dr Howell's findings:

> Evidence indicates that cooked, enzyme-free diets contributed to a pathological over-enlargement of the pituitary gland, which regulates the other glands. Furthermore, there is research showing that almost 100% of people over 50 dying from accidental causes were found to have deficient pituitary glands.

Diets of cooked, enzyme-dead foods tend to make you fat, regardless of how carefully you count calories. American farmers discovered long ago that hogs will simply not fatten when fed raw potatoes, but that a diet of cooked potatoes will make them very fat very fast. Active enzymes in raw foods permit food to digest so efficiently in the stomach that not only are the gastric ills of putrefaction and fermentation avoided, but the calories are also burned so efficiently by the body that fat does not accumulate. Indeed, much of the 'fat' on obese bodies is not adipose tissue, but bulky accumulations of mucus and toxic waste bulging out through the intestinal walls, jowls, lymph nodes and other parts of the body where such wastes are stored. Raw calories and cooked calories are as different as fresh air and polluted air. 'From my work,' remarks Dr Howell, I've found that it was impossible to get people fat on raw foods, regardless of the calorie intake.'

Since Western scientists are so fond of testing their theories on rats and then applying the results to humans, let's take a look at how rats fare on cooked food. When two groups of rats are fed respectively on exclusive diets of raw and cooked foods, the raw food group lives an average lifespan of three years, while the cooked food group rarely makes it beyond the age of two. In human terms, that would mean an extra 20–30 years of life! Dr Pottenger's cat experiments with raw and pasteurized milk provided precisely the same results. Think about that the next time you opt for a hamburger and fries instead of a fresh fruit or vegetable salad.

When not busy digesting enzymeless food in the stomach, the body's enzymes roam through the bloodstream and protect the entire system from all sorts of disease and toxic damage. This is one of the great benefits of fasting: the body's entire enzyme capacity devotes itself to cleaning house, digesting and eliminating dead and damaged tissues and putrefied proteins, and helping in the construction of new cells. Obviously, if you live on a daily diet consisting of denatured enzymeless foods, your entire enzyme capacity is constantly preoccupied with digestive duties, thereby permitting all sorts of putrid wastes and damaged cells to accumulate in other tissues to the point of severe toxemia. It is a well-known fact that cancerous tumors almost always develop in tissues that are severely toxified, such as smokers' lungs, drinkers' livers and gluttons' colons.

In order to compensate your system for the enzyme drain caused by cooked foods, especially cooked animal products, Dr Howell recommends taking one to three capsules of enzyme supplements with all big meals, unless the meal consists *entirely* of raw foods. A small side-salad does not provide sufficient enzyme activity to digest a steak. Enzyme supplements should be swallowed at the beginning of the meal so that they dissolve in the stomach by the time food arrives. Dr Howell recommends plant-derived enzymes over pancreatic enzymes derived from animal sources because 'plant enzymes can work in the acidity of the stomach, whereas pancreatic enzymes work best in the alkalinity of the small intestine'. By the time food reaches the small intestine, much of the digestive work has already been done in the stomach, and therefore it's best to use enzyme supplements that activate in the stomach.

Though raw foods are by far the best source of active enzymes, there are certain ways of lightly cooking foods that do not entirely decimate their natural enzyme factors. The three main conditions that kill enzymes during cooking are intense heat, extreme dryness, and long cooking time.

Thus the Western world's favorite cooking methods – baking and roasting – are the worst enzyme offenders.

The solution to this problem is typically Taoist: balance the excess Yang of heat and dryness with the soothing Yin element of water. That means applying fire to heat water, then applying the hot water to cook the food, such as steaming and poaching (but not boiling). When you steam or poach food, temperatures never exceed 212°F, compared with the 350–500°F temperatures generated in an oven and the even higher temperatures of charcoal or gas grilling. Steaming and poaching cut down the time required for cooking and, while both steam and hot water do indeed kill enzymes on exposed surfaces of food, the moisture seals and preserves many of the enzymes deep inside, where intense surface temperatures do not reach. Poaching and steaming also permit cooking without the extra addition of oils, fats, bastes or batters, which only impede digestion and add unwanted dead calories to food.

The other cooking method that preserves a portion of enzymes in food is the traditional Chinese 'stir-fry'. While temperatures are very high, cooking times are very brief – usually 30 seconds to 1 minute – which does not cause the evaporation of all vital juices and seals enzymes inside meat and vegetables. As long as stir-fried vegetables are 'crispy,' it indicates that their internal cellular structure is still intact, with enzymes locked inside. If meats are still rare or bloody inside, they too retain some of their natural enzyme factors.

Even fast-foods need not offend the rules of trophology and enzyme nutrition. For example, you do not necessarily need bread to make a 'sandwich'. Throughout Southeast Asia, people use fresh crispy lettuce leaves to wrap up all sorts of delicious ingredients, many of them raw, to make wholesome delicious meals that can easily be taken 'on the run'. The lettuce combines favorably with everything and provides both active enzymes and fibrous bulk. In Japan, pressed sheets of dried seaweed (*nori*) are used in a similar manner to wrap all sorts of different ingredients, including poached asparagus, raw lettuce and cabbage, raw fish, beansprouts, minced onions, tomatoes, ground raw beef, avocado and other wholesome enzyme-rich foods that are both nutritious and delicious. Called 'hand rolls' (*temaki*), they not only digest much better in the stomach and provide far more nutrition than hamburgers, submarines, 'fishwiches' and other culinary abominations, they also taste much better in the mouth. Try it, you'll love it!

Eating Right for Health and Longevity

Those who eat according to nature's way rarely report symptoms of gastric distress, but in America almost everyone now takes it for granted that a big meal is going to cause them some sort of gastric discomfort, and many Westerners routinely arrive at restaurants and dinner parties armed with antacids and other stomach remedies.

In order to help guide the reader on to the path of natural, healthy eating habits that promote longevity without sacrificing the pleasure of eating, the following pages present practical guidelines for the correct way to combine and consume the most important categories of food in the human diet: proteins, carbohydrates, fats, fresh fruits, and raw vegetables.

How to eat proteins

Jehovah spoke unto Moses, saying, 'I have heard the murmurs of the children of Israel: speak unto them, saying: "At evening ye shall eat flesh, and in the morning ye shall be filled with bread."' In other words, Jehovah instructed Moses in the rules of trophology, telling him to teach his people to eat their proteins and carbohydrates at separate meals. He also forbade them to consume milk and flesh together. This is the earliest and soundest dietary advice ever recorded in Western civilization, but unlike Orientals, who still respect the wisdom of their ancient sages, Western folks spurn the teachings of the past as 'outdated' and 'unscientific'. On the other hand, as the great American nutritional scientist Dr Tilden pointed out, 'Nature never produced a sandwich!'

Proteins are potent foods and require special conditions to digest and release their nutrients. The best choices for combining animal proteins with other foods are non-starch vegetables such as greens, squash, cabbage, sprouts, etc., and it's best to consume these vegetables raw in the form of a large salad. Concentrated animal proteins should only be consumed at one meal per day, though light vegetable proteins such as beancurd (*tofu*) may be eaten more often. Indeed, light vegetable proteins may completely replace meats in the human diet: 1½–2 pounds of raw nuts and seeds per week, for example, provide all the protein and fat required by anyone and eliminate the metabolic craving for meat, eggs and other animal proteins. Be sure to pre-soak all raw nuts and seeds in water overnight before consuming.

How to eat carbohydrates

Starchy carbohydrates should not be combined with any concentrated proteins. The best items to blend with starch-foods are non-acid fruits and fresh raw or lightly cooked vegetables. If you like potatoes or pasta or pastries, then make a meal of them, but do not add eggs, meat or cheese to the meal.

Most people prefer to take their carbohydrate meal for breakfast in the morning, either as toast or cereal. Even a well-functioning stomach requires approximately 12 hours to recover digestive equilibrium after ingesting imcompatible combinations of food, and therefore a bad blend at breakfast will ruin your digestion for the rest of the day, regardless of what you eat for lunch or dinner. Among the worst breakfasts is dry cereal flavoured with refined sugar and soaked in pasteurized milk. Jam on toast is almost as bad. Children suffer most from the ravages of such breakfasts, because many adults either skip breakfast entirely, or eat nothing but plain toast and coffee, which is a perfectly agreeable combination.

As with protein, you should not have more than one starch-based meal per day, and you should try to avoid combining two widely different types of starch at a single meal. Since protein and starch are the major antagonists in trophology, it's best to separate the protein and starch meals by 10–12 hours, such as the bread breakfast and flesh dinner recommended by Jehovah to Moses.

With starch-foods, it is even more important than with protein not to wash it down with water, fruit juice, milk or other fluids. Digestion of starch *must* begin in the mouth in order to continue in the stomach. A mouthful of fluid taken along with a bite of starch dilutes the salivary secretions so much that the starch hits the stomach with insufficient infusions of the alkaline ptyalin enzyme, permitting the starch to ferment instead of digest in the stomach. All carbohydrates should be chewed well and thoroughly ensalivated before swallowing.

How to eat fats

Fats may be consumed in combination with carbohydrates, vegetables and fruits, but should be avoided with concentrated proteins; with light proteins, fat is relatively compatible.

In the fat category, avoid all margarines and other butter substitutes and all 'hydrogenated' oils. Hardened hydrogenated vegetable oils are processed in such a manner that your stomach would have to generate temperatures of 500°F to break them down, i.e. they are indigestible. The best fats are butter and cold-pressed vegetable and nut oils in their fluid state.

How to eat raw vegetable salads

Both Dr Herbert Shelton and V. E. Irons strongly recommend everyone eat a large salad of fresh raw non-starch vegetables every day, preferably just before the main protein or carbohydrate meal. In addition to providing active enzymes and fibrous bulk, raw vegetable salads are excellent sources of vitamins, minerals, amino acids and other vital nutrients in their most assimilable forms.

It is most important to eat your salads *immediately* after cutting up the ingredients. Raw vegetables that are sliced and shredded then left sitting for hours prior to a meal rapidly lose many of their valuable enzymes and other nutrients due to oxidation.

Be careful with the type of dressings you use on salads, especially when combining them with protein meals. Excess oil or vinegar or cream interfere with digestion of protein in the stomach.

Raw salads are particularly beneficial to growing children. They provide abundant supplies of vital nutrients required for growing bones and tissues, and they keep young colons swept clean of the toxic debris created by eating candy and other junk food. Though it may strike you as illogical, raw vegetables are in fact a much better source of organic calcium for growing bones then the denatured pasteurized cow's milk which so many doctors and parents force children to drink for that purpose. Milk does indeed contain a lot of calcium, but pasteurization renders it virtually inaccessible to the body. If your children have trouble with acne, pimples and other skin eruptions and are chronically constipated, try taking them completely off pasteurized milk for a few months and replace it with fresh raw vegetable juices, especially carrot juice, and see the results for yourself. Raw certified milk is equally good for clearing up skin problems, but it's almost impossible to buy these days. Furthermore, by providing *real* nutrition that actually enters the bloodstream and feeds the tissues, raw vegetables and their juices effectively stave the notorious 'sweet tooth' syndrome that plagues the health of children whose meals of denatured processed foods ferment and putrefy instead of digest and metabolize. The chronic craving for sweets is a clear-cut sign of nutritional starvation.

How to eat fruits

The human digestive tract evolved around a diet of fruits and their close relatives, nuts and seeds. It is a biological fact that fresh raw fruits and nuts contain all the vitamins, minerals, natural sugars and amino acids required for human nutrition. 'Experts' continue to claim the contrary, saying that since fruits contain little 'protein' *per se*, they are therefore insufficient to maintain human health. While it is true that fruits contain very little *complete complex protein* molecules, such as that found in meat and eggs, it is equaly true that the body cannot utilize the complex proteins found in meat and eggs. It must first spend a lot of time digesting and breaking down these proteins, then restructuring the constituent amino acids into the unique proteins required by the human organism. Fresh raw fruits and nuts provide those very building blocks in the form of free-floating amino acids, complete with all the synergistic enzymes and vitamins with which they are associated, thereby saving the body all the time, energy and digestive distress required to process complex animal proteins.

Owing to ignorance of trophology and basic nutrition, fresh fruits have been unfairly accused of all sorts of culinary crimes. The self-styled nutritional 'expert' Dr William Henry Porter, in his book *Eating to Live Long*, condemned fruit as 'one of the most pernicious and reprehensible dietetic follies', and Dr Percy Howe of Harvard University observed that most people have trouble digesting oranges *with their meals*, though he did note that this trouble disappeared entirely when the oranges were consumed alone.

Many fruits, especially melons and acid fruits, will indeed cause digestive distress, ferment and thus provide little nutrition when consumed indiscriminately with incompatible foods. But when eaten alone *and* in sufficient quantities, fresh raw fruits provide all the enzymes, vitamins, amino acids and energy that any body needs for optimum health and vitality. They are also highly cleansing and detoxifying, which is why many people experience diarrhea and discomfort during the first few weeks of an exclusive fruit diet.

The Swedish heavyweight bodybuilder Andreas Cahling, winner of the highly coveted Mr Europe and Mr Universe titles, is an exclusive frugivore. He eats neither meat nor dairy products, not even grains or vegetables! Yet his body is every bit as strong and his health as robust as his carnivorous competitors, who feel obliged to consume many pounds of meat, dozens of eggs and quarts of milk every day to provide protein.

The biggest mistake people make when going on an exclusive diet of fruit is not to eat sufficient quantities. The other mistake is to throw away the most nutritionally beneficial parts. Fruit is composed primarily of water. Frugivores like Andreas Cahling therefore chomp their way through half a dozen bananas or a dozen apples or 3–5 pounds of raw grapes at a sitting. They always eat the white fibers between orange sections, the cores of apples and pears, the seeds and skins of grapes, because these parts contain the most potent enzymes and most of the amino acids. Seeds, cores and fibers of fresh fruits should be well chewed to liquid consistency before swallowing.

Fruits deliver their best nutritional benefits when consumed on an empty stomach, for much of it passes directly onward to the small intestine for digestion. But unless you eat nothing else but fruit and fruit juice all day, you should limit your fruit comsumption to one or two exclusive fruit meals per day. Eating fresh fruits or drinking their juices between starch and protein meals can severely inhibit digestion because the stomach will still be busy working on the starch or protein when the fruit lands there. You should also eat sweet fruits and acid fruits at separate sittings and never sweeten any fruit with sugar or honey, for other sugars do not blend well with fruit in the stomach.

If you eat carbohydrates for breakfast and proteins for dinner, then you may construct a very healthy lunch entirely of fresh raw fruits. This habit is especially beneficial for meat-eaters, for the fruit meal will provide active enzymes, fresh fibrous bulk and fruit acids to help clean the by-products of putrefactions from the intenstinal tract and bloodstream. As an extension of this once-a-day fruit meal diet, you might wish to declare one day each week as 'fruit day' and consume nothing but fresh raw fruits all day long.

All this is much easier to implement than it seems. The biggest hurdle is not physiological but psychological. As Walter Bagehot once remarked, 'The pain of a new idea is one of the greatest pains in human nature . . . Your favorite notions may be wrong, your firmest beliefs ill founded.' And your favorite foods may be the root cause of your greatest pains! It's a fact of life that people find it much easier to believe a lie they've heard a thousand times than a fact they've never heard before. One must first unlearn all the bad dietary habits instilled since early childhood, then familiarize oneself with the real facts concerning diet and nutrition. And there is no need to take anyone else's word about all this. If you simply follow the Tao of diet and the rules of trophology for a few months, your own body will provide all the evidence you need, and, unless you simply don't care about your health and longevity, you will quickly adopt these new eating habits as a permanent and natural part of your daily life.

Taoist diets do not require strict self-denial or culinary boredom. Using your imagination and your knowledge of trophology, it is easy to construct compatible, digestible, nutritious meals that are very pleasing to the palate. And how much trouble is it to set some fresh fruit, nuts and seeds on the table from time to time, instead of cooking up a storm? And by leaving the cupboard bare, you will be motivated to shop a bit more frequently for fresh, enzyme-rich produce instead of relying on canned, processed, refined foods that provide no nutrition while causing nothing but misery in your digestive tract.

Eating out at even the fanciest restaurants is also no excuse for commiting culinary crimes against your body. You can order a perfectly balanced and trophologically compatible meal at almost any restaurant that prepares food to order. That of course eliminates all fast-food outlets where everything is prepared long in advance from pre-processed products. But in an Italian restaurant you can build a good starch-based meal of pasta and tomato sauce (without cheese or meat, please), supplemented with a plate of antipasto and a big vegetable salad. At a steak house, help yourself to a large steak if you like, but forgo the bread and potatoes and specify your steak to be cooked very rare, and supplement it with a fresh vegetable salad. If you find yourself at a big buffet table laden with all sorts of tempting desserts that you *know* you will not be able to resist after the main courses, then skip the main courses and take two or three desserts after first preparing your stomach with the enzymes and roughage of a large salad. Where there's a will there's a way, and now that you know the Way, the rest is up to your own will to practice it.

Food as Medicine

Sun Ssu-mo, the Tang Dynasty Taoist physician who correctly diagnosed and cured the nutritional-deficiency disease beriberi 1,300 years ago, a full millennium before European doctors did in 1642, wrote in *Precious Recipes*:

> A truly good physician first finds out the cause of the illness, and having found that, he first tries to cure it by food. Only when food fails does he prescribe medication.

Hippocrates, the father of Western medicine, said precisely the same thing when he told his students. 'Thy food shall be thy medicine', but contemporary Western physicians seem to have forgotten his words of wisdom, as well as those by Dr Charles Mayo, one of the most celebrated American physicians of the twentieth century:

> Normal resistance to disease is directly dependent upon adequate food. Normal resistence to disease *never* comes out of pill boxes. Adequate food is the cradle of normal resistance, the playground of normal immunity, the workshop of good health, and the laboratory of long life.

Nutritional therapy used to be part and parcel of Western medical practice, but conventional Western physicians today don't even inquire about their patients' eating habits when making a diagnosis, nor do they dispense dietary advice with the powerful synthetic drugs they so casually prescribe.

A Federal Research Committee appointed by the National Research Council and headed by Dr Myron Winick, director of the Institute of Human Nutrition at Columbia University's College of Physicians and

Surgeons, reported in July 1985 that American medical schools do not provide physicians with even the most rudimentary education in nutritional therapy, despite growing awareness of its importance among the general public. Indeed, the six major causes of premature death in the United States today have all been linked to dietary factors: heart disease, cancer, strokes, diabetes, arteriosclerosis and cirrhosis of the liver. A major change in American dietary habits would have a powerful preventive impact on these deadly diseases, but that would require a tremendous revolution in the lucrative medical, pharmaceutical and food industries.

Reports Dr Winick, 'The faculty of many American medical schools are still philosophically not as committed to the whole area of preventive medicine as they are to diagnosis and treatment.' The heart of preventive medicine lies in diet and nutritional therapy, not pharmacology and surgery, and the preventive approach to health requires that the patient, not the physician, play the major role. Small wonder the American medical establishment so stubbornly resists this threat to its multibillion dollar industry!

To give the reader an idea how effectively various common foods may be utilized both as curative and preventive medicine, three of the most potent therapeutic foods are briefly introduced below: garlic, grapes and cherries. Appendix III provides a complete list of medicinal foods, categorized according to the ailments they remedy.

Garlic

Garlic has been prescribed as medicine since the dawn of recorded history in China, and probably long before that. Egyptian medical texts dating from 1550 BC list garlic as a major ingredient in 22 prescriptions, and it is a well-known fact that countries where garlic is consumed in large quantities suffer a significantly lower incidence of cancer. Chinese texts clearly state that in order to be fully effective, garlic must be consumed raw.

Modern science confirms the efficacy of this ancient remedy. American biochemists have discovered that 'allicin', the active component in garlic, works as a powerful antibiotic and fungicide. In fact, allicin has proven even more effective than penicillin in suppressing certain types of disease-carrying agents. However, allicin appears only in freshly cut or crushed *raw* garlic, again confirming the wisdom of ancient Chinese medical advice. When you cut a clove of raw garlic, a neutral vegetable substance called alliin mixes with a plant enzyme called allinase to produce the potent allicin factor. The characteristic odor of fresh cut raw garlic is caused by this powerful enzyme reaction. The garlic pills, garlic oil and other odorless garlic extracts sold in health-food stores are devoid of the allicin compound and are therefore therapeutically useless.

In old China, tuberculosis was effectively treated with hot compresses of fresh raw garlic applied to the back. The volatile therapeutic factors penetrated the skin and entered the lungs, killing the baccillus that causes tuberculosis. Garlic is also effective in ridding the alimentary canal of worms and other parasites, preventing colds and influenza, and giving a tonic boost to the libido. Regular daily consumption of fresh raw garlic provides round-the-clock protection against a host of contagious diseases and parasites.

Grapes

This may surprise you, but grapes rank among the most potent of all medicinal foods when properly used for therapy. Raw grape juice has been called 'vegetarian milk' owing to its ability to sustain nursing infants deprived of mother's milk, and it is a far superior option to pasteurized cow's milk. The sugars contained in raw grapes are precisely those used in cellular metabolism: mostly pure glucose, with some fructose and levulose. These natural sugars are immediately absorbed into the bloodstream, ready for metabolic use.

Among the most effective therapeutic applications of grapes is to cure constipation and gastritis, which are common complaints for those who live on Western diets. When severe gastritis strikes, simply stop eating and drinking everything else for a day or two and start eating fresh raw grapes. The black variety of grapes are by far the most potent. Start with a pound or two and work up to three or four pounds per day. In the case of gastritis, the seeds and skins should be spat out and only the juice and pulp swallowed. This therapy usually eliminates all symptoms of gastritis within 24–48 hours. If thereafter you avoid the denatured foods and improper combinations that cause the problem in the first place, gastritis will usually not recur.

Black grapes are wonderfully effective detoxifiers, especially for the digestive tract, liver, kidneys and blood. When used for this purpose, the seeds and skins should be carefully chewed and swallowed along with the juice and pulp, for they contain potent bioactive agents with specific detoxifying properties. They also alkalize the digestive tract and bloodstream, a highly desirable benefit in this day of chronic acidosis. The diarrhea and discomfort one often experiences during the first few days of grape therapy are due entirely to the powerful detoxifying properties of grapes: the worse you feel, the more toxic you are.

Cherries

Used therapeutically, cherries are nutritive, detoxifying, laxative and stimulating to the nervous system and vital organs and glands. Their potent antiphlogistic and antiputrid properties make them an excellent adjunct in combating the harmful effects of putrefaction of animal proteins in the intestinal tract. Cherries are safe for diabetics because the sugar they contain is levulose, which can be absorbed directly into the bloodstream without first being transformed by insulin.

As with grapes, dark cherries are the most medically efficacious variety, and they too must be consumed raw in order to gain their therapeutic benefits. You may chew them or drink their freshly extracted juice. Pasteurization, however, destroys the bioactive elements that make cherries such strong medicine. Fed to infants, raw cherry juice protects their sensitive systems against all sorts of digestive disorders, including those caused by pasteurized cow's milk, and enhances their resistance to infections.

It must be remembered that neither grapes nor any other therapeutic food will work their medical magic unless you also eliminate the bad dietary habits that cause your problems. All therapeutic foods work best when you fast for a few days and make them your exclusive diet. If you suggest this cure for gout or arthritis to a typical American doctor, he is likely to laugh in your face, but in the Soviet Union the medical community takes the grape cure very seriously, as they do colonic irrigations and other natural forms of hygiene. There are huge health resorts in Russia devoted entirely to the grape cure, and they are generally booked years in advance by Soviet citizens who habitually spend their holidays at such spas to rid themselves of the chronic ailments and toxic accumulations caused by contemporary urban lifestyles.

A word on vitamin and mineral supplements is in order here. Most of the so-called 'natural' vitamins on sale today are in fact either synthetic products or else crystalized extracts of natural products, such as bran, liver, butter and citrus fruits. The extraction process requires the use of powerful chemical solvents such as ether, benzine and methyl alcohol, precipitants such as barium chloride, lead and aluminium salts, and distillation at high temperatures. These chemical processes denature the vitamins, isolate them from their natural synergists, and destroy their related enzymes.

It has been observed for decades that all laboratory animals fed on 'scientifically balanced' diets of dry chow, to which synthetic vitamins and minerals have been added, habitually eat their own feces. Why? Because despite their 'enriched' diets, their food contains nothing raw or fresh and therefore no enzymes. Hence, they instinctively recycle their own limited stores of vitamins and enzymes by consuming their own feces.

The evidence against the efficacy of synthetic vitamins is overwhelming. In 1942, the *Journal of Immunology* reported the following results of tests on rabbits: when synthetic vitamin C was administered, ascorbic acid levels in the blood did not rise; when fed on plain *raw* cabbage, ascorbic acid levels in the blood rose significantly. In 1951, Dr E. Cruckshank reported in *Food and Nutrition* that when young chickens were fed synthetic vitamin D they reached an average 345 grams in weight, compared with 400 grams for a group fed with natural vitamin D extracted from cod-liver oil. Of the synthetically fed group of chickens, 60 per cent died before reaching maturity, while not a single one of the naturally fed group died prematurely.

It is a popular practice today to take mega-doses of vitamins and minerals on the assumption that these alone will guarantee health and longevity. They will not. Balance, not quantity, is the key to vitamin therapy, and this conforms entirely with the basic premises of Tao. 'Balance' not only means taking the full range of vital vitamins in correct proportions, it also means balancing your vitamin supplements with correct dietary habits, proper nutrition, regular exercise and a healthy lifestyle. As Dr Charles G. King points out, 'The same intake of a given nutrient may be optimum, toxic, or inadequate, depending on the intake of other nutrients.' Among those other nutrients, active enzymes are perhaps most important of all, for they are absolutely indispensable for the proper metabolism of vitamin and mineral supplements and they are the elements in which modern diets are most deficient. Unless you eat nothing but raw food, enzyme supplements extracted from natural sources are just as important as vitamin and mineral supplements.

Fresh wholesome foods contain all the known and *unknown* factors required for optimum health and longevity. Vitamin B12, for example, was 'discovered' and isolated in 1954, but prior to that people derived their daily doses of this vital element *unknowingly* from wholesome foods. Fresh unadulterated foods probably contain dozens of vital nutritional factors not yet 'discovered' and isolated by scientists. People who rely on diets of processed refined foods supplemented by synthetic vitamins deprive themselves of all the potent unknown factors for health and longevity contained in Mother Nature's menu.

Therefore, your best bet is to rely primarily on a diet of wholesome primary foods supplemented with vitamins and enzymes derived from natural sources and taken in small doses several times throughout the day. The body cannot absorb mega-doses of any sort of supplement and instead excretes the surplus with the urine and feces. As in every other aspect of life, Tao demands balance and harmony in diet, not a mega-dose of Yin or Yang.

Diet and Mental Health

Psychoanalysis as practiced in Western medical circles does not exist in the traditional Chinese medical system. When a patient in the Orient displays symptoms of emotional stress, mental confusion, panic, paranoia, and so forth, 'the truly good physician first tries to cure it by food'. After carefully analyzing the patient's dietary habits, the Chinese physician usually finds a critical deficiency of vital nutrition or an extreme imbalance in the pharmodynamic energies contained in the foods consumed. He then proceeds to tonify deficiency and redress imbalance with strict dietary guidelines supplemented with herbal therapy.

It was in Europe, where by Taoist standards diets are deplorably unbalanced, that psychotherapy evolved as a formal branch of medicine divorced from physiology. This medical dichotomy is typical of the dualism that lies at the core of Western thought.

Despite the dualistic currents in Western thinking, a small handful of dedicated nutritional scientists in America and Europe today have finally rediscovered the 'missing link' between body and mind, physical and mental health, and that link turns out to be nutrition. Dr George Watson of the University of Southern California states the case clearly in his excellent book *Nutrition and Your Mind*:

> We have found functional mental illness to be a reflection of disordered metabolism, principally involving the malfunction of enzyme systems.

The emphasis on enzyme systems is particularly significant, in light of the enzyme-dead diets of Western societies, which suffer most from mental disturbances.

To understand how these links function, we must take a close look at how the brain works. The brain can burn only glucose, which is also known as 'blood sugar'. In fact, the brain, which accounts for only 2½% of body weight, consumes 25% of all available blood sugar. Unlike other tissues, the brain cannot switch over to fat or other fuels when glucose supplies in the blood run dry. Since blood can only carry enough glucose to last for about four hours, any interruption to the steady supply of glucose in the bloodstream results in immediate impairment of brain functions. The very first symptom of mental impairment due to glucose deficiency in the brain is loss of emotional control.

The brain gets its glucose from three sources. Some is absorbed directly into the bloodstream and delivered to the brain from such glucose-rich foods as grapes and honey. Another source is the breakdown of carbohydrates and their refinement into glucose. A third source is glycogen, which is produced and stored in the liver from the breakdown of proteins and fats. When the relatively limited supplies of glucose from glucose-rich foods and carbohydrate digestion are exhausted, the liver converts stored glycogen into glucose and secretes it into the bloodstream to insure a steady supply of blood sugar to the ever-active, ever-hungry brain.

In order to break down protein and fat to produce glycogen, the liver must itself burn glucose to fuel this vital metabolic process. A person who follows a fad diet that excludes all carbohydrates and sugars, for example, is unable to furnish sufficient supplies of glucose to process the proteins and fats he consumes. Consequently, his brain is starved of all three sources of glucose – natural sugar foods, carbohydrates and liver glycogen. If on the other hand the diet calls for the elimination of protein and fat, then the body has inadequate stores of liver glycogen to take up the slack when glucose in the blood is all consumed.

Eliminating fat entirely from the diet is the ultimate folly, for fat is one of the very best sources of food energy. Fat yields three times the amount of energy as sugar and twice as much as protein, and it combusts faster and more completely than almost any other food. The key to consuming fat is to avoid incompatible combinations of foods that interfere with its digestion, such as consuming it together with concentrated proteins. When taken in correct combinations from wholesome natural sources, fat will not make you fat. Recall that Eskimos traditionally ate raw blubber and thrived on it. Sufficient supplies of fat are necessary for 'brain power', and Dr Watson's extensive research has established a definite link between too little fat in the diet and chronic mental disturbance.

Psychiatrists attach great importance to all sorts of abnormal mental *symptoms*, such as depression, mania and neurosis, when in fact these symptoms are usually psychologically meaningless manifestations of severe nutritional imbalance and deficiency. A typical example is the chronic violent behavior associated with critical niacin deficiency. Ten years on the psychiatrist's couch will do nothing to cure this condition, but a sufficient daily dose of niacin will.

Let's take a look at a concrete case described by Dr Watson in *Nutrition and Your Mind*. A young man was referred to Dr Watson suffering from severe mental depression and morbid claustrophobia. So afraid was he of small spaces that he had been unable to remain in his own bathroom long enough to take a shower or bath for over five years! Upon inquiry, the patient revealed that his daily diet, day in and day out, all year long, consisted entirely of only three items: hamburgers, black coffee and pasteurized skim milk. Due to prolonged malnutrition, Dr Watson discovered that the patient's cells had almost entirely lost their capacity to convert food into energy. Dr. Watson immediately put him on a balanced diet of protein, fat, carbohydrate, fresh fruits and vegetables, supplemented with natural vitamins and minerals, and the young man soon recovered his capacity for normal metabolism. His chronic mental depression and morbid claustrophobia disappeared entirely and permanently. Instead of spending years and wasting a fortune talking to a 'shrink', the patient was cured in only a few weeks at minimal cost.

Fully 80 per cent of Dr Watson's cases have been permanently cured of virtually every known form of mental illness using nutritional therapy, including some 'basket cases' referred to him by frustrated psychiatrists. Compare his excellent track record with the results of psychoanalysis: a report by Dr H. J. Eysenck in the *International Journal of Psychiatry* in 1965 evaluated the results of 19 different studies involving over 7,000 psychiatric patients and came to the conclusion that psychotherapy proved of *no lasting value whatsoever* in helping any of the patients recover from any mental disorder. By contrast, Dr Watson's nutritional approach to precisely the same ailments often effects permanent cures within only a few days or weeks. And while this approach is still regarded as heresy within the orthodox Western medical establishment, it has always been standard procedure in Taoist healing arts.

Dr Watson's work led him to discover for himself the traditional Taoist 'trinity' of essence, energy and spirit from an entirely modern scientific angle. His realization that 'essence' (enzymes and other nutrients) must provide the vital 'energy' required to support the 'spirit' (mind) is reflected in the following passage from his book:

> What one eats, digests, and assimilates provides the energy-producing nutrients that the bloodstream carries to the brain. Any interference with the nutritional supply lines or with the energy-producing systems of the brain results in impaired functioning, which then may be called poor mental health.

Concludes Dr Watson, 'What you eat determines your state of mind and who you are.'

Truly, 'food for thought!'

APPENDIX I:

Food Categories and Combination Chart

Food Categories

I. *Proteins*: foods that contain 15 per cent or more protein matter
    Concentrated proteins: meat, fish, fowl, eggs, milk, cheese
    Light proteins: nuts, beans, peas, soy beans products, avocados, whole grains

II. *Carbohydrates*: foods that contain 20 per cent or more starch and/or sugars
    Starch: peanuts, bananas, potatoes, all pasta products, rice, breads, cakes, pies, refined cereals, etc.
    Sugars: whole, brown and raw cane sugar, fructose, honey, maple syrup, dried sweet fruits (dates, raisins, figs, prunes)

III. *Fats*: animal or vegetable oils
    Animal: butter, cream, lard, tallow, fatty meats
    Vegetable: Olive, soy bean, sunflower seed, sesame, safflower, corn, and all nut oils

IV. *Vegetables*: lettuce, celery, cabbage, broccoli, spinach, bean sprouts, cucumber, asparagus, onion, eggplant, turnip, watercress, leek, zuccini, string bean, green pepper, radish, carrot, okra, artichoke, olive, etc.
    Exceptions: potatoes act as a starch; tomatoes act as an acid fruit

V. *Fruits*
    Acid fruits: orange, grapefruit, lime, lemon, berries, cranberry, pineapple, tomato
    Sub-acid fruits: apple, pear, peach, cherry, grape, apricot, nectarine, plum, etc.
    Melons: watermelon, musk melon, honeydew melon, cantaloupe, papaya, etc.
    Exceptions: bananas act as a starch; dried figs, dates, raisins and prunes act as sugars

Food Combination Chart

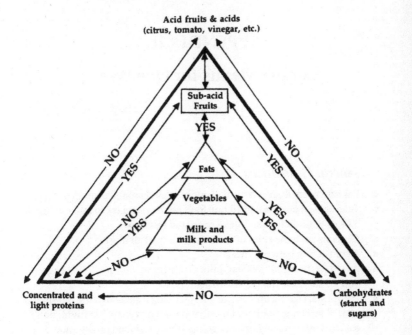

Notes:

1. 'No' denotes incompatible combinations.
2. 'Yes' denotes compatible combinations.
3. Milk is best taken completely alone as a protein food, preferably as raw certified milk.
4. Melons are not included in the 'fruit' headings above; they should always be eaten alone for optimum digestion and assimilation.
5. Bananas, figs, dates, prunes and raisins are sugar/starch foods of the very best quality, and should not be mixed with proteins.
6. Vegetables combine well with everything, except for potatoes (a starch) and tomatoes (an acid).
7. Fats should be avoided with concentrated proteins, but are relatively compatible with light proteins.
8. The closer to the fresh, raw state a food is consumed, the more compatible it is with other varieties of food; therefore, try to make at least 50% of your diet consist of fresh, raw foods consumed in the fresh, raw state. That will provide the active enzymes and moist, raw fiber required to compensate for incompatible combinations of cooked foods.

APPENDIX II:

Sample Menus for One Week

General Guidelines:

- Take no more than one meal of concentrated animal protein per day.
- Take at least one meal of all raw food per day, and try to make at least 50% of your daily food intake consist of raw foods.
- Observe the basic rules of food combining at all meals.
- Avoid eating between meals.
- Avoid pasteurized milk and milk products, as well as cooked eggs. If you do eat these things, eat them alone.
- Do not start eating immediately upon rising from bed in the morning; wait at least one hour, and use that hour for exercise. At night, don't eat food immediately prior to going to bed; last food intake should be 2–3 hours before bedtime.

Day 1

Breakfast: Coffee, tea, hot water or molasses in hot water as beverage (no sugar or milk in coffee or tea)

    Whole-grain bread, very well toasted, with dairy butter (no margarine) or any raw nut butter except peanut butter, 1–3 slices

    1–2 ripe bananas

    Handful of soaked raw nuts (excepts peanuts) or seeds

Lunch: Large glass of fresh raw carrot juice

    Large raw vegetable salad, with olive oil/lemon juice/garlic dressing

Dinner: Steamed fresh fish, garnished with ginger, scallions, parsley, and/or fresh coriander

    Fresh vegetable, Chinese-style (i.e. lightly sautéd to preserve crispness)

    Raw vegetable salad, if desired

Day 2

Breakfast: Coffee, tea or molasses water

2–3 sun-dried figs and/or dates and/or black raisins

Handful of soaked raw nuts and/or seeds

Lunch: Large plate of fresh raw sub-acid fruits: grapes, apples, pears, peaches, plums, nectarines (no acid fruits or bananas or dried fruits)

Handful of soaked raw nuts or seeds

Dinner: Very rare piece of beef or lamb, garnished with pepper, mustard or other seasonings

Lightly steamed fresh vegetables

Raw vegetable salad, if desired

Day 3

Breakfast: Large glass of freshly squeezed orange juice

One fresh grapefruit or a bowl of fresh berries

Lunch: Roast chicken, rare steak, or a piece of grilled or steamed fish

Steamed or sautéd fresh vegetables

Raw vegetable salad, if desired

Dinner: Large glass of fresh carrot or other vegetable juice

Large vegetable salad with olive oil/lemon juice/garlic dressing

Handful of soaked raw nuts or seeds

Day 4

Breakfast: Glass of raw certified milk or bowl of yoghurt made from raw certified milk

Plate of fresh sub-acid fruits

Lunch: Large glass fresh carrots or other vegetable juice

Raw vegetable salad

Handful of soaked raw nuts or seeds

Dinner: Brown rice, wild rice or fresh pasta with a vegetable sauce, fresh scallions, parsley and/or other fresh garnishes (no meat)

Steamed or sautéd fresh vegetables

Day 5

Breakfast: Coffee, tea or molasses water

Boiled kasha (whole buckwheat kernels), flavored with molasses or honey, raisins, chopped dates and/or figs

1 ripe banana, if desired

Lunch: Large plate of sub-acid fruits OR

Large raw vegetable salad

Large glass of carrot, cucumber or other vegetable juice

Dinner: Lightly sautéd fresh shrimps or prawns, with garlic, ginger and scallions (also chilies, if desired)

Broccoli and/or cauliflower, lightly steamed, garnished with freshly ground roasted sesame seeds

Raw salad, if desired

Day 6

Breakfast: Plate of fresh sub-acid fruits

Handful of soaked raw nuts or seeds

Glass of molasses water

Lunch: 2–3 slices of whole-grain bread, very well toasted, with dairy butter or raw nut butter (except peanut butter)

1–2 ripe bananas

Dinner: Fresh avocado stuffed with poached shrimps, chopped celery, scallions and/or other vegetables and dressed with olive/lemon/garlic dressing or good quality mayonnaise

Piece of steamed or grilled fresh fish

Steamed or sautéd fresh vegetable

Day 7

Breakfast: Fresh honeydew melon, papaya, musk melon or cantaloupe – as much as you want, but combined with nothing else

Molasses water

Lunch: Large raw vegetable salad with dressing

Handful of soaked raw nuts or seeds

Dinner: Tofu (beancurd) prepared any way you like

Sautéd fresh vegetables

Mushrooms: sautéd, steamed or in a casserole with broccoli, cauliflower, string beans and/or asparagus

APPENDIX III:

Therapeutic Foods and Juices

The therapeutic foods and juices introduced below are listed according to their natural affinities and therapeutic effects within the body's six major functional systems: digestive, excretory, respiratory, circulatory, nervous and reproductive. Within each category, foods and juices are listed according to the diseases and degenerative conditions they help cure and prevent. All therapeutic foods should be consumed as fresh as possible, without incompatible combinations of other foods, and all juices should be consumed raw immediately after extraction.

Digestive System: *stomach, intestines, liver, gallbladder, pancreas*

Colic

Abdominal pain caused by excess gas and acid owing to fermentation and putrefaction of improperly combined foods.

Carrot (10 oz), beet (3 oz) and cucumber (3 oz) juice: this blend of juices is very rich in the organic alkalizing elements sodium, potassium and phosphorus; neutralizes acid, helps expel gas, promotes peristalsis; 2 pints daily.

Yoghurt: benefits all forms of indigestion; restores friendly intestinal bacteria; soothes inflamed intestinal lining; 6–8 oz daily.

Spinach (bulk or juice): detoxifies digestive tract; restores pH balance; soothes intestinal inflammation; promotes peristalsis; must be taken raw, either in salad, or as 6 oz juice mixed with 10 oz carrot juice, 1–2 pints daily.

Other beneficial foods: zucchini, raw tomatoes, raw apples (on empty stomach), dark grapes.

Foods to avoid: pasteurized milk, cooked eggs, overcooked meats, refined sugars and starches.

Diabetes and pancreatitis

Inability of pancreas to produce sufficient insulin to metabolize sugars, owing to long-term excess consumption of refined sugars and starches; inflammation of pancreas due to excess demand for pancreatic enzymes in the stomach.

String beans (bulk or juice): rich in potassium, help restore deficient pancreas exhausted by excess demand for insulin and other enzymes; alkalize the pancreas; as bulk, steam lightly; as juice, extract raw, 1 pint daily; may be mixed with carrot juice for flavor.

Brussels sprouts (bulk or juice): rich in alkalizing elements with specific affinity for the pancreas; steam lightly for bulk consumption; extract raw juice, and mix with carrot juice, if desired; 1 pint daily.

Molasses: use unsulphured molasses only; all cases of diabetes and pancreatitis are associated with iron deficiency; molasses is one of nature's richest sources of organic iron and copper, which work together; take 2 tbsp molasses in large cup of warm water, 1–2 times daily; absolute abstention from refined starch and sugar required; this regimen has corrected diabetes, pancreatitis and hypoglycemia (low blood sugar) in 1–2 months; flavor molasses with ½ tsp vanilla or almond extract, if desired.

Other beneficial foods: active yeast dissolved in warm water (one small packet of powder per cup); raw tomatoes; cucumbers; raw spinach; asparagus.

Foods to avoid: All refined starch and sugar; overcooked meat; cooked potatoes; bananas, figs, dates, raisins; salt, pepper, mustard.

Gastritis

Gastric distress in stomach owing to excess gas and acid formed by incompatible combinations of foods, stimulating spices, alcohol, coffee and other irritants.

Yoghurt: soothes inflammation; neutralizes toxic gas and acids; promotes efficient digestion. Plain yoghurt only, may be flavored with a little molasses, if desired.

Carrot, beet and cucumber juice: powerful alkalizing blend; neutralizes stomach acidity; promotes digestion in stagnant stomach; 10 oz/3 oz/ 3 oz, 1–2 pints daily.

Spinach (raw or juice): detoxifies intestinal tract; restores pH balance; soothes inflammation; consume raw in salad, or as juice, 6 oz with 10 oz carrot juice, 1–2 pints daily.

Grapes: dark grapes, raw, 1–2 pounds daily, with no other food, for 1–3 days; or raw juice equivalent; powerful organic alkalizing and detoxifying elements.

Apple cider vinegar: contains malic acid (all other vinegars contain acetic acid), which is highly beneficial to digestion; balances stomach pH; 2 tsp in glass of water, 2–3 times daily, as needed.

Other beneficial foods: almonds, molasses, raw apples, raw tomatoes, papaya.

Foods to avoid: deep fat fried foods; pickled and smoked foods; salt-preserved foods; vinegar (except apple cider vinegar); hot peppers, mustard; alcohol, coffee; sweet carbonated soft drinks.

Liver trouble (cirrhosis and hepatitis)

Hardening, congestion and impairment of liver owing to excess consumption of refined starches (especially white flour), refined sugars, hydrogenated fats and overcooked meats, and insufficient raw food in diet; also due to excess use of alcohol and drugs, including nicotine.

Yeast: active yeast is a potent source of B vitamins and pangamic acid, all of which are vital for liver function and help reduce liver inflammation; alkalizes the liver and stimulates liver functions; 1 packet of granular active yeast in a glass of warm water, twice per day, on empty stomach only; do not mix with other foods.

Tomato: raw tomato is especially effective in reducing inflammation of liver due to hepatitis and cirrhosis; best taken for 1–3 days exclusive of other food, either bulk or raw juice; may be mixed with carrot juice for flavor and extra therapeutic benefit.

Carrot juice: fresh raw carrot juice is one of the best liver detoxifiers when consumed in quantities of 2–3 pints daily. Such dosage sometimes results in an orange tinge in the skin; contrary to popular belief, this is not caused by carotene, any more than beets turn you red or spinach green; the orange tinge is due to toxic bile being purged from the liver by the mega-dosage of carrot juice; the bloodstream cannot excrete the bile fast enough through kidneys, so it is purged through skin; when liver is clean, you won't turn orange, regardless how much carrot juice you drink.

Summer squash: especially rich in sodium, summer squash is an excellent alkalizing remedy for acidosis of liver and blood due to depressed liver function. Lightly steamed, no salt or spices.

Other beneficial foods: beets (raw juice or bulk); cabbage; zucchini; string beans (bulk or juice); calves liver; raw spinach; sunflower seeds; soy beans.

Foods to avoid: Deep fat fried foods; overcooked meats; refined sugars and starches; alcohol; drugs; foods with chemical additives and preservatives.

Obesity

Excess adipose tissue deposited throughout the body, especially abdomen, buttocks and thighs, owing to excessive consumption of refined starch and sugar and habitual consumption of incompatible food combinations; obesity is sometimes due to glandular disorders, but such disorders are often also the direct result of poor dietary habits and may therefore be corrected with the same nutritional therapy; fasting and colonic irrigations are very helpful as the first steps in correcting both obesity and glandular disorders, followed by nutritional therapy.

Carrot juice: raw carrot juice cleanses the entire digestive tract of morbid wastes, detoxifies the liver, and balances the endocrine system, all of which help cure and prevent obesity; 2 pints daily.

Carrot, beet and cucumber juice: a major symptom of obesity is severe acidosis of blood and tissues; this blend has potent alkalizing properties in the bloodstream and kidneys, thus promoting efficient metabolism and excretion of wastes, 10 oz/3 oz/3 oz, 2 pints daily.

Spinach: raw spinach is one of nature's best antidotes for lower bowel stagnation, which is a common cause of obesity; consume raw in salads, or 6 oz juice mixed with 10 oz carrot juice, 1–2 pints daily.

Cabbage juice: raw cabbage juice detoxifies the stomach and upper bowels of putrefactive wastes, thereby improving digestive efficiency and facilitating rapid elimination; mix half/half with carrot juice; 1 pint daily.

Other beneficial foods: all raw vegetables and raw fruits which provide the active enzymes, organic alkaline minerals and moist raw fiber required for digestive and metabolic efficiency.

Foods to avoid: all refined starch and sugar, especially white bread and sweet pastries; overcooked meats; fatty meats; chocolate; pasteurized milk, cooked eggs; alcohol.

Ulcers (gastric)

Severe inflammation and irritation of the lining of the stomach and duodenum owing to fermentation and putrefaction of incompatible combinations of foods, excess consumption of chemical additives and preservatives, excess alcohol, and excessively stimulating spices.

Cabbage juice: has potent cleansing and reducing properties; best taken half/half with carrot juice, 1–2 pints daily.

Yoghurt: soothes inflamed ulcers; restores pH balance.

Grapes: raw dark grapes, pulp or juice, 1–2 pounds daily, exclusive of other food, 1–3 days.

Other beneficial foods: raw goat's milk; raw egg yolk; raw black cherries or juice; papaya.

Foods to avoid: vinegar (except apple cider vinegar); smoked and pickled foods; overcooked meats; hot peppers, mustard, curry; coffee, alcohol.

Excretory System: colon, kidneys, bladder, lymph nodes, skin

Acne, boils, pimples

These skin conditions are caused mainly by excessive putrefactive waste matter in the body's excretory channels, and extreme acidosis of blood due to accumulation of toxic wastes; when wastes are retained and the colon is clogged, the body purges toxins through the skin and lungs, where these toxins cause abscesses, tumors, inflammation and eruptions. Also due specifically to poor metabolism of fats.

Wheat germ oil: Rich in inositol, which enhances metabolism of fats, thereby reducing excretory burden on skin; contains pyridoxine, which enhances peristalsis and thus improves digestion and assimilation of nutrients and elimination of wastes; 1–2 tsp daily, after meals; may also be rubbed directly onto skin eruptions.

Wheat germ: same benefits as wheat germ oil, but less concentrated; also rich in silicon, which builds strong fingernails and healthy hair.

Cucumbers (bulk or juice): raw cucumbers are rich in potassium, sodium and phosphorus, which neutralize blood acidosis; potent diuretic properties, which facilitate excretion of wastes through kidneys, so that they need not be purged through skin; also good for nails and hair; in raw bulk, or as juice, mixed 1/3 cucumber to 2/3 carrot, 2–3 pints daily.

Garlic: purifies the bloodstream and purges body of toxic waste; garlic ethers reach the skin soon after consumption, killing bacteria attracted to festering eruptions; must be taken raw.

Green (sweet) pepper juice: in combination with equal parts carrot juice; 1–2 pints daily.

Other beneficial foods: active yeast (in warm water); soy beans; fresh lemon juice (no sugar); alfalfa tea; raw potato slices rubbed directly on skin eruptions and raw potato juice (½ pint daily).

Foods to avoid: deep fat fried foods; refined starch and sugar; hydrogenated fats; cooked fatty meats, especially hamburgers on white buns; hot peppers; chocolate.

Allergies

Hives, rashes, runny nose and other irritations after consuming certain foods, usually fresh raw foods; raw foods are such excellent and efficient detoxifiers that they cause a cathartic excretion of accumulated toxins, usually through the skin (for example, orange liver bile excreting through the skin owing to large intake of raw carrot juice); such 'allergies' disappear entirely when the body is thoroughly detoxified; fasting and colonic irrigations are the best way to start the process, followed by nutritional therapy.

Carrot juice: detoxifies the liver, blood and intestinal tract; balances pH throughout the system; 2–3 pints daily.
Cucumber juice: purges blood and kidneys of acids and other toxins, thereby enhancing excretion of wastes; balances pH; may be mixed with carrot juice, 2 pints daily.
Wheat germ oil: rich in inositol, which improves fat metabolism, preventing accumulation of toxic wastes; improves oxygen absorption in blood, which facilitates efficient, toxin-free metabolism.
Other beneficial foods: fresh lemon or grapefruit juice (no sugar) in distilled water; raw egg yolk; raw potato juice; barley tea.
Foods to avoid: refined starch and sugar; pasteurized milk; cooked eggs; overcooked meats; hydrogenated fats; chemical additives and preservatives.

Appendicitis

Acute inflammation of the appendix owing to excessive accumulation of putrefactive wastes in the colon; first and foremost defense is a therapeutic fast with twice-daily colonic irrigations to quickly remove the offending toxic waste matter, followed with therapeutic foods and juices to restore colon and appendix health.

Spinach: provides the organic mineral salts required for repair and maintainence of the colon; raw bulk, or as 6 oz juice mixed with 10 oz carrot juice, 2 pints daily.
Molasses: molasses in warm water is a natural, mild laxative which helps keeps bowels functioning regularly, which prevents accumulation of the toxins in colon that cause appendicitis; 2 tbsp in warm water, twice daily.

Raw vegetables: a large salad of bulk, raw vegetables taken once or twice a day provides the moist raw fiber required by the colon to maintain regular bowel movements.

Other beneficial foods: sun-dried figs; prunes; raw tomato; raw apple; papaya.

Foods to avoid: incompatible combinations, especially of animal protein and concentrated starch pasteurized milk; cooked eggs; cooked fatty meats.

Arthritis

Caused by deposits of inorganic calcium in the cartilage of joints, where they eventually form 'spurs' that cause intense pain and inhibit movement of joints; these deposits are caused by incomplete digestion of incompatible foods and accumulation of toxic wastes throughout the system; the body dumps these inorganic minerals in the joints, where they won't pollute the bloodstream; excess consumption of concentrated starch and sugar and too much cooked meat in the diet are major factors.

Celery juice: rich in organic sodium, which dislodges inorganic calcium deposits from joints and holds them in solution until eliminated through kidneys; 1 pint daily; 2 pints if mixed with carrot juice.

Grapefruit juice: fresh raw grapefruit juice (no sugar) is highly effective in dissolving deposits of inorganic calcium in joints; mix half/half with distilled water, 1–2 pints daily.

Bone meal: bone meal is a rich source of readily assimilable organic calcium and other vital minerals that are indispensable for proper bone and joint formation; mix 1–2 tsp into any raw juice in the morning.

Cherries: raw black cherries contain active enzymes that help dissolve calcium spurs in joints; eat about 1 pound on empty stomach and take no other food for at least 12 hours, continue for 1–3 days in severe cases.

Grapes: when eaten exclusively for 1–5 days, depending on severity, raw black grapes provide amazing therapeutic relief for acute arthritis; 2–3 pounds per day; chew skin, seeds and pulp very well before swallowing.

Other beneficial foods: molasses; alfalfa (tea or sprouts); asparagus; whole barley; whole lemon, lime or orange puréed in blender with 1 cup distilled water (including peel, fibers and seeds).

Foods to avoid: incompatible combinations, especially of protein and starch; pasteurized milk; cooked eggs; ice cream; salt; excessive consumption of cooked foods, especially animal proteins.

Bladder inflammation (cystitis)

This common condition is the result of excess acidity in the bladder due to incomplete digestion of meats and starch; the by-products of incomplete digestion form uric acid crystals which irritate the lining of the bladder and eventually form painful bladder stones.

Carrot, beet, cucumber juice: this blend exerts a potent alkalizing influence in the bloodstream and the kidneys, thereby neutralizing the excess uric acid that inflames kidneys and bladder and forms stones there; 10 oz/3 oz/3 oz, 2 pints daily.

Watermelon: one of nature's safest and most dependable diuretics, watermelon has a remarkable ability to wash out the bladder quickly and completely; the most effective therapeutic use is to refrain from all other food and drink for 24 hours and eat a few small chunks of fresh watermelon every 5–10 minutes throughout the day; this will cause an incredible excretion of fluids from the bladder.

Cucumber (bulk or juice): raw cucumbers are an excellent diuretic with specific affinity for the bladder; as juice, mix 1/3 cucumber with 2/3 carrot, 2 pints daily.

Pears: ripe raw pears are almost as good as watermelon for correcting bladder inflammation; use them in conjunction with a 24-hour fast, a bite or two at a time, like watermelon therapy.

Other beneficial foods: asparagus, raw beet juice (8 oz sipped slowly throughout the day), barley water.

Foods to avoid: salt, soy sauce; strong coffee and tea; salt-preserved foods; cooked meats.

Colitis

Inflammation of the colon owing to prolonged chronic constipation and a critical deficiency of live active enzymes and moist raw fiber in the diet; the first and foremost measure against this dangerous condition, which often results in surgical colostomies, is to thoroughly clean out the colon of putrefactive wastes and solid obstructions with a 7-day fast and twice-daily colonic irrigations, followed by dietary adjustments to prevent recurrence.

Carrots (juice or bulk): grated raw carrots are an excellent preventive against colitis, providing both live enzymes and moist raw fiber for proper bowel function; best when supplemented with 1–2 pints daily of raw carrot juice.

Carrot and spinach juice: raw spinach juice is nature's best remedy for chronic constipation and inflammation of the colon; 6 oz spinach/10 oz carrot, 2 pints daily.

Molasses: a mild but dependable laxative, molasses also provides vital mineral salts required to restore and maintain colon health; 2 tbsp in warm water, twice daily.

Figs: fresh or sun-dried figs are also an excellent natural laxative for sluggish bowels; the tiny seeds gather toxic wastes and mucus in the colon and drag them out with feces.

Cabbage juice: raw cabbage juice effectively breaks up accumulations of putrefactive wastes in the intestines; its high sulphur and chlorine content makes it an excellent bowel cleanser; works so fast that foul gas often expelled soon after ingestion; 1 pint daily, or 2 pints mixed half/half with carrot juice.

Other beneficial foods: papaya; almonds; sunflower seeds; apple cider vinegar (2 tsp in distilled water); squash.

Foods to avoid: pasteurized milk; cooked eggs; cooked meat; refined starch and sugar, especially white flour and sweet pastries.

Constipation

Excessive consumption of devitalized and cooked foods, especially in incompatible combinations, results in sluggish bowels and chronic constipation; the colon fills with feces and toxic by-products of fermentation and putrefaction, which impairs peristalsis, irritates the colon, and eventually poisons the bloodstream by osmosis; colonic irrigations are the first step in correcting constipation, followed by nutritional therapy.

Figs: fresh or sun-dried figs cleanse the bowels of toxic waste and mucus and serve as a natural laxative; for an excellent therapeutic drink for constipation, put 3 figs in a blender with one ripe banana, 2 tbsp molasses and 1 cup water and blend till smooth.

Molasses: 2 tbsp in warm water, twice daily.

Spinach: raw spinach is nature's best remedy for irritated and sluggish bowels; as juice mix 6 oz spinach with 10 oz carrot, 2 pints daily.

Carrot: grated raw carrots supplemented with 2 pints raw carrot juice should be consumed daily by those with chronic constipation.

Other beneficial foods: papaya; squash; raw apples; ripe bananas; raw almonds.

Foods to avoid: never use mineral oil as a laxative: it robs the digestive tract of all oil-soluble vitamins, such as A, E & D, and is not as effective as figs or molasses; also avoid pasteurized milk, cooked eggs, overcooked meats, and refined starch.

Fever

Fevers are the result of the body trying to 'incinerate' waste matter stirred up in the system as the result of other conditions, such as colds, flu and infectious diseases. Hippocrates wrote, 'If you feed a fever, you'll have to starve a cold', which has been misquoted as 'Feed a fever, starve a cold'. Thus, the best remedy for any fever is complete fasting, plus colonic irrigations to accelerate elimination of waste matter from the body. If you 'feed a fever', you'll only make things worse.

Citrus juice: the only thing a fever patient should be given is freshly extracted lemon, lime, orange or grapefruit juice, diluted half/half with distilled water, with no sugar or ice; citrus fruit acids help loosen, dissolve and eliminate mucus and other toxic wastes throughout the system.

Foods to avoid: all foods and beverages, except for distilled water and the juices mentioned above.

Gout

Closely related to rheumatism, gout is the inflammation of bones and ligaments in joints, owing to formation of acid crystals; this is caused mainly by diets that contain too much fatty meat, salt and alcohol, and insufficient quantities of raw, enzyme-active foods.

Carrot, beet, cucumber juice: the potent alkalizing properties of this blend help rebalance pH in blood and tissues and dissolve acid crystals in joints; 10 oz/3 oz/3 oz, 1–2 pints daily.

Parsley juice: raw parsley facilitates oxygen metabolism and stimulates adrenal secretions; both actions relieve the discomfort of gout and help correct the excess acidity of blood and tissues which causes it; mix 4 oz parsley juice with 12 oz carrot juice, 1 pint daily.

Celery juice: rich in organic sodium, iron, calcium and magnesium, it corrects blood acidosis, dissolves deposits of inorganic calcium in joints, and provides the organic calcium required for repair of damaged ligaments and bones; mix half/half with carrot juice, 1–2 pints daily.

Other beneficial foods: cabbage; fresh citrus juices (no sugar); raw black cherries (exclusively for 24 hours); raw black grapes (exclusively for 1–3 days); alfalfa tea or sprouts.

Foods to avoid: fatty meats, especially pork; organ meats, especially liver; cooked spinach; cooked tomatoes; dry beans; alcohol; salt.

Hemorrhoids

This increasingly common affliction is caused by stagnation and coagulation of blood fibron in the tiny capillaries that feed the anus and lower rectum; this is mainly the result of sticky toxic waste in the bloodstream, owing to excess consumption of refined starch, especially white bread and other flour products; in addition to dietary adjustments, daily practice of the anal sphincter exercise and defecation in the squatting position help correct and cure this condition.

Carrot and spinach juice: this blend benefits all colon conditions; restores proper blood pH; eliminates the sticky wastes that clog anal capillaries; 1–2 pints daily, 6 oz spinach to 10 oz carrot.

Celery juice: hemorrhoids are sometimes result of insufficient supplies of organic sulphur, iron and calcium in the diet; celery juice provides abundant supplies of these elements; may be mixed half/half with carrot juice, 2 pints daily, or 1 pint straight.

Apple cider vinegar: 2 tsp in a glass of water, 2–3 times daily, prevents excessive bleeding in hemorrhoids by balancing the bloodstream and lowering blood pressure.

Other beneficial foods: turnips; watercress; parsley.

Foods to avoid: refined starch and sugar, especially white bread and sweet pastries; all pasta; chili peppers; persimmons.

Kidney inflammation (nephritis)

This and related kidney conditions, such as kidney stones, are the result of excessive retention of uric acid in the kidneys, owing to an overload of acid wastes in the blood from incomplete digestion of improperly combined foods; left unattended, uric acid forms painful crystals or 'stones' in the kidneys.

Asparagus: contains asparamid, nature's most effective kidney diuretic; asparagus gives urine a strong odor of ammonia, which indicates that excess uric acid is being rapidly expelled; asparamid breaks up oxalic acid crystals in kidneys and muscles (cooked spinach and cooked tomatoes leave oxalic acid in the system); steam a bunch of fresh asparagus for 3 minutes or less and consume immediately, once daily.

Red beet juice: raw red beet juice has strong natural affinity for the kidneys; it is one of nature's best kidney cleansers, dissolving acid crystals and quickly eliminating the 'gravel' from the kidneys; its affinity for kidneys is reflected in red coloration of urine; take 8 oz raw beet juice, 2–3 tsp at a time, over a 24-hour period, with no other foods.

Watermelon: for nephritis, the watermelon cure is an excellent adjunct to asparagus therapy; eat nothing but lightly steamed asparagus and bites of raw watermelon for 24–48 hours.

Cucumbers: raw cucumbers, in bulk or juice, are excellent kidney diuretics and alkalizing agents; may be mixed with carrot and beet juice, 2 pints daily.

Other beneficial foods: apple cider vinegar; barley water; parsley; carrot juice; lecithin; cabbage; black grapes.

Foods to avoid: salt and salt-preserved foods; soy sauce; shellfish; strong coffee and tea; cooked spinach and tomatoes; alcohol; hot peppers.

Rheumatism

Closely related to gout, rheumatism is caused by heavy retention of uric acid, which eventually is absorbed into muscles, where it crystallizes. The condition is further aggravated by heavy consumption of cooked animal proteins, which cannot be properly digested and metabolized when the system is saturated with excess uric acid.

Carrot, beet, cucumber juice: this potent alkalizing blend dissolves uric acid crystals in muscle tissue and kidneys; 10 oz/3 oz/3 oz, 2 pints daily, taken in 6 equal doses throughout the day.

Lemon juice: dissolves and neutralizes uric acid crystals, thereby facilitating their rapid elimination through the kidneys; take the juice of one whole lemon in a tumbler of warm distilled water (with no sugar), 4–5 times throughout the day; efficacy is doubled if taken mid-way between doses of carrot, beet, cucumber juice.

Spinach: raw spinach helps dissolve uric acid crystals in blood and tissue and cleanses the lower bowels of the putrefactive wastes that contribute to accumulations of excess acidity; 6 oz with 10 oz carrot juice, 1–2 pints daily.

Other beneficial foods: parsley; asparagus, grapefruit juice (mixed with distilled water); cabbage; dark grapes, raw tomatoes.

Foods to avoid: cooked meats; refined starch and sugar; salt and salt-preserved foods; hot peppers; mustard.

Toxemia

This is a condition of general toxicity throughout the system, caused by auto-intoxication of the bloodstream, owing to huge accumulations of toxic waste matter in the intestinal tract; toxemia is characterized by severe acidosis of the blood, chronic fatigue, irritability and depression, skin eruptions, body odor, bad breath and poor digestion; the foremost measure against toxemia is therapeutic fasting with daily colonic irrigations, followed by nutritional therapy and permanent adjustments in dietary habits.

Carrot, beet, cucumber juice: restores pH balance in blood; dissolves acid crystals; cleanses bowels; builds strong blood plasma; 10 oz/3 oz/3 oz, 2 pints daily.

Carrot and spinach juice: cleanses and tonifies lower bowels; detoxifies bloodstream; balances pH; restores peristalsis and general colon health; builds strong blood plasma; 10 oz/6 oz, 2 pints daily.

Cabbage juice: a powerful cleanser and detoxifier for the stomach and upper bowels, raw cabbage juice is especially effective against protein putrefaction; 5 oz with 11 oz carrot juice, 1–2 pints daily.

Other beneficial foods: parsley; celery juice; asparagus; grapefruit juice (in distilled water); black grapes (exclusively 1–3 days); black cherries (exclusively 1–3 days).

Foods to avoid: incompatible combinations, especially of animal protein and concentrated starch; pasteurized milk; cooked eggs; overcooked meats; refined sugars, especially sweetened soft drinks.

Respiratory System: lungs, bronchial tubes, throat, nose, sinuses

Asthma

Extreme difficulty in breathing owing to inability to fully evacuate the lungs of stale air; accumulations of mucus in the lungs and consequent blockage of air passages block outflow of air, not inflow; pasteurized milk and refined starch are prime dietary causes.

Horseradish and lemon juice: the potent ethers in fresh grated horseradish dissolve mucus in the sinuses and bronchial tubes quickly and effectively; mixing it with fresh lemon juice doubles its efficacy; grate fresh horseradish into a bowl, add enough fresh lemon juice to make a paste, take ½ tsp 2–3 times a day, as needed.

Carrot and radish juice: fresh raw radish juice is similar in effect to horseradish, but milder; it is too strong to take straight, however, and should be blended 5 oz with 11 oz carrot juice, 1 pint daily.

Cranberries: cranberries contain one of nature's most potent vasodilators, which open up congested bronchial tubes so that normal breathing is restored; cranberries are excellent curative and preventive therapy for the entire breathing apparatus; bring fresh cranberries to boil with just enough water to cover them, simmer 2–3 minutes, pour off excess water, purée cranberries in blender, strain off skins, and keep pulp in refrigerator; when asthma or other respiratory difficulty occurs, mix 2 tbsp in a cup of warm distilled water and sip slowly.

Garlic: raw garlic contains potent ethers and enzymes that dissolve mucus in lungs and bronchial tubes and help restore normal breathing; also kills bacteria in air passages, preventing respiratory infections; 3–5 cloves daily.

Other beneficial foods: wheat germ oil; pumpkin seeds; sunflower seeds; celery juice; turnips; raw spinach.

Foods to avoid: pasteurized milk and all dairy products; cooked eggs; refined starch, especially white flour.

Bronchitis

Inflammation of the bronchial tubes owing to excess mucus in the lungs, caused by vicarious elimination of toxic wastes from the bloodstream to the lungs; toxins irritate and inflame tender lung and bronchial tissues as they excrete, permitting infection by bacteria to occur; colonic irrigations have proven highly effective as a fast method of eliminating the excess toxic wastes from the system, so that they do not get pushed out through skin and lungs.

Carrot and dandelion juice: raw dandelion juice counteracts blood acidosis and helps alkalize the entire system, with particular affinity for the lungs; 4 oz with 10 oz carrot juice, 1–2 pints daily.

Horseradish and lemon juice: same effects and dosage as for asthma.

Carrot and radish juice: same as for asthma.

Cranberries: same as for asthma.

Other beneficial foods: celery juice; raw radishes; raw spinach; whole lemon purée (mix in blender with cup of distilled water); watercress.

Foods to avoid: same as for asthma.

Colds

Colds are caused not by germs, but rather by accumulations of toxic mucus in the nasal passages that prevent the normal bathing and cleansing of nasal and sinus passages by clear moving mucus; germs then attack these toxic wastes, generating even more mucus and inflaming nasal and sinus passages; the best cure for a severe cold is a 3-day therapeutic fast with twice-daily colonic irrigations, followed by nutritional therapy to prevent recurrence.

Horseradish and lemon juice: same as for asthma.

Lemon juice: take the juice of one or two lemons and mix with a glass of warm distilled water, then sip slowly, 2–3 times daily; helps dissolve and eliminate excess mucus throughout the system, thus preventing its vicarious excretion through the lungs and nasal membranes.

Whole lemon purée: purée a whole lemon (with skin, fiber and seeds) in blender with a cup of distilled water, and drink slowly; flavor with 1 tbsp molasses, if desired, but no sugar; dissolves mucus, restores mucus membranes; biflavonoids in skin and fiber assist in restoring tissue integrity in respiratory system.

Other beneficial foods: carrot juice; raw radishes; cranberries (as for asthma); raw spinach; raw garlic; molasses.

Foods to avoid: pasteurized milk and all dairy products; all cooked food; all refined starch and sugar; eat nothing but raw fruit and raw vegetable juice.

Coughs

Coughs are caused mainly by the body's attempt to rid itself of excess toxic mucus through the lungs and bronchial tubes; the toxins irritate tender lining of throat, causing the throat to 'cough it up'.

Pineapple: fresh ripe pineapple is rich in bromelin, a proteolytic (protein-digesting) enzyme; bromelin literally 'digests' dead and diseased cells and foreign microbes in the throat; cut pineapple into cubes, chew well, and let juice dribble down throat, but spit out the pulp; or gargle with the freshly extracted juice of ripe pineapple, and spit it out.

Persimmons: raw, very ripe persimmons soothe sore throats and contain enzymes that break down damaged cells and foreign microbes.

Horseradish and lemon juice: for coughs and accompanied by heavy mucus congestion in lungs and sinuses; same usage as for asthma.

Whole lemon purée: same as for colds.

Other beneficial foods: grapefruit and orange juice; raw tomatoes; raw garlic; carrot and radish juice (as for asthma).

Foods to avoid: pasteurized milk and all dairy products; refined starch, especially white flour; cooked meats; cooked eggs.

Influenza

The 'flu' is caused primarily by the body's vulnerability to flu germs owing to extreme toxemia of the system, which results in excessive retention of toxic wastes, which impair immunity; flu strikes hardest in winter, because in winter the body excretes wastes more slowly and people eat less fresh, raw foods; toxic tissues, mostly in respiratory

THE TAO OF HEALTH, SEX AND LONGEVITY

apparatus, become breeding grounds for air-borne pathological bacteria; as with all such conditions, the most effective first step in treatment is a short therapeutic fast with daily colonic irrigations to remove the source of toxemia, followed by therapeutic nutrition.

Horseradish and lemon juice: same as for asthma.

Carrot, celery, parsley, spinach juice: this blend is super-rich in potassium, which quickly reduces acidity throughout the system, thereby commencing the detoxification process required for a complete cure and recovery; this blend also contains the full range of organic minerals and other nutrients required to sustain convalescing patients, without stuffing them full of solid foods; 8 oz/4 oz/2 oz/4 oz, 1–2 pints daily, taken in small doses throughout the day.

Other beneficial foods: lettuce juice; carrot and radish juice; whole lemon purée; grapefruit juice (in distilled warm water); distilled warm water.

Foods to avoid: all cooked and solid foods; pasteurized milk; coffee, tea; sweet soft drinks.

Pneumonia

Severe inflammation of lung tissues owing to vicarious elimination of highly toxic wastes through the respiratory system, which becomes infected by pathogenic bacteria as a result; due largely to excessive long-term consumption of pasteurized milk, refined starch and sugars; at the turn of the century, Dr J. H. Tilden of Denver, Colorado, treated thousands of cases of pneumonia using only two methods: fasting with daily colonic irrigations, and nutritional therapy; no drugs, no surgery; and he never lost a single patient! Therefore, fasting and colonic irrigation are the first and foremost defense against this dangerous disease.

Horseradish and lemon juice: same as for asthma; provides quick relief from mucus congestion.

Carrot, celery and radish juice: dissolves mucus; alkalizes bloodstream and respiratory tract; accelerates detoxification and thus restores natural immunity; 8 oz/5 oz/3 oz, 1 pint daily.

Carrot and spinach juice: detoxifies colon and restores normal bowel functions, thereby taking excretory load off the respiratory system; 10 oz/ 6 oz, 2 pints daily.

Other beneficial foods: cranberry (as for asthma); raw garlic; whole lemon purée (as for colds); molasses.

Foods to avoid: all refined starch and sugar; pasteurized milk and all dairy products; all cooked foods, especially meat and eggs.

Tonsillitis

Excessive retention of wastes and extreme acidosis permit germs to enter the body through the throat, thereby inflaming the tonsils, which are the first line of defense against incoming airborne germs; surgical removal, especially in children, is harmful, because the tonsils are glands that are intimately involved in endocrine balance; removal can adversely affect growth and normal development in children, especially in girls; colonic irrigation has proven highly effective in curing tonsillitis by removing the offending accumulations of toxic wastes that inflame the respiratory system when in excess.

Pineapple: ripe pineapple contains the protein-digesting enzyme bromelin, which digests diseased cells and foreign microbes in the throat; same usage as for coughs.

Garlic: the ethers from raw garlic quickly permeate the entire system, killing germs in the throat and decongesting the respiratory system.

Carrot and spinach juice: the best blend for detoxifying the colon and restoring normal bowel functions, which takes excretory pressure off the respiratory system, especially the lymph vessels in the throat; 10 oz/6 oz, 1–2 pints daily.

Other beneficial foods: carrot juice; ripe persimmons; grapefruit juice (in distilled water); cranberry; carrot, celery, parsley juice.

Foods to avoid: pasteurized milk; refined starch and sugar; cooked eggs and meat; strong coffee and tea.

Circulatory System: heart, pericardium, blood vessels

Anemia

A condition also known as 'tired blood', anemia is caused by a critical deficiency of red blood corpuscles, especially the oxygen-carrying element hemoglobin; symptoms include chronic fatigue, lethargy, depression and loss of sexual drive; this condition is due entirely to poor dietary habits, especially the exclusive consumption of cooked, denatured, processed foods, pasteurized milk and refined starch; heavy smoking may also be a contributing factor.

Molasses: molasses is nature's richest source of organic iron and copper, which work together to build 'strong blood', especially the iron-dependent protein hemoglobin; 2 tbsp in a glass of warm water, twice daily.

Wheat germ oil: enhances the blood's capacity to carry oxygen, thereby correcting blood deficiency; 1 tsp of pure wheat germ oil after breakfast and again after dinner.

Lecithin: builds strong blood plasma and dissolves sticky deposits in arteries, thereby enhancing blood's capacity to assimilate and transport oxygen and nutrients; liquid lecithin from soy beans is best; raw egg yolks is another rich source.

Fennel juice: use 'Florence Fennel', also known as 'Finocchio'; specific affinity for bloodstream, builds strong blood plasma; may be taken straight, 1 pint daily, or mixed half/half with carrot juice, 2 pints daily.

Red beet juice: builds red blood corpuscles and tones up overall blood quality; 8 oz, taken 2–3 tsp at a time throughout the day; or as carrot, beet, cucumber blend.

Spinach: rich in organic iron and other vital minerals; builds strong blood plasma, especially iron-dependent hemoglobin; raw bulk in salads, or 6 oz juice with 10 oz carrot juice, 1–2 pints daily.

Other beneficial foods: pomegranate; lettuce juice; dandelion juice; asparagus; cabbage; chrysanthemum tea; black grapes; raisins; raw egg yolks wheat germ.

Foods to avoid: pasteurized milk; strong coffee and tea; refined starch, especially white flour; canned, smoked, preserved and otherwise processed foods.

Angina pectoris

Painful contractions and cramps in the valves and muscles of the heart and/or pericardium, due primarily to polluted blood, and sometimes to excess pressure from gas in the colon.

Carrot, celery, parsley, spinach juice: this potent potassium-rich blend quickly detoxifies and alkalizes the bloodstream, thereby correcting a major cause of angina pectoris; builds strong blood to nourish the heart muscles; 8 oz/4 oz/2 oz/4 oz, 1 pint daily.

Garlic: raw garlic consumed daily in sufficient quantities has been shown to eliminate the acute pain of angina pectoris within 5 days; it cleanses the blood, removes sticky deposits in blood vessels, and thus enhances the quality and quantity of blood supplied to the heart; 6–8 cloves daily (minced into salad dressings, or crushed and put into gelatin capsules for swallowing).

Black fungus: also called 'Tree Ears' because it grows from the bark of trees, this Chinese delicacy contains active elements that remove deposits from the walls of blood vessels, thus enhancing the supply of blood to the heart and other tissues.

Wheat germ oil: according to research of nutritional therapist Dr Marsh Morrison, 1 tsp of wheat germ oil per day provides about as much oxygen to the heart as an oxygen tent, thus relieving spasms and cramps in heart muscles and valves.

Other beneficial foods: raw spinach; wheat germ; lecithin; pecans; active yeast (in warm water, on empty stomach); sunflower seeds; raw egg yolk.

Foods to avoid: refined starch and sugar, especially white flour; pasteurized milk and dairy products; cooked eggs and meat.

Arteriosclerosis

The hardening of blood vessels owing to deficiency of organic calcium and other vital organic minerals, and an excess of calcium and inorganic cholesterol, derived primarily from denatured foods, especially pasteurized milk, cooked eggs and overcooked fatty meats; these deposits of inorganic calcium and cholesterol continue to accumulate, hardening and narrowing the blood vessels and permitting clots to develop.

Carrot, celery, parsley, spinach juice: alkalizes bloodstream; removes deposits from blood vessels; 8 oz/4 oz/2 oz/4 oz, 1 pint daily.

Garlic: purifies blood and removes accumulations of sticky inorganic deposits from walls of blood vessels, thereby restoring elasticity and free flow of blood.

Black fungus: a fungus that grows on bark of trees, it contains elements that purify blood and remove sticky deposits from blood vessels.

Beet and carrot juice: raw beets purify the blood and build strong blood plasma, enhancing capacity to carry oxygen; best mixed half/half with carrot juice, 1–2 pints daily.

Other beneficial foods: raw spinach; celery; lettuce; black grapes; pumpkin seeds; raw tomatoes; seaweed (kelp).

Foods to avoid: pasteurized milk and all dairy products; cooked eggs; animal fat, especially lard; cooked meat, especially pork; all preserved and canned foods; salt.

Blood pressure (high)

Excessive pressure of blood against the walls of blood vessels, owing primarily to diets of denatured and overcooked foods, which deposit inorganic minerals and cholesterol against walls of blood vessels, narrowing and hardening them and raising blood pressure; also caused by excess retention of toxic by-products of protein putrefaction in the digestive tract and liver.

Carrot, celery, parsley, spinach juice: same benefits and usage as for arterio-sclerosis, which is usually accompanied by high blood pressure.

Spinach: raw spinach corrects pH imbalance in the digestive tract and bloodstream, thus eliminating a major source of the toxic wastes that leave deposits in blood vessels and raise blood pressure.

Beet and carrot juice: same effects and usage as for arteriosclerosis.

Molasses: builds and balances the bloodstream, eliminating toxic conditions that lead to high blood pressure; 2 tbsp in cup of warm water, twice daily.

Other beneficial foods: raw garlic; wheat germ oil; wheat germ; pecans; sunflower seeds; raw tomatoes; seaweed (kelp); lecithin.

Foods to avoid: refined starch and sugar; pasteurized milk; fatty meats; salt and salt-preserved foods; alcohol; stimulating spices such as hot peppers, curry, mustard.

Headache

There are dozens of different types of headache, but most are caused primarily by excess pressure in the tiny capillaries that feed the brain; this pressure is caused by impurities in the bloodstream, which not only block the tiny capillaries but also deprive the brain of oxygen and glucose.

Spinach: raw spinach, as bulk or juice, purifies the bloodstream and builds up the oxygen-carrying element of hemoglobin, thus enhancing supply of oxygen and blood to the brain.

Carrot, beet, and cucumber juice: this blend breaks down acid crystals in kidneys, thus improving their ability to cleanse the blood of the impurities that often cause headaches when they reach the brain; also purifies blood and builds hemoglobin, thus enhancing oxygen supplies to brain; 10 oz/3 oz/3 oz, 1–2 pints when headache approaches.

Lecithin: 20 per cent of brain tissue consists of lecithin, which when taken in combination with vitamin C has remarkable rejuvenating effects on the brain; organic lecithin also rinses away inorganic cholesterol deposits in coronary arteries, thereby enhancing supply of oxygenated blood to the brain; liquid lecithin extracted from soy beans is most convenient form of supplement.

Garlic: raw garlic is one of nature's best blood vessel cleansers; taken in conjunction with lecithin, it not only eliminates toxic conditions that often cause headaches, but also enhances memory, learning and other mental functions.

Other beneficial foods: lettuce juice; molasses; pecans; wheat germ; sunflower seeds; raw egg yolk (for lecithin and organic cholesterol).

Foods to avoid: refined starch, especially white flour; refined sugar, especially sweet soft drinks; cooked eggs; pasteurized milk; cooked fatty meats.

Heart disease

The various forms of heart disease are primarily the result of toxic impurities clogging blood vessels; this deprives the heart muscles and valves of oxygen and puts excessive chronic strain on the heart, which has to pump much harder than normal to push blood through a clogged circulatory system – a healthy heart pumps about 3,000 gallons of blood every 24 hours, but a heart under the stress of a clogged circulatory system must pump up to 25,000 gallons in 24 hours just to maintain sufficient circulation; obviously, such an 8-fold increase in heart strain soon leads to heart exhaustion and disease; the prime source of the blood impurities and deposits that cause heart disease is a diet composed entirely of denatured and cooked foods.

Carrot, celery, parsley, spinach juice: the most potent blend of juices for potassium, which quickly restores proper blood pH, helps remove deposits from blood vessels, and builds strong blood plasma, especially hemoglobin; 8 oz/4 oz/2 oz/4 oz, 1–2 pints daily.

Carrot, beet, cucumber juice: dissolves acid crystals in kidneys, enabling them to cleanse the blood more efficiently, thus removing impurities that can accumulate to cause heart disease; 10 oz/3 oz/3 oz, 1–2 pints daily.

Molasses: rich in organic iron and copper, as well as potassium, all of which alkalize the bloodstream and build strong blood plasma, which in turn benefits the heart tissues; 2 tbsp in warm water, twice daily.

Grapes: the 'grape cure' (nothing but 1–3 pounds of raw black grapes for 5–7 days) has been shown by experiments in the Soviet Union to have a direct tonifying effect on the muscles and valves of the heart; also purifies and balances the bloodstream.

Wheat germ oil: greatly enhances delivery of oxygen to the heart; best when used in conjunction with raw garlic; 1 tsp wheat germ oil and 2–3 cloves raw garlic, once or twice a day, after meals.

Pecans: raw pecans are nature's richest source of readily assimilable organic pyridoxine (vitamin B6), an element that plays an essential role in converting the amino acids from consumed proteins into usable form for the body; thus, raw pecans assist in the regeneration of damaged cells in diseased hearts; 10–15 raw pecans (or 20–30 pecan halves) per day.

Other beneficial foods: raw spinach; cabbage; ripe bananas; wheat germ; lecithin; sunflower seeds; raw garlic.

Foods to avoid: refined starch, especially white bread and sweet pastries; refined sugar, especially sweet carbonated soft drinks (regular as well as 'diet' types); cooked eggs; pasteurized milk; cooked fatty meats; salt.

Varicose veins

This condition is caused by deposits of inorganic calcium, cholesterol and other inorganic elements in the walls of veins, causing them to clog up and bulge outward through the skin; refined starch and sugar are primary dietary culprits.

Spinach: raw spinach detoxifies and stimulates the lower bowel, so that wastes are eliminated there rather than accumulating and polluting the bloodstream; builds and balances blood; as juice, mix 6 oz with 10 oz carrot juice, 2 pints daily.

Red beet juice: another potent purifier and builder of blood, raw beet juice eliminates the blood toxemia that causes varicose veins; best taken half/half with carrot juice, 1–2 pints daily; or sip 8 oz of the straight beet juice slowly throughout the day.

Garlic: raw garlic dissolves the deposits of inorganic calcium and cholesterol that lead to varicose veins.

Parsley juice: raw parsley juice is one of the most potent of all vegetable juices for enhancing oxygen metabolism, cleansing the blood, dissolving sticky deposits in veins and maintaining elasticity of blood vessels, especially delicate capillaries; it's too strong to take straight and should be mixed with 4 oz to 12 oz carrot juice, or with other blends, 1 pint daily.

Other beneficial foods: lettuce juice; turnips; watercress; black grapes (exclusively for 1–5 days, depending on severity), Black Fungus; molasses; lecithin.

Foods to avoid: pasteurized milk; refined starch, especially white flour; refined sugar; cooked eggs and overcooked meats; hydrogenated fats.

Nervous System: brain, nerves, eyes

Eye trouble

Most eye trouble is due to insufficient circulation and nutritional deficiency in the eye muscles and the optic nerve; the optic nerve is one of the most powerful nerves in the body and uses up to 30% of available glucose (blood sugar); when blood sugar runs dry, all nerves must rely on glycogen from the liver; any interruption in glycogen supply due to liver dysfunction is often reflected in eye trouble; Chinese physicians always look first to the liver when treating eye problems; a polluted bloodstream can also cause serious eye problems.

Sunflower seeds: sunflower seeds are rich in organic vitamin A and other vital eye nutrients; Dr Marsh Morrison has shown that 2 oz of raw sunflower seeds per day, in conjunction with abstention from all animal proteins, clears up many eye problems within two weeks.

Carrot, celery, endive, parsley juice: this blend provides potent nourishment to the entire optic system, including nerves and muscles; carrots provide organic vitamin A as carotene, endives are rich in other nutrients with specific affinity for the eyes; 8 oz/4 oz/3 oz/2 oz, 1–2 pints daily.

Dandelion juice: rich in potassium, calcium, sodium, magnesium and iron, raw dandelion juice alkalizes the bloodstream and provides a blend of organic nutrients of specific benefit to the nervous system, of which the optic nerve is the busiest component; mix half/half with carrot juice, 1–2 pints daily.

Spinach: raw spinach is another good source of organic vitamin A for the optic system; also builds strong blood due to rich supplies of organic iron, and this enhances circulation of oxygenated blood to the eyes.

Other beneficial foods: carrots; watercress; apricots; turnip greens; calves liver.

Foods to avoid: deep fat fried foods; refined starch and sugar; hot peppers; alcohol; mineral oil (as laxative).

Fatigue

Chronic fatigue is an indication that the body's 'batteries' have run down and resistance is lowered, and thus serves as a warning that disease might strike at any time; it is primarily due to a critical deficiency of active enzymes in the diet and an overabundance of 'dead' processed, over-cooked foods, in incompatible combinations; such diets, typical of modern times, literally starve cells of nutrition and energy and permit toxic wastes to accumulate in the tissues; consequently, the body is unable to generate and direct energy for work or play; all available energy must be used just to keep the body alive.

Pecans: nature's most potent source of organic pyridoxine (vitamin B6), which is essential for all nervous functions and plays a key role in utilizing amino acids derived from consumed proteins; since all vital

THE TAO OF HEALTH, SEX AND LONGEVITY

functions are controlled by the nervous system, pecans provide the element required by nerves to transform nutritional 'essence' to functional energy and regulate the body; 10–15 raw pecans, or 20–30 pecan halves daily is a therapeutic dose.

Carrot, beet, cucumber juice: this blend provides a potent boost of active enzymes and organic nutrients to the bloodstream, while also alkalizing and cleansing the kidneys, which in turn improves blood quality and helps relieve fatigue; 10 oz/3 oz/3 oz, 1–2 pints daily.

Carrot juice: raw carrot juice is perhaps the best overall therapeutic food in the world; it alkalizes, cleanses, nourishes and stimulates almost every system in the body; as such, it is an effective antidote for the nervous exhaustion caused by diets deficient in vital raw foods; 2–3 pints daily.

Raw egg yolk: a potent source of organic lecithin, which is a major component in brain and nerve tissue; also stimulates sluggish adrenal glands, which alleviates fatigue; 2 yolks daily, blended into carrot juice.

Other beneficial foods: raw spinach; active yeast (in warm water, on empty stomach); molasses; wheat germ; soy beans; lecithin.

Foods to avoid: denatured, processed, preserved, canned and cooked foods should compose less than 50 per cent of daily diet in order to cure and prevent chronic fatigue due to nutritional deficiency.

Hypertension

Besides stress and other psychological factors, hypertension is caused by the irritation of various nerve centers owing to nutritional deficiency, retention of toxic wastes and lack of organic alkaline elements; for example, severe hypertension that leads to violent outbursts has been quickly cured in many patients with sufficient doses of niacin (vitamin B3); pyridoxine (vitamin B6) in organic form relieves the hypertension associated with nervous stress.

Pecans: a potent source of organic pyridoxine, pecans rank among the very best of therapeutic foods for hypertension and other nervous disorders; 10–15 whole raw pecans per day.

Yeast: active yeast dissolved in a cup of warm water and taken on an empty stomach provides a powerful dose of all important B vitamins in organic form; brewer's yeast, though more palatable, is technically 'dead' and thus not as potent a source of nutritional elements; 1 small packet of granular active yeast per cup warm water, twice a day.

Lecithin: the most basic building block of brain and nerve tissue, organic lecithin may be taken as liquid extract of soy beans or in the form of raw egg yolks (as for fatigue).

116

Wheat germ oil: nature's best source of organic vitamin E, which is essential for optimum nerve function; 1 tsp daily after breakfast, another after dinner.

Carrot, beet, cucumber juice: alkalizes the kidneys and blood, thus eliminating the excess acidity that is usually a contributing factor to hypertension; also provides organic minerals and active enzymes which enhance nervous functions; 10 oz/3 oz/3 oz, 2 pints daily.

Other beneficial foods: carrot juice; celery juice; molasses; wheat germ; black grapes; apricots; apricot kernels (for vitamin B17); turnip greens.

Foods to avoid: hot peppers; mustard; cooked meats, especially pork; all preserved and canned foods; strong coffee and tea; refined sugars, especially sweet soft drinks; alcohol.

Insomnia

Inability to sleep owing to nervous tension and/or excess acidity in the system.

Pecans: 10–15 whole raw pecans per day provide all the organic pyridoxine (vitamin B6) the nervous system needs for normal function; this helps eliminate the nervous tension that causes insomnia.

Molasses: besides iron, copper and potassium, molasses is rich in organic pyridoxine and calcium, which enhance nervous functions; organic calcium is well known as a promoter of sound sleep; a glass of milk, if pasteurized, will not deliver organic calcium to the system owing to lack of the vital lactase enzyme, which is required to extract calcium from milk; 2 tbsp in warm water, before bed.

Bananas: ripe bananas are very rich in potassium, sodium and magnesium, all of which restore health and balance to nutritionally exhausted nervous systems; also rich in the amino acid tryptophan, which is known to promote sleep.

Other beneficial foods: lecithin; wheat germ; grapefruit; parsnips; soy beans; honey.

Foods to avoid: vinegar (except apple cider vinegar); cooked meats, especially at dinner; refined starch, especially white bread and sweet pastries; hot peppers; strong coffee and tea; alcohol.

Neuralgia

Acute pain in and around nerves that are inflamed and impaired owing to nutritional deficiency and excess acidity.

Lecithin: provides the basic building block for nourishment and repair of damaged nerves.

Wheat germ oil: potent source of organic vitamin E, which is required for nourishment and repair of nerves and increases oxygen supply to nerves; 2 tsp daily, one after breakfast and the other after dinner, in conjunction with lecithin.

Pecans: provide organic pyridoxine, which nerves require to utilize amino acids.

Carrot and celery juice: rich in organic sodium, magnesium and iron, which help restore blood pH, thus eliminating acidity, and nourish the nerves; mix half/half, 1–2 pints daily.

Other beneficial foods: raw spinach; raw parsley; wheat germ; molasses; active yeast (in warm water, on empty stomach).

Foods to avoid: cooked fatty meats; refined starches and sugars; synthetic additives and preservatives; salt; hot peppers; mustard.

Neuritis

Acute pain caused by the formation of uric acid crystals in muscles, which then press against nerve endings; excess consumption of cooked meat is the prime dietary cause of excess uric acid, and hence of neuritis.

Carrot, beet, cucumber juice: a potent alkalizing blend with specific affinity for the blood and the kidneys; facilitates elimination of uric acid from blood and kidneys; 10 oz/3 oz/3 oz, 2 pints daily.

Carrot, celery, parsley juice: an alkalizing blend of raw juices with specific affinity for the nervous system; contains organic minerals required for repair and maintainence of nerves; 9 oz/5 oz/2 oz, 1–2 pints daily.

Lemon: raw lemon juice diluted with warm distilled water is an excellent all-around alkalizer and mucus dissolver, but only when taken without sugar; though acidic in the natural state, lemon juice has strong alkalizing properties in the stomach and bloodstream.

Wheat germ oil: provides organic vitamin E, required for repair and maintenance of nerves; 1 tsp after breakfast.

Other beneficial foods: pecans; lecithin; grapefruit juice (diluted with distilled water); molasses; carrot and spinach juice.

Foods to avoid: vinegar (except apple cider vinegar); refined starch, especially white flour; refined sugars, especially sweet soft drinks; chocolate and candy; cooked meat and eggs.

Reproductive System: genitals, suprarenal glands, prostate, ovaries, testes, uterus, urogenital canal

Impotence

A condition of male sexual dysfunction, in which erection cannot be attained, or maintained sufficiently to complete sexual intercourse; other than psychological factors, common contributing causes include nervous exhaustion, depletion of sexual glands due to excessive ejaculation, insufficient nutrition for the reproductive organs and glands, and excess acid toxicity; therapeutic fasts in conjunction with colonic irrigations have corrected even the most stubborn cases of impotence, when followed up with proper nutrition.

Carrot, beet, cucumber juice: this is one of the strongest kidney alkalizers and cleansers and helps heal damage to the urogenital canal, bladder, prostate, suprarenal glands and other parts directly affected by excess acid toxicity in the kidneys; also provides vital organic nutrients for their repair and maintainence; 10 oz/3 oz/3 oz, 2 pints daily.

Bananas: ripe raw bananas are very rich in potassium, tryptophan and other nutrients that restore the nervous system and thus help eliminate impotence; they also contain enzymes that help manufacture sexual hormones.

Pumpkin seeds: nature's most nourishing food for the male prostrate gland, dysfunction of which is a common cause of impotence; 2–3 oz of raw seeds daily.

Oysters: raw oysters are rich in zinc, which is vital for prostrate health and sexual functions; they also contain active enzymes and hormones of benefit to the reproductive system.

Wheat germ oil: a potent source of organic vitamin E, which is vital for manufacture of sexual hormones, and also helps eliminate nervous exhaustion; 1–2 tsp daily, preferably after meals.

Lecithin: male semen consists largely of lecithin, and thus lecithin helps build strong and abundant semen, deficiency of which is one cause of impotence.

Bee pollen: contains enzymes and other elements that stimulate production of sexual hormones; 3–6 capsules per day.

Other beneficial foods: sunflower seeds; carrot juice; raw spinach; shrimp (preferably raw or very lightly steamed); seaweed (kelp); ginger root; celery seeds; raw garlic; beet juice; raw egg yolk; black grapes, black cherries.

Foods to avoid: refined starch and sugar, especially white bread, sweet pastries and sweet soft drinks; overcooked meat, especially hamburger meat on white bread; all meat and other foods preserved with potassium nitrate (saltpeter); vinegar (except apple cider vinegar); strong coffee and tea.

Infertility

Insufficient sperm or ova to effect conception during intercourse; this is largely a result of nutritional deficiency and excess retention of toxic wastes throughout the system, especially in sexual glands; it can also be caused by a collapsed colon, which puts excess pressure on prostate in males and fallopian tubes in females, preventing the free flow of sperm and ova; some couples, infertile for 10–15 years of marriage, have suddenly found themselves 'with child' after three to five 7-day fasts with daily colonic irrigations, followed by proper nutritional therapy.

Carrot, beet, cucumber juice: the best blend for cleaning and alkalizing the kidneys, sexual organs and sexual glands – all of which are influenced by kidney function and condition; 10 oz/3 oz/3 oz, 2 pints daily.

Asparagus: contains aspartic acid, an amino acid that neutralizes toxic wastes in the bloodstream and eliminates them through the kidneys; one of nature's best kidney diuretics; lightly steamed, no salt.

Bee pollen: a potent stimulator of sexual hormone production in men and women; 3–6 capsules daily.

Raw egg yolk: rich in organic lecithin, which builds strong semen; 2 per day, stirred into carrot juice.

Bananas: rich in tryptophan, a vital amino acid involved in nerve function, but also vital for fertility in both men and women; chronic tryptophan deficiency often causes infertility in men and women.

Wheat germ oil: rich in organic vitamin E, essential for production of sperm and ova; 2 tsp daily, one after breakfast and one after dinner.

Other beneficial foods: raw spinach; celery; pumpkin seeds; sunflower seeds; raw fish (*sashimi*)

Foods to avoid: pasteurized milk (prolonged use of which has been shown to be a contributing factor to infertility – recall Dr Pottenger's experiments on cats); overcooked meats; cooked eggs; refined white starch, especially white flour.

Leucorrhea

Excess formation and discharge of mucus in the female genital tract; this is almost always the direct result of poor dietary habits and the consequent retention of toxic wastes in the system; denatured foods consumed in incompatible combinations, with insufficient supplies of active enzymes, are the major cause of this condition.

Horseradish and lemon juice: a potent dissolver of mucus throughout the system; use in similar manner as for asthma and other respiratory ailments.

Carrot, beet, cucumber juice: alkalizes the kidneys and sexual organs, thus eliminating acid mucus from the reproductive system; 10 oz/3 oz/3 oz, 2 pints daily.

Whole lemon purée: one of nature's best therapeutic foods for the female sexual organs and glands, whole lemon purée contains active bioflavonoids, which have specific affinity for the uterus and vagina; dissolves vaginal mucus; restores pH balance; regulates the female reproductive system; purée whole lemon in blender with 1 cup distilled water and 1 tbsp molasses (if desired), 1–2 times daily.

Other beneficial foods: grapefruit juice (in distilled water); whole grapefruit or orange purée (same as lemon purée method); apple cider vinegar (2 tsp in glass of distilled water, twice daily); carrot and spinach juice.

Foods to avoid: pasteurized milk and dairy products; cooked eggs; fatty meats, especially pork; hydrogenated fats, especially margarine; refined starch, especially white bread and sweet pastries.

Menstrual disorders

Excessive bleeding during menstruation, excessively dark menstrual blood, foul menstrual odor and irregular menstrual cycles usually indicate a condition of blood toxemia as well as endocrine imbalance, which itself is often a result of blood toxemia; these problems generally respond very well to a program of fasting and colonic irrigation to cleanse the bloodstream and rebalance the endocrine system, followed by nutritional therapy.

Fennel juice ('Florence Fennel' or 'Finocchio'): fennel juice is a highly effective blood builder, and thus helps correct menstrual disorders; best mixed half/half with carrot juice, 1–2 pints daily.

Carrot, beet, cucumber juice: an excellent all-around blend for cleaning and balancing sexual organs and glands, via its natural affinity for the kidneys; 10 oz/3 oz/3 oz, 2 pints daily.

Carrot and spinach juice: specific affinity for blood and lower bowels, this blend eliminates the source of blood toxemia in the colon, thereby neutralizing the blood toxemia that causes menstrual problems; 10 oz/ 6 oz, 1–2 pints daily.

Whole lemon purée: this remedy has worked wonders in correcting all sorts of menstrual disorders, including excess bleeding, foul odor, dark blood, irregularity and the stress of menopause; same use as for leucorrhea.

Molasses: builds and balances the blood, especially the vital hemoglobin component; 2 tbsp in warm water, twice daily.

Other beneficial foods: whole orange or grapefruit purée; seaweed (kelp); beet juice; black grapes (exclusively for 1–3 days); wheat germ oil.

Foods to avoid: pasteurized milk; cooked eggs; fatty meats, especially pork; hydrogenated fats; refined starch and sugar.

Prostate disorders

This increasingly common problem has four prime causes: nutritional deficiency; excess toxicity; excess ejaculation; pressure from a collapsed colon. Prostitis can quickly lead to impotence in men and can also make urination painful and difficult, and eventually impossible, requiring surgical removal of the prostate, which in men is tantamount to castration as far as sexual potency is concerned; colonic irrigation is very beneficial in cases due to excess toxicity and/or collapsed colons.

Pumpkin seeds: raw pumpkin seeds have been recognized in East and West for centuries as the very best therapeutic food for the prostate; they are very rich in unsaturated fatty acids, organic iron and pangamic acid (vitamin B15), all of which are vital for prostate function; 2–3 oz raw seeds daily.

Wheat germ oil: contains organic vitamin E, essential for prostate health; 2 tsp daily, one after breakfast and the other after dinner.

Yeast: active yeast contains abundant supplies of almost all B vitamins in organic form; these are very helpful in restoring prostate health; 1 packet of granular active yeast in a cup of warm water, on empty stomach, twice a day.

Carrot, asparagus, lettuce juice: this blend detoxifies and alkalizes deficient kidneys, as well as the entire urogential tract, which runs straight through the prostate; 8 oz/4 oz/4 oz, 1–2 pints daily.

Lemon juice: the juice of two lemons in 6 oz of warm distilled water, taken at 3–4 hour intervals for 24–36 hours, with no intake of any other food or beverage, has potent alkalizing and cleansing effects in the urogenital canal, prostate and related sexual parts.

Red beet juice: an 8 oz glass taken 2–3 tsp at a time, throughout the day, with no intake of other food, detoxifies and alkalizes the prostate via its affinity for the kidneys and urogenital tract.

Other beneficial foods: lecithin; filbert (Hazel) nuts; sunflower seeds; grapefruit juice (in distilled water); black grapes (exclusively for 1–3 days); bee pollen; soy beans; carrot juice.

Foods to avoid: pasteurized milk and other dairy products; cooked meats, especially pork; refined starch; especially white flour; all foods with artificial additives and preservatives.

Cancer/AIDS/Herpes

Cancer

According to both traditional Chinese medicine as well as more enlightened studies in the West, cancer occurs when a mass of cells in various tissues become so toxic and starved of organic nourishment that they can no longer breathe properly, i.e. they can no longer eliminate wastes and absorb nutrients. Hence, they literally 'ferment' in their own toxic wastes, mutate, and become cancerous tumors. This condition can be caused by a number of factors: primary cause is chronic poor diet, heavy in cooked meats, eggs, and refined starches and sugars and poor in raw food, enzymes, organic nutrients. Insufficient circulation of essence and energy due to lack of exercise and shallow breathing are contributing causes. Chronic stress and depression also play a role by poisoning the bloodstream with toxic by-products of adrenalin and other 'fight or flight' reactions.

First and foremost therapy is detoxification with a series of 7–10 day fasts with daily colonic irrigations. Thereafter a diet of raw fruit and vegetable juices is indicated. Breathing exercises are extremely beneficial to cancer patients, in conjunction with detoxification and proper organic nutrition, because they circulate the nutrients to the cells, and suffuse all tissues with abundant supplies of *chee*.

Carrot juice: this is perhaps the best vegetable juice for detoxifying tissues. It also helps alkalize the bloodstream, which in cases of toxemia is always highly acidic. Raw carrot juice delivers abundant supplies of readily assimilable vitamins, minerals, and enzymes to diseased cells, giving them the fuel they require to sluff off wastes and rebuild cells. 75-year-old Jay Kordish, who today promotes raw juice diets in America, was cured of bladder cancer at age 25 with a blend of raw carrot and apple juice, taken a glass at a time every hour 13 times a day under the supervision of the great raw juice therapist Dr Max Gersen. Drink at least 1½ quarts freshly extracted raw carrot juice daily, in conjunction with breathing and other exercises, for as long as therapy is required.

Grapes: raw grapes, especially the dark variety, are renowned as excellent cancer therapy when taken as an exclusive diet for prolonged periods. Entire sanatoriums in Russia are devoted to this cure. Grapes detoxify all tissues and organs and restore organic integrity to starved cells. In 1925, South African Johanna Brandt cured herself of cancer with an exclusive grape diet and wrote a book about it called *The Grape Cure*. She recommends 2–4 pounds of dark grapes per day, for a week to a month or more, chewing the skins and seeds as well.

Cabbage juice: fresh raw cabbage juice has been proven to cure severe ulcers in the stomach, duodenum, and intestines. As such, it is also an effective therapy for cancers of the stomach and intestinal tract. High concentrations of organic chlorine and sulphur in raw cabbage cleanse the mucus membranes of the stomach and intestinal tract, where cancerous tissues often form. It is generally recommended to take cabbage juice in combination with raw carrot juice, due to its strength. 4 oz cabbage juice/8 oz carrot juice, 3 times daily.

Raw beet juice: beet juice is highly beneficial as a liver detoxifier and blood cleanser. In cases of cancer, therefore, it purifies the bloodstream so that the blood can do its work of detoxifying the body and delivering nutrients to starved cells. By detoxifying the liver, it further promotes clean blood, which is filtered by the liver. Also indicated in cases of liver cancer. 8 oz of pure beet juice, twice daily, or 6 oz beet/6 oz carrot, 3 times daily. Tablets and dry crystals of pure beet juice extract are also very good.

Foods to avoid: all animal products, especially proteins and fats, i.e. no cooked meat, fat, eggs, milk, etc.; all refined sugars and starches; carbohydrates; oils; eat only fresh raw fruit and vegetables, juices and extracts.

AIDS

AIDS is a disease of the immune system which has only recently been recognized. Therefore, no specific cures have yet been proven to be effective. The raw juice therapy recommended below is not claimed as a cure but rather as a highly effective adjunct to whatever other therapies are being used. Since AIDS directly attacks the immune system, it is a logical approach to tonify the immune system as a basic part of therapy. Tonifying the immune system involves a two-pronged approach: removing morbid wastes from the system which suppress immunity and resistance; ingesting organic nutrients which repair and strengthen the immune system. Fasting is by far the most efficient method of removing morbid wastes from the body, and raw fruit and vegetable juices are by far the most potent sources of the organic nutrients required to repair the body.

Carrot juice: as the best overall vegetable juice for detoxifying the system and repairing damaged tissues, carrot juice is an excellent supplement to the diet of AIDS victims. It has specific affinity for the adrenal glands, which by virtue of their hormone secretions bolster the entire immune system and help regulate the whole endocrine system. It detoxifies the liver, which is responsible for filtering and nourishing the blood. It is the blood which carries immune factors to the various tissues of the body. At least 1½ quarts of freshly extracted carrot juice per day is recommended.

Beet juice: beet juice has strongly detoxifying properties, especially in the liver, bloodstream, and kidneys, owing to its high organic chlorine content. It is rich in potassium, which balances metabolism. Its organic iron content help build 'strong blood' by enriching the red corpuscles, which by virtue of their hemoglobin carry oxygen to the tissues. Take 8 oz twice daily, preferably on empty stomach, or mix 8 oz with 8 oz carrot juice and take twice daily.

Grapes: raw dark grapes are such an effective remedy for so many serious ailments when taken as an exclusive diet for up to one month that this therapy is well worth trying in cases of AIDS. 'Incurable' cancers have in many cases been completely cured with this therapy, when properly administered. Since AIDS is also regarded by conventional medical practice as 'incurable,' raw grape therapy may be helpful, although no studies have yet confirmed this. Therapy indicates 2–4 pounds of grapes per day, for up to one month at a time.

Garlic: fresh raw garlic, in bulk or juice, is one of the most effective natural antibiotics on earth. It has been shown to kill many germs which are resistant to penicillin. It also eliminates intestinal parasites. Among the many symptoms of AIDS are a wide range of infections caused by the body's lack of normal immune factors. Daily doses of raw garlic or garlic juice help protect the body from all sorts of germs and parasites to which AIDS victims are vulnerable. This prevents the onset of severe infections during other forms of therapy against the AIDS virus itself. Note that the garlic must be fresh and raw. Odorless refined substitutes do not contain the active enzymes responsible for its therapeutic benefits. 6–12 cloves of fresh raw garlic daily, either crushed and stuffed into gelatin capsules for ingestion, or extracted juice. It's best to take it in two doses to ensure steady absorption throughout the day.

Foods to avoid: eliminate all cooked meat and eggs and all pasteurized milk and milk products, in order to avoid protein putrefaction in the system, which damages the immune system; all refined sugars and starches; deep-fried foods; artificial preservatives and additives.

Herpes

Herpes is a sexually transmitted disease which attacks the nervous system and in its active stages manifests itself as festering skin eruptions and lesions, usually on and around the genitals and mouth areas. It is contagious only in its active stages but relatively harmless when dormant. Its connection with the nervous system is why it tends to become active and erupt into lesions when the victim becomes 'nervous' due to stress. Several drugs have been developed to suppress herpes but so far there is no permanent cure. The juice therapy recommended below is helpful in suppressing active symptoms and helping the body to fight the infection, but it is not claimed as a cure.

Carrot juice: as an overall detoxifier and source of organic nutrients, fresh carrot juice is a good dietary supplement for victims of herpes. By cleansing the body of morbid matter, carrot juice reduces the severity of skin eruptions when the disease becomes active. Take at least 1½ quarts daily, preferably in 2 or 3 doses, on empty stomach.

Pecans: rich in pyridoxine, pecans rank among the best of therapeutic foods for the nervous system. Daily intake of raw pecans helps balance nervous system functions and hence reduces the symptoms of nervous stress, which is a prime cause in activating herpes symptoms. One or two handfuls of raw pecans, eaten throughout the day, is recommended.

Wheat germ oil: rich in vitamin E, wheat germ oil is almost always beneficial to patients with nervous ailments. It also contains inositol, which improves the body's fat metabolism and thereby takes some excretory burden off the skin. When lesions occur, wheat germ oil may be rubbed onto them externally to promote rapid healing. 1 tbsp morning and night.

Apple cider vinegar: rich in organic potassium, apple cider vinegar enhances metabolic efficiency, which in turn calms the entire system, thereby preventing dormant herpes from becoming active. When sores and lesions do occur, apple cider vinegar may be rubbed directly onto the skin to disinfect them and promote rapid healing. This should be done in conjunction with internal dosage as well. 2–3 tsps apple cider vinegar in an 8 oz glass of distilled water, 2–3 times per day.

Foods to avoid: overcooked meats, cooked eggs, pasteurized milk; refined sugars and refined starches; deep-fried foods; coffee, alcohol, sweet soft drinks; artificial additives.

_____ ◒ _____

CHAPTER 2:

Fasting and Excretion

Purging the bowels eliminates the source of poison, thereby permitting blood and energy to regenerate naturally. By cleaning the bowels we repair the body.

[Chai Yu-hua]

Modern lifestyles put tremendous toxic strain on our vital organs and glands. The stomach is perpetually stuffed with denatured foods taken in incompatible combinations, the liver is swollen and strained with the effort of breaking down massive intakes of animal protein and fat as well as drugs and poisons, the pancreas balloons to abnormal size owing to the constant demand for digestive enzymes to process enzymeless foods, and the colon gets lined with layer upon layer of glue-like crud that poisons the bloodstream.

The Colon: Sewer or Cesspool?

Of all the vital organs in the body, the one that suffers the most abuse from modern dietary habits is the colon. Our colons were intended by nature to function as smoothly flowing sewer systems, in order to promptly flush digestive wastes from the body. Instead, they have become stagnant cesspools, the physiological equivalent to a festering pile of uncollected garbage or a broken toilet that continues to be used for defecation. The average American male colon today carries within it about 5 pounds of putrid, half-digested red meat, plus another 5–10 pounds of foul toxic waste impacted for years in the folds of the colon with mucus.

Why does toxic waste from bad food taken in wrong combinations accumulate in the colon? V. E. Irons explains this in his newsletter as follows:

When food that is not wholesome or is harmful to the body reaches the stomach, word is immediately sent from the stomach to the mucus manufacturer, warning, 'Get busy, the enemy is on the way!' We know that mucus starts to be produced immediately and the colon is lined with it. 12–18 hours later, when the poisoned or harmful food from the stomach finally enters the colon, the latter is well prepared with a layer of mucus lining it, so that the body does not absorb any of the poison. Were this to happen once or even several times a month, this mucus, having been used, would disintegrate and slowly be discharged from the colon with no harm done.

But it is now certainly apparent that nature never intended that protective mechanism to be used as continuously as it is today . . . The result is that layer on top of layer is secreted until its accumulation thickens to ⅛" to ¼" thick. Sometimes this layer or layers gets to ⅜" to ½" in thickness, becoming as hard and black as a piece of old hardened rubber you see on a highway, torn from a truck tire . . .

We have had specimens preserved in alcohol from several inches to a few feet in length, while the longest we have had was 27 feet, in one piece. Sometimes it will come out as a pile weighing as much as 11 pounds and continuing to come out for several days to a week. . . .

Regardless of your financial standing, regardless of your past health history, regardless of your age or sex, *YOU* (meaning the reader and 95% of the USA) do have this hardened mucus in your colon, and you will be amazed by what comes out of you.

Even the United States Health Service, in a rare display of candor, admitted several years ago that 'over 90%' of Americans are walking around with clogged colons. Irons cites the experience of one of the most famous and highly respected surgeons in American history, Dr Harvey Kellogg of Battle Creek, Michigan, who wrote, 'Of the 22,000 operations I have personally performed, I have never found a single normal colon.' And that was back at the turn of the century, long before American eating habits had become completely corrupted by processed, denatured foods as today. As Irons puts it, 'About the only place you see a normal healthy colon today is in an anatomy book!'

Figure 2.1 illustrates a normal healthy colon, as depicted in anatomy books. Compare that with the distorted tubing in Figure 2.2, which shows reproductions of actual X-rays of the colons of apparently healthy people. Note the tortuous twists and bends in the tubing, the enormous

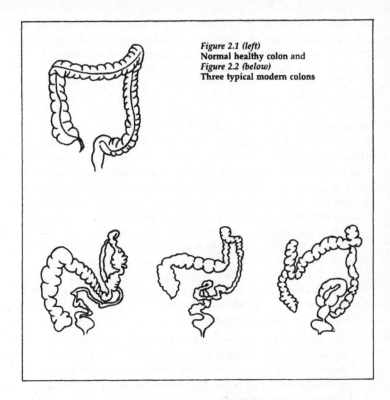

Figure 2.1 (left)
Normal healthy colon and
Figure 2.2 (below)
Three typical modern colons

sacculations of impacted mucus and trapped feces, the pinched and withered sections that have completely degenerated. Appalling? Then take note, for odds are 95 per cent certain that you are looking at a reflection of your own colon.

What goes in must come out – eventually. In the meantime it can fester inside for years and cripple or even kill you.

Toxemia is the real culprit in almost all chronic diseases and degenerative conditions. It explains, for example, why under precisely the same conditions of exposure some people 'catch' colds and other contagious diseases while others remain completely immune. It is not the 'germs' that are at fault, as Louis Pasteur claimed, for germs of all sorts float constantly on the air and enter our food and water at all times. It is the *lack of normal resistance* due to auto-intoxication of the bloodstream that opens a 'window of vulnerability' in the body and permits germs to invade.

Anyone who consistently breaks the laws of nature will ultimately be sentenced to chronic disease and early death by Mother Nature. No type or quantity of drugs, surgery, or other remedial medical care can save you from the self-imposed death-sentence of auto-intoxication. The only way to win a reprieve is by 'good behavior', which means thoroughly reforming your bad habits and 'cleaning up your act'.

However, it is an illusion to believe that you can clear out these fetid obstructions and purge the imbedded toxins from your colon simply by eating bran, raw vegetables and other fibrous foods. Bran and raw vegetables are so rich in fibrous bulk that they cannot get through the tiny holes remaining for passage of feces in most colons. Instead they back up, fester and contribute further to the problem. It's pointless to embark on a major new dietary program until you have first flushed all the accumulated, impacted debris and poisonous residues from your former dietary habits out of your digestive tract. There is only one way to do this and that is by fasting and flushing out your colon with colonic irrigations. When you put new oil into your car engine, you don't just pour it on top of the old filthy oil, but first drain the old stuff out. The least you could do is treat your own body with the same respect and care you give your car.

As V. E. Irons says: 'You will probably continue with wrong combinations of food as long as you live and so will continue to need a series of colon cleanings.' In his book, *Colon Health: The Key to a Vibrant Life*, 116-year-old Dr Walker is equally adamant:

> The elimination of undigested food and other waste products is equally as important as the proper digestion and assimilation of food . . . The very best diets can be no better than the very worst if the sewage system of the colon is clogged with a collection of waste and corruption.

Fasting

Fasting is the world's most ancient and natural healing mechanism. All animals except modern man fast instinctively when sick. To this day, primitive tribes in the Amazon, central Africa and remote parts of Asia maintain 'sick houses' on the outskirts of their villages, where ailing tribesmen retire for prolonged and total fasts until they recover their health and vitality. Hindu yogis are famous fasters and colon cleaners. Therapeutic fasting has always been an important part of Taoist training regimens. Masters made their students fast for prolonged periods to purify body and clarify mind before introducing them to the most advanced techniques.

The ancient Greeks fasted for health and longevity, and were known for their robust physical health. Galen, Paracelsus and Hippocrates, who are recognized as the founding fathers of Western medicine, prescribed and practiced fasting for all serious ailments and recommended it as an excellent preventive regimen. Pythagoras required his students to fast for 40 days to purify body and mind prior to receiving his highest teachings. Plato and Aristotle, whose thought forms the very warp and woof of Western philosophy, fasted regularly to enhance physical health and stimulate mental powers. The Bible mentions fasting 74 times, and Jesus himself fasted frequently, sometimes for up to 40 days at a time. So did Buddha. Fasting is a universal, natural response to sickness and debility, not a cultural or religious 'trip'.

Fasting triggers a truly wondrous cleansing process that reaches right down to each and every cell and tissue in the body. Within 24 hours of curtailing food intake, enzymes stop entering the stomach and travel instead into the intestines and into the bloodstream, where they circulate and gobble up all sorts of waste matter, including dead and damaged cells, unwelcome microbes, metabolic wastes, and pollutants. All organs and glands get a much-needed and well-deserved rest, during which their tissues are purified and rejuvenated and their functions balanced and regulated. The entire alimentary canal is swept clean, and what comes out the lower end should astonish and disgust first-time fasters sufficiently to make fasting and colon cleansing a life-long habit.

Perhaps the most important benefit of fasting is that it thoroughly cleans and purifies the bloodstream. Blood is responsible for delivering nutrients and oxygen to every cell in the body, and it must also carry away metabolic wastes from the cells for excretion in the kidneys and lungs. Blood is also the body's immunological watchman, circulating white blood cells, enzymes and other immunity factors on 24-hour-a-day 'search and destroy' missions against invaders. Dirty blood simply cannot perform these functions properly. As a result, malnutrition sets in, resistance plummets, toxemia becomes a chronic condition, and germs have a field day invading your most vulnerable tissues. Unless you live an ascetic life far from civilization and avoid all dietary folly, your blood and other tissues are bound to accumulate toxins and gradually lose their functional vitality. If you don't purge yourself of these toxins on a regular basis, toxemia gets worse and worse, until the body cannot stand it any longer and either purges itself spontaneously in the form of diarrhea, acne, pimples, boils, 'liver spots', foul perspiration, body odor, bad breath, and so forth, or else it simply gives up the battle and succumbs to cancer, tuberculosis and other fatal conditions.

An Associated Press release dated 28 May 1986, reports the following results of forced fasting on laboratory rats in a recent study on aging in America:

When the diets of laboratory rats are severely restricted, they live *far longer* than do otherwise identical animals that are allowed to eat as much as they want. In fact, researchers say such food limits are the *only way* they know of significantly extending these rodents' normal lifespans.

Fasting also re-establishes proper pH balance in the blood. As we have seen, the Yin and Yang of diet and digestion boil down to acid/alkaline balance in Western scientific terminology. Blood acidosis has become a major bane of contemporary civilization and is responsible for all sorts of misery. When acid builds up to intolerable levels in the blood, the bloodstream deposits the acid as crystals in the various joints, where they form spurs that literally 'cement' your joints together and supplant the natural synovial fluids that lubricate joints. The result is painful, debilitating arthritis. Fasting permits enzymes to enter the joints and dissolve these crystals, thereby restoring the synovial fluids and recovering joint mobility. Fasting also eliminates acidosis from the bloodstream itself. In fact, the unpleasant side-effects felt during the first three days of a fast are due entirely to these acid crystals and other toxins entering the bloodstream *en masse* for elimination.

Fasting is excellent therapy for mental illness. In Russia, where fasting is called the 'hunger cure', spectacular results have been achieved. In 1972, Dr Yuri Nikolayev of the Moscow Research Institute of Psychiatry reported successful treatment of over 7,000 patients suffering from various psychic disorders such as schizophrenia and neurosis.

Suffering from impotence or infertility? You might take a look for the culprit in your colon. Clogged, toxic colons negatively influence both male and female sexuality by pressing against and thereby interfering with sexual organs and glands. Many cases have been reported in which married couples who had been childless for 10 or 20 years owing to 'infertility' suddenly found themselves 'with child' after a few therapeutic fasts combined with colon cleansings.

The tenth-century AD Sung Dynasty physician Chang Tsung-cheng wrote extensively on the therapeutic benefits of cleansing the colon of accumulated debris and poisons, and he recommended this therapy for all sorts of seemingly unrelated ailments, including indigestion and constipation, breathing problems, headaches and fevers, stiff and painful joints, mental and emotional abnormalities, and so forth. He wrote:

> All physicians know that the unobstructed circulation of fresh blood and vital-energy are the most important factors in health. But if the stomach and bowels are blocked, then blood and energy stagnate.

The traditional Taoist method of cleansing the colon involved fasts combined with powerful herbal purgatives that dissolved mucus and dredged debris from the colon. These methods are mentioned as far back as the third century BC, in the *Yellow Emperor's Classic of Internal Medicine*.

Today, chemical laxatives and cathartics have become among the most popular drugs in the Western world, where constipation has become a chronic problem for young and old, male and female alike. Unlike the natural herbs Chinese physicians use to purge the bowels in conjunction with therapeutic fasts and nutritional therapy, these Western drugs are inorganic chemicals that are entirely incompatible with the human system. They work by irritating the lining of the colon so severely that it literally recoils like a wounded snake, expelling the offending drug along with whatever loose debris happens to be in the way. They do nothing whatsoever to remove the deeply impacted encrustations of putrefied protein wastes, toxic residues of fermentation, and layers of dried mucus. With continued use, these drugs gradually weaken the bowels so much that they fail to function at all without the artificial stimulus of ever-stronger chemicals. And when those no longer work, the hapless patient's next step is into the surgery room for a colostomy.

Fortunately, there is a better way to purge the colon and restore normal bowel movements, a Way based entirely on nature's most abundant and life-giving element – water. It is an entirely mechanical, non-chemical method that completely cleanses the colon of blocked feces and impacted toxic wastes without any harmful side-effects whatsoever. That method is colonic irrigation.

Plumbing Your Colon with Water

If you stand long and still enough near rivers, lakes and ponds where herons and simular long-beaked birds fish and feed, you will notice a curious habit. From time to time, a heron will suck up a beak full of water, twist its neck around and insert the beak into its own anus, squirting the water deep into its bowels to flush out the putrid debris and other residue from its fish-based diet. Who taught these birds to do that? Nature did. And a Taoist respects no teacher more than nature.

The very sound of the word 'colon' prompts embarrassment these days. Suggest that someone run 5 gallons of warm water through it, and embarrassment turns to suspicion or sheer panic. American doctors are reluctant even to discuss the matter, and they flatly refuse to administer colonic irrigations to patients on request. They believe, as one New York physician put it, that colonics 'went out with the horse-and-buggy' a century ago. American doctors also reject nutritional therapy, herbal remedies, fasting, therapeutic breathing, meditation and other 'outdated' methods that they no longer understand. In the Soviet Union, however, it remains standard procedure in *all* hospitals and clinics to administer a thorough colonic cleansing to *all* patients, regardless of their ailments, immediately upon entering any hospital. Soviet physicians realize that no cure for any ailment can be properly administered to a filthy, highly toxic body, which simply cannot assimilate and utilize medications. Nor does a body devitalized by chronic toxemia have sufficient strength and energy to fully recover from such radical procedures as anesthesia, surgery and chemical therapy.

As a case in point for colonics, take pneumonia. At the turn of the century, before cancer and heart disease replaced it, pneumonia was the biggest killer in America. Back then, Dr J. H. Tilden of Denver, Colorado, who specialized in pneumonia and treated more patients for this disease than any other physician on record, *never lost a single patient* to this dreaded ailment. He achieved his remarkable record by relying entirely on fasting and colonic irrigations, followed by strict diets of raw natural foods. Today, pneumonia still takes a heavy toll among the elderly and weak, despite all the modern drugs used to treat it.

In 1935, at the age of 40, V. E. Irons suffered from a rare and extremely painful form of arthritis now known as 'ankylosing spondylosis'. This condition is caused by unassimilated calcium (such as that from pasteurized milk) being deposited on the spinal vertebrae, where it gradually builds spurs that cause the entire spine to stoop forward, until, after 10–20 years, the victim is bent over double for life. Having been told that there was no cure, Irons went off to research his conditions on his own, and, like anyone else who looks hard and long enough for the *real* source of chronic degenerative disease, he found it lurking in his own clogged colon. As he recalls:

> Within two months I had no more pain from displacement and within 14 months practically no spurs. All done with cleansing, fasting, and natural foods – no drugs!

Colonics must not be confused with enemas. At best, enemas flush out the rectum and a small part of the descending colon, but they do not reach the transverse and ascending portions. Enemas can also be a real mess to handle. Colonics, on the other hand, send water coursing all the way through the entire length of the colon in a continuous flow. Instead of only a few quarts, a thorough colonic irrigation passes about 5 gallons of water through the colon during a single session.

If you are unwilling to administer your own colonics at home, and since your doctor will not or cannot administer them for you, you will have to find a colonic clinic. Clinics generally administer pump-powered colonics, which require careful supervision from a trained therapist. They cost about $35 per session, which comes to about $350 for the minimum ten irrigations you will need to effect a thorough cleansing of the colon.

Figure 2.3 **The 'Colema Board'**

There is, however, a much better, easier, cheaper, more convenient and private way, thanks to the 'Colema Board' © (Figure 2.3).* A Colema Board costs about $135 and may be used for life by the whole family in the convenience and comfort of your own home. It works entirely by gravity, not pumps, and is completely safe to use alone. It comes with detailed instructions and is so simple to use that children can do it by themselves. Best of all, the board is always there, ready to be used whenever the need arises. In 1981, V. E. Irons enthusiastically endorsed the Colema Board system:

> My seven-year-old son Robert frequently takes home colonics –
> all by himself. I'm 87 and I take them all the time. So, if you're
> anywhere between the ages of 7 and 87, you should have no
> problems . . . It is completely safe.

So, if you wish to rid yourself of the 5–15 pounds of hard, rubbery, toxic waste impacted in your colon owing to a lifetime of wrong eating habits, and simultaneously eliminate the source of most of your chronic ailments, discomfort and fatigue, while also preserving youthful vitality and prolonging your life, order a Colema Board and read on!

The Seven-Day Fast and Colon-Cleansing Program

The 7-day fast and colon cleansing program is an integrated system of self-purification that combines the benefits of fasting, fibrous intestinal

---

* Colema Boards may be ordered through Colema Boards, Inc., P.O. Box 1879, Cottonwood, California 96022, USA. Fax 530 347 5921/email: colema@awwwsome.com (Only supplier in the world of this patented product.)

cleansers, nutritional supplements and daily colon irrigation. It is a complete program of blood and tissue detoxification that rejuvenates each and every organ, gland, tissue and cell in the body.

Why seven days? Seven is a sort of 'magic number' throughout the realm of nature. Women's menstrual cycles occur in four units of seven, as do the moon's orbits around the earth. It takes exactly seven days to cleanse the entire bloodstream by fasting, and it requires seven days thoroughly to rid the lymph system of toxins. On a larger scale, it takes seven months to balance the endocrine system through proper nutrition and exercise and seven years to replace every cell in the body.

This particular purification program was developed by V. E. Irons, who explains it as follows:

> For seven days, you eat nothing at all, but you won't feel hungry because you take a product called Intestinal Cleanser. This is a powder that's ground from a special grade of psyllium seed. The cleanser clings to the colon walls, holds moisture there, and softens and loosens the waste matter.
>
> The Intestinal Cleanser should be taken five times a day, every three hours. You put a heaping teaspoon of Cleanser in a jar with a good tight cover. Add ten ounces of water, with a little bit of your favorite fruit or vegetable juice for flavor. You also add a tablespoon or two of another of our products called Bentonite, which is made from volcanic ash. Bentonite is like a magnetic sponge that removes toxins from your entire digestive tract. Shake the mixture well and drink it. Then follow it with a glass of water.
>
> A seven-day fast sounds severe, but it's really not too bad because the Intestinal Cleanser swells up in your system, so that you feel full. Also you take tablets of a supplement called Greenlife®, which is a concentrate of the juices of wheat, rye, oat, and barley grasses . . .
>
> If you're reluctant to plunge into a seven-day fast, you can take the Intestinal Cleanser and Bentonite twice a day, morning and evening, for a month, while continuing to eat other foods. Many people see so much improvement from this simple program, that they become willing to go on a seven-day fast.

During the 7-day fast with nutritional supplements and intestinal cleansers, you administer two 5-gallon colonics per day on the Colema Board, which works entirely by gravity, not pumps. To the 5 gallons of warm (100–105°F) water you add some strong boiled coffee, which stimulates the bowels' natural peristaltic contractions and contains acids that help cut through mucus and cleanse the colon wall. If you are overly sensitive to caffeine, you may substitute fresh garlic juice, fresh lemon juice, Bentonite or Epsom salts.

Greenlife®, which is produced and marketed by V. E. Irons, Inc.* under the 'Vitratox' label, is one of the best food supplements money can buy. It is the dried extract of juices squeezed from the tender young shoots of cereal grasses grown in organically fertilized soil without pesticides. The juice is dried in vacuum within seconds of extraction to retain maximum potency of vitamins, minerals, amino acids and the all-important enzymes. This product, though extracted entirely from grasses, contains 25–35 per cent pure unadulterated protein – much more than meat or eggs! To provide the complete complement of trace elements as well, seaweed powder is drilled directly into soil and compost heaps, and a 5 per cent proportion of seaweed is also added to the Greenlife® powder itself before tableting. Greenlife® provides everything your body needs in precisely the correct balance, yet it is so pure and alive with active enzymes that the nutrients are quickly assimilated through the stomach and small intestine without requiring digestive effort by the body. These nutrients provide a steady stream of potent building blocks to replace dead and damaged cells and repair injured tissues during your fast.

The Intestinal Cleanser and the Bentonite are remarkably effective cleansing agents. Powdered psyllium seed husk is almost 100 per cent pure fibrous bulk. It is not absorbed or digested but instead expands in the gut and dredges your bowels of debris as it passes through. When it reaches the colon, the warm water from the colonics helps it loosen impacted toxic wastes from the colon wall, and propel it out through the rectum.

Bentonite, which is derived from volcanic ash, contains an ingredient called montmorillonite, a molecule of which is 1/500th the size of a water molecule and carries a negative charge that is 200 times greater than its positive charge. It's miniscule size enables it to reach into nooks and crannies of your tissues that even water cannot penetrate, while its strong negative charge enables it to pick up 200 times its own weight in toxic positive ions. As we have seen, pollutants always take the form of big, bulky positive ions, and these are readily neutralized by active negative ions. Bentonite works in the bowels along with the psyllium seed powder, but it also enters the bloodstream to neutralize and facilitate rapid elimination of the toxic wastes that enter the blood from the cells.

Some advocates of fasting, such as Paul Bragg, do not recommend colonics or any supplements whatsoever during cleansing fasts. Instead.

* V. E. Irons' complete line of Vitratox internal cleansing products are available from Colema Boards Inc. (see footnote, page 135).

they advise nothing but distilled water. However, four or five water-fasts without colonics or intestinal cleansers are required to remove the same amount of toxic waste from the colon as one fast supplemented with intestinal cleansers and colonics. Paul Bragg's program calls for four 7–10-day fasts per year, plus one 24–36-hour fast per week throughout the year. In addition, Bragg follows a very strict diet of mostly raw foods between fasts.

An alternative is to do your first few fasts with colonics in order to effect a thorough cleansing of the bowels, after which you may experiment with straight water-fasts. A good program would be to take one 7-day fast each year with colonics and supplements, plus two or three 3-day fasts during the rest of the year drinking distilled water. Fasting once a week for 24–36 hours with nothing but distilled water is also an excellent year-round maintenance program between major fasts.

For those who have never attempted a fast but wish to benefit from the marvelous health it brings, here are a few helpful hints to keep in mind when you get started. Remember, fasting is a personal, private matter that only *you* can do for *yourself*. It's also the *only* way effectively to purge your entire body of accumulated toxins and purify your bloodstream.

- The first day is simple. It takes at least 24 hours for the body to commence detoxification and start pouring toxins into the bloodstream for elimination.
- The second and third days are the most difficult. By then your bloodstream will be carrying up to *ten times* its normal load of toxins, as the entire body excretes accumulated poisons into the blood for disposal. You will feel weak, fatigued, stiff, light-headed and perhaps a bit nauseous, much like a heavy hangover. This is *not* due to nutritional deficiency, so do *not* make the most common mistake of first-time fasters, which is to break the fast prematurely by eating something to 'pick you up'. The moment you eat something, the unpleasant symptoms of detoxification disappear – not because of the nutrients in the food but because the food signals the body to halt the detoxification process and gear up for digestion and metabolism instead. The worse you feel during the first three days, the more toxic are your tissues, and the better the program is working. Hang in there and you will soon feel better than ever!
- During your first fast with colonics, the first two or three days often fail to produce the dramatic evacuations of foul toxic wastes expected. That's not because your colon is clean, but because the dried mucus and toxins are so deeply impacted in the folds of your colon that it takes six to eight colonics just to start jarring them loose. One

of Irons' most severe cases failed to evacuate anything of significance through four full 7-day programs, but then on her fifth fast an avalanche of black hard poisons came pouring out with every colonic. Generally, you will start passing these toxified encrustations of mucus on the fourth or fifth day and continue to do so till the end of the fast. This deathly junk is collected in a collander under the board, and you should carefully inspect it after each colonic. By seeing what comes out of you each time, you will be strongly motivated to continue through to the end of the program.

- If by the end of the seventh day you are still expelling a lot of waste, you may choose to continue the program for up to 10 days, or else stop and wait till your next fast. Do not attempt fasts of more than 10 days by yourself until you have done at least half a dozen 7–10-day fasts. The less toxic your system becomes, the easier it is to maintain fasts.

- Don't expect to get everything out during the first fast. It takes about six 7-day programs, with mini-fasts in between and careful attention to diet, to effect a thorough cleansing of the colon and completely detoxify the tissues. Paul Bragg recounts how, after five years of four annual 7-day fasts, he went on a 10-day fast, on the seventh day of which, 'I had a terrific bowel evacuation, and at the end of this evacuation, I felt a heavy cool sensation in my rectum and out passed a third of a cup of quicksilver [mercury] from the Calomel [a medication] that I had taken during my childhood.' When it comes to purifying your body from a lifetime of self-pollution, 'once is not enough!'

- If you are afraid to administer your own colonics with the Colema Board, then look for a qualified colonic therapist and have him perform the first series for you in a clinic. After that you will realize how easy and safe it is and you can do the next series at home.

- The program is safe and effective for children, pregnant women, and the elderly. For children aged 4–10, cut the dosage of supplements and intestinal cleansers by half. Pregnant women should take enough extra nutritional supplements 'for two', but should not embark on the program during the final three months of pregnancy.

- Consume no solid food whatsoever during the program. Except for an ounce or two to make your intestinal cleanser mixture more palatable, avoid all fruit and vegetable juices as well. Besides cleansing your colon, you want to give all your digestive organs and all your vital glands a complete 7-day rest so that their tissues may be detoxified and their damaged cells replaced. If you 'cheat', you'll only be cheating yourself.

- Excessively obese and/or chronically ill persons should not attempt a 7-day fast the first time. Such persons are so permeated with toxins that a 7-day fast would raise the toxin levels in the blood to dangerous or even fatal levels. If you feel that your body is extremely polluted with poisons, start out with several 3-day fasts spread over a period of 3–4 months, with a diet of mostly raw vegetarian foods in between. This program will detoxify your tissues sufficiently for you to tolerate a complete 7-day fast. Highly toxic people should *always* use the internal intestinal cleansers and administer colonics during their fasts to facilitate rapid excretion of poisons.

- Break any fast with a light meal of raw vegetables, especially carrots, cabbage and lettuce, followed a few hours later with either some fresh mild fruit (apple, grape, pear, etc., but no dried fruits) OR a couple of lightly steamed vegetables, such as squash, tomato, string beans. You may also have a few slices of *well-toasted* whole-grain bread with a little bit of nut butter but no dairy butter. Thoroughly toasting bread converts much of the hard-to-digest starch into readily digestible sugars. Make the second day a vegetarian day as well, then on the third day you may commence eating one meal a day with meat, chicken, fish or cheese for protein. After your fasting programs, try to make fresh raw foods comprise at least 50 per cent of your overall diet and be aware of food combinations whenever you are eating. Plain yoghurt is an excellent way to restore friendly intestinal fauna to your colon after fasting. Last but not least, continue to take the psyllium seed powder once or twice a day for about a week after fasting to restore rhythmic regularity to your bowel movements.

Do the complete 7–10-day fast with colonics once or twice a year for the rest of your life, which will grow healthier, livelier and longer every time you do it. Between major fasts, go on several 3-day maintenance programs, with or without colonics, or try fasting once a week for 24–36 hours. During the year, whenever you feel 'down in the dumps' or feel a cold or other ailment taking hold, stop eating immediately and flush out your colon on your Colema Board. You'll be amazed how effective this is in curing and preventing all sorts of ailments.

Mini-Fasts and Semi-Fasts

The program outlined above is actually a 'semi-fast' because it includes nutritional supplements and internal intestinal cleansers. Other popular semi-fasts include raw vegetables and fruit juice fasts, such as the famous 'grape cure'. Vegetable and fruit juice fasts are an excellent way to purify the body and eliminate toxic conditions before they become pathological. Select only one variety of raw vegetable or fruit juice, and stick to it throughout the program, which may last anywhere from 3 to 10 days, depending on your condition and your determination. Select something that has natural affinity for the organs and glands that need the most therapy.

Dark grapes, for example, are the best choice for people with gastro-intestinal and liver ailments. In the Soviet Union, there is a sanitorium in Yalta that specializes exclusively in the grape fast. Patients begin by eating 1 pound of fresh raw grapes and work up to 10 pounds per day. Besides detoxifying the entire body and curing gastro-intestinal ailments, the grape cure greatly enhances metabolism and strengthens the heart muscles. Some patients in America have credited the grape with curing otherwise 'incurable' cancers.

Most people who try a fruit or vegetable juice semi-fast feel marvelous the first two days, then start 'crashing' by the third or fourth. That's because it takes two or three days for detoxification to commence but, once it does, the bloodstream becomes heavily loaded with poisons excreted from the cells for disposal through the kidneys. When this happens, just grin and bear it for a few more days, and you will soon feel better than ever before. In order for *any* fast to work, you *must* go through this two-or-three-day period of cathartic discomfort; otherwise, you'll carry these poisons with you right into an early grave. For some excellent guidance on the therapeutic uses of raw vegetable and fruit juices, get a copy of Dr Norman Walker's *Fresh Vegetable and Fruit Juices*.

Mini-fasts are short fasts lasting from 24 hours to 3 days. Going on a once-a-week mini-fast of 24–36 hours is an ancient Oriental health practice that is still quite popular among enlightened circles in the East. It used to be known in the West as well. The Greek biographer Plutarch wrote, 'Instead of medicine, fast for a day.' Paul Bragg highly recommends this once-a-week regimen as a 'maintenance program' between annual 7-day fasts. This habit gives the body a chance to 'catch up' with all the various things you put into your alimentary canal during the week. It's not an easy habit to start, but once it's established it makes you feel so much healthier and energetic during the rest of the week that it's hard to break.

It is entirely up to you and your health conditions whether or not to administer colonics during semi-fasts and weekly or monthly mini-fasts. If you are ailing from anything, colonics will flush out the toxic culprits responsible for your ailments. Otherwise, use your own judgement. But remember: colonics greatly enhance the overall cleansing effects of *any* fast, especially in the colon, so if you do not want to devote a lot of time each year to fasting, then it's best to fast in conjunction with colonics.

Excretion: 'Squatters Do It Better'

Take a look at nature and you will see that all animals squat to defecate. Even our closest ancestors, the primates, squat down with their knees drawn up to their chests when 'nature calls'. What you may not realize, however, is that even today most human beings still defecate in this natural manner, especially in Asia, Africa and the Middle East. (See Figure 2.4)

Figure 2.4 **Squatting Posture for proper defecation.** This may be done on any type of toilet

It is only in the industrialized West, where the modern toilet was invented, that people 'sit down' to defecate just as they sit down to eat. No wonder the entire Western world suffers from chronic constipation, hemorrhoids, bleeding piles and other problems caused by trying to evacuate the bowels in the sitting position. While the sit-down toilet may well save your legs the effort required to squat down properly, it is a device of terrible torture for your bowels, and the problems it causes are hardly worth the effort saved.

When sitting on a toilet, the lower end of the descending colon is bent, requiring a major muscular effort to evacuate the bowels. The strain of this effort can burst or clog the minute capillaires that feed the anal sphincter, causing hemorrhoids to form there. When squatting, the colon aligns itself naturally with the rectum and anus, which opens completely and effortlessly in the squatting posture. In this manner, no strain is required for evacuation. You will pass much more feces in a single squatting than you could possibly pass in a single sitting. Owing to the full spread of the cheeks, squatting also leaves less of a mess than sitting, so you'll save money on toilet paper as well.

To squat on a sit-down toilet, simply raise the seat and stand up on the rim, then squat down slowly until your knees are pressed against your chest. When barefoot, squat on the seat instead of the rim. A sink, handle or shelf nearby may serve as an armrest to help with balance. If your knees and back are too weak to support your weight in the squatting position, then build a simple wooden frame around the toilet with supports for your arms. Bowel movements are so rapid, efficient, effortless and voluminous in this posture that once you start doing it this way you will never again torture your bowels in the sitting position.

The following tips will make the squat work even better for you. If you suffer chronic gas and constipation, keep a steel ball or a smooth round rock near your bed. First thing in the morning before rising, roll that weight around your abdomen in the direction of colonic flow, i.e. from lower right corner up to the ribcage, across the transverse colon, and back down the left towards the rectum. This is an excellent method for expelling pockets of gas, loosening impacted feces and stimulating the bowel muscles to move prior to your first visit to the toilet.

Another good method for alleviating chronic constipation is to use your fingertips to gently massage the soft region between the anus and the tip of the spinal column (coccyx). This directly stimulates the colon and helps sluggish bowels to evacuate more thoroughly. In addition, practice the anal sphincter exercise introduced in Chapters 4 and 7 by rhythmically contracting and relaxing the sphincter several times a day. This stimulates glands in the anus to secrete natural lubrication, which greatly facilitates movement of dry stools. This exercise also flushes stale blood from the anal sphincter, thereby preventing formation of hemorrhoids.

Last but not least, whenever you feel the need for a laxative *despite* all the above measures, start first with laxative *foods*, and only as a last resort try a mild herbal laxative in conjunction with a dose of psyllium seed husk solution. *Never* use commercial chemical laxatives: they quickly create a chronic dependence on synthetic stimulation of the bowels, which only makes constipation a chronic condition.

If you follow these simple suggestions in conjunction with proper nutrition you will never again suffer constipation and all the attendant ills of toxemia it fosters. A clean, unobstructed colon is one of the most important prerequisites on the road to health and longevity. As the alchemist and prolific Taoist writer Ko Hung wrote:

> Those who aspire to longevity
> must keep their bowels clean;
> those who wish to delay death
> must keep their bowels unobstructed.

CHAPTER 3:

— ◐ —

Breathing

> You can live two months without food and two weeks without water, but you can live only a few minutes without air.
>
> [Master Hung Yi-hsiang]

According to the Taoist view, the nutrition provided by air through breathing is even more vital to health and longevity than that provided by food and water through digestion. Breathing influences the body's bioelectric balance just as diet influences its biochemical balance.

There are basically two functional types of breathing: cleansing and energizing. Cleansing breath detoxifies the body and stresses exhalation. Energizing breath collects and stores vital energy and focuses more on inhalation. Though people today take breathing for granted, everyone unconsciously practices both types of breath spontaneously throughout the day, whenever toxins in the bloodstream reach a critical level or energy is running low. Thus, a sigh is a spontaneous cleansing breath, for it involves a quick inhalatory gulp followed by a long, forceful exhalation. By contrast, a yawn is a spontaneous energizing breath – a long, slow, deep inhalation, briefly retained in the lungs, followed by a relatively short exhalation.

Chee-gung, which means both 'breathing exercise' and 'energy control', has been a formal branch of Chinese medicine for over 2,000 years. Recall that the Chinese word *chee* means 'breath' and 'energy' as well as 'air'. One of the earliest references to this form of medical therapy appears in an inscription found on 12 jade tablets dating from the mid-sixth century BC:

> In breathing, one should proceed as follows: hold the breath down and let it collect together. When it collects, it will expand. When it expands, it sinks down. When it sinks down, it grows quiet. When it grows quiet, it will solidify. When it solidifies, it

begins to grow. As it grows, it is drawn inward and upward and will reach the crown of the head. Above, it presses against the top of the head. Below, it presses downward.

Whoever follows this method will live a long life. Whoever goes against it, will die prematurely.

Like all Taoist health regimens, breathing is based on the balance of Yin and Yang and the harmony of the Three Treasures. Just as correct diet enhances the body's store of nutritional essence, so correct breathing enhances the body's supply of vital energy. Since breath and energy form a bridge between body and mind, breathing may be controlled either mentally or physically and is the only vital function that straddles the border of voluntary and involuntary control. Left unattended, breathing occurs as spontaneously and naturally as heartbeat; when controlled by mind, breathing becomes as deliberate as walking and can be made to regulate all other vital functions, including pulse, blood pressure, digestion metabolism, ejaculation, hormone secretion, and so forth. Owing to its pivotal role between body and mind, breathing comprises the single most important element in Taoist health and longevity regimens.

The internal alchemy schools of Taoism that flourished during the early centuries AD regarded air as the ultimate 'essence' of nature. Their aim was to purify their bodies and minds to the point that they could live on nothing but air and water, a diet they referred to as 'supping wind and sipping dew'. *Chee*, the vital energy contained in air, was literally regarded as a 'nutrient'. This ancient Taoist idea found an odd Western echo in the so-called 'Breatharian' doctrine propagated by the Natural Science Society in Maitland, Florida, during the 1930s. On 3 May 1936, they introduced a woman to the press who they claimed was 68 years old and had not eaten a bite of solid food for 56 years. According to press reports, she looked and behaved like an innocent child.

While only the most highly accomplished adepts ever reach the goal of relying entirely on wind and water for sustenance, even the most ordinary men and women can cultivate breath control as an effective means of promoting health and prolonging life. The act of breathing not only extracts *chee* from air, it also drives and distributes *chee* through the body's invisible network of energy channels, called 'meridians'. Meridians transport vital energy throughout the body and, when they get blocked, a condition called 'energy stagnation' occurs. Energy stagnation results in insufficient blood circulation, which in turn causes such common ailments as lethargy, chronic fatigue, irritability, headaches, poor digestion, weak libido, and so forth. Since 'energy commands essence', poor blood circulation and all its attendant ills can usually be remedied by correct breathing.

Along the Channel of Function, which runs from the tongue down the front of the body to the genitals, lie three vital energy centers called the upper, middle and lower *dan-tien*, or 'elixir fields'. The upper point lies directly between and behind the eyes and is associated with the pituitary and pineal glands; the middle point is located in the solar plexus and is associated with the heart; the lower one lies about two inches below the navel, midway between abdominal wall and spine, and is associated with the sexual organs and glands. The lower center, which acts as a sort of magnet for collecting energy, is called *chee-hai*, literally the 'Sea of Energy', and this is the spot the mind focuses upon during breathing exercises.

Taoist adepts attach extraordinary importance to the navel. The Ching Dynasty physician Chang Chin-chiou described the role of the navel in his commentary on the *Yellow Emperor's Classic of Internal Medicine*:

> Man is born attached at the navel to an umbilical cord, and the navel is connected to the lower Elixir Field, which is the Sea of Energy. Thus the navel forms the Gate of Life. The fetus receives life through the opening of this Gate, and the infant enters this world by its closing. Therefore, in its capacity as a spring of living energy, this region is the source of man's well-being and his discomfort, his strength and his weakness. When the energy here is strong, the whole system is strong. When it is weak, the whole system grows weak.
>
> The navel is where Fire and Water meet, where Yin and Yang reside. It is the sea of essence and energy, the door of life and death.

Taoists discovered the vital role played by the lower abdomen in breathing simply by observing nature, specifically animals and newborn babies. Watch a dog or cat breathe while resting, and you will notice that their abdomens – not their chests – expand and contract rhythmically. The longer they remain at rest, the slower and deeper grow these abdominal contractions.

Breathing therapy is orthodox medicine in Chinese tradition. Besides assimilating and circulating vital energy, deep breathing massages internal organs and glands, purges tissues of toxins, purifies the bloodstream, stimulates hormone secretions, and greatly enhances resistance and immunity. Our old centenarian mentor Dr Sun Ssu-mo wrote about therapeutic breathing in *Precious Recipes*:

> When correct breathing is practiced, the myriad ailments will not occur. When breathing is depressed or strained, all sorts of

diseases will arise. Those who wish to nurture their lives must first learn the correct methods of controlling breath and balancing energy. These breathing methods can cure all ailments great and small.

The Science of Breathing

In the Orient, breathing is regarded as a science. China has its *chee-gung* and India has *pranayama*, but the Western world doesn't even have a specific term to denote breath control, nor do Western physicians understand how atmospheric energy serves as a vital 'nutrient' for human health. Ironically, Western science has recently uncovered abundant evidence that clearly verifies ancient Taoist notions about air, breath and energy and their central roles in health and longevity.

The essential element in air that carries the vital charge of *chee* turns out to be neither oxygen, nor nitrogen, nor any other gaseous chemical, but rather the negative ion – a tiny, highly active molecular fragment that carries a negative electrical charge equivalent to that of one electron. By contrast, pollutants such as dust, smoke and toxic chemicals are borne on the air in the form of large, sluggish, polymolecular ions that carry a positive charge. In polluted air, positive ions slow down, trap and neutralize the active negative ions, thereby robbing the air of vitality. Breathing such air is equivalent to eating junk food full of 'empty calories'. In clean country air, the average ratio of negative to positive ions is about three to one; in polluted city air, it drops drastically to about one negative ion against 500 positive ions!

The vitality of negative ions in air is also destroyed by air-conditioning, central heating and closed spaces. It has long been observed that working all day in air-conditioned or heated offices and factories often leaves people totally exhausted, even though they only sit at desks or stand at automated assembly lines, whereas farmers who spend the same number of hours outdoors doing strenuous physical labor do not suffer this end-of-the-working-day syndrome of complete depletion. That's because it's not the work that exhausts the office and factory worker, but rather the lack of vitality in the air they are required to breathe all day. In Japan, where *chee* is understood, most big office buildings, factories and high-rise hotels are now equipped with negative ion generators to replenish the vital negative ions drained from the air by heating, air-conditioning and pollution. Perhaps this is one of the secrets to Japan's incredibly high productivity.

In nature, air is naturally ionized by the action of short-wave electromagnetic radiation from the sun and by other cosmic rays, which bombard air molecules and impart vital energy to the fragments. The movement and evaporation of large bodies of water also ionize the air above them. A third method of natural ionization is the unobstructed flow of wind over wide open spaces. The most potent atmospheric *chee* is thus found at high altitudes, where solar and cosmic radiation are strongest, winds are constant, and water takes the form of rushing streams and open lakes. That is why you feel so refreshed and revitalized after spending a day in the mountains, even after a long hike.

During the early years of the space program, it was frequently observed that, despite their robust health and physical fitness, astronauts became thoroughly exhausted after only a few hours in their space capsules, regardless whether they were orbiting up in space or training down on the ground. It took scientists several years to figure out the problem, although they would have found the answer immediately had they consulted a Taoist adept or Indian yogi. A report by a firm that manufactures negative ion generators for the space program, quoted in Andre van Lysebeth's excellent book on breathing *Pranayama: The Yoga of Breathing*, declares:

> Being wholly metallic, each space capsule is an absolutely ideal Faraday cage in which even the best trained pilot quickly shows signs of physiological disturbances, particularly tiredness and early exhaustion. This has been observed in a similar competent manner and openly admitted by the Russians. Glenn and Carpenter tired very quickly, and tiredness as well as exhaustion and physiological disturbance were such in the case of the space pilot Titov that he was actually air-sick after only six orbits.

When an artifical cosmic atmosphere charged with abundant negative ions was created within the space capsules with negative ion generators, these symptoms disappeared entirely, thereby enabling astronauts to remain in space for days, weeks, and even months at a stretch. Since electricity is a universal form of 'self-existing energy' not dependent upon life, the physiological benefits of artifically induced electrical fields are exactly the same as natural fields.

It is the polarity of Yin and Yang that makes *chee* move. In Western science, this polarity is called 'potential gradient', i.e. the potential difference in voltage between two points. In clean open air, potential gradient rises several hundred volts per meter, but in polluted air and closed spaces it is virtually zero. Potential gradient thus determines the 'strength' of an electric field, and the strength of the electric field determines how active the negative ions within it are and how strongly they flow between points. The report quoted above continues:

It has been established beyond doubt that an electric field exists between the earth and the atmosphere. This natural electric field is normally positive [Yang] in relation to the earth [Yin], and its strength is usually of the order of several hundred volts per meter.

The potential gradient is therefore higher in such places as mountains, beaches, parks and other open spaces, where negative ions flow freely from the positive Yang pole of the atmosphere to the negative Yin pole of the earth. All living organisms in between serve as conductors for this energy. For example, in a strong electric field where the potential gradient is several hundred volts per meter, a person 2 meters tall would be subject to a gradient of 400–500 meters between head and foot, which greatly enhances the free flow of vital energy. The above report concludes:

The electric current caused by the presence of an electric field passes through all the cells, the organs, and the whole of the nervous system, and stimulates the metabolism as well as all other physiological functions of living organisms . . .

If the field is too weak, tiredness, indolence, and lack of vitality will be manifest. This is the main cause of tiredness and numbness felt in cars, planes, tanks, submarines, and trains, and now in space capsules.

Negative ion generators for automobiles are now commercially available, and they greatly reduce the risk of 'highway fatigue' during the long drives. If airlines were to install them in airplanes, the problem of 'jet lag' would no doubt be greatly reduced as well.

Even if you live in a strong climate with a strong natural electric field, your entire system may be deprived of its benefits if you wear rubber shoes and synthetic fibers and live in air-tight enclosures surrounded by plastic furniture and fixtures, all of which insulate the body from atmospheric electricity as surely as rubber insulates electrical wires. For a taste of true vitality, try walking barefoot, hatless and lightly clothed in cotton across an open lawn or field while the morning dew is still on it, breathing deeply and rhythmically as you walk. Since our bodies serve as conductors for the atmospheric *chee* raining down constantly from above, we must also discharge excess energy through our feet to the earth. Dew-laden grass works like a powerful magnetic pole when you walk on it barefoot, drawing energy down through the body from the sky. That's why it is best to practice *chee-gung* outdoors, preferably barefoot and lightly clothed in natural materials.

The tissues that assimilate the negative ion energy of *chee* from air during breathing are located in the lining of the nasal cavities and sinuses, which is why inhalation must always be through the nose in breathing exercises. Though skin and lungs also absorb small amounts of *chee*, when it comes to detecting and extracting the bionic energy carried in air, 'the nose knows best'. For example, the nose is sensitive enough to catch the scent of a rose all the way across a garden and distinguish its bouquet from a carnation. That's because scent is *chee* and has bioactive properties when whiffed through the nose's sensitive olfactory terminals.

The bioactive energy of scent and the nose's ability to absorb it for therapeutic benefits are proven by the efficacy of aromatherapy, which has been used for millennia throughout the Orient to cure disease. Medieval Arab physicians noted the potent medicinal properties of scents when they observed that perfumers and incense makers rarely suffered the ravages of cholera and other plagues which regularly swept through the Middle East. Aromatherapy uses the essential oils of certain fragrant plants to cure specific aiments by exposing aromas in volatile form to the olfactory nerves in the nose, which are directly linked to the brain and the energy meridiens. These essential oils are secreted in plants by special glands in the roots, stems, leaves and flowers. Botanists compare these secretions to the hormones secreted in animals.

The *Yellow Emperor's Classic* states, 'essence transforms into energy'. In other words, when the essential oils of aromatic plants are permitted to evaporate into the air, they release their energy as fragrance, and this energy is absorbed by the olfactory nerves when a waft of fragrance enters the nose. Aromatherapy works only with scents derived from natural living sources, such as flowers, seeds and roots. Synthetic scents have 'smell' but no energy, and any sensitive nose can readily tell the difference. In 1960, the French medical journal *L'Hôpital* published an article on aromatherapy by Dr J. Valent, in which he explains this mechanism as follows:

> Carried by the bloodstream, the ionized plant aroma impregnates every corner of the body, powerfully revitalizes the polarized and discharged cells, replenishes electronic shortages by recharging the bioelectromagnetic batteries, and disperses cellular residue by dissolving the viscous and diseased substances of body fluids. It oxidizes poisonous metabolic waste products, increases energy balance, frees the mechanism of organic oxidation and of self-regulation, and reaches the lungs and kidneys, whence it is excreted or exhaled without trace.

That's a fancy way of saying that natural aromas carry a potent, concentrated charge of active bioelectrical energy which enters the body through the lining of the nose and quickly exerts powerful therapeutic effects on all cells and tissues. An obvious example of this is smelling salts: a mere whiff of this powerful aromatic agent instantly revives the faint by jolting the brain with a strong pulse of bioenergy absorbed directly through the nose.

Thus we begin to realize the importance of the nose in correct breathing and energy balance and the importance of air as a source of vital bioenergy. Now let's take a closer look at the marvelous but much maligned nasal apparatus. Rhinologists (nose specialists) list about 30 distinct vital functions of the nose, including moisturizing and warming incoming airstreams, filtering dust, modulating air flow, registering smells, and many more. It takes about 150 per cent more effort to breathe through the nose than through the mouth, so obviously Mother Nature had a specific purpose in mind when designing this apparatus, otherwise she would not permit such an extravagant expenditure of energy.

There are three big bulges inside the nose, convoluted like sea-shells, which stir and baffle incoming airstreams so that they become 'turbulent' and cover a much greater interior surface area. Called 'turbinates', these bulges also impart warmth and moisture to incoming air so that it does not shock the sensitive lungs with cold or dryness. That is the reason why people from cold northern and dry desert climates have long prominent noses with narrow nostrils: the cold and/or dry air from their environments enters the nose more slowly and must travel a greater distance over the warm, moist turbinates prior to entering the lungs. By contrast, natives of hot, humid climates tend to have short, flat noses with wide nostrils, because the air they breathe is already warm and moist. In cold and/or dry climates, adepts should always exhale through the nose in order to replenish the heat and moisture borrowed from the turbinates during inhalation with heat and moisture from the lungs. In hot, humid climates, mouth exhalation is not only permissible, but sometimes preferable, as a method to expel excess heat from the body.

The entire nasal cavity is lined with mucus membranes which trap dust, debris and microbes and eliminate them through the nose along with stale air, or down the throat into the stomach with mucus. When the nose is healthy, this mucus coating is constantly moving and is replenished regularly by fine hairs called 'cilia', which sweep dirty mucus down the throat for digestion and elimination in the stomach. When the mucus coating gets too dry, the characteristic 'crust' of a clogged nose develops, making it impossible for the cilia to sweep mucus away. This condition results in accumulation of toxic debris in the nasal passages, which in turn renders the respiratory system vulnerable to colds and influenza. When the mucus is too fluid, 'post-nasal drip' is the result.

The capacity of nasal membranes to absorb *chee* and resist infection is determined by the quality and quantity of nasal mucus, which is largely dependent on diet and excretion. An unbalanced diet full of mucus-forming foods such as starch, sugar and pasteurized dairy products causes the nasal mucus to become thick and heavy. When excretory functions are blocked by constipation, shallow breathing, water retention, antiperspirants, and so forth, mucus must take up the extra burden by excreting toxins that are normally handled elsewhere, resulting in the cathartic discharge of tainted mucus characteristic of head colds, coughs and bronchitis.

Here's another interesting nasal fact: the nose is the only organ in the entire body other than the sexual organs and breasts that contains erectile tissue. All physicians are familiar with the phenomenon known as 'Honeymoon Nose', in which the excessive stimulation of sexual organs experienced by newlyweds causes a sympathetic swelling of the erectile tissue in the nasal passages. In the nose, erectile tissue controls the size, shape and angle of the air passages, thereby regulating air flow through the nasal passages. It is erectile tissue that automatically alternates air flow between right and left nostrils by alternately shutting off one side. This natural phenomenon has only recently become known to Western physicians, who call it 'infradian rhythm,' but Taoists have been aware of it for millennia. The alternate blocking of one nostril occurs naturally about every two hours throughout the day, and it is intimately linked to the mechanisms of right-brain/left-brain functions. When air flows in through the right nostril, the body is geared for action. When air flows in through the left side, the body is prepared for physically passive mental functions. In Taoist parlance, the left nostril is identified with Yin, the right with Yang, and each is associated with a major energy channel that runs down the side of the spine. If both nostrils are not clear and properly functioning, breathing becomes unbalanced, assimilation of *chee* is impaired, and the equilibrium of Yin and Yang energies throughout the body is upset.

It is important to be aware of this natural switch-over between left and right nostril because sometimes one side gets stuck, in which case you must take measures to re-open it and re-balance your breathing. If air flow is permitted to continue exclusively on one side for six or seven hours due to blockage or inflammation of the other nostril, disease of some sort usually sets in, and depression and lethargy are a certainty. The simplest way to open a blocked nostril is to lie down on the side that is clear and breathe deeply through the nose. This tends to open up the clogged upper passage and close off the one below. Alternative nostril breathing is another good way to clear obstructed nostrils and balance breathing between left and right sides, and so is the 'Bellows' breath. You may also use acupressure to clear the nostrils by applying deep thumb pressure to the *feng-chir* ('Wind Pond') points on the back of the head. These points are located where the base of the skull and the cervical vertebrae meet (Figure 3.1). Stretch the neck, find the points with the thumbs, then press deeply and rub hard four or five times. Release and repeat several times.

Figure 3.1
Pressing 'Wind Pond' points to clear sinuses

The Neti Nasal Douche

By far the best way to keep your nose clean and keep the nasal passages clear and unobstructed is to give yourself a regular nasal douche, known in yoga lore as the 'neti'. The neti nasal douche is a particularly important form of hygiene for deep breathers, especially in this age of air pollution, smoking and mucus-forming diets. The neti loosens and flushes away encrustations of dried mucus, dissolves and expels dust, grease and other pollutants, and thoroughly washes the sensitive olfactory endings, thus enhancing their capacity to extract and assimilate *chee* from air.

Here's how to perform the neti: heat two cups of clean (preferably distilled) water to body temperature and dissolve ½ to ⅔ teaspoon of salt in it, more or less 'to taste.' The point is to approximate the temperature and salinity of the nasal passages so that the cleansing solution does not cause osmosis of fluids between itself and the nasal membranes. Pour the warm saline solution into a small teapot or a special 'neti pot'. Squat down on the ground, tilt your head to one side, and insert the spout of the pot into the upturned nostril. Continue tilting your head sideways until the saline solution starts to pour into the upper nostril and drain out through the lower one. Heavily clogged nostrils will not permit such a free flow from side to side, in which case you must block off the lower nostril with your free thumb and gently suck the solution in through the upper nostril (Figure 3.2). Keep sucking through the nostril until you feel the warm solution trickle down into your throat, but do not swallow it. Instead, spit it out on the ground as it dribbles down. Be careful not to inhale air while pouring the solution into the nose. After draining about half the solution

Figure 3.2 Neti Nasal Douche

through one nostril, switch sides, tilt your head the other way, and flush out the other side.

When the solution is finished, alternately block one nostril with a thumb and vigorously blow air out through the other. You'll be astounded by some of the junk that comes out: besides the usual 'snot', you'll sometimes find gritty black particles, wads of dust and lint, blobs of grease, fibrous strings, and other pollutants impacted inside the nasal caverns. After blasting residual water and debris from both nostrils, dry the nasal passages by standing with hands on hips and bending forward, then vigorously raising and lowering the head while exhaling hard through the nose. This whole process sounds much more difficult than it actually is: the major hurdle is mental, not mechanical, and the most essential requirement in performing the neti is to keep calm and keep your mind on what you're doing.

The enormous enhancement of olfactory sensitivity after a thorough nasal douche should suffice to convince anyone of its therapeutic efficacy and its vital importance to breathing and overall health. Scents that passed you by unnoticed before suddenly play aromatic symphonies in your nose, and your sense of taste – half of which involves the nose – improves multifold. Most important, however, is the enormous enhancement of vitality experienced by those who practice breath control with clean nasal passages.

If you practice breath control and perform the neti regularly, you may kiss head colds goodbye. Regardless what Western doctors say about 'germs' being the cause of colds and other respiratory diseases, the *root cause* is a pathological toxicity of the nasal membranes, which causes them to become inflamed and impacted with a dry crust of toxic mucus that forms an ideal environment for germs. As these toxins accumulate, they severely damage nasal membranes and render the nasal passages vulnerable to attack by germs. Germs are a symptom, not a cause of head colds. One or two thorough nasal douches each week, performed as part of your regular regimen, will keep your nose clean and make it invulnerable to 'catching' the colds that have become so 'common' in this age of air pollution and denatured diets.

The Art of Breathing

In principle breathing is a science, but in practice it is an art. Now that we have reviewed the scientific nature of *chee* and investigated the vital role in breathing of the nose, it's time to learn the art of breathing.

What distinguishes ordinary shallow breathing from deep abdominal breathing is the role played by the diaphragm. The diaphragm is a resilient yet flexible muscular membrane that separates the chest from the abdominal cavity. When lungs expand, they push the diaphragm downward; when lungs contract, they pull it up into the chest cavity (Figure 3.3).

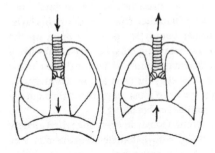

Figure 3.3 **Diaphragm Breathing:**
(left) inhalation/expansion,
right exhalation/contraction

Though most Western physicians still regard the diaphragm as a relatively unimportant muscle that is only passively involved in respiration, a cursory glance at nature suffices to reveal the fact that man was meant to breathe primarily with his diaphragm, not his rib-cage and clavicles. Owing to laziness, ignorance, smoking, pollution, constipation and other factors, adults these days invariably become shallow chest breathers, rather than the deep abdominal breathers we were meant to be. Chest breathing employs the intercostal muscles between the ribs to forcibly expand the upper rib-cage, thereby lowering air pressure in the chest so that air enters by suction. However, this leaves the lower lungs, which contain by far the greatest surface area, immobilized. Consequently, one must take about three times as many chest breaths in order to get the same quantity of air into the lungs as provided by a single diaphragmic breath. Dr A. Salmanoff describes the respiratory functions of the diaphragm as follows:

> It is the most powerful muscle in our body; it acts like a perfect force-pump, compressing the liver, the spleen, the intestines, and stimulating the whole abdominal and portal circulation.
>
> By compressing the lymphatic and blood vessels of the abdomen, the diaphragm aids the venous circulation from the abdomen towards the thorax.
>
> The number of movements of the diaphragm per minute is a quarter of those of the heart. But its haemodynamic power is much greater than that of cardiac contractions because the surface of the force-pump is much greater and because its propelling power is superior to that of the heart. We have only to visualize the surface of the diaphragm to accept the fact that *it acts like another heart*.

Clavicular breathing, which is characteristic of asthma and emphysema victims, is even less efficient than chest breathing. In clavicular breathing, the clavicles (collar bones) are raised to open up the narrow upper portion of the lungs. Breathing must be very rapid – like a panting dog – in order to get sufficient quantities of air into those narrow little top pockets of the lungs controlled by the clavicles. And with such a small surface area exposed to air, the heart must pump blood through the lungs much more rapidly than in deeper breathing.

Clavicular breathing occurs spontaneously in everyone when anxiety or stress strikes. Conversely, those who habitually breathe this way become prone to chronic anxiety. Next time you feel anxious or 'up-tight', you can easily prove the connection between anxiety and shallow breathing simply by observing your breathing patterns. Then take a few deep abdominal breaths, hold them for a few seconds, and exhale long and slow. Immediately you'll notice anxiety melt away!

Unfortunately, most adults have long ago forgotten how to use their diaphragms to breathe – indeed many people don't even know they have such an organ. Women are especially inclined towards shallow clavicular breathing. This tendency is related to pregnancy, during which time diaphragmic breathing becomes impossible due to the expanding uterus. Women also tend to wear clothing that constrains the waist, where even the slightest pressure suffices to drive breathing up to the rib-cage and clavicles.

A complete, deep, abdominal breath should employ all three modes of breathing in a smooth, unbroken expansion of the lungs that begins at the bottom, not the top. The deep breather first inhales air slowly into the lower lungs by letting his diaphragm expand and balloon downward into the abdominal cavity. When the diaphragm is fully expanded, the intercostal muscles come into play to open the rib-cage and fill the mid-lungs with air. As the rib-cage reaches full expansion, the breather makes a small final effort to raise his clavicles a bit so that air flows into the narrow upper pockets of the lungs. At this point, the shoulders tend to hunch up and the neck contracts, so when the breath is complete, you should deliberately relax and lower the shoulders and stretch out the neck. Then gently sink the 'bubble' of breath in your chest down towards the navel by pushing it down against the diaphragm.

By cutting down the number of breaths required per minute by more than half, diaphragmic breathing greatly enhances respiratory efficiency, saves work on the heart, and conserves vital energy. Taoists measure lifespan not by counting birthdays but by counting breaths and heartbeats: every breath and heartbeat saved now prolongs life later. Diaphragmic breathing gives a powerful propellant boost to blood circulation, sending it coursing strongly throughout the system without causing work for the heart, and it greatly enhances lung capacity. For every extra millimeter the diaphragm stretches during inhalation, lung capacity increases by a volume of 250–300 ml. Recent studies in mainland China show that most beginners in deep breathing increase the stretch of their diaphragms by an average 4 mm after only six–twelve months of practice, which means that in less than a year they increase lung capacity by 1000–1200 ml.

Before proceeding with a detailed analysis of four-stage diaphragmic breathing, let's review the four fundamental postures used in performing breathing exercises: standing, sitting, lying and walking. The ancient sages suggested 'Stand like a pine, sit like a bell, lie like a bow, and walk like the wind'. Here's what they meant:

Standing

Standing is the best posture for therapeutic breathing exercises, for it permits complete circulation of blood to all parts of the body and encourages free flow of energy through the meridians. Standing also provides maximum benefit from the potential gradient between Heaven (head) and Earth (feet). The stance used by Taoist adepts is called the 'Horse' because it resembles the posture one adopts when straddling a horse (Figure 3.4). The ancient masters used to say, 'A man is only as strong as his horse', referring not to the animal but to the man's stance.

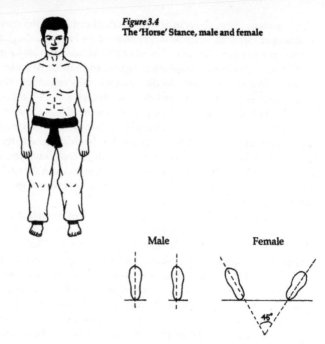

Figure 3.4
The 'Horse' Stance, male and female

Male   Female

45°

Place feet shoulder-width apart. Men should align the feet parallel to each other, women should splay the toes outward at a 45-degree angle. Slightly bend the knees into a semi-squat, so that all body weight is supported by the thighs, freeing the spine and pelvis. Knees and thighs should be slightly tucked inward, as if gripping a galloping horse. Let arms hang loosely down, with palms facing backward. Keep shoulders completely relaxed and slightly rounded, so that chest is at ease. 'Stand like a pine' means keeping the spine straight as a pine from crown to coccyx. Keep pelvis loose, 'unlocked', and tucked forward in order to straighten out the sway in the lower spine.

Sitting

There are two basic sitting postures: cross-legged 'lotus' postures and chair or stool postures. The lotus has three variations: easy lotus, half lotus and full lotus (Figure 3.5). Half-lotus is most frequently employed. Full lotus requires long practice and substantial stretching of knee ligaments, while easy lotus tends to constrict blood vessels where ankles

Figure 3.5
The three 'Lotus' Postures
(top left) Easy Lotus
(top right) Full Lotus
(left) Half Lotus

press against calves, causing numbness. The lotus is a very stable posture, with body weight spread evenly on the ground and spine rising erectly from a firm foundation. Hence the ancient masters described it as 'sitting like a bell'.

It helps to sit on a firm cushion placed on top of a phone book. This tilts the pelvis forward, keeps the spine erect and helps prevent numbness in the legs. Head should be held straight, shoulders slightly rounded, chest relaxed, eyes loosely directed at the ground in front, hands comfortably placed on thighs or knees, or else cupped palms-up in the lap below the navel.

The other method involves sitting on a firm stool or chair with thighs parallel to the ground and calves perpendicular (Figure 3.6). This is the best position for beginners to adopt when practicing deep breathing, at least until they develop sufficiently strong thighs and knees to maintain the Horse stance for prolonged sessions. The seat of the chair should be firm, not cushioned, and you should sit on the edge, with soles of feet flat on ground about shoulder-width apart, parallel for men, splayed at 45 degrees for women. Keep spine erect from coccyx to crown and place hands comfortably on thighs. Men should wear loose pants or nothing at all and let their testicles hang freely over the edge of the chair to facilitate

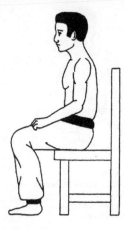

Figure 3.6 **Sitting on Chair Posture for Breathing**

energy flow from sacrum upward along spine. Women, however, should wear underpants to inhibit escape of *chee* through the vagina. The great advantage of this posture is that it can be maintained for long periods of time without numbing, cramping or fatiguing the legs.

Lying

Unless you are ill or incapacitated, the lying posture is not generally recommended for breathing therapy, for this position does not permit free circulation of essence and energy, nor does it take advantage of potential gradient.

There are two variations. One is to lie flat on your back with head slightly elevated on a small firm pillow, legs fully stretched out, arms

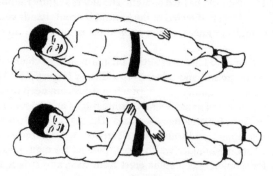

Figure 3.7 **Lying on Side Posture for Breathing and Sleeping**

resting by sides. The preferred method is to lie on your right side, with right hand tucked between pillow and temple and left arm resting along the upper side. Legs may be placed in one of two positions: either stretch lower leg out fully and bend upper leg so that upper ankle rests near lower knee; or else rest the upper leg evenly against the lower leg, with knees touching and slightly bent (Figure 3.7). In the side position, the diaphragm deeply massages the abdominal organs during breathing exercise. Owing to the smooth curvature of spine and legs in this posture, ancient masters refered to it as 'lying like a bow'.

Walking

Walking is an adjunct to all stationary breathing postures. Deep breathing should be practiced in the standing or sitting position, then gradually applied to other activities, such as walking, driving a car and sexual intercourse. Walking is the first step in the process of general application of breathing to ordinary activities. Breathing correctly while walking demands absolute attention to what you're doing, which makes it a sort of 'moving meditation'. Breathing deeply and regularly while walking is an excellent way to cultivate functional harmony of body, breath and mind, and it improves overall physical coordination. When properly performed, this sort of breathing makes you feel very light and limber, as though you were 'walking like the wind'.

Regardless which posture you adopt for breathing exercises, always bear in mind the following basic pointers:

- Prior to practice, remove all jewellery, watches and glasses, and loosen belts and collars. Avoid any constrictions against the surface of the body, especially the waist, and avoid any synthetic materials that might insulate you from the earth's electric field.
- Whenever possible, practice outdoors, preferably barefoot, or in socks or leather shoes. Allow maximum exposure to the ionizing element of wind, water and sunlight, but avoid exposure to cold breezes. Practicing near abundant vegetation is very beneficial because plants enrich the air with oxygen and exude their own variety of *chee*. That's why urban Chinese like to practice in public parks. When indoors, practice near an open window in a well-ventilated room.
- Timing is important. By far the best hours to practice breathing are between 3:00 a.m. and 7:00 a.m., when positive Yang energy rises most strongly in the atmosphere, and between 11:00 p.m. and 1:00 a.m., when cosmic Yin energy switches over to Yang. For best results, practice twice a day: first thing in the morning, before

breakfast; and last thing at night, before bed. Do not practice within the first hour after a meal, and avoid all cold drinks for at least 20–30 minutes after a session. Deep breathing packs warm energy into the 'Sea of Energy' below the navel, and a cold drink tossed on top of that can cause severe conflicts of energy.

- Pregnant women and people suffering from any sort of fever or internal bleeding should not practice deep breathing.
- Keep spine erect but not rigid at all times. Cramped or stooped spines block energy along the spinal channels, thus preventing free flow of energy from the sacrum up to the head. It's especially important to keep the back of the neck stretched, for that's where energy enters the brain from the lower centers. The proper way to stretch the back of the neck is to draw the chin inward towards the throat.
- Eyes should be kept unfocused and half-lidded during breathing in order to avoid visual distractions. Direct eyes loosely towards the ground or floor a meter or two in front of feet. Internalize attention by mentally visualizing the region of the navel and the organs behind it.
- Shoulders tend to hunch during the final stage of inhalation, which tenses the neck and blocks energy flow into the head. Be sure to keep shoulders loose, relaxed and low throughout the session.
- Keep lips closed but don't clench teeth. Tongue should be kept firmly pressed against palate, behind the upper teeth, throughout the exercises. Raising tongue to palate stimulates secretion of salvia from two ducts below the tongue. This is called 'sweet dew' (gan lu) and should be swallowed because it contains highly active enzymes of great benefit to the stomach. However, any mucus coughed up from the lungs or drawn down from the nose should be spat out, for unlike saliva mucus is a waste product. The tongue against the palate also forms a bridge connecting the two channels of the Microcosmic Orbit, which meet at the roof of the mouth. Unless the tongue is firmly pressed against palate, energy has no avenue for crossing from palate to throat.
- Focus ears on the internal sounds of breath and heartbeat rather than letting them distract the mind by listening to external sounds. Try to practice in a quiet place without artificial external noise, although the natural sounds of wind, water, birds, etc. can actually help harmonize the spirit. Some adepts use earplugs to help internalize awareness during breathing and meditation.
- By exerting a bit of conscious control over the nasal apparatus, you may greatly enhance deep breathing. During inhalation, deliberately flare the nostrils wide open. This increases the intake of air and enhances its turbulence within the nasal passages, permitting

162

greater extraction of *chee*. Note how animals distend and contract their nostrils rhythmically with every breath, 'testing' the air as they 'take' it in. Owing to the atrophy of nostril muscles in civilized man, breathing is inhibited. Conscious flaring of the nostrils also helps focus mental attention on the breathing process.

- At the core of the entire breathing process lies the mind. The mind is a slippery little devil with a very short attention span and a strong penchant for drifting aimlessly in ever-shifting seas of thought and fantasy. Chinese Taoists call it a 'playful monkey' and Indian yogis compare it to a 'wild horse' that refuses to be tethered. We already know that 'spirit commands energy'. Therefore, if the mind is 'absent' during breathing exercise, energy has no commander and strays about aimlessly, scattering and leaking instead of gathering and circulating. Recent studies in mainland China show that when deep breathing is performed with the mind firmly focused on a certain part of the body, that part registers a strong electric charge and grows warm. This accords well with the findings of Dr Chang Rui, director of the imperial medical institute during the Southern Sung Dynasty (1127–1279):

Mind is the leader of energy. Where mind goes, energy follows. When a certain part of the body is ailing, use the mind to draw energy to the affected area and it will correct the condition.

Taoist masters refer to the eyes, ears, nose, tongue and body as the 'Five Thieves' of breathing and meditation because they literally 'rob' you of the mental attention required to command breath and control energy. Adepts must therefore learn to 'imprison' the Five Thieves internally by consciously directing sensory awareness inward and focusing on organs and energy centers rather than external objects.

Do not be discouraged if at first your mind keeps galloping off in all directions. It's much like raising a child: you must apply a balanced blend of discipline and patience to the task, day by day. Soon you will learn your own personal tricks for controlling your mind, such as 'bribing' it to shut up for half an hour in exchange for the promise of a favorite indulgence later. When you start feeling heat in certain organs or parts of the body and energy tingling up the spinal channels into the brain, it means that you have begun to achieve unity of mind and breath, spirit and energy. Ultimately you will be able to send energy coursing to whichever organ, gland or limb requires therapy simply by focusing mental attention there as you breathe.

The harmony of mind and breath is the fundamental key to breathing exercise and energy control. Without clarity and presence of mind, breathing becomes no more than a hygienic physical exercise that tonifies lungs, massages organs and assists circulation of blood. In order to reach the stage of practice in which breathing is used to assimilate, gather and distribute energy throughout the body's energy networks, the mind must be in complete command of body and breath, and *you* must be in complete command of your mind.

Four-Stage Breath Control

Most Taoist breathing exercises are performed in four distinct stages: inhalation, retention, exhalation and pause. It is important to perform each stage correctly and to link them together smoothly, so let's take a detailed look at each stage.

Inhalation

In English, the word 'inhalation' was once synonymous with 'inspiration', which proves that even in Western civilization the intimate links between breath and spirit were once clearly recognized.

After adopting your posture of choice, with abdomen relaxed, shoulders loose and spine erect, empty your lungs completely with a forced exhalation and a strong contraction of the abdominal wall. Then let the abdomen relax again and commence a *slow* inhalation through flared nostrils, drawing air deep down into the bottom of your lungs by expanding the diaphragm downward and letting the abdomen balloon. When lower lungs are full, continue inhaling smoothly and let the rib-cage expand to fill the mid-lungs, then inhale a bit more to fill the top. It is not necessary or desirable to fill the lungs completely on each inhalation, and you should *never* force inhalation beyond comfortable capacity. About two-thirds full is the right measure for an inhalation.

The final step in inhalation is to sink the big 'energy bubble' of breath gently down into the abdominal cavity. This will cause the abdominal wall to balloon out.

Retention

When properly performed, even brief retention of breath provides profound therapeutic benefits to every organ, gland and functional system in the body.

Taoists refer to breath retention as 'womb breathing' (*tai hsi*) because the lungs don't move. In Western scientific jargon, it's called 'the dive response' (based on research with seals) or 'cellular respiration'. The fetus in the womb receives oxygen and energy directly through the umbilical cord, not the lungs, and therefore all respiration in the fetus takes place on the cellular level only. What occurs inside the body during breath retention is complex, subtle and of central importance to the efficacy of breathing exercises. Heartbeat slows by more than half, blood pressure is substantially reduced, and cellular respiration is automatically triggered. Cells throughout the body start 'breathing' by themselves, spontaneously breaking down sugars to release oxygen and automatically excreting cellular wastes into the bloodstream for disposal. The heat and perspiration experienced after 10–15 minutes of deep-breathing exercise is a direct result of enhanced cellular respiration.

Nature has equipped the human species with the same 'dive response' mechanism used by seals underwater, but civilization has let this rejuvenating response atrophy. Children, however, retain it while very young, as evidenced by stories of 5-year-olds who fall into freezing cold rivers and remain underwater for up to two hours, and are then rescued and revived, with no brain damage. With sufficient practice, adults may recover this mechanism as well. However, prolonged retention of breath should not be attempted by anyone without the personal guidance of a qualified teacher and many years of preliminary practice in breath control. For our purposes, retentions of 3–10 seconds suffice, and these may be practiced alone safely, without special instruction from a master.

Promoting cellular respiration is a primary goal of breath retention, but it also has other purposes. In the lungs, retention enriches the blood with extra oxygen and purges it of extra carbon dioxide by prolonging the time for gas exchange. In the tissues, retention increases the partial pressure of oxygen against the capillary walls, thus improving gas exchange between bloodstream and cells.

Cellular respiration generates body heat. This heat is first felt in the lower abdomen, then spreads slowly to the extremities, often causing perspiration, even on a cold winter day. Where does this heat come from? It radiates from the 'cauldron' of every cell in the body! Tibetan yogis gather this cellular heat into the Sea of Energy with a highly sophisticated breathing exercise called *tummo-yoga*, the 'Fire in the Belly'. Adepts are tested for success in this yoga as follows: they sit stark naked in the snow by a frozen lake in mid-winter, while assistants soak bedsheets in the freezing water through a hole in the ice. The sheets are then draped over the adept's body, and he must thoroughly dry each sheet with *tummo* heat generated from within. This continues all day long until a specified number of sheets are dry.

In 1966, the Soviet Union invited Prime Minister Nehru's personal guru, Swami Brahmachari, to Moscow to train Soviet cosmonauts in deep-breathing techniques as preparation for prolonged space travel. This fact alone reflects how seriously the Russians take these matters. The Swami arrived in Moscow in mid-winter wearing nothing but a thin cotton gown, while his hosts shivered on the tarmac in overcoats, fur hats and woolen scarves. Anxious for the Swami's health, they immediately offered him an overcoat, but the Swami politely declined and said, 'I manufacture my own heat as I need it.' His secret: breath control and cellular respiration.

When you retain breath, the carbon dioxide count in the blood rises, which automatically signals the respiratory center in the brain to make the lungs exhale. At that moment, the adept imposes his will to override the exhalatory reflex, and every time he does this, he enhances voluntary control over breathing. The next step in the 'internal alchemy' of breath control occurs spontaneously: stimulation of the pneumogastric nerves, or 'parasympathetic nervous system'.

The autonomous nervous system has two branches: sympathetic and parasympathetic. The sympathetic nerves run down the spine and constitute the body's 'action' circuit: they increase pulse, stimulate adrenalin and heighten respiration in preparation for physical activity, while at the same time suppressing digestive, eliminative and other basic functions. The parasympathetic branch consists of the pneumogastric nerves. These also run down the spine and control such vital functions as digestion, peristalsis, elimination and metabolism. When this branch is activated, the 'action' circuits shut down and the entire body is calmed.

The sympathetic system and the pneumogastric nerves are antaganistic. The former stimulates physical and mental activity at the expense of basic vital functions, while the latter calms the body and mind while stimulating basic functions. Modern urban lifestyles cause excessive, chronic excitation of the sympathetic system, resulting in a pathological condition known in Chinese medicine as 'fire-energy excess' and in Western medicine as 'sympathicotonic syndrome', symptoms of which include chronic stress, nervous excitation, heart palpitations, constipation, indigestion, dry mouth and sexual dysfunction. How many of these symptoms do you take for granted in your daily life?

Deep breathing re-establishes natural balance between the sympathetic and pneumogastric branches of the nervous system, which makes breathing a highly effective form of preventive therapy against the constant stress and strain and consequent ills experienced by harried city dwellers throughout the world today.

Recent medical tests conducted in China show that just 15 minutes of deep-breathing exercise cause abundant secretions of the protein-digesting enzyme pepsin, as well as other vital digestive juices, and that it greatly enhances peristalsis throughout the digestive tract. This effect occurs during the retention phase and makes breathing an excellent remedy for indigestion, constipation and other digestive ailments.

Remember, however, never to force retention beyond natural capacity. Work with average retentions of 3–5 seconds, and, after several months of regular practice, you may occasionally try a few retentions of 7–10 seconds, but do not venture beyond that without personal supervision from a qualified teacher. Furthermore, bear in mind that it is not the duration or volume of breath retained that works such therapeutic wonders, but rather the smooth, rhythmic regularity of the entire breathing process, as well as three key physical techniques that are applied during the brief retention phase.

Exhalation

In Taoist breathing exercises, exhalation is more important than inhalation. Shallow chest breathing leaves a perpetual residue of stale air and toxins deep down inside the lungs, and this must be thoroughly emptied in order to fill the lungs properly with fresh air.

When you feel that it's time to exhale, the first step is to relax the Three Locks. Then slowly, almost imperceptibly, commence exhaling gently through the nostrils or mouth, keeping tongue pressed to palate, gradually increasing the force (but not the speed) of the exhalation until a strong, steady stream is established. Empty the lungs in reverse order of inhalation: start at the top and end at the bottom. At the end of exhalation, pull the entire abdominal wall inward in order to push the diaphragm upward into the chest and thereby expel the last residues of stale air from the lower lungs. This final contraction of the abdomen also compresses the inner organs and disgorges them of the extra blood pumped into them during inhalation. Finally, let the abdominal wall relax and the organs fall back into place, without inhaling yet.

If the breath tends to burst out in an explosive gust, it means you've retained too long.

In cold, dry weather, exhalation should always be done through the nostrils in order to replenish heat and moisture borrowed from the turbinates on the way in. However, in warm, humid climates, you may opt for mouth exhalation, which enhances expulsion of toxins, permits more thorough evacuation of air and helps dissipate excess body heat. By keeping tongue pressed to palate, outgoing airstreams through the mouth are baffled and modulated to facilitate slow, steady exhalation.

Pause

When the lungs are completely empty, block the throat by closing the glottis, so that air does not rush back into the vacuum left in your lungs. Now pause for a few seconds to permit the abdominal wall and the diaphragm to relax again, then slowly commence the next inhalation through the nose. If you have to gasp for the next inhalation, then you have paused too long.

The Three Locks

During breath retention, the Three Locks trigger the biochemical and bioelectric reactions that impart therapeutic benefits to the body's internal organs and energy network and enhance circulation of blood and energy throughout the system. They should be applied towards the end of the inhalation stage, held during retention and released as exhalation commences.

The anal lock

The entire pelvic cavity is strung with a resilient webbing of muscles that in fact forms another diaphragm, called the 'urogenital diaphragm'. It supports and controls the anus, rectum, perineum and urogenital apparatus. As lungs fill and the diaphragm expands, enhanced pressure in the abdomen pushes down on the soft pelvic floor. Not only does this negate enhanced abdominal pressure, it also stretches and ultimately weakens the muscles and tendons of the urogenital diaphragm. Even worse, it permits the escape of *chee* through the anus and urogenital passages, both of which penetrate the lower diaphragm just as the esophagus penetrates the upper diaphragm.

To maintain increased abdominal pressure on the internal organs and glands and prevent the loss of *chee* through the lower orifices, you must firmly apply the anal lock. The anus is controlled by two sphincter rings. The exterior ring seals the external orifice, and the interior ring – located about one inch higher – seals off the main orifice and is directly linked to the urogenital diaphragm. Contraction of the inner ring delivers a powerful stimulation to the sacral nerves and glands and prevents the loss of *chee* below. It tightens and tones the tissues of the entire urogenital diaphragm and prevents its prolapse due to downward pressure from the upper diaphragm and abdominal organs.

Here's how to apply the anal lock: as inhalation reaches capacity, focus attention on the anus and contract the external sphincter ring. This is easy. Next, make a stronger, deeper, more deliberate contraction about an inch above the first. You will immediately feel a powerful contraction throughout the pelvic floor.

When breath is retained, the pneumogastric nerve receives direct stimulation at its point of origin in the brain. When you apply the anal lock at the same time, the sacral root of this powerful nerve receives a similar stimulation, thereby greatly enhancing all bodily functions controlled by the pneumogastric nerve. Contraction of the urogenital diaphragm with the anal lock also puts direct stimulatory pressure on a little-known but very important gland called the 'Luschka Gland', which hangs like a cherry at the very tip of the coccyx, or 'tail-bone'. In van Lysebeth's book on breathing, Dutch physician and yoga therapist Dr R. Polderman writes:

> It is an irregular mass of cells situated at the tip of the coccyx . . .
> When practicing the anal sphincter lock, its nerve endings are stimulated. This coccygean body is linked directly to the asymmetric ganglion – an autonomous nerve center – by its nerve fibers.

By properly applying the anal lock, you deliver profound therapeutic benefits to all vital parts and functions connected with the sacral region, including excretion, peristalsis, prostate function, menstruation, testicular and ovarian secretions, ejaculation, urination, and so forth. Furthermore, the anal lock exercises precisely those muscles, tendons, nerves and sphincters required for male ejaculation control, which becomes easier and easier as a man masters breath control.

Practicing the anal lock prevents and cures hemorrhoids, which are caused by stagnation of blood in the minute capillaries of the anal sphincters. Every contraction and relaxation of these sphincters flushes out stale and draws in fresh blood. Practice the anal lock a few times at the end of every bowel movement, using the squatting position. This helps propel residue feces downward and outward for a final evacuation and replenishes the sphincters with fresh blood and energy after their excretory work is done. All animals rhythmically contract and relax the anus at the end of bowel movements, and so should humans.

The abdominal lock

With the spine forming a rigid wall in back, the descending diaphragm providing pressure from above and the anal lock keeping pressure in from below, the abdominal lock provides the fourth barrier to loss of abdominal pressure and *chee* during breath retention.

It is in control of the abdominal wall that most newcomers to Oriental breathing techniques usually go wrong. In order to faciliate diaphragmic breathing, beginners tend to keep the abdominal wall completely relaxed through all four stages of breath control. This does indeed make it easier to flex the diaphragm downward, but it also causes an abnormal ballooning of the abdominal muscles (see Figure 3.8a), which can eventually lead to development of a 'pot belly'. Distension of the gut during retention also negates the benefits of enhanced abdominal pressure against the organs. Moreover, deep breathing increases the volume and circulation of blood within the abdominal cavity, thereby engorging the organs with blood. Unless the abdominal wall is locked during retention, there is insufficient abdominal pressure to squeeze excess blood out again, and consequently the organs may get congested with blood.

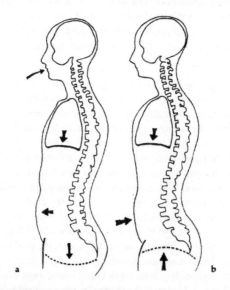

Figure 3.8 **Abdominal Movement in Breathing**
(*a*) Inhalation: Abdomen expands, urogenital diaphragm descends.
(*b*) Retention: Lower abdominal wall is retracted slightly and urogenital diaphragm is raised with anal lock.

Here is the correct procedure for applying the abdominal lock during breath retention: when the lungs are full, the diaphragm stretched and the anal lock applied, deliberately draw the *lower* portion of the abdominal wall (the part below the navel) inward (Figure 3.8b). This will push the abdominal organs inward and upward against the downward and outward pressure caused by the diaphragm and thereby maintain enhanced pressure within the abdominal cavity. Note that contraction of the lower abdominal wall causes a slight distension of the upper abdominal wall, just below the sternum. This is perfectly normal and correct. The upper part of the abdomen is much more rigid than the lower and its slight distension during the abdominal lock does not negate abdominal pressure.

The suprarenal glands, owing to their position on top of the kidneys, receive the most direct stimulation from the descending diaphragm when the abdominal wall is locked into place. Secretions from the suprarenal include vital sex hormones as well as cortisone, which relieves arthritic inflammations in the joints. The abdominal lock also stretches and stimulates the vertebrae and ganglia of the spinal column by providing a sort of internal traction to the spine.

Let's take a closer look at how the diaphragm acts as a 'second heart' when abdominal pressure is enhanced and maintained with the abdominal lock. The vena cava is a major vein which penetrates the diaphragm and draws stale blood up from the abdominal organs to the heart and lungs. It therefore serves as an outlet for the extra pressure applied to blood circulation in the abdomen during breath retention. Retention with the locks in place substantially increases pressure in the abdominal cavity, while pressure in the chest cavity remains normal. This differential naturally pushes blood up the vena cava from the area of high pressure in the abdomen to the area of normal pressure in the chest. The force of this propulsion, which acts like a suction pump, is many times stronger than any heartbeat, and it extends throughout the entire circulatory system. When the pressure differential between abdomen and chest is reversed during exhalation and release of the locks, freshly oxygenated blood pours back down into the abdominal organs. This pump effect is especially important during winter and in the early morning, when up to 50 per cent of the body's blood supply remains stored in the liver and pancreas.

The brain is irrigated by 2,000 liters of blood each and every day, and this blood must pass through many miles of capillaries. The cerebral cortex, for example, contains 1,000 meters of capillaries per gram! Normally, the heart must work hard and constantly to keep the brain irrigated through this vast circulatory network, a job made even more strenuous by gravity. For sedentary people who get little exercise, the circulatory strain on the heart is even greater, especially when doing cerebral work. Deep diaphragmic breathing takes the workload off the heart and transfers it to the diaphragm, which performs the task much more efficiently and virtually effortlessly by manipulation of pressure differentials between abdomen and chest.

Do not confuse abdominal control with abdominal rigidity. Some people have such rigid abdominal walls that they can neither expand nor contract them. Such rigidity freezes the diaphragm in place and permits nothing but shallow upper-chest breathing. Common symptoms of rigid abdomens and frozen diaphragms include chronic constipation, indigestion, poor circulation, shortness of breath, chronic fatigue, insomnia, headaches, weak libido, low resistance, and frequent anxiety.

On the other hand, a flabby, soft abdominal wall is just as difficult to control as a rigid one. Soft abdomens tend to protrude during retention and are too weak to control with the abdominal lock. Success in breath and energy control requires strong yet flexible abdominal muscles. Every adept of breathing should include specific exercises in his or her regimen to strengthen the abdominal muscles. Sit-ups, for example, are an excellent exercise for toning up the abdomen.

The neck lock

The third lock is the neck lock. This is the easiest of the locks to apply, for it is not involved in maintaining abdominal pressure.

To apply the neck lock, first contract the throat muscles and close the glottis over the bronchial tubes. Then tuck the chin slightly in towards the throat without bending the neck forward. This locks the throat while simultaneously stretching the back of the neck. Be sure to keep shoulders relaxed, otherwise they will hunch up and tense the back of the neck.

The neck lock has several beneficial effects. It partially constricts the carotid arteries in the throat, thereby preventing enhanced abdominal pressure from causing an excessive rush of blood into the brain, which could cause dizziness, discomfort and undue pressure on sensitive cerebral capillaries. The neck lock diverts excess blood bound for the brain out to the limbs and other parts of the body, while still permitting abundant cerebral circulation. The neck lock also gives the entire spinal column an extra stretch during breath retention, thereby stimulating all nerve and energy centers along the way and encouraging energy to rise up through the Governing Channel from sacrum to brain. Closing the glottis and tightening the throat literally 'locks' the breath deep down inside the lungs, making it much easier to control. Without the neck lock in place, retained breath exerts exhalatory pressure all the way up to the nostrils and eustacian tubes, which is unpleasant and undesirable. In compressing the carotid arteries, the neck lock helps regulate the heart by causing it to beat more slowly and deeply. It also puts light pressure on the carotid sinus nerve, which helps to direct mental awareness inward during breath control.

The best exercise for developing the neck lock is a classic yoga posture called the 'Plow', which is introduced in Chapter 4. This exercise also stretches and limbers the entire spinal column from head to coccyx, opening up energy centers and stimulating vital nerves. Make the Plow an integral part of your daily regimen.

Rhythmic Regularity

Transitions from retention to exhalation and from exhalation to inhalation should always be slow, smooth and deliberate, not sudden, sharp and uncontrolled. The actual duration of each stage is not as important as *relative* duration and *smooth* transition. At first, your lungs, diaphragm, abdomen and circulatory system will resist the rigors of deep diaphragmic breathing due to long neglect, but with patience and daily practice they will soon adjust and thrive on it. In the beginning, it is most important to focus on rhythmic regularity of all four stages of breath control, rather than on prolonging each stage.

The whole universe and all its parts function rhythmically, and all organisms thrive to the extent that they harmonize their own internal rhythms with the grand patterns of nature. Sleep cycles are tuned to the rhythms of day and night, menstrual cycles follow the rhythms of the moon, and heartbeat follows the rhythms of breathing. The mind is naturally attracted to rhythms, and therefore rhythmic breathing greatly enhances the ability of the mind to focus inwardly and become totally absorbed in the breathing process.

Mentally counting off seconds is one way to measure the relative durations of the various stages of breath control, but this can be distracting. A better way is to count heartbeats, a practice that requires that you shut off external sensory input, silence the 'internal dialogue' and focus attention inward on breath and heartbeat. One of the best ways to cultivate this inner awareness is to focus attention on the region of the navel and try to visualize it expanding and contracting with each breath. As one Taoist master used to tell his disciples, 'Focus attention on the lower abdomen and you will eventually learn everything there is to know about your body.'

As soon as mind wanders away from breath, breath immediately loses its rhythm, so try to pay attention to what you're doing when practicing breathing exercises. After long practice, you will become so familiar with the various rhythms involved in breathing that you will be able to judge the relative durations of each stage without counting seconds or even thinking about it.

There are several basic rhythmic patterns you can use in deep breathing. One is to make exhalation about twice as long as inhalation, with a brief retention and a pause between stages. This pattern of prolonged exhalation gives a strong boost to blood and energy circulation, expels toxins from lungs and bloodstream and stimulates the pneumogastric nerve. Another pattern often used in breathing is to make all four stages of equal duration. This pattern enhances assimilation of *chee*, regulates heart beat, lowers blood pressure and enhances gas exchange in the lungs.

Beginners should be prepared for several signs when commencing deep breathing regimens. There is a tendency to perspire and feel hot flashes in various parts of the body, especially after retention. This is caused by heat released during cellular respiration and by the accelerated movement of vital energy throughout the meridian network. You'll probably belch and break wind during the first few minutes of a breathing session. This is caused by deep massage of the abdominal organs by the descending diaphragm and shifting pressure differentials between chest and abdomen. It is a sign of correct practice and a great way to expel noxious gases from both ends of the alimentary canal. Sometimes you'll feel 'goose-bumps' or currents traveling up your spine, or down your arms and legs, or over the top of your head. This is *chee* moving through the meridians, propelled by the power of breath. The signs that disturb beginners most are occasional feelings of dizziness in the head, numbness or tingling in the extremities and tremors in the muscles, but again this is no cause for worry. It is the direct result of opening up long-neglected energy channels and pumping *chee* through them. As parts of the body chronically deprived of blood and energy are activated, they tend to tingle, just as when your foot 'goes to sleep' and then you stand up on it. With prolonged practice, all your channels will open up and energy will flow smoothly and evenly through the system, after which these tingly, dizzy feelings will disappear.

The Warrior's Breath and the Scholar's Breath

There are two fundamental modes of breathing in *chee-gung*: the Warrior's Breath (*wu-hsi*) and the Scholar's Breath (*wen-hsi*). The Warrior's Breath is forceful, strong, audible and driven by powerful, deliberate contractions of the diaphragm and abdominal wall. The Scholar's Breath is natural, gentle, silent and relatively effortless.

The Warrior's Breath is best for therapeutic breathing exercises aimed at strengthening the body, collecting and storing *chee*, boosting blood circulation and promoting overall physical health and vitality. It requires exclusive mental attention to the breathing process.

The Scholar's Breath is used primarily for meditation and for practicing rhythmic breathing during ordinary activity, such as reading, walking, working, and so forth. The Scholar's Breath does not require as exclusive attention as the Warrior's Breath, for it is more natural, but the mind should remain alert in the background to insure that all four stages of breathing are rhythmically executed. The diaphragm remains the key driving force in the Scholar's Breath, but it does not expand and contract to the same degree as in the Warrior's Breath.

The Warrior and the Scholar Breath are simply two different methods of performing any breathing exercise, rather than being breathing exercises in themselves. The essential difference is that the Warrior Breath is basically stimulating to the system and prepares the breather for 'battle' i.e. activity. The Scholar Breath is calming to the system and hence appropriate for contemplation, concentration, meditation, and so forth. The main technical difference is the force behind the breath.

These two types of breath may be combined within a single breathing session. For example, to commence a session of meditation, it's a good idea to first stimulate the energy centers and get circulation moving with a few minutes of the forceful Warrior's Breath, then slip gently into the more passive Scholar's Breath. Use the Scholar's Breath to wind down and cool off the system after performing a prolonged series of exercises with the Warrior's Breath. Employ the rhythmic Scholar's Breath during ordinary activity throughout the day, but boost your energy and circulation from time to time with a few minutes of Warrior's Breath. Eventually you will become familiar with the subtleties of each type of breath and know intuitively when to apply them.

Basic Breathing Exercises

Different breathing exercises have different benefits. Some exercises, for example, specifically enhance assimilation and circulation of oxygen and *chee*, some focus on rapid expulsion of toxins from lungs and bloodstream, while others sedate or stimulate the system. By practicing a variety of different breaths, the adept realizes the full spectrum of benefits and learns how to use each one for practical applications.

Those who have never practiced deep abdominal breathing should first familiarize themselves with the diaphragm by performing the following exercise. Lie down flat on your back on a carpet, floor, lawn or other firm surface, but not a mattress. Completely relax your body, with legs slightly parted, arms down by your sides, and neck comfortably stretched. Place a palm on your abdomen just below the navel, and press the other palm against your rib-cage. Now thoroughly empty your lungs, then start inhaling *slowly* through your nose, directing the airstream down to the bottom of your lungs. Unless your diaphragm and abdominal wall have become completely frozen, you will feel your lower abdomen swell up as you inhale. When the abdomen stops expanding, continue the inhalation and feel the rib-cage expand as the mid-lungs fill with air. Retain the breath for a few seconds, then commence a long, slow, controlled exhalation through the nose. This time you'll feel the rib-cage shrink first, followed by the contraction of the lower abdomen. This is the correct sensation of deep abdominal breathing. Next, place a smooth round rock or a telephone book over your lower abdomen and repeat the exercise with hands down by your sides, raising and lowering the weight with expansions and contractions of the abdominal wall. Practice these two exercises daily for a couple of weeks, until you have a firm grasp of how the diaphragm and abdominal wall function during deep breathing, then commence regular practice of the exercises introduced below.

The Bellows

This is a classical breathing exercise designed to purify the lungs and bloodstream of toxins – an especially important exercise in this age of environmental pollution. It should be practiced during long-life exercises, at the beginning of deep breathing exercises, and whenever your breathing and circulation feel stagnant.

Posture: Horse stance, or sitting.

Technique: Place tongue firmly against palate and keep it there throughout the exercise. Start by forcefully expelling all air from the lungs with a strong contraction of the abdominal wall. You may exhale through nostrils or mouth: in cold, dry weather use nostrils only; if air is warm and moist, mouth exhalation is preferable. Immediately after expulsion of air, let lungs fill again naturally by virtue of the vacuum left inside and exert a small additional effort to fill them about half full only. Lungs should never be more than half full during the Bellows, and effort should not be expelled on inhalation. Focus entirely on abdominal exhalations that completely evacuate the lungs. No pause or retention of breath is involved in this exercise.

When lungs are half full, immediately contract the abdominal wall again to forcefully expel another gust of air. Then let air flow in again, and repeat continuously at a rate of about 20 breaths per minute. It should sound and feel like a bellows slowly fanning the flames of a fire with voluminous gusts of air.

If while performing this exercise you feel like you're 'losing your breath' and need to 'catch' it again, simply pause and take a long, slow, deep inhalation, hold it a few seconds, and exhale thoroughly, then continue the Bellows.

This breath may be performed for two or three minutes any time of day or night to expel toxins and rejuvenate the energy system, and it should also be incorporated into your regular regimen. Since the Bellows leaves the bloodstream super-oxygenated, it's a good idea to re-establish normal oxygen/carbon dioxide in the blood by doing a few deep inhalations with brief retentions after each session of Bellows breathing.

Pointers: Due to deep contractions of the abdominal wall, the abdominal lock does not come into play here, but you should keep the anus and neck about halfway locked.

Try not to grimace. Tense facial muscles constrict the nasal passages and cramp energy channels in the head. Keep shoulders relaxed and rely entirely on abdominal contractions to drive the air from your lungs.

Benefits: The Bellows expels stale residual air from the deepest recesses of the lungs and effectively clears and opens all air passages in throat and head. It purges alveoli of accumulated toxins and thus makes excellent therapy for smokers and city dwellers. The rise in oxgen levels during the Bellows revitalizes blood and tissues and stimulates metabolism. Extra oxygen infusions are also very calming to the 'action' circuits of the sympathetic nervous system, while stimulating the digestive and other vital functions of the pneumogastric system.

The Bellows tones and strengthens the all-important diaphragm and abdominal muscles, and thus enhances overall breath control. It amplifies the propulsive power of the diaphragm on venous and arterial circulation, and thus insures circulation of blood to even the most minute capillaries.

Rhythmic contractions of the abdominal wall increase oxygenation of abdominal tissues, which helps burn off excess abdominal fat. The vigorous contractions also provide therapeutic massage to the internal organs and glands.

The Bellows refreshes the brain by irrigating it with oxygen-rich blood. Vigorous exhalations set up a series of powerful waves throughout the circulatory system, and these waves travel up the carotid arteries into the brain, where they actually cause the brain to expand and contract rhythmically, providing a highly beneficial cerebral massage that helps distribute vital cephalo-rachidian fluids evenly throughout the brain tissues. There is however no danger whatsoever to the brain during this exercise, because blood pressure remains constant – only the *rate* and *volume* of blood circulation increase.

Note how lucid you feel after the Bellows. Try it when you feel physically exhausted, mentally muddled or emotionally upset. You'll be amazed at how quickly it restores equilibrium and boosts energy levels.

Chee Compression Breath

This is a fundamental deep diaphragmic breathing exercise for assimilating and circulating vital energy from the air and packing it into the organs, glands and muscles by internal compression. The mind should focus exclusively on incoming and outgoing airstreams and visualize energy moving through the meridians with each breath. After long practice, your mind will learn to lead energy rather than merely follow it through the system, thus realizing the Taoist precept that 'energy follows where mind leads'.

Posture: Standing, sitting, lying, walking. Standing and sitting are best.
Technique: Empty the lungs completely, then commence a long, slow inhalation through flared nostrils. Visualize a luminous stream of pure energy flowing deeply into your lungs as you inhale.

When lungs are comfortably full, apply the Three Locks and swallow hard. The act of swallowing helps move the 'energy bubble' deeper down into the lower abdomen. During the brief retention phase, shift attention down to the region of the navel and imagine energy gathering there in the form of heat and light.

Then gently release the Three Locks and commence a long, slow, controlled exhalation through the nose, keeping tongue firmly against palate. Visualize energy spreading out through the entire body via the meridian network as you exhale. If a particular part of the body is ailing, try to direct energy there by focusing mental attention on it during exhalation.

Pause briefly, relax the abdomen, then repeat. At first do only three or four *chee* compression breaths in a row, then relax lungs and energy channels with five or six Bellows breaths, then do another three or four *chee* compressions. Gradually work up to six or seven compressions in a row, and do two or three sets in a session.
Benefits: This exercise charges the body with concentrated doses of *chee*, distributes it throughout the meridian network, and packs it into organs, glands and other tissues. It also stimulates the central nervous system and helps cultivate internal awareness of the harmony of body, breath and mind.

Fusing Fire and Water

This is a moving exercise in which the hands help raise and lower *chee* between the Sea of Energy (water) and the heart (fire).

Posture: Horse stance, or sitting.
Technique: Exhale thoroughly and bring your hands together just below the navel, with palms up and fingertips about an inch apart. Commence inhaling slowly through the nose and slowly raise your upturned hands up the torso until they reach the nipples. Time it so that inhalation is complete and hands reach the heart about the same time.

Apply the Three Locks and retain the breath 3–5 seconds, then turn the palms over to face downward and slowly push them back down the torso as you exhale slowly through the nose, timing it so that hands reach bottom as lungs empty. Pause briefly, relax abdomen, then turn the palms back up and commence another cycle. Repeat six to ten breaths.
Pointers: Breathe and move hands in unison. Keep shoulders, arms and neck muscles loose and relaxed, and 'sink' the breath down as deeply as possible during retention.
Benefits: This exercise moves energy up and down between the 'fire' of heart and the 'water' of the navel region, thus blending and balancing these two types of energy. It regulates and deepens heartbeat and develops awareness of the Sea of Energy as the body's *chee* headquarters.

Fractional Breathing

This is a good exercise for beginners to use in developing breath retention. Each breath is inhaled or exhaled incrementally, with 'mini-retentions' between segments.

Posture: Standing or sitting are best, but lying and walking may also be employed.
Technique: For fractional inhalation, commence a deep abdominal inhalation, but stop when lungs are only ¼ to ⅓ full. Apply Three Locks, sink the breath down, and retain briefly. Then release locks, but instead of exhaling, continue the inhalation for another ¼ to ⅓ increment, pause, lock up, retain, release locks, and continue in this manner until lungs are full, then do a long, complete, uninterrupted exhalation.

For fractional exhalation, reverse the process. Take a complete, uninterrupted inhalation, lock and retain briefly, then exhale about ¼ to ⅓ of the breath, stop, lock and retain, then exhale another increment, until lungs are empty.

After two or three fractional breaths, relax the breathing apparatus with a few Bellows breaths, then do another round or two.

179

Pointers: Never practice both fractional inhalation and exhalation on the same breath. Fractional inhalation is stimulating to the system and should be practiced in the morning, or whenever you need a boost. Fractional exhalation is tranquilizing and should be used at night or whenever you need to calm down.

Benefits: This exercise quickly accustoms the novice to the techniques and sensations of breath retention and the Three Locks. The serial shifts in pressure and locks promote circulation of blood and energy and stimulate cellular respiration, which causes body heat and benefits metabolism.

The Great Tai-Chi Circle Breath (Figure 3.9)

This highly fluid exercise synchronizes body, breath and mind and balances Yin and Yang energies throughout the system. It is one of the best breathing exercises in the entire Taoist repertoire, and if you practice only one breath control technique, then this should be it.

Posture: Standing, with heels together, toes splayed at 45 degrees, knees bent, spine erect. Bring hands together in front, below the navel, palms up, with right hand cupped in left.

Technique: Empty lungs thoroughly, and commence a long, slow inhalation through flared nostrils. As you inhale, slowly raise the hands out to the sides, palms up, and inscribe as wide a circle as possible as you raise them up above your head. At the same time, slowly straighten up the knees, so that knees are straight, hands raised above and lungs full at about the same time. Tuck in the pelvis and apply the Three Locks as you retain briefly and swallow audibly. Be sure to keep neck as stretched as possible, despite the raising of the arms.

Then release the locks and commence a slow, controlled exhalation through the nose; at the same time bring hands, palms down, slowly down in a straight line past face, throat, heart, solar plexus, navel and back down to the starting position, while at the same time slowly bending the knees back into a semi-squat. Empty lungs with a final abdominal contraction, pause to relax the abdominal wall, then turn palms upward again, cup them and commence another inhalation. You may take a short shallow breath between the end of exhalation and beginning of next inhalation to help relax breathing apparatus, if you wish. Repeat for as long as you wish, the longer the better, but do at least a dozen.

Pointers: Dr Huang Hsi-yi of Taipei cites three basic pointers for this most excellent of breathing exercises: stay natural, round and soft. That means breathing should be as natural as possible, not forced; that joints and muscles should be kept as loose and 'soft' as possible; and that arms must inscribe as round and wide an arc as possible.

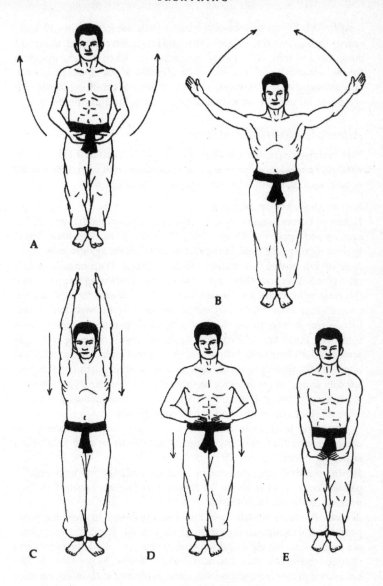

Figure 3.9 **The Great Tai-Chi Circle Breath**

Benefits: This breath balances the various polar aspects of Yin and Yang energy throughout the system: upper and lower, left and right, inner and outer, hot and cold, etc. It clears obstructions in the energy channels and thereby enhances equitable energy distribution. It also opens up the ribcage and expands the chest cavity, which benefits all breathing exercises. It is a powerful exercise for assimilating *chee* from the atmosphere.

Alternate Nostril Breathing

This exercise alternates the flow of air between right and left nostrils, which in turn balances the energy channels associated with right and left nostrils and right and left hemispheres of the brain.

Posture: Horse stance, or sitting.

Technique: Empty lungs completely, then take a deep breath through both nostrils and apply the Three Locks. Place thumb of right hand firmly against right nostril, fold index and middle fingers against palm, then close off left nostril with fourth and little fingers. With nostrils sealed, retain for 3–5 seconds. Now open left nostril by releasing fingers from it (keeping right nostril well sealed with thumb), release locks, and commence long, slow, controlled exhalation entirely through left nostril. Exhale completely, pause to relax abdomen, then commence a deep, controlled inhalation through the open left nostril, keeping right side sealed. When lungs feel full, seal off left nostril again, apply locks and retain briefly, then open up the right nostril by removing thumb (keeping left side shut), and commence controlled exhalation through right side. When empty, pause to relax, then inhale again through open right side, close off, lock and retain, and exhale through left.

Repeat at least a dozen times, six on each side, performing one complete inhalation and one complete exhalation on each side before switching nostrils.

Pointers: Apply Three Locks during retention and keep tongue pressed to palate. Focus eyes loosely on the hand controlling your nostrils, to help internalize awareness of breath.

Benefits: Alternate nostril breathing is a great way to clear the nasal passages and balance air flow through the nostrils. Right and left nostrils are associated with right and left energy channels along the spine, and alternate breathing thus balances energy as well as air flow. It also balances right/left hemisphere functions in the brain. Nasal membranes are exposed to far more concentrated doses of air when one nostril is shut, and thus more *chee* is extracted than in double-nostril breathing. Much of this *chee* is transmitted directly to the brain and central nervous system by the olfactory nerves, giving the entire system a potent boost.

Vibratory Breathing

There are five 'healing' sounds used in Taoist tradition, five in Tibetan practice, and even more in Hindu *pranayama*. Of all syllables in the world, the one that provides the greatest therapeutic benefits in vibratory breathing is the ancient syllable 'Om'.

Don't worry: by mouthing this syllable, you will not be participating in some pagan ritual, nor supplicating some foreign god. As used here, this sound has purely therapeutic functions.

Posture: Standing or sitting is best, but walking or lying may also be used.
Technique: Empty lungs thoroughly, then take a comfortably deep breath and retain it briefly. Open the mouth and round the lips, keeping the throat partly blocked with the neck lock to baffle and slow down the exhalation, then commence exhaling as you loudly pronounce 'oooooooohh . . .' as deeply and resonantly as possible. By controlling throat and vocal cords, you may prolong this audible exhalation for a remarkably long time. About ¾ through the exhalation, shut the mouth and continue exhaling through the nose, loudly humming the rest of the syllable nasally, 'hmmmmmmmmmmmm . . .'. When lungs are empty, relax with a few Bellows breaths, then fill up and perform another long, loud, resonant 'Om', starting the 'ooooh . . .' through the mouth and ending with 'hmmmm . . .' through the nose. Do three to six at a session.
Benefits: This syllable sets up a deeply resonant vibration in the larynx, and this vibration is transmitted directly down into the lungs, where it gently 'massages' the delicate alveoli and shakes loose mucus and debris. The vibrations travel up into the brain as well, where they massage the brain cells. This in turn stimulates all branches of the central nervous system. Owing to its proximity to the vibrating larynx, the thyroid gland receives an especially strong stimulation, which enhances its secretions and balances metabolism. In the brain, the vibrations also lend direct stimulation to the pineal and pituitary glands, thereby balancing the entire endocrine system.

Reverse Abdominal Breathing

This is a very old and rather esoteric Taoist breathing exercise and should not be practiced regularly until you have mastered normal abdominal breathing.

Posture: Horse stance, or sitting.
Technique: Empty lungs thoroughly, then commence a slow, deep inhalation through the nose. But instead of letting your lower abdomen expand

during inhalation, deliberately contract it inward as your lungs fill. Strong downward pressure from the diaphragm is required here to prevent the contracting abdominal wall from pushing the organs up into the chest cavity. When lungs are full, apply the anal and neck locks (abdominal lock will already be in place), swallow hard to sink *chee*, and retain briefly.

During exhalation, gradually relax the abdominal wall and let it expand outward, rather than pulling it inward as in normal abdominal breathing. Pause, relax and commence another cycle, about a dozen breaths per set.

Pointers: Focus the mind fully on the navel during this exercise, in order to coordinate abdominal contraction with the inhalation stage and expansion with the exhalation stage.

Benefits: The dramatic pressure changes between abdomen and chest caused by this type of breathing greatly amplify the packing and draining of blood and energy in the abdominal organs and greatly enhance the force-pump effect of the diaphragm on venous circulation. These pressure shifts also massage the organs and glands, increase secretions of gastric juices and stimulate peristalsis.

The Grand Celestial Tour (Figure 3.11, pages 186 and 187)

This is the 'grand-daddy' of traditional Taoist breathing exercises, combining six classical breathing postures in smooth succession.

Posture: Standing only. Although arms and torso shift to various positions during this sequence, thighs remain stable, knees slightly bent and feet firmly planted shoulder-width apart throughout the series.
Technique:
(1) *'Horse'*: The starting position is the Horse stance, with knees bent and arms hanging loosely by the sides. Perform six–ten deep diaphragmic breaths in this posture.
(2) *'Embracing the Jug'*: After the last exhalation in the Horse, slowly raise both arms up in front of you, with palms down, as you commence the next inhalation. Stop raising arms when they reach throat level, turn hands inward so palms are towards face, and form a wide circle with arms, as though embracing a big jug. Do six–ten deep breaths.
(3) *'Pressing Palms to Heaven'*: After the last exhalation, turn palms outward and continue raising arms up above head on the next inhalation. With hands above head and palms towards the sky, form a little 'porthole' with thumbs and index fingers, keeping elbows slightly bent and arms rounded. Look through the 'porthole' and perform six–ten deep breaths, tilting the pelvis back during inhalation and tucking it forward during

exhalation. Owing to upraised head, the neck lock is not used in this position.

(4) *'Pressing Palms to Earth'*: After last *inhalation* in above posture, commence controlled exhalation and slowly bend torso forward at the waist until you are bent over with palms towards earth. Let head and neck dangle loosely without tension. Perform three–six breaths only, not too deep, and without retention, keeping anus half locked, then slowly raise arms and torso back to above position as you inhale. Do a few breaths with palms pressing to heaven, then inhale deeply and slowly lower the arms out to the sides on the exhalation.

(5) *'Surrendering Weapons to the Emperor'*: Lower the arms until hands reach shoulder level, with palms facing outward to the sides, so arms form a cross with spinal axis. Hold hands at 90-degree angle to wrists and push palms as far outward as possible without tensing shoulders and arms. Keep hollows of elbows facing upward. Inhale, apply the Three Locks and retain briefly, then exhale slowly, repeating six–ten diaphragmic breaths. Focus attention on energy channels that run from shoulders, down the arms and into the thumbs and index fingers.

(6) *'Plucking Stars'*: This is the most difficult step in this exercise, but also the most beneficial to the internal organs. It should also be practiced as a complete exercise in itself. If you find it too difficult at first, skip it until you're ready. With lungs full in the above position, commence a long, controlled exhalation as you twist and bend the torso forward and down to the left, so that your right hand goes down towards the ground and left hand soars up to the sky to 'pluck a star'. Continue exhaling and bending and twisting until you have reached the posture depicted in Figure 3.10;

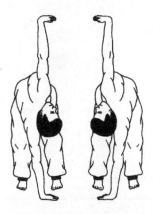

Figure 3.10 **Plucking Stars**

185

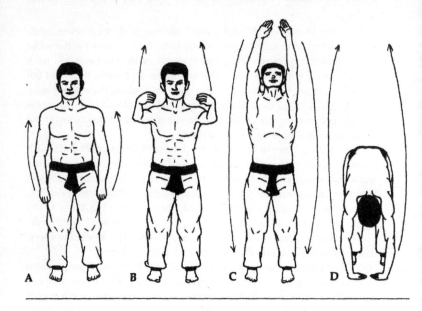

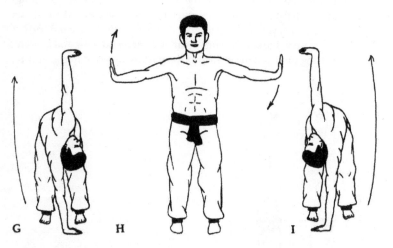

Figure 3.11 The Grand Celestial Tour
(a) Horse Stance, *(b)* Embracing the Jug, *(c)* Pressing Palms to Heaven, *(d)* Pressing Palms to Earth, *(e)* Return Palms to Heaven, *(f)* Surrendering

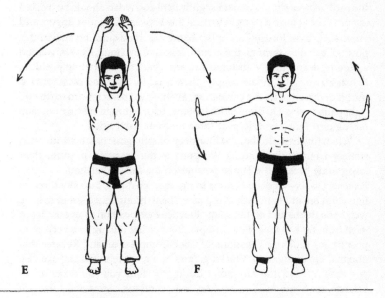

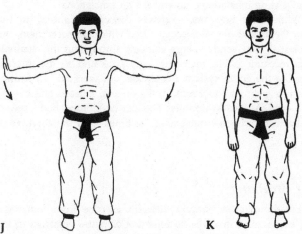

Weapons to the Emperor, *(g)* Plucking Stars, left side up, *(h)* Return to Surrendering to the Emperor, *(i)* Plucking Stars, right side up, *(j)* Return to Surrendering Weapons to the Emperor, *(k)* Return to Horse Stance with left palm pressing toward the sky and right palm pressing toward the earth. Knees should remain slightly bent and wrists should be twisted inward. Try to form a straight vertical line between the index fingers and nose. Keep eyes focused on upper hand. Do three quick breaths in this posture, exhaling through the mouth, followed by a long, slow inhalation as you raise and turn your torso and arms back to the starting position. Exhale completely, inhale deeply, then bend forward and twist torso in the other direction on the exhalation, pushing left palm toward earth and right palm to sky. Do three quick breaths, then return to starting position on the next inhalation. Repeat three times on each side.

When finished, do three or four deep diaphragmic breaths with arms stretched out in 'Surrendering Weapons to the Emperor' posture, then lower arms back to the Horse posture on the final exhalation.

Pointers: Do six–ten deep breaths in the erect postures, but only three or four short breaths bent over. Keep knees bent throughout the tour to keep weight on thighs and off the spine. Practice each position as an exercise in itself from time to time. For example, 'Embracing the Jug' is a very good posture for prolonged sessions of Chee Compression and Reverse Abdominal Breathing, and 'Plucking Stars' is a great rejuvenating exercise any time of day. If at any point during the tour you feel dizzy or off balance, do a few Bellows breaths, then continue. Arms and torso are shifted upward on inhalations, downward on exhalations.

Benefits: While most breathing exercises concentrate energy in the three Elixir Fields and the Microscopic Orbit which connects them, the Grand Celestial Tour sends energy coursing throughout the channels of the Macrocosmic Orbit, including legs, arms and all the internal organs, giving the entire system a complete '*chee* workout'. In winter, this series is a great way to warm up the organs, muscles and energy systems in even the coldest weather. The tour harmonizes body, breath and mind and coordinates movements of limbs with the rhythms of breath.

Circular Breathing

Circular breathing is an entirely different exercise from four-stage breathing exercises. It involves no retention or pause whatsoever; instead, inhalation and exhalation follow one another in a smooth, unbroken sequence that makes the entire breath cycle 'circular'.

Circular breathing has an immediate and powerful stimulating effect on the body's energy system, so powerful that it often causes dizziness, tremors and numbness in various parts of the body, effects very similar to hyperventilation. Therefore, it should be practiced only in the sitting or lying positions.

To perform a round of circular breathing, commence breathing through the nose at about the same rate as the Bellows breath, except make the exhalation and inhalation stages as even, equal and balanced as possible, with no pause at the end of either. Repeat five or six times in a row, then take a long, slow, deep inhalation, filling lungs comfortably full and exhaling in a long, slow, complete exhalation immediately thereafter. Without pausing, commence another set of five or six quick shallow breaths, followed by another long, deep breath. Do three or four sets at a time, two or three times a day. As your energy channels open up and your physical body grows accustomed to the surge in energy flow, symptoms such as dizziness and tremors will gradually cease. Even then, however, adepts should proceed no further with this breath without personal supervision from a qualified teacher.

Establishing a Regular Regimen

Like eating, sleeping and brushing your teeth, breathing exercises should become an integral part of your daily regimen. Though at first it may seem difficult to establish the habit, after only a few months the benefits become so obvious that it's hard to break. Once body and mind grow accustomed to that daily energy booster, your whole system feels like a flat tire without it. It takes far less time than eating, watching TV or reading the newspaper, yet this small investment of time and effort yields tremendous benefits for all aspects of your daily life.

By no means should you attempt to incorporate each and every exercise into each and every workout. Focus on the ones that give you the best results, try different combinations and sequences, practice some in the morning and others at night, and adjust your program as you progress. It is much better to perform two or three exercises correctly than to rush through half a dozen haphazardly.

Ideally, you should practice a round of breathing exercises at least twice a day: first thing in the morning before breakfast, and last thing at night before bed. In between, it's a good idea to engage in some sort of vigorous athletic exercise, such as tennis, swimming or weight-lifting, in order to give the muscles and cardiovascular system a thorough workout. However, vigorous sports which compact muscles and strain joints should *always* be preceded and followed by a few minutes of stretching, loosening, and breathing exercises, and such sports should be regarded primarily as recreational rather than therapeutic. Field sports are not an adequate substitute for long-life and breathing exercises.

The 3rd-century AD alchemist Ko Hung wrote:

> From midnight until noon, energy waxes; from noon until midnight, energy wanes. When energy is waning, breathing exercises are of no benefit.

In other words, *chee-gung* should be practiced between midnight and noon, when positive Yang energy prevails in the atmosphere. Ko Hung's observation accords precisely with the findings of Western science, which has determined that the concentration of negative ions (i.e. *chee*) in the air peaks between 3:00 and 6:00 a.m. Disciplined adepts of breathing rise around 4:00 a.m. to take advantage of this airborne power.

The morning session should be practiced immediately after rising from bed. You can make this a bit easier by first stretching your limbs and doing a bit of deep breathing while still lying comfortably in bed. It's a sobering fact that the overwhelming majority of fatal strokes occur between 8:00 and 9:00 a.m. when up to half the body's blood is still 'asleep' in the liver and pancreas. Some preliminary breathing and stretching in bed is not only a good preventive against such strokes, it also prepares you to commence a complete morning regimen of exercise. A sample exercise regimen that includes yoga, calisthenics, breathing and long-life exercises is suggested in the next chapter.

In this modern work-a-day world, people tend to leap out of bed the moment the alarm rings, jump into the shower, and rush off to work, while their bodies are still technically 'asleep'. This sort of routine puts a tremendous strain on heart and brain, and the damage is cumulative. Half an hour of early morning breathing and exercise not only prevents such self-inflicted damage to heart and brain, it also stimulates gastric secretions in preparation for breakfast and kicks peristalsis into gear for morning bowel movements. Those who plead, 'I don't have time for all that in the morning', will sooner or later find themselves unable to get up at all any more in the morning.

The evening round of breathing takes advantage of the great cosmic switch-over from Yin to Yang energy, which occurs roughly between 11:00 p.m. and 1:00 a.m. Breathing at this time prepares body and mind to derive maximum benefit from sleep by slowing, deepening and regulating respiration and heartbeat and relaxing the mind. Today, 7.2 million Americans suffer from chronic sleep disorders, some of which cause victims to awaken spontaneously up to 500 times during the night without realizing it. The most common disorder is called 'sleep apnea', a result of irregular breathing and consequent deficiency of oxygen to the brain. Apnea victims find themselves suddenly waking up with a start at night, gasping desperately for breath. All sleep disorders, including snoring, leave their victims thoroughly exhausted in the morning, regardless how long they stay in bed. Regular rhythmic tuning of breath and heartbeat before bed corrects the irregular breathing patterns and weak pulse that lead to oxygen and energy deficiency during sleep. Deep breathers enjoy uninterrupted sleep at night, wake up with abundant energy and need less sleep. Twenty minutes of deep diaphragmic breathing before bed reduces the time required for a thorough rest by about one hour.

Breathing sessions should last at least 15–30 minutes. It takes at least 5 minutes to establish rhythm and synchronize body and breath, and another 5 minutes to tether the 'monkey-mind'. However, it's also a good idea to keep pulse, digestion, respiration, metabolism and other vital functions balanced throughout the day by doing a few minutes of deep abdominal breathing from time to time. For example, you could spend your 'coffee break' up on the roof of your office building or in front of an open window breathing and stretching rather than stuffing yourself with sugar, starch and caffeine. You may improve bowel movements by doing a minute or two of deep breathing as you squat on a toilet. You can practice breathing while reading, driving and making love.

Here's a helpful hint for sluggish beginners: start with a set of ten or twelve deep, slow breaths, rest for a few minutes, then do another set. You will find that the second and all subsequent sets are much easier to perform because the first round squeezes large supplies of glucose and red blood cells from the liver and pancreas into general circulation, which energizes the entire system.

In order to get the most out of the time you invest in deep-breathing practice, always bear in mind the following basic points:

- Keep the shoulders loose, relaxed and low and keep the neck well stretched.
- Keep the tongue pressed against the palate at all times.
- Keep the chest relaxed by slightly rounding the shoulders.
- Keep the spine erect and perpendicular from coccyx to crown by stretching the neck and tucking in the pelvis.
- Keep the hands and face relaxed.
- Keep the Three Locks in place during retention.
- Keep the 'mind's eye' focused internally on the region of the navel.

A Bonanza of Breathing Benefits

Throughout the ages, Taoist texts have pointed out the vast superiority of breathing over drugs in medical therapy. Shen Chia-shu, a Ching

Dynasty adept and physician, insists that breathing therapy should be properly prescribed by all physicians:

> Breathing and related exercises are 100 times more effective as medical therapy than any drug. This knowledge is indispensable to man, and every physician should study it thoroughly.

While the orthodox Western medical establishment still regards deep-breathing therapy as 'voodoo medicine', a few Russian and European physicians have already rediscovered this ancient remedy, and they are moving ahead with it. In his book *Yoga Self Taught*, Andre van Lysebeth cites the conclusions of French physicians Dr Peschier and Walter Michel:

> Every organic or functional disorder leading to conditions of illness is susceptible to the influence, if not always the cure, of controlled breathing.
>
> Controlled respiration is the most outstanding method known to us for increasing organic resistance. Reduce the organic resistance by any means whatsoever and you will see germs, which up to that moment had been non-injurious, now developing into agents of infection. . . .
>
> There is always a natural immunity attributed to ionic balance in the blood, and dependent on breathing . . . It confers on the balance of the acid/base (i.e. Yin/Yang) a regularity which is re-established with each breath. . . .

This is precisely how ancient Taoist physicians described the root causes of disease – not as external 'attack' by germs, but as internal degeneration and toxicity that create critical imbalances that *permit* external attack. When such pathological conditions within the system are eliminated through diet, breathing and other regimens, optimum biochemical balance is restored to blood and tissues and the body automatically recovers its natural immunity. The stubborn Western view, fostered by Pasteur, that disease is primarily an 'attack' by germs that must be 'killed' with powerful drugs and surgical removal of damaged parts only reflects the abysmal lack of preventive care in the West. Such 'cures' do nothing whatsoever to correct the imbalances and toxicity that permit disease to occur in the first place. The net result of this approach is that diseases recur over and over again, often in different disguises and different parts of the body, trapping the patient for life in a vicious cycle of drugs and surgery that rapidly depletes his vital energy and deprives him of vital parts of his body. This approach to medical care degenerates and destroys the human system much faster than any disease.

As final motivation for beginners, let's briefly review the bonanza of therapeutic benefits realized by deep breathers at no financial cost whatsoever:

(1) Deep breathing stimulates vital hormone secretions throughout the endocrine system by exciting the pneumogastric nerve and providing direct massage to glands in the abdomen and sacrum, thereby balancing all vital functions, including sexual potency and fertility.

(2) Excitation of the pneumogastric nerve dramatically improves digestion, metabolism and excretion. Diaphragmic massage to the stomach and liver further enhances digestion and promotes peristalsis.

(3) Deep breathing permits deep, uninterrupted sleep and reduces time required for a complete rest.

(4) Awareness, thought, memory and other mental faculties are greatly heightened by deep breathing, which massages and irrigates the brain.

(5) Deep breathing calms the emotions and brings them under conscious control. A few deep abdominal breaths taken amid the throes of emotional excess quickly restore equilibrium.

(6) Deep breathing strengthens, stretches and tones the diaphragm, which in turn improves breath control and deepens abdominal massage. Recent studies in China show that the average flex of the diaphragm in people who do not practice deep breathing is only 3 cm. After only two months of daily practice, diaphragm flex increased to between 6 and 9 cm.

(7) Deep breathing literally 'saves breath' by slowing down and deepening respiratory patterns. This effect lasts for several hours after the exercises. In a study conducted in India, the average volume of air per breath rose from 482 ml before deep breathing up to 740 ml after only 15 minutes of practice, while the number of breaths per minute dropped dramatically from 15 to 5.

(8) Deep breathing has tremendous benefits for the heart and circulatory system: 20–30 minutes of deep breathing reduces the pulse by an average 10–15 per cent, and this effect continues for several hours after practice. A major study in China showed an enormous increase in the red blood cell count after only 30 minutes of deep breathing, a benefit that greatly enhances the blood's capacity to fix and carry oxygen. As we have seen, a properly utilized diaphragm functions as a 'second heart', and every beat of the heart you save now prolongs your life by one beat later.

Once you have established a regular daily regimen, you may gradually adapt and apply the exercises to other activities. Athletes, for example, may improve performance by practicing 20–30 minutes of breath control prior to athletic events. This habit relaxes the nerves, calms the heart, boosts circulation and enhances energy reserves, insuring optimum performance under pressure. East German and Japanese athletes have been using this method for decades. Singers and stage actors know how to apply deep diaphragmic breathing during performances, but many are not aware that 10–15 minutes of deep breathing in the dressing room before going on stage will prepare them for even better performance.

Painters and calligraphers in China routinely practiced *chee-gung* prior to taking up brush and ink in order to 'quiet thought, calm the heart, harmonize energy, and concentrate the spirit'. The inner tranquility they achieved thereby is clearly reflected in the elegance and serenity of their work, especially in calligraphy and landscape painting.

Chinese writers and poets have practiced the art of breath control ever since the dawn of writing in China. The earliest recorded reference to breathing as a literary aid appears in the famous third-century AD treatise on literature entitled *The Carved Dragon of the Literary Mind*:

> Breathing regulates the arts and letters by clearing and harmon-
> izing the mind and by balancing and channeling vital energies.

I hope this precept is reflected in the quality of writing in this book, which was conceived and written entirely under the influence of *chee* fueled by breath control. Su Tung-po, a twelfth-century adept and one of China's most beloved poets, didn't commence Taoist breathing regimens until mid-life, but in his memoirs he extols the virtues of deep breathing in no uncertain terms, and his words ring with the conviction of direct experience:

> At first, one feels little effect, but after practicing breathing exercises regularly for 100 days or so, the efficacy of this method is beyond measure, and its benefits are a hundred times greater than taking any medicine . . .
>
> The method is actually quite simple, but it must be practiced regularly over a period of time in order to realize its deepest benefits. If you try it for just 20 days, already your spirit will feel different, the region around your navel will feel warm during practice, your waist and legs will feel light and limber, and your eyes and complexion will grow bright and lustrous.
>
> These benefits are permanent for as long as one continues to practice.

CHAPTER 4:

———————— ◐ ————————

Exercise

The Tao of nurturing life requires that one keep oneself as fluid and flexible as possible. One should not stay still for too long, nor should one exhaust oneself by trying to perform impossible tasks. One should learn how to exercise from nature by observing the fact that flowing water never stagnates and a busy door with active hinges never rusts or rots. Why? Because they exercise themselves perpetually and are almost always moving.

[Sun Ssu-mo]

In this excerpt from his priceless masterpiece *Precious Recipes*, the Tang Dynasty physician Sun Ssu-mo succinctly distills the essence of Taoist exercise principles. Natural rhythmic movement is the foundation for cultivating essence and energy. Balance and moderation are also key factors. In a volume of the *Spring and Autumn Annals*, we find the following passage:

Essence and energy, body and breath, are indivisible: when the body does not move, essence cannot flow; when essence cannot flow, energy becomes stagnant.

Taoist exercises aim at keeping essential fluids (blood, hormones, lymph, etc.) and vital energy circulating. The prime focus is thus internal, not external. By getting essence moving like a mountain stream through controlled deep breathing balanced with rhythmic physical movement, body and breath are harmonized and vital energy is circulated to every organ and tissue in the body.

The Hard Way versus the Soft Way

When man is born, he is soft and flexible;
When he dies, he grows hard and rigid.

195

So it is with all things under Heaven.
Plants and animals are soft and pliant in life,
But brittle and dry in death.
Truly, to be hard and rigid is the way of death;
To be soft and flexible is the way of life.

[*Tao Teh Ching*]

In practice, the physical aspect of Taoist exercise takes a completely opposite approach from Western forms. Taoist exercises loosen, stretch and relax the body; Western exercise tightens, compacts and tenses the body. Taoist exercises are slow and rhythmic; Western forms are fast and fitful. Taoist regimens collect and store vital energy, leaving you feeling refreshed; Western exercises such as running, weight-lifting and field sports deplete energy and leave you feeling 'wiped out'.

All Taoist exercises are essentially 'aerobic', because they all involve carefully regulated breathing patterns. As such, in addition to the various benefits different exercises have for different parts of the body, *all* Taoist exercises benefit the cardio-vascular system and oxygenate the bloodstream. For the heart, the major benefits come from using the diaphragm as a force-pump for circulation. As these exercises become habitual, the body breathes more and more deeply with the diaphragm, even in ordinary activity, and this takes a tremendous load off the heart.

The essential difference between Taoist and Western exercises is most evident in the joints and associated muscles of the spinal column. By loosening and stretching the vertebrae and relaxing the associated spinal muscles, you may restore optimum nerve and energy impulses to the vital organs. Tense spinal muscles not only block nerve and energy channels, they also deplete vital energy because it takes a lot of energy to keep these muscles tight.

Complete physical relaxation is an absolute prerequisite for proper breath control and energy circulation, which in turn is essential for cultivating strong spiritual and mental powers. As Cicero said, 'Only the man who learns how to relax is able to create, and for him ideas reach the mind like lightning.' This is a genuine Taoist remark, for it clearly links physical relaxation with mental clarity, body with mind, essence and energy with spirit. It also acknowledges the electromagnetic properties of the vital energy that feeds the spirit of the physically relaxed man.

Soft-style exercise has an interesting history in China. It originally developed from a sort of therapeutic dance designed to ward off the ill effects of flooding well over 3,000 years ago, when Chinese civilization was centered in the flood-prone basin of the Yellow River. In a 2,000-year-old text dating from the Warring States Period appears the following passage:

> In ancient times, due to flooding of rivers and streams, excessive Yin and heavy dampness filled the air, causing energy stagnation among the people and making their joints and bones stiff and painful. Therefore, they practiced certain dances to relieve these symptoms.

These therapeutic dances were called *dao-yin* (literally, 'to guide and gather'). They consisted of various movements learned by watching animals in nature. 'Guide and gather' referred to the therapeutic effects of these dances, which gathered essence and energy and guided it rhythmically throughout the entire body to dispel 'evil *chee*' and rebalance the system. They conformed precisely to the Taoist principle of blending body and breath, balancing essence and energy. *Dao-yin* thus became the ancient foundation of Chinese calisthenics and martial arts.

The Martial Arts

What Westerners often fail to grasp about Chinese martial arts is that their primary purpose is to serve as defense against disease and degeneration, not against bullies and bandits, and that they are based upon precisely the same forces that lie at the heart of medicine, meditation and all Taoist arts. This point is well put in *The Wandering Taoist*:

> Learning martial arts means self-assurance, not arrogance. It is not the boxer who is dangerous, rather, it is the weakling. Insecure, the latter must constantly 'prove' himself.

As master martial artist Hung Yi-hsiang of Taipei says, 'The best fighters never have to fight!'

To Taoists, the martial arts are simply the Yang complement to the Yin arts of medicine and nutrition and the active physical complement to the passive spiritual arts of meditation. From the point of view of the Three Treasures, the medical/nutritional arts nourish essence, the martial arts 'martial' energy, and the meditative arts cultivate spirit.

The fusion of body and breath in exercise is traditionally attributed to the Buddhist monk Bodhidharma (Ta Mo), who arrived in China from India during the fifth century AD. In addition to Buddhist scriptures, Bodhidharma introduced yoga and pranayama breathing to China. The resulting blend of indigenous Chinese *dao-yin* animal forms with the yoga and rhythmic breathing brought from India by Bodhidharma gave birth to the Chinese martial arts as we know them today.

The indivisibility of the Three Treasures is the key that links the medical, martial and meditative arts in Taoist tradition. All three aspects support and complement one another and approach the same goal of harmony and balance from different angles. In China, most masters of the martial arts study and practice traditional Chinese medicine and devote time to the cultivation of spirit through meditation. Most Chinese physicians also practice soft-style exercises and deep breathing, and Taoist mystics keep their bodies in shape by practicing martial arts and taking medicinal herbs. As with everything else in Taoism, exercise is a package deal in which the total is greater than the sum of its parts. It cannot be fragmented into parts without losing its therapeutic benefits.

Bodhidharma ended up at the famous Shao Lin Temple in central China. Part of his program was to get the Chinese monks there back into physical shape, for they were all cramped and half-crippled from prolonged meditation in lotus without any exercise. Though Buddhist, Bodhidharma was deeply influenced by Chinese Taosim, and to this day he remains the patron saint of the martial arts in China, Korea and Japan. His glum, scowling face with his big, penetrating eyes and perpetual five-o'clock shadow remains a favorite theme in traditional scroll paintings.

In order to learn the traditional martial arts forms of China, especially the subtle internal schools, such as Tai-Chi (Form of the Supreme Ultimate), Ba-Gua (Form of the Eight Trigrams) and Hsing-Yi (Form of Mind), personal guidance from a qualified master is an absolute necessity. However, you may learn some of the various soft-style *exercises* associated with the martial arts by following the instructions and illustrations provided below and practicing them regularly. These confer great health benefits and complement your nutritional, breathing and meditative regimens. A few useful hatha yoga postures are provided as well. The exercises are presented in four categories: warming up; loosening and stretching; long-life exercises; and relaxation. The final section presents a sample daily regimen of breathing and exercise for the reader to consider in organizing his or her own personal program.

All Taoist exercises involve careful coordination of body, breath and mind in order to cultivate and harmonize the Three Treasures of essence, energy and spirit. These three aspects are inseparable. If you falter at one level during the exercises, the other two are immediately thrown off balance. For example, if your mind ponders tonight's dinner menu or recalls last night's sexual encounter during your exercises, body and breath lose their 'commander' and cannot synchronize. If you go through the physical motions without breath control, the body must burn stored energy rather than utilize fresh supplies of *chee* provided by proper breathing, and, if you fail to properly loosen, stretch and relax the body, breath will not be able to circulate blood and energy to the limbs, organs and other tissues.

Warming Up

Before commencing any exercises – breathing, yoga, calisthenics or football – it is important first to warm up the body. This principle is similar to warming up your car engine in winter: it heats your biological 'motor', gets your 'oil' moving, and 'tunes' the moving parts. This warm-up set requires about 3 minutes to perform, and it may be practiced as an exercise in itself any time, any place to relax a cramped, fatigued body and stimulate circulation of blood and energy. The entire set is performed in the standard Horse stance (see Chapter 3).

Spine and Torso Twist (Figure 4.1)

This is one of the single most beneficial physical exercises in the entire Taoist repertoire. It should be practiced several times daily as a preventive measure against congestion in the digestive tract, misalignment of the spinal vertebrae, and stiffness in the hips and sacrum.

Technique: Adopt the Horse stance, relaxing the shoulders and arms as much as possible. Using *only* the thighs for torque, twist the trunk and torso slowly left and right. Torso and spine should be passively propelled left and right by the torque action of thighs and waist. Gently increase the torque and extend the twist, letting your arms flail out loosely to the sides by centrifugal force. Elbows, wrists and shoulders should be totally loose and arm muscles relaxed throughout the exercise. Hands will slap loosely against chest and back when they reach the limit of torque, adding a little extra twist to the upper torso at the end of each swing. As soon as the twist in one direction is complete, start turning the trunk the other way, using thighs and hips only. Do 30–50 twists per set.

Pointers: Knees well bent, arms loose, spine and neck erect. The head follows the torso far enough around in each direction to see directly behind you. Perform gently and rhythmically.

Benefits: You may hear crackling sounds along your spine during the first few twists. That's the sound of your vertebrae realigning themselves into proper position. Spinal vertebrae frequently fall out of line during the

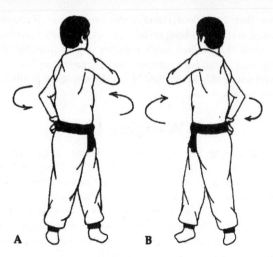

Figure 4.1 **Spine and Torso Twist**
A and *B* depict the final extent of twist in either direction

course of a day, especially for people with sedentary lifestyles. The spinal twist corrects this chronic condition.

The twist also stretches and limbers all the supporting muscles along the spinal column, thereby freeing any nerves pinched by muscular tension there. It opens up vital energy channels along the spine, permitting free flow of *chee* between the 'roots' of the sacral region and the 'blossom' of the brain.

Within the torso, this exercise stretches the rib-cage, expands the lungs and provides a highly stimulating massage to the abdominal organs.

This exercise is especially beneficial first thing in the morning, because the powerful rhythmic torque forces accumulated blood in the abdominal organs to flow outward and upward to the arms and head and downward to the legs, without requiring any extra work from the heart. This makes it a good preventive against early morning stroke. It's also a good way to redistribute blood and energy after long hours at the desk or in a car or after any other sedentary activity that congests blood and stagnates energy.

The Windmill

Technique: Stand in the Horse stance with arms hanging loosely by your sides. Swing both arms upward and around in as wide a circle as possible. Continue swinging them like a double windmill round and round, maintaining smooth, regular momentum and a wide arc. Do 20–30 swings.

Pointers: Shoulders *must* be kept loose in this exercise, especially on the upswing. Inscribe as wide an arc as possible. During the downswing, let the chest protrude and the rib-cage expand fully.

Benefits: The windmill stretches and warms up the intercostal muscles, which control the rib-cage during deep breathing. It limbers and loosens chest muscles to facilitate breathing. It also stretches arm and shoulder muscles, making it easier to keep them loose during subsequent breathing exercises. Heart and lungs are opened and stimulated, enhancing breath control.

Reverse Windmill

Technique: Start from same position, but raise the arms in the opposite direction coming up and around from behind and down the front. Same pointers apply.

Benefits: Benefits are basically similar to regular windmill, but instead of focusing on stretching the front of the rib-cage, this version opens up the back part of the rib-cage and limbers all the muscles connecting the upper spine to the shoulders and neck.

Chest Expander (Figure 4.2)

Technique: Stand in the Horse and raise your arms out in front of you at eye

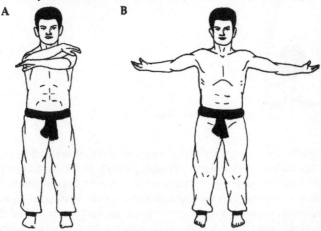

Figure 4.2 Chest Expander:
note palms down when hands cross *(A)*, palms up when open *(B)*

A   B

level, palms down (Figure 4.4a). Swing arms out to both sides, turning palms upward, until they reach full limit of stretch. Keep arms parallel to ground throughout the exercise, and fling them as far back as they'll reach. This will expand the chest completely (Figure 4.4b). Then swing them back to the front, turning palms downward, and let the hands cross over one another so they don't collide. Continue swinging back and forth, expanding and contracting the chest, 20–30 times per set.

Benefits: This exercise prepares the upper chest for deep breathing and facilitates smooth transition from the diaphragmic to intercostal phase in deep breathing. It stretches the powerful chest muscles, preventing them from tensing during breathing exercises. It also helps loosen the shoulder joints.

Forward Bend (Figure 4.3)

Technique: Stand in the Horse and fold your arms loosely across your chest. Straighten and lock the knees, then bend over forward until your folded arms are hanging loosely down, with elbows dangling a foot or two above your feet. Now start 'reaching' down to the ground with folded forearms by rocking gently up and down. Keep head and neck loose and dangling downward. Each downward thrust should stretch spine and legs to their natural limits. Do about a dozen rhythmic dips in this manner, then shift torso slightly to the right and repeat, then to the left, then back to the central position.

Figure 4.3 Forward Bend

Benefits: This is a quick way to stretch spinal vertebrae and their supporting muscles. It opens nerve and energy circuits all the way from the heels up to the head; these are important channels for energy control during deep breathing. This exercise also massages the abdominal organs and squeezes accumulated blood from them, pushing it into general circulation without requiring extra work from the heart. Gravity flushes the brain with abundant supplies of oxygen and glucose and flushes out carbon dioxide and other metabolic wastes.

Abdominal Lift (Figure 4.4)

Technique: Adopt the Horse stance, then lean forward, and place hands on the thighs just above the knees, with thumbs next to fingers along the inner thigh. Forcefully expel the breath completely, block the throat with the glottis, and immediately pull the entire abdominal wall back towards the spine and up into the diaphragm. Empty lungs will facilitate this upward thrust of the diaphragm by vacuum.

Apply the anal lock tightly and hold the abdominal wall contracted for 5–15 seconds. Then, without inhaling yet, relax the abdominal wall and let the organs fall back into place, after which you should commence a slow, deep inhalation. Repeat two–three times.

Another version is to rapidly contract and relax the abdominal wall while maintaining this posture and keeping the lungs empty. This provides the organs with an invigorating massage.

Pointers: It's important to thoroughly evacuate the lungs and lock the throat shut before pulling the abdominal wall inwards and upwards.

Benefits: This exercise squeezes stagnant blood from the internal organs like water from a sponge. Stagnant blood is disgorged into the vena cava for recirculation and oxygenation in the lungs. It strengthens and tones

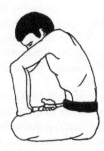

Figure 4.4 **The Abdominal Lift**
(left) Standing and *(right)* sitting

the diaphragm, improves its flex and thus facilitates deep breathing. It improves the tissue tone of all abdominal organs by massaging them and is a good preventive measure against gastritis, constipation and digestive congestion.

Loosening and Stretching

Loosening and stretching are the hallmarks of Chinese soft-style calisthenics. While loosening exercises are focused primarily on the joints, stretching concentrates on the muscles, tendons and ligaments. Bodily mobility and physical coordination depend entirely on flexibility of the joints and the tone of the tendons, which attach joints to muscles. Furthermore, blood, energy and nerve impulses can only circulate freely when joints are loose and flexible and muscles are stretched and relaxed.

First, let's take a close look at stretching. While Western calisthenics abruptly *contract* and relax the muscles, Taoist exercises slowly *stretch* and relax them. Stretching the muscles first squeezes out stagnant venous blood, permitting the subsequent relaxation phase to draw in fresh arterial blood. By contrast, heavy muscular contractions compact the vessels that feed the muscles, obstructing blood circulation and therefore impairing cellular respiration in muscle cells. Consequently, Western exercises lead to a rapid build-up of lactic acid, a metabolic by-product of muscle contraction that causes muscular fatigue.

Regularly stretching rather than compacting muscles causes the whole body to grow progressively more supple, rather than stiff, and keeps nerve, blood and energy channels open and unobstructed.

For stretching major tendons and muscle groups throughout the body, nothing beats the postures of traditional hatha yoga. When practicing these stretches, always bear in mind the following three basic rules, in order to derive maximum benefit without any risk of injury:

- Proceed *slowly*, *deliberately* and *gently* with each stretch. First empty the lungs, then commence the stretch until you have reached your limit of flexibility. Pause briefly to relax and inhale, then try to stretch just a little bit further on the next exhalation. While holding the fully stretched posture, breathe slowly and rhythmically, but do not retain the breath. Exhalation should be about twice as long as inhalation during stretches.
- Relax for 20–30 seconds between stretching exercises. This permits a surge of fresh blood to enter the muscles and deliver oxygen and glucose, while flushing out carbon dioxide and lactic acid.
- Focus mental awareness on the specific muscles and tendons being

stretched in each posture. This will increase your capacity to stretch and enhance the flow of blood and energy there, because 'energy follows where mind leads'.

Stretches

The Plow (Figure 4.5)

Technique: Lie flat on your back on a firm surface with feet together. Place palms firmly on the floor by your hips for support. Slowly raise your legs up off the floor, using the abdominal muscles to lift, and swing them up over your head until the toes touch the floor behind your head, or as far back as they'll reach. Relax briefly and inhale, then try to stretch a bit further on the exhalation. Keep knees locked, legs straight and arms stretched on the floor. Hold this posture for 1–2 minutes, breathing slowly and rhythmically through the nose. Each inhalation will stretch the spine a bit more, while each exhalation will relax it a bit.

Benefits: This is the best spinal stretch of them all. It stretches and aligns the vertebrae from the lower back all the way to the top of the neck, at the same time stretching and toning the muscles that support the spine and opening up vital-energy channels. It is also an excellent exercise for developing the Neck Lock. Many types of headache are instantly relieved by this posture. Breathing in the plow posture provides an invigorating massage to the stomach, draws fresh blood into the spinal muscles and cleans out the thyroid gland.

Figure 4.5 The Plow

The Cobra (Figure 4.6)

Technique: Lie flat on your stomach with forehead on the floor and palms placed flat at about shoulder level, as though you were doing push-ups (Figure 4.6 top). Completely relax the spine. Now raise up your head and stretch it back until you're looking upward, then raise the top part of the torso off the floor, using only the back muscles for lift. When you've reached the limit, continue bending upward by pushing up with your

Figure 4.6 **The Cobra:** *(top)* starting position, *(centre)* full stretch, *(bottom)* incorrect posture

hands until your spine is fully arched. Do not raise the lower abdomen off the floor and do not straighten and lock the elbows. Stretch the neck up as far as it will go and look at the ceiling or sky. Don't let the neck contract and the shoulders hunch up, as in Figure 4.6 (bottom), which shows the wrong posture. Hold the position for 30–60 seconds.

Benefits: The Cobra stretches spine and neck in the opposite direction from the Plow. Thus the two are complementary exercises. It opens up the throat, stretching all the muscles, tendons and blood vessels there, and stimulates the thyroid gland. By contrast to the Plow, the back muscles are contracted instead of stretched and the abdominal muscles are stretched instead of contracted.

The Forward Bend (Figure 4.7)

Technique: Sit on the floor with legs stretched out in front of you, feet 2 or 3 inches apart. Stretch the spine and neck, then slowly bend forward at the waist as you exhale. Try to bend as much from the waist as possible, instead of curving the spine, which should bend only during the final phase. Slide hands down along shins as you bend, grasp the soles of the feet, and use the arms to pull the torso forward toward the feet, aiming forehead to knees (Figure 4.7). Keep knees locked and legs straight, or else you'll lose traction. When you've reached your limit, relax briefly, inhale, then try to bend a bit further on the next exhalation by pulling forward with the arms. If at first you cannot touch head to knees or reach hands to feet, go as far as you can and stop. Prolonged practice will stretch and revive those atrophied muscles and tendons in the back of the legs and spine, until you're able to fold up like a jack-knife. Hold for 1–2 minutes.

Figure 4.7 **The Forward Bend**

Benefits: The Forward Bend focuses on stretching the lower spine, thereby completing the work begun by the Plow, which exerts its strongest stretch on the upper spine and neck. As such, it is both an excellent preventive and an effective palliative for chronic lower back pain, sciatica and discomfort in the kidneys. Like the Plow, it stretches nerves, muscles and tendons from heel to head and massages the stomach. Breathing in this posture provides direct diaphragmatic massage to kidneys and the sexually vital suprarenal glands.

Single Leg Forward Bend (Figure 4.8)

Technique: Stand in front of a table, wall, fireplace mantle, or similar solid support which stands anywhere from waist level to eye level. The higher the support the more difficult the bend, but the better the results. Start with waist level and work up. Raise one leg up so that the heel rests on the support, keeping torso and hips facing the support rather than at an angle to it. Slowly bend forward from the waist and move the hands

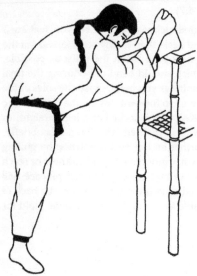

Figure 4.8 Single Leg Forward Bend

down along the upraised leg until fingers wrap around the toes. Place forehead on or just below the knees and pull the toes back toward the head to increase the stretch of tendons and muscles along the back of leg. Perform 6–10 slow deep breaths, then raise the head and lower the leg back down. Switch legs and repeat. Perform one or two stretches per leg during each exercise session.

Benefits: One of the most common problems for sedentary people is the shrinking and atrophy of tendons along the backs of the legs, a condition that keeps muscles and nerves chronically tense and blocks energy channels. This exercise stretches those vital tendons and opens nerve and energy channels from feet to hips and spine.

Double Team Back Bends (Figure 4.9)

Technique: This exercise requires two people of approximately equal height and weight. Stand back to back, link arms at the elbows and cross forearms tightly against the ribs and chest. While one person relaxes, the other tightens his grip on their linked arms and slowly bends forward, lifting the other person off the ground and pulling him onto his own back (Figure 4.9). Hold the person suspended in this position briefly, being

Figure 4.9 **Double Team Back Bends**

careful not to bend too far forward and flip over, then slowly straighten up and let him down again. Without pause, the other person now bends forward and lifts his partner up in the same manner. Repeat five or six times or as often as you wish in both directions.

Benefits: This exercise provides an excellent backward spinal stretch without any muscular effort whatsoever, complemented by a forward bend. It loosens spinal vertebrae and muscles, while stretching their attached ligaments and tendons.

Figure 4.10 **The Pylon**

The Pylon (Figure 4.10)

Technique: Stand with feet splayed out in opposite directions, thighs parallel to ground, calves perpendicular. Place hands on thighs just above knees, as in the abdominal lift exercise. Keep spine erect, the head straight and butt well tucked in. Squat until you stretch the tough tendons and large muscles connecting inner thighs to pelvis. Do Bellows breathing and practice anal lock contractions to give the entire urogenital diaphragm an excellent workout. Hold the posture until your thighs begin to tremble, then bring heels and toes back together to a normal stance. Relax tendons and muscles by kicking feet out loosely to the sides. *Benefits*: The Pylon stretches the cramped muscles and tendons between thighs and pelvis and opens up energy channels along the inside of the legs from the perineum to the feet. It tones up the urogenital diaphragm and enhances one's sense of balance.

Figure 4.11 Dip Splits

Dip Splits (Figure 4.11)

Technique: Stand straight with feet together. Take one giant step forward with left leg and dip down into a split by sliding the right foot backward until you've reached the position illustrated in the figure. If necessary, brace a hand against a chair or wall for balance. Front thigh should be parallel to ground, front shin perpendicular, rear knee suspended just above the ground. Extend arms out to the sides for balance, arch spine back a bit, and rock gently up and down five or six times. Then repeat with the right leg forward. Do two or three splits in each direction. *Benefits*: This exercise stretches the large muscles and tendons on the front and outer part of the thighs, and thus complements the effects of the Pylon. It strengthens ankles, arches the feet and exercises the muscles that support the lower back and pelvis. It improves balance and stimulates energy meridians between pelvis and feet.

The above exercises limber, relax and energize all the major muscles and tendons involved in supporting the head, neck, spine, pelvis and legs and provide a fast, effective preparation for any athletic activity. When practiced in conjunction with the loosening exercises given below, they provide a complete workout.

Loosening Exercises
Spine and Torso Twist

This has already been introduced as a warming-up exercise, but it's also one of the best loosening exercises for the spine, neck and shoulders.

The Pendulum (Figure 4.12)

Technique: Stand relaxed with feet parallel, shoulder-width apart, and knees locked. Bend forward at the waist until your back is about parallel to the ground, letting arms and hands dangle loosely downward. Relax the neck and let the head hang down as well. Using hips and lower back muscles only, start twisting the entire torso from side to side, causing arms and head to swing back and forth like pendulums (Figure 4.12). After about a dozen full 180-degree swings from side to side, stop propelling the torso and let the 'pendulum' gradually decrease

Figure 4.12 **The Pendulum**

swinging until hands come to rest again. Repeat this two or three times.

Benefits: The Pendulum loosens and limbers the vertebrae of the neck and spine, as well as the joints of the shoulders, elbows and wrists. It stretches and loosens the massive muscles of the upper back and shoulders, which should remain relaxed throughout the exercise. Tension here is the cause of many chronic discomforts. It also stimulates the energy meridians running from spine into head, and from shoulders down to arms and hands.

Shoulder Roll (Figure 4.13)

Technique: Horse stance, arms hanging loosely by sides. Start rolling the shoulders alternately up, back, down and around, like the action of a driveshaft (Figure 4.13a). Roll them in as wide an arc as possible. Then reverse direction, rolling shoulders alternately forward (Figure 4.13b). You may also practice this exercise by simultaneously rolling one shoulder forward and the other backward.

Benefits: The Shoulder Roll is a good way to loosen up the shoulder muscles, limber the tendons that attach them to the sockets and loosen the joints. This is the region of greatest tension in people today, owing to chronic stress and overstimulation.

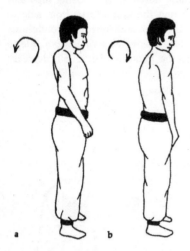

Figure 4.13 Shoulder Roll

Upper Back Loosener (Figure 4.14)

Technique: Stand erect with heels together and toes splayed out at 45 degrees. Relax your arms, reach back and clasp your hands behind your

Figure 4.14 **Upper Back Loosener**

back with palms together. It helps to interlace the fingers. Stretch the neck up, roll both shoulders backward, and try to bring your elbows together. You won't be able to touch elbows, but that is the direction in which to move. Hold the position for 3–5 seconds, then relax shoulders and arms and roll them forward again. Repeat three–six times.

Benefits: This maneuver loosens the upper vertebrae and their surrounding muscles, thereby unblocking pinched nerves in this chronically tense area and restoring neural communication with organs and glands. It opens up the rib-cage, thereby facilitating deep breathing, and loosens the shoulder joints. Try this exercise from time to time during the day, especially after sitting at a desk for hours or when feeling 'uptight'.

Long-Life Exercises

Having warmed up, stretched and loosened your entire bodily framework and its related network of energy channels, you are ready to proceed with a round of deep diaphragmatic breathing exercises, such as those described in the previous chapter. Or you may proceed with a series of long-life exercises, as introduced below. Long-life exercises may be practiced in combination with deep breathing, or as a preliminary to it.

Long-life exercises are so named because they promote longevity by extending the functional life of the various vital organs, glands, joints, muscles and other parts of the body. Most of them combine mobile

213

loosening and stretching movements with rhythmic diaphragmic breathing, but some of them involve pressing vital points to stimulate energy flow to various parts of the body. Long-life exercises synchronize body and breath, essence and energy, under the guidance of mind. They may be practiced any time, any place, for a quick physical tune-up and energy recharge. The most beneficial times to practice them are early morning, before breakfast, or just before bed at night.

The following long-life exercises are labeled according to the parts of the body upon which they focus primary benefits, although all of them extend their benefits throughout the system via the energy channels. Breathe rhythmically and naturally throughout the exercises, pausing to take a few deep diaphragmic breaths whenever you feel the need for a recharge of *chee*.

The Head

Face and Throat Stretch (Figure 4.15)

Technique: This may be practiced standing in the Horse, sitting or lying down in bed. Tilt the head upward and stretch the face vertically as much as possible, as though taking a deep yawn. Open eyes and mouth wide (Figure 4.15a). Then contract the facial muscles into a grimace. Repeat about a dozen times, stretching various individual muscles as you become aware of them. Then tilt head all the way up and jut the chin out as far as it will go, stretching the 'strings' of the throat between larynx and lower jawbone (Figure 4.15b). Relax and repeat a dozen times.

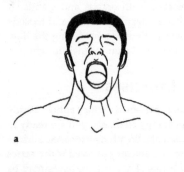

a

b

Figure 4.15 Face and Throat Stretch

Benefits: Stretches and relaxes the myriads of tiny muscles that control the face and jaws. Helps prevent and get rid of wrinkles, irrigates face muscles with fresh blood and draws energy up to the face and head.

Tones the throat and strongly stimulates the thyroid and parathyroid glands, thereby regulating metabolism.

Eye Roll

Technique: May be practiced standing, sitting or lying. Open eyes wide and start rolling them clockwise in a wide arc, gradually increasing speed. Do two–three dozen, then repeat in the other direction.

Benefits: Stretches and tones the muscles that control the eyeballs, thereby improving vision. Enhances blood circulation to the eyes and related nerves. Draws vital energy into the brain. Balances circulation of Yin and Yang energies throughout the system.

Pressing Vital Head Points (Figures 4.16–4.17)

Technique: Practice these in standing or sitting postures.

(a) Make a fist with both hands, with the knuckles of the index fingers protruding. Press these knuckles firmly against the vital points at the temples, about 1½ inches back from the outer corners of the eyes. Press, hold the pressure for a few seconds, then release. Repeat three–four times. (Figure 4.16).

Figure 4.16 **Pressing Temple Points**

Benefits: Stimulates and balances energy flow in the head. Clears obstructions to energy in head. Provides quick relief for certain varieties of headache due to nervous tension.

(b) Press the knuckle of index finger of one hand firmly against the vital point that lies in the depression at the center of the upper lip, just below the nose. Press hard, hold briefly, release, and repeat three–four times. This is the end point of the Channel of Control. (Figure 4.17).

Benefits: Pressure here helps stimulate the Channel of Control to pulse energy up into the head from the spine. It also clears obstacles to energy flow.

(c) Place palms on head with fingers laced and use thumbs to find the two vital points located in back of the head, where the cervical vertebrae meet the base of the skull. Press hard, rub, then release, repeating several times. (Figure 3.1).

Benefits: Pressure here clears blocked nasal passages and helps balance air flow between right and left nostrils.

Figure 4.17 **Pressing Upper Lip Point**

Ear Press and Skull Drum (Figure 4.18)

Technique: Practice standing or sitting. Press palms tightly against ears, then pull palms away abruptly. Repeat three–four times. Then press palms to ears and place index and middle fingers firmly against base of skull at 'Jade Pillow' point. Snap index fingers off middle fingers so that index fingers drum against skull, causing a loud drumming sound inside.

Benefits: Balances air pressure in the eustachian tubes and ear canals. Relieves ringing in the ears and alleviates certain varieties of headache. Helps prevent fainting and dizzy spells. Expels stagnant *chee* from Jade Pillow points.

Figure 4.18 **Ear Press and Skull Drum**
(left) Index Fingers crossed over Middle Fingers, ready to snap
(right) Index Fingers snapped against head to 'drum the skull'

Teeth and Gum Grind

Technique: Sitting, standing or lying down. Clamp jaws shut so that teeth are pressed together. Grit the teeth and grind them together, causing the jaw muscles to bulge at the temples. Release, and repeat as often as desired.

Benefits: Strengthens teeth and gums, tones jaw muscles and improves circulation to the gum tissues. Also helps draw energy up to the head and focus mental attention inward.

Tongue Stretch and Roll

Technique: This may be done standing, sitting or lying down. First, stretch the tongue out of mouth as far as possible, retract and repeat five–six times. Then roll the tongue around the mouth clockwise along the external gumline, then repeat counter-clockwise.

Benefits: Strongly stimulates beneficial salivary secretions from the ducts below the tongue. This should be swallowed to benefit digestive functions in the stomach. The powerful enzymes contained in these secretions help eliminate bad breath by digesting the bacteria in the mouth and stomach that cause this offensive condition. Since the tongue muscle is directly connected to the heart muscle, this exercise limbers the heart.

Face Rub

Technique: This should be done either standing or sitting. Rub the palms of the hands together briskly to generate heat and draw energy into the palms, then rub the index and middle fingers in circles around closed eyes, going with the grain of the eyebrows, about a dozen times. Recharge the palms with another brisk rub and do the same thing around the ears, moving up from the temples around and over the ears, down behind and back again, a dozen times. Rub palms again, then place index and middle fingers on either side of the nose and rub briskly up and down between inner corners of eyes and lower corners of nostrils.

Benefits: Rubbing the palms together charges them with *chee*. Rubbing around the eyes with charged palms improves vision and enhances blood and energy circulation to the eyes, thereby relieving fatigue caused by eye strain. Rubbing around the ears enhances hearing and stimulates mental energy. Rubbing the sides of the nose draws blood and energy to the sinuses in preparation for breathing exercises. In winter, the nose rub is an especially effective preventive against head colds.

Head and Neck Twist

Technique: Standing or sitting. Stretch the neck and direct eyes straight ahead, unfocused. Turn the head 90 degrees to the right by twisting the neck around until both eyes can see the right shoulder. Then turn the head 180 degrees back around to the left, until both eyes can see the left shoulder. Repeat 10–20 times, slightly increasing the torque each time, but be careful to keep the exercise 'soft'.

Benefits: Stretches and limbers the muscles and tendons throughout the neck and cervical vertebrae, stimulates the nerves there, and massages the thyroid and larynx.

Nose Massage

Technique: Standing, sitting or lying. Rub palms together till warm, then place the open palm of one hand directly on the tip of the nose, press lightly and rub around in a circle about a dozen times in each direction. This will cause the entire tip of the nose to roll around along with the palm.

Benefits: Stimulates sinus nerves, opens the nasal passages, loosens dried encrusted mucus, and serves as a good preventive against head colds in winter.

Abdomen, Waist and Lower Back

Spine and Torso Twist

Already introduced, this is an excellent all-around exercise to stimulate energy and blood circulation in abdominal organs, hips and spinal column.

Abdominal Massage

Technique: This may be done standing, sitting or lying down on your back. Rub palms together briskly to generate heat and charge them with *chee*. Bare the abdomen and place left palm over the navel, with right palm over the left hand. Start inscribing small circles around the navel, moving in the direction of colonic flow, i.e. from lower left. Gradually increase the diameter of the circles until your hands are following the actual path of the colon.

Benefits: Stimulates the Sea of Energy center and balances abdominal energy. Stimulates stomach and bowels, enhances peristaisis and promotes regular bowel movements.

Lower Back Massage

Technique: Standing or sitting. Rub palms together to charge them with heat and *chee*. Raise your shirt and place palms firmly against the soft part of the lower back, about three inches to either side of the spine and just below the rib-cage. Use palms and fingers to massage this region vigorously, moving the hands up and down rhythmically in opposite directions.

Benefits: In cold weather, this massage quickly builds up body heat by drawing Yang energy into the lower spinal channels and warming the kidneys. It stimulates blood and energy circulation in the lumbar and sacral region, and provides excellent therapy for chronic stiffness and pain in the lower back.

The Bump and Grind (Figure 4.19)

Technique: This can only be done standing. Adopt the Horse stance, with all your weight resting on your thighs, and raise arms up above head so palms are facing the sky. Start rotating the hips and swiveling the pelvis round and round in circles, extending the diameter of the swivel as widely as possible, as though you were swinging a 'hula-hoop' around your waist. Do a dozen or two rotations, then repeat in opposite direction.

Figure 4.19 **The Bump and Grind**

Anal Sphincter Contractions

Technique: This may be practiced standing, sitting, lying down or walking. Inhale and briefly retain the breath, while performing a quick series of deep anal sphincter contractions. Hold the last contraction tightly for a few seconds, then completely relax the sphincters as you exhale. When lungs are empty, perform one more deep contraction and release it before commencing next inhalation. Do this two–three times. In the lying position, you may direct the stimulation of the contractions directly to the colon by performing them with knees drawn up against the chest, with arms wrapped around

Benefits: Expels noxious gas and helps prevent constipation. Exercises the urogenital diaphragm and provides an excellent prostate massage for men. Prevents formation of hemorrhoids by flushing out stale blood from the anal sphincters and associated muscles and eliminating energy and blood stagnation from this vital spot. Helps men gain control over the urogenital canal, for use in ejaculation control, and helps women gain voluntary control over the vaginal 'Love Muscle'. Prevents prolapse of the rectum and the uterus. For pregnant women, this is a good way to prepare the pelvic muscles and tendons for childbirth. Practice this exercise frequently throughout the day, with or without the deep breathing.

Back Bows (Figure 4.20)

Technique: Spread feet more than shoulder-width apart and place hands on ground shoulder-width apart in front. Arch the spine upward and push back on hands, bending neck and head downward between the arms (Figure 4.20 top). Now push forward on hands and feet, while at the same time arching the back down toward ground instead of up toward the sky and stretching the neck and head upwards (Figure 4.20 bottom). Then push back on hands, arch spine the other way and repeat, bowing the spine up and down and moving the body forward and back, 10–15 times. Martial artists practice this exercise on their fingertips instead of flat on palms, in order to build up tendons in hands and forearms.

Benefits: Excellent spinal exercise and vertebrae massage. Also, stretches and contracts the spinal cord and attached muscles. Alternately stretches and contracts the Channel of Function in front and the Governing Channel in back, thereby facilitating flow of energy within the Microscopic Orbit. Promotes circulation to the brain by bobbing head up and down. Tones and strengthens muscles and tendons in arms and legs.

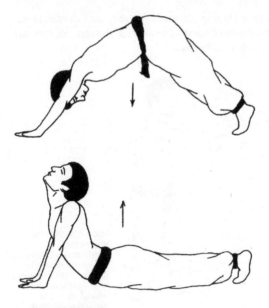

Figure 4.20 **Back Bows**
(top) Starting posture, up
(bottom) Down

Arms and Hands

Pushing Mountains (Figure 4.21)

Technique: Adopt a firm Horse stance and bring both hands up to waist level, palms up, elbows tucked in. As you slowly twist hips and torso to the left, push your right hand forward, turning the palm around to face straight ahead as you turn. Continue to push the right hand forward at a rising angle from the hips until the arm is fully extended in front of you at throat level, with the hollow of the elbow upward and fingers slightly spread, as in Figure 4.21 (left). Then draw the extended arm back down to starting position at the hip, turning the palm up and twisting the hips and torso to the right, while at the same time pushing the left hand up and forward in a similar manner to the first extension. The two hands should cross paths about a foot in front of the abdomen at solar plexus level. Keep shoulders relaxed and low, elbows in with hollows up, throughout the exercise. This feels very awkward at first but with practice it will grow smoother and more rhythmic. Eventually you will feel a distinct stretching sensation in the energy channels running from shoulders out to tips of the index and middle fingers whenever hands reach full forward extension, like stretching a rubber band.

Figure 4.21 **Pushing Mountains**
Note that both figures are side views; actual direction of thrust should be straight ahead with left and right arms, hands crossing each other at level of navel

Benefits: This is a very old Taoist and martial arts exercise, highly recommended by the ancient masters for building up and balancing *chee*, especially through the arm channels. Prolonged practice will enhance rapid flow of *chee* into the hands whenever they are extended for battle or work. It's a good exercise for those with poor circulation in the hands and excellent practice for synchronizing movements of limbs and joints. The twisting of torso massages abdominal organs and limbers the spinal column.

Pressing the Hands 'Valley of Harmony' Points (Figure 4.22)

Technique: You may do this standing, sitting or lying. One of the strongest energy points on the entire body is located at the base of the 'V' formed on the back of the hands by the bones of the thumb and index finger, about 1½ inches up from the webbing that connects them. You can find it by probing your thumb deeply into that soft depression until it strikes a point that is sharply sensitive to pressure. This is called the 'Valley of Harmony'. Press this point hard a dozen times or so on both hands.
Benefits: Pressing the Valley of Harmony sends energy coursing up the

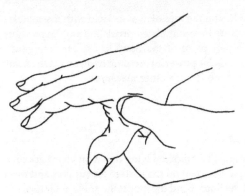

Figure 4.22
'Valley of Harmony' point
on hands

arm channels into the head, stimulating the brain. This maneuver relieves many types of headache and toothache on the side that's pressed. It also enhances flow of *chee* to the hands, which is important for martial artists, painters, physicians and craftsmen. Since it lies along the channel that controls the large intestine, it helps regulate this important excretory organ.

Pressing the Wrists 'Inner Gate' Points (Figure 4.23)

Technique: Standing, sitting or lying. The 'Inner Gate' is located 2 inches up from the wrinkle that marks the boundary between bottom of the hand and the inner surface of the wrist, and directly between the two central tendons of the wrist. Probe the index or middle fingertip in there until you find the point, which will be sharply sensitive to pressure, and apply deep acupressure there a dozen times or so.

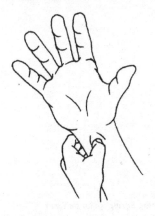

Figure 4.23
'Inner Gate' point on wrists

Benefits: The Inner Gate lies on the meridian associated with the pericardium ('heart sack'). Pressure here stimulates circulation and helps regulate heartbeat. It is the best point of the body to use for emergency treatment of heart attacks. Quick powerful pressure here can get the heart pumping again before it's too late for other measures.

Legs and Feet

Foot and Ankle Flex

Technique: This exercise must be practiced lying down on your back on a firm flat surface. Place palms down on the surface for support and raise one leg a few inches off the floor. Bend the foot at the ankle as far forward as it will go, then retract and bend it back as far as it will go. Curl the toes forward on the extension and bend them back on the retraction. Repeat 20–30 times, fairly briskly, then repeat with the other foot. Next, swivel each foot around in circles from the ankle joint, one at a time, 20–30 times each.

Benefits: Stretches and limbers the many minute muscles and tendons in the feet and ankles, stimulates nerves and blood circulation in the feet, which makes it good therapy for those who suffer from chronic cold feet, especially in winter. Stimulates energy channels running from legs into feet and back up to vital organs. This is a good way to help wake up the body in the morning before getting out of bed.

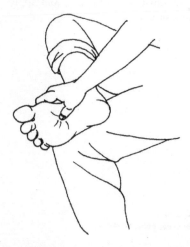

Figure 4.24
'Gushing Spring' point on feet

Pressing the 'Gushing Spring' Point on the Feet (Figure 4.24)

Technique: Sit on a chair or on the floor and cross one leg up over the other knee so that the sole is exposed and within reach. In the center of the sole is the point called 'Gushing Spring'. Press deeply into it with the ball of the thumb and rub hard a few times, release, and repeat a dozen times or so. Then do the other foot.

Benefits: This point is related to the kidneys and suprarenal glands. Pressure here calms the entire body and helps balance the energy network. Highly recommended at night before bed for those who suffer insomnia.

Figure 4.25
'Supreme Thrust' point on feet

Pressing the 'Supreme Thrust' Point on Feet (Figure 4.25)

Technique: Sit on chair or floor and locate the point on top of the foot known as 'Supreme Thrust', which is the most powerful point on the liver meridian and is equivalent in effect and location to the Valley of Harmony points on the hands. It lies between the tendons of the big and second toes, about 2 inches up from the webbing that connects those toes. Press thumb or fingertip deeply into this groove until you find the point, then apply acupressure to it a dozen times or so. Then do the other foot.

Benefits: This point will provide a 'thrust' of energy when feeling fatigued. Vigorous daily pressure here is good therapy for those suffering from hepatitis or other liver ailments. Cures certain types of headache and is a good palliative for hangovers.

The Pylon

Introduced previously as a stretching exercise, this is also regarded as a long-life exercise. Breathing in this posture energizes the leg channels, tones up the urogenital diaphragm, and helps 'sink'; energy down to its headquarters in the lower abdomen.

Total Relaxation

For truly 'uptight' people who find it virtually impossible to relax their bodies and minds by means of deep breathing and rhythmic calisthenics alone, there are two postures whose sole purpose is to induce total relaxation of body and mind by permitting all muscles to unwind like springs released. These postures may be practiced any time of day or night for quick relief of stress-related muscular tension and all its attendant symptoms. They provide a convenient method for high-strung people to unwind sufficiently to practice deep breathing and soft calisthenics.

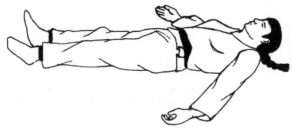

Figure 4.26
The 'Corpse'

The Corpse (Figure 4.26)

This aptly labeled posture is without a doubt the most effective method ever devised for highly tense people to teach themselves how to relax. Those who master this method will gain ready access to a state of relaxation even deeper than sleep – a state of relaxation many people never experience until death.

Select a room where no one will disturb you for at least half an hour. It should be quiet, well-ventilated , sufficiently warm and quite dark. In the office, simply draw the curtains, close the door and tell your secretary or colleagues that you wish not to be bothered for a while. At home, make sure you are insulated from interruption by children, pets and ringing telephones. In a hotel, tell the operator to hold all calls till further notice.

Remove shoes, neckties, watches, belts, jewellery and anything else that binds the body. Lie down flat on your back on the floor or carpet (mattresses and couches are too soft). Legs should be slightly parted, arms lying relaxed down by your sides. If necessary, drape a light blanket over yourself to prevent chills. Carefully extend the neck so that the head rests comfortably without contracting the neck muscles. If necessary, place a small pillow or a rolled towel under the nape to keep the neck from contracting. Breathe deeply and slowly from the abdomen, but with as little conscious effort as possible. This is not a breathing exercise, so do not retain, count or time your breaths. However, do try to make the exhalation stage about twice as long as inhalation, and breathe only through the nostrils. Close your eyes and focus your mind on the rising and falling of your abdomen.

When your posture is comfortable and your breathing slow and natural, you are ready to start unwinding all those spring-like muscles in the body. Start by focusing mental attention on the muscles and joints of the feet, then mentally soften and relax them. This is more a matter of 'letting go' than trying to 'do' something. Gradually move attention up to the ankles and calves, then the thighs, hips and abdomen, mentally 'watching' these various muscles soften and relax. Continue up to the chest, throat and finally the face. You will be amazed how many muscles there are in the face and how tight they are. Let the lower jaw drop slightly open, but without parting the lips. Feel the mini-muscles around the eyes and cheeks grow soft and 'melt' as you relax them. Next, start down at the fingers and hands, move up the arms to the shoulders, and back again to the face and throat, which merit a second round of attention owing to the chronic tension there.

The first time you try, this may not bring the desired results. Repeat the process again as often as necessary each session to get your body fully relaxed. Relaxing the muscles permits their blood vessels to dilate, allowing abundant supplies of fresh blood to enter, which warms them and makes them heavier. As you progressively relax the muscles, therefore, your entire body will feel warmer and heavier. As you approach this stage of relaxation, it is of utmost importance to remain *absolutely still*, for the slightest physical movement tenses at least several muscles and this tension quickly spreads throughout the body in an involuntary chain reaction. Once you've gained a 'feel' for this exercise, 20–30 minutes usually suffices to achieve the desired state of total relaxation.

Whatever happens, do not leap up suddenly from the Corpse posture to answer the telephone or a knock at the door. Such abrupt tensing of a totally relaxed body not only completely negates the therapeutic benefits of the exercise, it can also be harmful to the heart. When you are ready to 'come back to life', start by rhythmically wriggling fingers and toes, then swiveling ankles and wrists, then flexing the major muscles of the arms and legs. Stretch the face and throat, contract into a grimace, then stretch again. Sit up and take a few deep breaths, then slowly stand up on your feet. You should now feel as refreshed as after a 2-hour nap, as soft and supple as a cat, as calm as a tortoise.

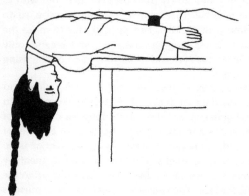

Figure 4.27
The Head Hang

The Head Hang (Figure 4.27)

This is easier and takes less time than the Corpse, though it is not as complete an exercise. The Head Hang focuses specifically on those muscles responsible for the most frequent forms of nervous and muscular tension – the region of the upper spine, neck and shoulders. These are the muscles most sensitive to stress-induced tension. When tense, they block circulation of blood and energy into the head and pinch the vital nerves that communicate between brain and body.

To perform the Head Hang loosen collar and belt and lie flat on your belly on a bed or across a desk or table, so that your head may hang freely over the edge. Keep your arms extended flat against your sides and your body flush to the bed or table. Let your head hang down completely relaxed. As neck and shoulder muscles gradually unwind by grace of gravity, your head will hang further down and feel heavier. Breathe slowly and naturally through the nose without straining. Hold the posture for 5–10 minutes.

Lying in this posture stretches the entire back of the neck, where chronic tension in dozens of tiny tendons and muscles translates into all sorts of nervous disorders, mental malaise and fatigue. The Head Hang takes pressure off the cervical vertebrae, allowing them to stretch out and realign themselves, thereby restoring optimum communication through the spinal nerves. This stretching also opens up the energy channels there, drawing *chee* into the brain. The partial constriction of the carotid arteries in the throat in front prevents an excess flood of blood from rushing to the brain. People with shoulders perpetually hunched and necks constantly cramped as a result of chronic stress and nervous tension will benefit tremendously by practicing the Head Hang once or twice a day.

A Sample Regimen

After studying and experimenting with the various breaths and exercises introduced in this and the previous chapter, each reader should devise a regular daily regimen specifically tailored to his or her own individual requirements and lifestyle. No two people are exactly alike in physique or temperament, and only you yourself can determine which combination of exercises provides the best benefits to your system. This requires a period of trial-and-error practice with variously blended programs. As a general guideline, a sample regimen for the beginner is given below. However, never stick permanently to one rigid regimen, day after day, year in, year out. You should adjust your programs from time to time according to specific health requirements, seasons and other relevant factors, and you should experiment with new exercises as you progress.

When first exposed to this daily regimen of Tao exercise, most Western adepts toss their hands up in despair and say, 'But I haven't got time for all that!' In fact, most people have plenty of time for all this and more, if they re-arrange their priorities a bit. For example, one could spend one's 20-minute coffee break each morning up on the roof doing breathing exercises or meditating. One could sacrifice an hour or two of television each day, or skip going to the pub once in a while, or simply get up a bit earlier in the morning.

The best way to handle the problem of time is for each adept to devise two complete programs for himself: one 'full' workout and one 'abbreviated' workout. The full workout, including exercise and breathing but not meditation, should be at least one full hour, consisting of those exercises which the practitioner feels are most suitable for his or her situation. Then, throughout the rest of the day, do an afternoon and/or evening set, and/or some meditation, as time permits. But be sure to do at least one workout, preferably in the morning before eating.

Meanwhile, devise an 'abbreviated' program as well for those days when you are really pressed for time, or simply too tired to do more. Take your full workout and selectively delete about half of the exercises. Delete those that are somewhat redundant, and keep the ones you feel are most beneficial to your current condition. Do that in the morning for about half an hour, and try to squeeze in 10–15 minutes more during the day. The great advantage of Taoist exercise is its flexibility: you don't need to 'play a full set,' complete a 'match,' or wait for a partner. Instead, you can spend 15 minutes doing 5–6 exercises, go back to work, spend another 20 on breathing later, go home, then meditate a while at night, or do another brief workout before bed. Doing it right and doing it daily is of prime importance: how many exercises to do and how much time to spend on each workout is flexible and of secondary importance.

Morning Set

For those who find it hard to 'rise and shine' in the morning, certain exercises may be performed in bed. This is especially important for the elderly and weak. Remember, during sleep 30–50 per cent of the blood supply returns to the liver and pancreas, which is why the risk of fatal strokes is so high early in the morning, especially when one bounds out of bed without warming up.

Start by doing the Foot and Ankle Flex: this awakens major nerves and meridians from heels to hips to head. Stretch the arms out and flex fingers and wrists. Perform the Abdominal Rub, or roll a smooth heavy weight around the path of your colon. Then perform half a dozen deep abdominal breaths. These simple steps should suffice to awaken even the sleepiest zombie.

Immediately upon arising, commence with the warm-up set, followed by about 15–20 minutes of simple yoga stretches. Then, weather permitting, move outdoors for breathing and long-life exercises. If it's cold or raining outside, stand on a protected veranda or in front of an open window. Adopt the Horse stance, or prepare a stool or chair for sitting and perform a series of breathing exercises, such as this:

Bellows (1–2 minutes)
Chee Compression Breath (a dozen) with some sets of 3–5
    Bellows breaths in between
Alternate Nostril Breathing (a dozen or two, both sides)

Grand Celestial Tour (a complete or abbreviated tour, as you
    like)
Great Tai-Chi Circle Breath (about two dozen)

After breathing, do a round of long-life exercises, varying the regimen
from day to day, depending on mood, preference and physical needs.
This should take about 30 minutes. You may include a set of push-ups or
pull-ups to limber the muscles and stimulate the cardiovascular system.

The morning set takes about an hour (an hour and a half if a round of
meditation is included) and is followed by breakfast. Those who find it
difficult to move in the morning may be further motivated by the
following fact: when exercise is performed in the morning *before* breakfast
(i.e. after an all-night 'fast'), the body automatically burns off stored fat to
derive the necessary calories to perform the exercises. After food has
entered the stomach, the body automatically resorts to calories derived
from digestion and therefore does not burn much fat. You must abstain
from food for at least 12 hours before blood-sugar levels drop low enough
for the body to switch over to fat for fuel. So, if you wish to use these or
any other exercises to burn off unwanted fat, you will get by far the best
results in the morning before breakfast.

Afternoon Set

Afternoon belongs to the waning Yin period of the day (noon till midnight), which is fine for physical exercise but not the best time for
breathing and energy control. You may either participate in one of your
favorite sports such as tennis, racketball or swimming – or try something
like the following:

Warm-up set
Loosening and stretching (10 mins)
Long life exercises (10–15 mins)
Deep breathing (10 mins)

Deep breathing does not generate much energy in the afternoon, but it
still provides excellent therapeutic benefits to the circulatory system and
to the abdominal organs. It's always a good idea to prepare for any
vigorous athletic activity with the warm-up set followed with a few
minutes of deep breathing to rebalance energy and calm the heart.

But if it comes down to a choice between 'hard' vigorous sports and
'soft' rhythmic exercise, the latter is always the best choice, for it benefits
the internal organs, regulates the heart, deepens respiration, and promotes circulation of blood and energy. Long-term practice of field

sports without the benefits of loosening, stretching, and deep breathing gradually stiffens the joints and strains the heart.

Evening Set

This set is performed at night just before retiring to bed. It's best to do it outside under an open sky, but if weather or other conditions do not permit, do it on a veranda or before an open window. Use either the Horse stance and/or one of the sitting postures.

Spine and Torso Twist
'Bump and Grind'
Bellows breathing (1–2 mins)
Alternate Nostril Breathing (a dozen)
Great Tai-Chi Circle Breath (two dozen)

If you're having trouble getting to sleep, finish up in bed by giving the 'Gushing Spring' point on the soles of the feet a vigorous acupressure massage.

If you're rushed or running late, or simply feel too tired or lazy for a complete workout, spend 5–10 minutes doing just two exercises – the Spine and Torso Twist, followed by the Great Tai-Chi Circle Breath. This combination gives maximum benefits with minimum time and effort and comprises a good mini-workout any time of day or night.

CHAPTER 5:

—————————— ☯ ——————————

Taoist Healing Arts

Before an omen arises,
It's easy to take preventive measures.
What is still soft is easily melted;
What is still small is easily scattered.
Deal with things in their formative state;
Put things in order before they grow confused.

[*Tao Teh Ching*]

Until the twentieth century, wealthy households in China would retain a well-known physician to be on constant call for the entire family, much as major corporations today retain renowned attorneys on a permanent basis. The physician would visit the household regularly to check everyone's health, dispense preventive advice and formulas, check on diets and personal habits, and generally keep himself abreast of each individual's unique conditions. The moment anyone in the family fell seriously ill, the regular monthly payments to the family physician were *stopped*, until he restored the patient's health – at his own expense! Thus disease was regarded largely as a case of professional negligence by the family doctor. This system was not only a great preventive against disease, it was also a highly effective preventive against malpractice.

In the *Yellow Emperor's Classic of Internal Medicine*, the chief medical advisor Chi Po states the point succinctly:

To administer medicine to a disease that has already started is like tying to suppress a revolt that has already begun. Such an approach is comparable to the behavior of a person who starts digging a well only after he is thirsty, or who begins to forge his weapons after he is already engaged in battle. Would these actions not be too late?

In the Western world, people generally take health for granted until they lose it, by which time it is usually too late to fully restore it. What they fail to realize is that every cut of the scalpel, every drop of synthetic drug and every ray of radiation to which they submit their bodies also cuts and burns their vital-energy channels and undermines their spiritual strength as surely as it cuts and scars their flesh. In the long run, the invisible scars to the energy circuits are far more debilitating than any superficial physical symptoms.

The casual submission by patients in the Western world to surgery, chemotherapy, radiation, and powerful chemical drugs astounds Chinese physicians, who know perfectly well how devastating such therapies are to the body's delicate energy balance. Therefore, in the Orient, the 'New Medicine' incorporates Western diagnostic technology such as urine and blood tests and electronic monitoring devices to pinpoint the problem, then applies traditional Oriental therapies to cure the condition. Though Western medicine used to understand and apply natural cures, technology has dazzled modern Western physicians with supposed short-cuts to health, but this is an illusion, as is clearly evident from the health situation in America today. Therefore, as a general rule for health and longevity in medical care today, it's best to go to the modern Western clinic for a quick reading of what's wrong, then walk across the street to get it treated by a traditional therapist.

The history of Taoist healing arts in China is as old as the hills where the ancient sages started dabbling with herbs and alchemy. The first systematic written references to human disease and health care in China appear on oracle bone inscriptions dating back to 1500 BC. During the Han era, there appeared three major medical texts which summarized all the foregoing medical knowledge handed down in ancient China. These texts separated fact from superstition and codified medical principles so well that they are still used for reference by Chinese physicians today. Those works are *The Yellow Emperor's Classic of Internal Medicine*, *Shen Nung's Pharmocopeia*, and *Discussion of Fevers*. The last work, written around 200 BC by Chang Chung-ching, classifies diseases into six major categories – three Yin and three Yang – and lists 113 medical prescriptions using 100 different herbs. Many of those prescriptions are still in use today.

Precious Recipes, written by the great Tang physician Sun Ssu-mo, has already been quoted in great detail. This valuable text contains important information on every aspect of traditional Taoist health care, including herbs, acupuncture, nutrition, breathing, exercise, massage and sexual discipline. It correctly diagnoses beriberi, scurvy, goiter and other common vitamin and mineral deficiency diseases, and provides highly effective prescriptions against them. More than any other Taoist medical text on record, it forms a convenient handbook to health and longevity.

The next major historical milestone in Chinese medicine occurred during the Ming Dynasty with the publication of Lee Shih-chen's mammoth pharmocopeia, *Classification of Herbs*, which contains detailed information on the nature, effects and uses of almost 2,000 herbal, mineral and animal ingredients. This still remains the bible of professional Chinese herbalists.

By the time Lee's pharmocopeia was printed in the late sixteenth century, Chinese medicine was already entering its fourth millennium as a systematic science of health care. Western medicine, by contrast, was just beginning to shed the cloaks of superstition and witchcraft from the 'Dark Ages' and had just begun to make some headway against such common disorders as beriberi and goiter. During this time, there was plenty of borrowing from China. Quinine, the cure used for malaria, was literally stolen from southern China by a Jesuit missionary, who brought it back to Europe as his own 'discovery'. The method of extracting vaccines from the serum of cow's blood was also developed in China and brought to Europe by missionaries. In light of this historical record of borrowing, it truly surprises Eastern physicians today to witness the arrogance and incredulous shake of the head with which most Western physicians now greet suggestions from traditional Chinese medicine. This attitude is somewhat similar to the resentment immature adolescents feel towards the wisdom of their elders.

Throughout the Orient and in certain parts of the Western world today, Eastern and Western methods are beginning to meet and meld in a comprehensive new system of health care aptly dubbed the 'New Medicine', which will be further discussed at the end of this chapter. Suffice to say here that, while the 'New Medicine' is fast taking root in Asia, the Soviet Union and some parts of Europe, it remains not only unknown but also illegal in the United States. Small wonder then that today America remains one of the few places on earth where human health and longevity continue to deteriorate at alarming rates.

The Tao of Health and Disease

The basic principles involved in traditional Taoist healing arts are precisely the same as those in the martial and meditative arts. Medical principles revolve around the constant flux and interplay of Yin and Yang, depend upon the dynamics of the Five Elemental Activities, and involve the internal alchemy of essence, energy and spirit. Regardless of their symptoms, all diseases are rooted in a basic imbalance of Yin and Yang and other energies within the human system, and all therapies must therefore aim at re-establishing the natural primordial harmony of essence, energy and spirit that the body requires to protect and cure itself. The chart in Table 5.1 illustrates some of the basic Yin/Yang connections used in traditional Chinese diagnosis and treatment of disease. Note that the various symptoms all boil down to an excess of one or the other, and that the treatments work by balancing that excess with an equal dose of its own essential opposite.

Table 5.1 *Chart of Yin/Yang associations used in Chinese diagnosis and therapy*

Symptom	Cause	Type of medication	Desired effects
hot	Yang	Yin	cooling
cold	Yin	Yang	warming
full	Yang	Yin	sedative
empty	Yin	Yang	tonic
external	Yang	Yin	suppress
internal	Yin	Yang	expel

In order to be able to track down the root cause of disease and not be fooled by superficial symptoms, the physician must be thoroughly familiar with every organ and other part of the body and must know precisely how they function and influence one another. For example, according to the Taoist system, the symptoms of liver dysfunction include blurry vision, chronic depression and stomach disorders. A patient suffering from any one of these seemingly unrelated symptoms in the West would have to visit an ophthalmologist for blurry vision and get fitted for a pair of glasses he does not need, visit a stomach specialist for his stomach problem and take drugs that only suppress the symptoms without curing the cause, and visit a psychiatrist for his chronic depression and waste a lot of money on empty and therapeutically useless talk. In China, the same physician is qualified to treat all three conditions, which he recognizes as stemming from the same root cause. By treating the liver to restore its normal function, he eliminates all three symptoms.

Practitioners of traditional Chinese medicine must therefore master far more knowledge about human health and disease, body and mind, than those who practice a specialized branch of Western medicine. They must be thoroughly familiar with herbology, nutrition, anatomy, physiology, psychology, human emotions, sexology, meteorology and many other related fields. It requires an average 10–15 years of arduous study to properly prepare for and pass the qualifying exams in traditional Chinese medicine in the Orient today, compared with 4–5 years for Western medicine. Small wonder that even in the East today many prospective physicians opt for the easier, more lucrative Western approach.

Dr Hsu Hong-yen, a traditional Chinese physician trained in Taiwan and Tokyo, explains the fundamentally different approaches in Chinese and Western medicine as follows:

> Chinese medical theory contends that diseases are caused by environmental elements (wind, cold, moisture, heat, aridity, and fire) and by internal factors (pleasure, anger, anxiety, pensiveness, sorrow, fear, and terror). Treatment focuses not only on eliminating harmful toxins but also on strengthening vitality and the body's resistance to disease. Western treatment, on the other hand, mostly adopts a palliative localized treatment, treating the head for headaches and the feet for aching feet. Chinese medicine seeks a whole body treatment by adjusting the imbalance in the body that is causing the headache or the aching feet. Radical treatment employs not only medicines but also diet and exercise in therapy.

'Killing' germs with powerful synthetic drugs does little good in the long run because there are always more germs in the environment to re-infect the patient as soon as medication is withdrawn. The only measure that effects a permanent cure is to correct the internal conditions of imbalance and toxicity that permit the disease to develop in the first place. When that is accomplished, all symptoms will disappear entirely.

Originally, Western medicine also recognized root causes of disease. Hippocrates believed that disease was caused by an imbalance in the 'humors' of the human body, not by external factors. Thomas Sydenham, the seventeenth-century physician known as the 'English Hippocrates', wrote, 'Disease is nothing else but an attempt of the body to rid itself of morbific matter'. Rudolf Virchow, the eighteenth-century pioneer in cellular pathology, wrote as follows about disease:

> If I could live my life over again, I would devote it to proving that germs seek their natural habitat – diseased tissue – rather than being the cause of diseased tissue. For example, mosquitoes seek stagnant water, but do not *cause* the pool to become stagnant.

The analogy of stagnant water to diseased tissue is remarkably close to the Taosit analogy cited at the head of Chapter 4.

In *Food is Your Best Medicine*, Dr Henry G. Bieler, who may be regarded as the 'modern Hippocrates', comes to three basic conclusions about disease, based on over 50 years of clinical experience:

> The first is that the primary cause of disease is not germs. Rather, I believe that disease is caused by a toxemia which results in

cellular impairment and breakdown, thus paving the way for the multiplication and onslaught of germs.

My second conclusion is that in almost all cases the use of drugs in treating patients is harmful. Drugs often cause serious side effects, and sometimes even create new diseases . . .

My third conclusion is that disease can be cured through the proper use of correct foods.

Here we find echoes of the great Tang physician Sun Ssu-mo and many other Taoist statements on disease.

The real culprit in modern Western medical misunderstanding of disease was Louis Pasteur and his 'germ theory'. Though his 'discovery' of germs was in many ways useful, his thesis that germs were the cause of disease was wrong. And the reason that Western physicians and patients alike were so ready and willing to accept his theory is that it placed the blame for disease squarely on outside factors, thus absolving the patient of all responsibility for his condition. The true cause of disease is cellular pathology caused by internal conditions of toxemia, due mostly to incorrect dietary habits. That means the patient is responsible for his own condition and must correct it mainly through self-discipline – a fact modern man and woman are loathe to accept, much less put into practice.

In traditional Chinese health care, most treatment occurs at home, not in clinics or hospitals. A basic knowledge of nutritional and herbal therapy is common in most Chinese households, as is the concept of therapeutic breathing, massage and exercise. Most herbal remedies are prescribed by the doctor, filled by the herbalist, and then prepared by the patient at home. In a recent survey of illness episodes suffered during a one-month period by 115 typical Chinese families in Taiwan, 93% of the patients were first treated at home and 73% received their *only* treatment at home. Compare these figures with Western society, where people rush off to see a doctor for even the slightest complaint and where doctors almost always conclude the visit by saying, 'Come back to see me next week'.

In the East, anyone can walk into a herbal pharmacy and purchase anything they require for either prevention or cure. These drugs are safe and natural, and many of the most common and effective prescriptions are available in print to the general public. Only when a patient fails to figure out his own problem does he need to visit a doctor, who then prescribes therapy and advice that helps the patient cure himself. After all, no one is more familiar with your body than yourself. One of the biggest drawbacks of the Western approach is that patients come to rely entirely on doctors for every sort of ailment great and small, and blindly accept their advice about everything. When the doctor's advice fails, they blame him as a convenient scapegoat, rather than facing the fact that the main cause of their condition is a failure to protect themselves with preventive measures. Such an attitude can never lead to health and longevity.

A glaring example of the failure of the Western approach to health and disease is the so-called 'war on cancer' in America, where this deadly disease flourishes more than anywhere else on earth. Over the past 35 years, the National Cancer Institute has spent more than $20 billion researching a cure for cancer, while suppressing all homoeopathic and preventive approaches to the disease. Since 1962, the number of cancer deaths per 100,000 people in America has risen from 170 to 185, and in 1986 close to 1 million new cases of cancer were reported. Yet whenever someone suggests that a raw-food diet or a natural product like 'laetrile' (Vitamin B17), or deep breathing, or some other tried-and-true measure might cure and help prevent the occurrence of cancer, the NCI is the first to launch legal proceedings to suppress it.

Those who wish to break the vicious cycle of disease and degeneration caused by exclusive reliance on chemical and surgical 'cures' and conquer their dependence on the 'men in white coats' might wish to take a closer look at the traditional Taoist way, which provides a preventive path to health and longevity that can be easily followed by anyone with sufficient respects for Mother Nature to live by her immutable laws.

The Five-fold Path to Natural Health Care

Taoist health care employs five primary therapeutic methods to prevent and combat disease, maintain energy balance, regulate the vital organs and harmonize the Three Treasures of life. Those therapies are herbs and diet, breathing and exercise, acupuncture, massage, and heliotherapy (sunlight therapy).

Herbal Therapy

Herbal therapy, which in Taoist tradition always includes diet and nutrition, is the oldest and most widely used method in the Chinese system of health care. It evolved slowly over thousands of years by patient empirical observation of nature and trial-and-error experimentation, and its vast pharmocopeia provides the most abundant and the most effective herbal weapons against disease ever devised by man.

All Chinese herbs are categorized according to their basic biochemical natures and therapeutic effects, which determine what Chinese herbalists call their *gui-jing*, or 'natural affinities'. *Gui-jing* literally means 'return to meridians', and indicates which organ/meridian systems a particular drug has a natural affinity for after it has been ingested and metabolized. For example, drugs used for liver ailments have a natural affinity for the meridian associated with the liver. When the drug is combusted in the human system, its energy enters the liver meridian, and in this manner its therapeutic effects are carried into the liver, Each herb is also labeled according to its associations with the Five Elemental Activities. In herbs, these forces are represented by the Five Flavors: sweet, bitter, sour, pungent, salty. The relationships among the flavors, forces, affinities and effects of medicinal herbs are illustrated in Table 5.2.

There are numerous methods of administering herbal remedies. The most popular is to boil the mixed ingredients in a covered ceramic or earthenware crock until half the liquid has evaporated, then strain the broth and take it in two separate doses on an empty stomach. Herbalists measure and mix the dry ingredients in individual packets sufficient for one day's dosage, and patients simply take them home and boil them up like tea.

Steeping the herbs in strong alcoholic spirits for 3–6 months in order to extract their potent active ingredients is the favored way of preparing and taking tonic prescriptions. This concoction, aptly named 'Spring Wine' for its rejuvenating effects, is discussed in further detail in the section on Chinese aphrodisiacs in Chapter 8. Other methods of preparing herbal prescriptions include grinding them into fine powders then binding them into little pellets with honey, fermenting them with a flour paste, and chewing on the dry herb itself to extract the bioactive ingredients by salivary action.

The introduction of modern Western technology in the East has even further extended the range of Chinese herbal remedies by making it possible to refine highly purified, potent extracts from the raw herbs for use in potent patent medicines. These remedies are available over the counter throughout Asia and in some of the bigger 'Chinatowns' of the West. A good example of these patent remedies are 'Po-Chai Pills', the famous Chinese remedy for gastro-intestinal ailments, hangovers and related chronic ills of the grand gourmand.

Of all the various and sundry herbs in the Chinese pharmocopeia, none is better known or more widely used than ginseng. The 'man-root', so named for its striking resemblance to the human body, has been used as a preventive tonic against disease and degeneration of the body for over 5,000 years in China. To date, however, the only serious scientific studies of this plant in the West have been conducted in the Soviet Union and France.

Soviet scientists have recently isolated three active ingredients in

Table 5.2 *Chart of Five Flavors and Five Elemental Activities as used in Chinese herbal therapy*

Flavor*	Element	Related organ	Effects	Example
pungent	Metal	lungs; large int.	induce sweat; balance chi; scatter blockage	fresh ginger
sweet	Earth	stomach; spleen	digestive tonic; distribute nutrition	Chinese licorice
sour	Wood	liver; gallbladder	binding; astringent; anti-pyretic	unripened plums
bitter	Fire	heart; small int.	drying; anti-dysenteric	bark of Amur cork tree
salty	Water	kidneys; bladder	softening; laxative; diuretic	algae and seaweed

* pungent like ginger; sweet like sugar; sour like vinegar; bitter like lime; salty like salt

ginseng–panaxin, panaquilan and schingenin. In combination, these potent elements enhance circulation, stimulate the nervous system and increase hormonal secretions throughout the endocrine system. That's the 'essence' of ginseng. The same Soviet scientists also discovered that ginseng root emits minute amounts of a unique band of ultraviolet radiation and that this radiant energy specifically stimulates growth of healthy human tissues. This radiant energy is none other than *chee*, the energy of life, and it is this bioactive energy that gives ginseng its 'mysterious' healing powers. It is the same sort of friendly bioactive radiation found emanating from live active enzymes when they go to work in the human system.

All 'power plants' such as ginseng contain, in addition to their biochemical 'essence', powerful bioelectrical energies with specific affinity for living tissues. This energy stimulates the body's own energy system by entering the meridians. From there it travels to related organs and glands to confer therapeutic benefits. It is this sympathy between the living energies of certain plants and the energy channels of certain human organs that gives each drug its particular 'natural affinity' in the human system.

The Soviets have applied ginseng-energy to improving the performance of their athletes. After nine weeks of daily dosage of a ginseng extract, the performance of young Soviet athletes in training improved significantly. Dr Jelleff Carr, one of the few American scientists to study ginseng, believes it has great potential in combating senility. Says he, 'There are chemical ingredients in the plant that are responsible for the physiological effects enhancing intellectual acuteness and physical prowess.' He also correctly points out that it takes at least a full month of daily dosage to begin realizing its therapeutic effects.

The most convenient way to use ginseng is to get a herbalist to cut up a root into thin slices and chew on a piece several times a day. The action of salivary secretions releases the active components, much of which is directly absorbed through the mucus membranes of the mouth. You may also boil a few slices of the root for 15–20 minutes, then drink the broth and eat the pulp. In addition, you may buy ginseng powders, pills, liquid extracts, and even ginseng chewing gum from Korea. Cooling white ginseng is generally recommended for the summer, the warming red variety for winter. Average prices range from $5 to $25 per ounce, though in Hong Kong there are some rare varieties on sale at a hefty $25,000 per ounce!

An area of traditional Chinese herbal medicine of current interest to the Western world is herbal birth control. Medical scientists in Hong Kong are currently working on an extract from a common weed which promises to provide a safe, effective and very inexpensive herbal birth control potion for women. Chinese physicians on the mainland have also observed in recent years that people who consume a lot of cottonseed oil and workers who produce and process cottonseed oil show a much lower birth rate than the general populace. They discovered that gossypol is the active element responsible for the prophylactic effects on fertility, and that its effects work on the male of the species. Gossypol is now being tested in Hong Kong and China as a natural birth control agent for men.

For thousands of years the young women of Polynesia have enjoyed complete and uninhibited sexual freedom prior to marriage, with no worries about unwanted pregnancy. Their secret has been to eat a few handfuls of papaya seeds every day. The active ingredient responsible for their freedom from pregnancy is Vitamin B17, more popularly known as 'laetrile', the controversial drug banned in the USA owing to claims that it can prevent and help cure cancer. It works as birth control by directly interfering with the biochemical process by which a fertilized egg attaches itself to the wall of the uterus. In other words, even if conception takes place, the fertilized egg cannot attach itself to the uterus. The kernels inside apricot pits are another potent source of this component: two or three dozen kernels a day, chewed and salivated very well to extract the active ingredient, should provide sufficient protection against pregnancy.

Acupuncture

Acupuncture is another ancient branch of Chinese health care that has in recent years received a lot of scientific attention in the Soviet Union and Europe. It remains the only therapy in the world that deals directly with the human energy system. Conventional Western medicine treats the flesh with drugs and surgery and the mind with psychoanalysis, but it has nothing at all for the third treasure of life – energy. Yet, in the Chinese system, energy is the most important aspect of all, for it forms the vital bridge between essence and spirit. Since energy imbalance is regarded as the foremost cause of disease, direct manipulation of energy is naturally the foremost cure.

Acupuncture was first discovered on the battlefields of ancient China, when soldiers wounded by arrows reported that other longstanding chronic ailments had suddenly disappeared. Before long, Chinese physicians found that the body has a complex network of invisible energy channels through which *chee*, the vital energy of life, travels. They found 12 major and dozens of minor channels and discovered that each one was functionally related to specific organs and glands. These channels, though invisible to the eye, have been 'mapped' by Kirlian photography in the Soviet Union.

Along each meridian are spots called 'vital points', which when stimulated by acupuncture or acupressure cause vital-energy to flow, stop, accelerate, slow down, gather, scatter or otherwise behave in the manner prescribed by the physician, depending on how he manipulates the points. There are over 800 vital points on the human body, but only a few dozen are used in treatment of most conditions. By modulating the patient's natural bioelectric currents (*chee*) via the meridians and vital points, the physician effects the desired cure.

The electrical nature of human energy is the key to how acupuncture works, with the needles serving as either conductors, insulators, accelerators, inhibitors or antennae, depending on how and where they are inserted. By attaching electrodes to the inserted needles and running various currents through them from an outside electrical power source, the therapeutic benefits of acupuncture are even further enhanced. Dr Bjorn Nordenstrom of the Karolinska Institute in Stockholm, Sweden, has successfully used electronically enhanced acupuncture to shrink malignant tumors in cancer patients by inserting the needles directly into the tumors. The enhanced electrical field created around the tumor killed cancerous cells without affecting healthy tissues, while the pulsating electrical currents in the needles attracted white blood cells to the tumor to digest and eliminate the residues of cancerous cells. Of 20 breast and lung cancer patients tested, the tumors in 10 regressed significantly under electro-acupuncture therapy, and in 7 other patients the tumors disappeared entirely.

This evidence clearly indicates that one of the prime conditions that permits cancer to develop is severe disruption or complete blockage of normal bioelectrical activity in the tissues. Such disruptions literally 'starve' the cells in affected tissues of the vital bioelectric energy currents they require to maintain normal healthy functions. This in turn disrupts circulation of blood and inhibits cellular respiration. Consequently, the deprived cells literally 'ferment' in their own metabolic wastes, become pathological due to their own toxicity, and start to mutate, forming tumors. Acupuncture restores both the normal electric fields and the natural bioelectric currents that damaged tissues need to regenerate, and this in turn enables the body's natural defenses to arrive on the scene to dissolve and eliminate toxic cells and re-establish cellular integrity to the affected tissues.

Therapeutic Massage

Self-massage has been used since the earliest times by Taoist adepts to relieve fatigue, restore circulation, balance Yin and Yang energies, stimulate organs and glands, and tone the muscles and ligaments. One form of therapeutic massage is acupressure, which employs deep digital stimulation to vital points along the energy meridians to accomplish the same effects as acupuncture. The pressure-point maneuvers introduced in the section on long-life exercises in Chapter 4 are typical of therapeutic acupressure, which can be performed simply and safely by anyone in his or her own home.

The major form of massage is called *tui-na*, literally 'press and rub'. The name refers to the technique: the tip of the thumb is pressed deeply into a muscle, joint, nerve or meridian, then rubbed hard a few times and released. The maneuver is repeated rhythmically for 10–12 minutes, depending on the severity of the condition and the area of massage. *Tui-na* is applied primarily to the spine, major joints and central nerve networks rather than the meridians and vital points.

For example, Dr Huang Po-wen, a *tui-na* specialist in Taipei, spent a full year 'pressing and rubbing' the spinal cord and major branch nerves on a Canadian patient paralyzed from the neck down in a construction accident. After 6 months of daily *tui-na* therapy under the good doctor's thumbs, the patient could raise both arms above his head, after 9 months he suddenly recovered his capacity for ejaculation, and after 12 months he was able to stand on his feet for the first time since his accident, although he could not walk unassisted. There are no short-cuts to such treatments: it requires daily work, a huge expenditure of *chee* from the doctor, who actually drives his own energy into the patient's body through the thumbs, and long clinical experience. All the fancy electronic traction machines, computerized leg braces, and other gadgets used in

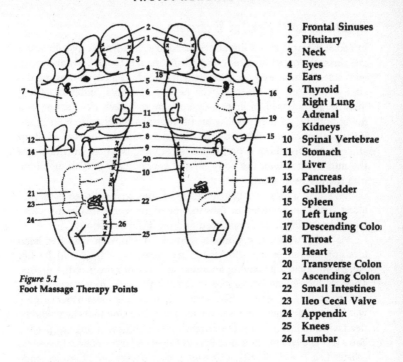

1 Frontal Sinuses
2 Pituitary
3 Neck
4 Eyes
5 Ears
6 Thyroid
7 Right Lung
8 Adrenal
9 Kidneys
10 Spinal Vertebrae
11 Stomach
12 Liver
13 Pancreas
14 Gallbladder
15 Spleen
16 Left Lung
17 Descending Colon
18 Throat
19 Heart
20 Transverse Colon
21 Ascending Colon
22 Small Intestines
23 Ileo Cecal Valve
24 Appendix
25 Knees
26 Lumbar

Figure 5.1
Foot Massage Therapy Points

physical therapy in the West cannot match the restorative healing powers of *chee* properly applied to the injured body.

Foot massage (also known as reflexology) is a specialized branch of Chinese therapy that has received some attention in the West in recent years. Six major energy meridians terminate in the feet: spleen, kidneys, liver, stomach, gallbladder and bladder – as do the major nerves of the autonomous nervous system. Massaging the feet therefore stimulates the organs and glands associated with those meridians and nerves. Cramped feet make for cramped organs, and these days almost everyone in the world except barefoot aborigines suffers to some degree from cramped feet. Indeed, ancient Taoist texts claim that a major cause of impotence in men is energy blockage in sexual organs and glands due to cramped feet and that vigorous massage of the toes and soles prior to intercourse helps solve this problem. Foot massage is easy to perform on yourself at home, and its benefits are manifold. Use either the thumbs or forefinger knuckles to press and rub deeply and rhythmically at the various vital foot points illustrated in Figure 5.1, which also indicates which organs and glands those spots influence.

Breathing and Related Exercises

In Taoist therapy, *chee* is literally referred to as 'medicine'. By cultivating *chee* through correct breathing and circulating it through body and mind with soft rhythmic exercises, the patient cures himself by generating the energy required by the body for healing. Patients under breathing therapy are advised to spend an hour or two each day 'sitting still doing nothing' as they practice breath control to balance their energies. If the patient is too weak to do the related calisthenics, or even to sit up straight, the breathing is performed in reclining position, in which case the mind rather than the body 'moves energy' (*yün-chee*) to distribute it to the diseased areas.

Let's take a look at a concrete case of cure accomplished by breath alone. The case occurred in Taiwan, one of the few places in the world where breathing is still prescribed and practiced as therapy.

Ms Yeh Pu-sheng, a Chinese woman from Taiwan who had been teaching school in the USA for many years, was diagnosed by her American doctors as having an advanced case of cancer of the uterus. They performed major surgery to remove the cancerous tissue, but it recurred with a vengeance. The doctors then told her that further surgery was impossible, that there was no hope of a cure, and that she would be dead within a few months. Distraught but still Chinese enough to give the Tao a try, she and her husband flew to Taipei and immediately looked up Master Lee Tse-ni. Because of her extremely severe condition, he made her sit and practice his prescribed breathing regimen for a full eight hours per day. After six long months, her cancer began to subside, and soon thereafter it disappeared completely, never to recur. She returned triumphantly to America in perfect health – to the absolute astonishment of her American doctors – and she is still teaching there today.

People often turn to Taoist healing arts as a last resort – out of sheer desperation to live. Prior to falling ill they never give Tao a thought. Owing to the life-and-death nature of their stuggle, such patients usually manage to master the methods taught very quickly, and they have no trouble mustering sufficient discipline to sit still and breathe deeply for up to eight hours per day. It is amazing what the body and mind are capable of when life is at stake. Such examples should, however, serve as lessons to ordinary healthy people who still claim they 'don't have time' for Tao. Practicing a little deep breathing every day is one of the best preventives against disease and premature death. Learning how to breathe correctly on your deathbed is a bit late in the game for health and longevity.

'Let There Be Light'

Taoist adepts realized the medical benefits of sunlight thousands of years ago. The *Tao Tsang* (*Treasury of Tao*), compiled over 2,000 years ago, contains numerous references to heliotherapy, which it refers to as 'the method of administering sunbeams'. It advises exposing both the naked body and the naked eyes directly to sunlight in order to assimilate vital solar energy. It states unequivocally that exposing the eyes to direct sunlight greatly 'benefits the brain' by stimulating secretions of 'vital essence' there.

There is indeed a direct scientific connection between sunlight entering the eyes and secretions of the pituitary and pineal glands in the mid-brain. For example, it has been observed for centuries in the West that during deep winter in the northern regions people suffer from ever-growing mental depression and physical lethargy as the days grow shorter. Having experimented with factors such as diet, temperature, sexual activity and exercise, Western medical scientists finally targeted sunlight as a possible causative factor. Patients exposed daily to panels of bright artificial light that included the *full spectrum* of natural sunlight (which includes all the colors of the rainbow *plus* the invisible ultraviolet and infrared bands) showed dramatic improvement in mood and vitality even in deepest, darkest winter.

Dr Michael Gitlin of the Neuropsychiatric Institute at UCLA has established that when the environment is dark the pineal gland secretes the hormone melatonin, which induces drowsiness, lethargy, apathy and depression, i.e. the 'winter blues'. In his report he states: 'The fascinating part of all this is that it's based on how much light hits the retina.' Seventy per cent of Dr Gitlin's patients responded favorably to daily exposure to full spectrum artificial light.

The key factor in heliotherapy is the invisible ultraviolet band, and the key receptor is the retina. A layer of cells in the retina called the epithelial cells become highly neuro-active when exposed to ultraviolet radiation, without in any way affecting vision. While the visible bands of light excite the retina's rods and cones to produce vision, the invisible ultraviolet band stimulates the adjacent epithelial cells, which transmit the stimulus as a powerful neural impulse through the optic nerve directly to the pituitary and pineal glands. Western medicine calls this newly discovered biosystem the 'oculo-endocrine system', but the mechanism has been known to Taoists for ages. This discovery has spawned a new branch of Western science called 'photobiology'.

Western science has photographer John Ott to thank for this discovery. He stumbled on the phenomenon while working on his now famous time-lapse films of growing plants and blooming blossoms. During his long research in time-lapse photography, he suffered such crippling arthritis in the hips that he could barely negotiate the three steps from garden to porch. Then one day he accidentally sat on and broke his sunglasses, which he habitually wore while working on his plants outdoors. Too busy to go buy a new pair, he did without them for a few weeks and continued his work. To his utter surprise and great scientific curiosity, he suddenly discovered that his arthritis had improved so rapidly that he was barely even aware of it any more. It did not take him long to realize why: sunglasses had blocked out all ultraviolet radiation from the light entering his eyes, leaving only the denatured visible band to enter and strike the retinas.

When full-spectrum light was restored to his retinas, ultraviolet energy stimulated the oculo-endocrine system via the optic nerve. The pituitary, which is the master regulator of the endocrine system, then secreted its vital hormones into the bloodstream, and these in turn stimulated the suprarenal glands to secrete their hormones, which include cortisone. Cortisone is the natural hormone that relieves inflamed arthritic joints.

Clearly, the *quality* of light entering the eyes is just as important to health as the quality of air entering the lungs and the quality of food entering the stomach. The body cannot live on denatured nutrients of any sort. Light devoid of its natural ultraviolet 'nutrients' is as 'dead' as food without its living enzymes and air without its active negative ions. In all three cases, the missing ingredient is a form of *chee*, the indispensable bioactive energy of life.

Russian science has probed much further into the field of light therapy than American science. In addition to exploring the oculo-endocrine system, they have made extensive studies of the therapeutic benefits of exposing the skin to full-spectrum light. In 1967, at a meeting of the International Committee on Illumination in Washington, DC, three Russian scientists presented the following findings:

> If human skin is not exposed to solar radiation (direct or scattered) for long periods of time, disturbances will occur in the physiological equilibrium of the human system. The result will be functional disorders of the nervous system and a Vitamin-D deficiency, a weakening of the body's defenses, and an aggravation of chronic diseases. Sunlight deficiency is observed more particularly in persons living in the polar regions and in those working underground or in windowless industrial buildings.

The problems resulting from ultraviolet energy deficiency are far more severe than you might expect. All types of glass, for example, filter out ultraviolet rays, including ordinary window panes, car windshields, eye glasses (clear or tinted), and contact lenses. People today spend most of their time indoors behind walls and glass, and when they do go out in the sunlight they usually wear sunglasses. The occasional weekend spent lying on the beach compensates for this deficiency no more than a properly balanced meal once every few weeks compensates for a regular diet of 'junk food'. If anything, it leads to severe sunburn, which can cause skin cancer. It should be noted that the artificial light sources that illuminate most offices, schools, hospitals and homes do not include the ultraviolet band and are thus good for nothing except visual illumination.

An alarming example of the trouble that can be caused by chronic ultraviolet deprivation is the severe hyperactivity, lack of concentration and fits of violence observed in today's young school children, who spend almost all their time in closed classrooms lit by fluorescent lights or in front of television tubes. So severe are the symptoms in many schools in America that high doses of amphetamines are routinely administered to these children. For some reason, amphetamines fed to hyperactive children in high doses have the reverse effect and calm them down, but the side-effects are highly toxic to the entire system, especially metabolism and endocrine balance. When ordinary fluorescent lights were replaced with full-spectrum lighting in typical classrooms where severe behavior abnormalities had been observed, violence and hypertension disappeared within weeks of the change in lighting, and former 'problem children' turned out to be model students. This positive result was observed in *every* classroom tested.

Television is another great enemy of the oculo-endocrine system. Not only are many of the rays from a TV screen dangerous, they flicker erratically, causing irregular and uneven stimulation of the retina. This choppy stimulus is transferred directly into the brain via the optic nerve, and irritates the hypothalamus. In scientific experiments conducted in the USA but ignored by both the television industry and the government agencies whose job it is to regulate this lucrative business, rats exposed to color TV for six hours a day became hyperactive and extremely aggressive for about a week, after which they suddenly became totally lethargic and stopped breeding entirely. Their endocrine systems had literally 'burned out'. What made this experiment doubly significant was the fact that the TV screens were covered with heavy black paper so that only *invisible* rays came through. This proves beyond doubt that the damage from TV rays is caused not by the visible spectrum but by invisible radiation contained within it.

In an article released by Associated Press writer Ben Frank on 24 April

1970, Dr H. D. Youmans of the Bureau of Radiological Health is quoted as follows:

> We found rays escaping from the vacuum tubes to be harder and of higher average energy than we expected. They penetrated the first few inches of the body as deeply as 100-kilowatt diagnostic X-rays. You get a uniform dose to the eyes, testes, and bone marrow.

The same article notes that Dr Robert Elder, director of the BRH, testified before Congress that even very minute doses of radiation, which fall far *below the legal limit*, deeply penetrate human tissues and that the damage they do is *cumulative*. That damage includes genetic damage that can influence fertility and be carried over to future generations. Recall now that over the past three decades there has been a dramatic and 'inexplicable' rise in infertility throughout the general population in America, where the present generation was virtually raised before the television tube. Even more ominous is the fact that cancer recently replaced accidents as the biggest killer of children under age 15 in America. These facts alone should suffice to alarm the nation into immediate action at home, in schools and at the work place, but then again, lethargy and apathy are among the symptoms of the problem.

The story of light gets worse every year. Global air pollution has significantly cut down the intensity of sunlight reaching the earth throughout the world today. Worse yet, air pollution specifically filters out the ultraviolet band. Scientists at the Mount Wilson Observatory in California report a 10 per cent loss in average light density over the past 50 years, and a whopping 26 per cent reduction in ultraviolet radiation. This ultraviolet deficiency in our sunlight has already begun to affect farming by greatly reducing yields and leaving plants more vulnerable to attack by pests. Some farmers now spread aluminium foil on the ground beneath growing plants to augment ultraviolet exposure, and they report an amazing five-fold increase in harvests. If plants are already suffering such obvious damage from ultraviolet deficiency, what unknown effects is it having on man and his sensitive oculo-endocrine system?

Taoists employ their own traditional measures to compensate for the light deficiency of modern times, and anyone can benefit from these methods. Before taking a look at two eye exercises used to 'administer sunbeams' to 'benefit the brain', let's briefly review a list of vital points to bear in mind regarding sunlight and health:

- Try to get some daily exposure of bare skin and naked eyes to direct sunlight. However, avoid sunburn, which is hazardous to the skin.

Sunscreens are not the answer, for they block ultraviolet radiation from the skin. The answer is balance: forget about that 'perfect tan' and approach sunbathing as a medical-hygenic activity, like taking a shower.

- Try to minimize time spent in denatured artificial light, especially fluorescent light. When stuck indoors behind concrete and glass for prolonged periods, take an occasional break before an open window or up on the roof to recharge your oculoendocrine system with ultraviolet energy.

- Watch TV as little as possible, or not at all. Best of all, throw your TV away – you will be doing yourself and your entire family a big favor in the long run. It may turn out that 'quitting TV' is as important to health and longevity as 'quitting smoking'.

- Toss out those fashionable sunglasses, which serve no therapeutic purpose whatsoever. If you wear reading glasses or contact lenses, specify that they be made from glass or plastic that transmits ultraviolet light. These materials are now commercially available.

- If you or anyone in your family suffers from any long-standing degenerative disease or condition, you may accelerate cures and help prevent recurrences by installing full-spectrum lighting in home and office. Such lights are now commercially available in America and Europe. In addition, you could have ordinary glass window panes replaced with plastic panes that transmit ultraviolet light in rooms where people spend the most time. These materials are also available commercially.

- In order to compensate for the 26 per cent reduction in overall ultraviolet radiation reaching the earth today, as well as for all the time spent indoors, practice the sun-blinking solar-energy eye exercises introduced below once or twice a day.

The following exercises should only be performed when the sun is shining brightly, not when obscured with clouds or heavy haze, and ONLY before 9:00 a.m. or after 4:00 p.m., when the sun is not at its height of intensity. Fans of Carlos Castaneda's 'Don Juan' series will recognize these exercises as similar to one of the basic energy-gathering exercises Don Juan taught Carlos.

1. Stand or sit comfortably outdoors with head tilted towards the sun, eyes closed. Angle your head so that eyes are aimed about 10–15 degrees above the sun, not directly at it. Now open your eyes quickly and blink very rapidly, for about 3 seconds, or about 10 times. Then

close eyes, tilt head away from sun, and pause for brief rest. Tilt head back towards sun, eyes closed, this time with eyes aimed 10–15 degrees below the sun. Repeat blinking sequence, look away, and repeat exercise to the left and to the right of the sun. This method insures even exposure of retinas to beneficial UV rays without focusing eyes directly at the sun. You may perform this exercise once or twice per session.

2. The second method is a bit more advanced. Adopt the same posture outdoors as above. Instead of blinking rapidly *at* the sun, roll your eye-balls in a circle *around* the sun for 3–5 seconds, then pause, look away and repeat 3–5 times. Employ the eye-rolling exercise given in the previous chapter as a long-life exercise. This method provides a more complete and even irradiation of the retina with ultraviolet energy. This method provides a more complete and even irradiation of the retinas with ultraviolet energy, but you must be careful not to let the eyes focus directly on the sun itself as they revolve around it.

These exercises run counter to the conventional Western wisdom that direct exposure to sunlight is harmful to the eyes. Hopefully the evidence presented above suffices to belie such ill-founded advice. If not, then consider the following two facts for additional support. First, it is *short-wave* ultraviolet radiation that is harmful to eyes and skin, and this portion of the band is completely filtered out by the atmosphere, especially by today's highly polluted atmosphere; only the beneficial *long-wave* ultraviolet radiation in the sunlight reaches the earth's surface. Secondly, when you look at the sun or anything else intensely bright, the irises instantly contract to narrow the opening of the pupil. This natural protective mechanism effectively cuts down the overall *intensity* of light entering the eyes to tolerable levels without cutting out any part of the *spectrum*. Furthermore, it is the chronic *deficiency* of ultraviolet exposure to the eyes caused by sedentary modern lifestyles that makes eyes so excessively sensitive to prolonged *occasional* exposure, such as a day at the beach or in the mountains. Heliotherapy calls for *brief* but *daily* exposure of the retinas to sunlight in order to balance the oculo-endocrine system.

The best test of course is to practice yourself and see what an improvement it makes in health and vitality. The wonderful thing about Tao is that it speaks for itself with results, not arguments. At first, the exercises might cause your eyes to water and throb a bit, but that is due primarily to long neglect of the epithelial cells in the retina, and to atrophy of the eye muscles themselves. A week or two of practice should eliminate these symptoms, but if they persist you should stop the exercises and have your eyes checked, especially the irises and retinas. If you make solar-energy-gathering eye exercises part of your daily regimen, your eyes will quickly adjust and you should then notice a significant enhancement in energy, awareness and resistance to disease.

The New Medicine

Throughout Asia, and to a lesser but growing extent in certain parts of Europe, traditional Eastern and modern Western medical systems are being blended into a whole new approach to health care popularly known as the 'New Medicine'. Basically, the New Medicine employs the most sophisticated Western medical technology in diagnosis and clinical research, while relying primarily on traditional Chinese methods to effect cures and prevent recurrence of diseases.

True, there are acute situations in which only radical Western-style surgery or chemical therapy can save the patient: for example, a bullet lodged near the heart or a virulent infectious disease. But for all the various and sundry *chronic* diseases and *degenerative* conditions that plague the human species and comprise well over 90 per cent of all human ailments, traditional Chinese therapies have proven time and again to be far more effective, safe and permanent than Western methods.

Electro-acupuncture is a good example of how the best of East and West may be harmoniously blended to create a new therapy that is greater than the sum of its parts. Another example is the use of Western technology to extract and refine highly potent essences from traditional Chinese medicinal herbs. These essences may be injected directly into the vital points used in acupuncture, from where they transmit their therapeutic benefits to related organs and glands via the meridian system, or they may be made into patent medicines for oral use.

In France, Sweden and the Soviet Union, such cures as electro-acupuncture, herbs, fasting, nutrition, exercise, massage and helio-therapy have become quite popular as the New Medicine takes root there. A patient in these countries might have his diabetes diagnosed by sophisticated Western technology but opt to have it treated by traditional methods such as nutrition, herbs and breathing. X-rays may be used to detect a malignant tumor but, instead of using radiation to try to 'kill' it as is the practice in America, patients where the New Medicine is available may opt for electro-acupuncture, fasting and other natural methods derived from Oriental tradition. At least they have the choice to select the therapy in which they have the most faith and which has provided the best results in similar cases throughout the world.

The stubborn resistance to new medical approaches displayed by the American, and to a somewhat lesser extent the British, medical establishments not only deprives their own patients of valuable alternative therapy, it also harms the medical profession itself. American medical schools are not preparing doctors with sufficient background in nutrition, heliotherapy, massage and other traditional methods which are becoming part and parcel of medical training elsewhere in the world. Owing to this myopic attitude towards 'alternative therapy' on the part of the American medical establishment, more and more Americans with serious ailments such as cancer are traveling to France, Germany, Japan and even Mexico for treatment. It is only a matter of time before this deficiency in American medical care causes a major crisis in public health and in the medical profession.

The New Medicine provides a path of compromise as well as discovery in medical care, and it paves the way to a whole approach that synthesizes the best elements of East and West, past and present. An excellent example of this synthesis is the China Medical College in Taichung, Taiwan, which includes a recently completed 220-bed hospital that offers both traditional Chinese and modern Western treatments side by side, with daily consultation between the two systems and instant computerized access to all relevant information. So successful has this hospital proven in the treatment of every sort of human ailment, both chronic and acute, common and rare, that three more such East/West hospitals have opened in Taiwan since then.

Chen Li-fu, chairman of the China Medical College's Board of Directors, speaks for all enlightened medical scientists and professional physicians dedicated to the pursuit of public health and longevity rather than personal pride and profit:

> Today in Taiwan, Chinese and Western medicine both play an important role in modern society. They both have their respective advantages and limitations. Traditional and Western physicians should abandon their prejudices and value the differences between their systems. They should treasure the mutual common sense of both systems, discard what is useless or harmful, and strive for the full growth and development of the best aspects of both systems, so as to incorporate the two in bringing forth a new medical science.

PART II

The Tao of Sex

陰陽之道

CHAPTER 6:

◐

The Tao of Yin and Yang

All the best medicines and good food in the world cannot help one achieve longevity unless one knows and practices the Tao of Yin and Yang.

[Ko Hung]

The Chinese have always held the Taoist view that sexual relations between male and female are the primary earthly manifestation of the universal principles of Yin and Yang. As such, the Chinese regard sex to be as natural and indispensable to human health and longevity as rain falling on the fields is to plant life. The intense sense of guilt attached to sexual matters in Judeo-Christian tradition is, in Chinese eyes, one of the most unpleasant and incomprehensible aspects of Western culture.

Traditional Western hypocrisy towards sex has prevented serious study of human sexuality in the Western world until only a few decades ago. Like everything else in Western philosophy, sex is viewed through the lens of dualism: it is seen as either sacred (in matrimony) or profane (out of wedlock), with no room for anything in between. The Chinese, however, do not draw distinctions between sacred and profane sex. As far as Taoists are concerned, the only important distinctions regarding sexual activities are those between healthy and unhealthy habits.

The Chinese approach the subject of human sexuality with a blend of curiosity and reverence, just as they do all natural phenomena. Since sexual relations are as fundamental to human life as eating and sleeping, Taoist adepts devoted a lot of time and thought to researching its every aspect and implication for human health and longevity. In a society happily free of sexual repression, Taoist physicians took a long and careful look at human sexual behavior, and they candidly recorded their findings in journals and books, couched in the usual florid Taoist terminology.

Consequently, the Chinese have been able to approach and study

257

sexual relations between man and woman with open eyes and open minds, and they have, over three millennia, become the world's most astute observers of human sexuality, as well as the most inventive lovers.

The Nature of Man and Woman

The essential difference between the sexual nature of man and woman lies in the different nature of male and female orgasm. When a man ejaculates, he ejects his semen-essence from his body. When a woman reaches orgasm, she too 'ejaculates' all sorts of sexual secretions internally, but these are retained within her body. For both men and women, sexual essence is an important storage battery for vital energy and a major source of resistance and immunity. In conventional sexual relations, a man ejaculates every time he has intercourse, regardless of whether his partner reaches orgasm or not and regardless of his own age or condition. This habit gradually robs him of his primary source of vitality and immunity, leaving him weak and vulnerable to disease and shortening his lifespan. Meanwhile, the woman gets stronger and stronger, both from her own orgasmic secretions and from her assimilation of potent male semen-essence.

The different nature of male and female orgasm is reflected in the various slang terms to describe that magic moment in both the Chinese and Western languages. The most common Chinese term for female orgasm is *gao-chao*, literally 'high tide', a graphic and poetic image drawn from nature. But when man ejaculates, the Chinese say that he has 'lost his essence', 'thrown it away', 'leaked semen', or 'surrendered'. If a man ejaculates before his partner reaches orgasm, the Chinese say that she has 'killed' him. The French refer to ejaculation as 'petit mort', or 'little death'.

By patterning their sexual relations on the models of Heaven and Earth and conforming to the nature of Yin and Yang, men may derive life-giving benefits from the sexual forces, rather than being forever at their mercy. Instead of depleting precious stores of essence and energy, sex may be used to replenish them. Classically, appropriate analogies were drawn between human nature and Mother Nature, which illuminated the basic qualities of man and woman. Appropriate principles drawn from those analogies were then applied to regulate human sexual relations. As the Han Dynasty adept Wu Hsien put it:

> The male belongs to Yang. Yang's nature is such that the male is easily aroused but also quick to retreat. The female belongs to Yin. Yin's nature is such that the female is slow to be aroused and also slow to be satiated.

Throughout the animal and insect world, nature has fashioned the female as a superior specimen uniquely equipped for the survival and propagation of the species. According to the 'law of the jungle', the male exists only to provide the seed for future generations and to protect the nest while the female nurses the young to maturity. Sexual intercourse occurs seasonally, and, while all females 'in heat' get fertilized, only a small fraction of the strongest males perform the task. Even among primates, only the strong, dominant males are permitted to fertilize the females, while weaker male specimens are either discarded or kept at a distance from the herd. Among many orders of insect, such as black widow and praying mantis, nature gives the male even shorter shrift: the moment he deposits his seed in the female, she promptly kills and devours him as a post-coital snack.

Only humans (and a few higher primates such as orangutans) engage in sexual intercourse all year long, day and night, in any season or weather, and only humans do it primarily for pleasure rather than procreation. Yet the human male, despite his inflated ego, is subject to the same inherent limitations that nature has imposed on his gender in all species.

Matriarchy is a social acknowledgement of female superiority and is therefore a natural pattern for the human species to follow. China's prehistoric matriarchy is still reflected in Chinese language and thought. The single most common word in the Chinese language is *hao*, which means 'good' in all its various senses. The ideogram for 'good' consists of the symbol for 'woman' placed next to that for 'child', indicating that the highest good is the generative relationship between mother (not father) and child. The ideogram that denotes the word 'surname' in Chinese consists of the symbols for 'woman' and 'birth' clearly indicating that family descent in prehistoric China was traced through the mother's line, just as it was in ancient Hebrew tradition prior to patriarchy. In all the ancient Chinese sex manuals, woman is always depicted as the guardian of sexual arcana and the supreme source of life-sustaining essence and energy. In these texts the woman plays the role of the great initiator and teacher of sex, while the man is described as a sexually ignorant bumbler.

Because of her sexual potency, woman was regarded as possessor of great stores of *teh* (power). The contemporary Taoist Jolan Chang, in his book *The Tao of the Loving Couple*, quotes some conclusions by Mary Jane Sherfey regarding the power of female sexuality:

> All relevant data from the 12000 to 8000 BC period indicate that precivilized woman enjoyed full sexual freedom and was often totally incapable of controlling her sexual drive. Therefore, I propose that one of the reasons for the long delay between the

earliest development of agriculture (c. 12000 BC) and the rise of urban life and the beginning of recorded knowledge (c. 8000–5000 BC) was the ungovernable cyclic sexual drive of women. Not until these drives were gradually brought under control by rigidly enforced social codes could family life become the stabilizing and creative crucible from which modern civilized man could emerge.

Although man took over control of the family, village, economy, religion and state, he still found himself at woman's mercy in bed. No amount of human artifice can mask or alter the fundamental facts of Tao. Hence, there arose a deep contradiction between man's artificial social superiority and his genuine sexual inferiority *vis-à-vis* woman, and this gave rise to the battle of the sexes that still rages in most boudoirs today. It also explains the deep fear and resentment that many men harbor toward women, despite women's supposed 'inferiority'. 'Macho' men simply cannot face the fact that women are sexually superior, nor do they dare admit the realities of their own inherent sexual weakness. This sad state of affairs is due primarily to sexual ignorance. Any man open-minded enough to take a serious look at the Tao of Yin and Yang – and self-disciplined enough to practice it – will find that the Tao completely eliminates the fundamental inequity between male and female sexual potency. The Tao enables the male member to become an all-weather instrument of equal competence to that of its female counterpart and permits man and woman to 'make love, not war', while at the same time protecting the health and prolonging the lives of both partners.

In the Western world, artists and athletes have so far been the only people who truly realize the debilitating nature of male ejaculation. In his autobiography, Charlie Chaplin wrote, 'Like Balzac, who believed that a night of sex meant the loss of a good page of his novel, so I believed that it meant the loss of a good day's work at the studio.'

On a more contemporary note, let's listen in on an interview with jazz musician Miles Davis which appeared in the April 1975 issue of *Playboy* magazine:

> Davis: You can't come, then fight or play. You can't do it. When I get ready to come, I come. But I do not come and play.
> Interviewer: Explain that in layman's terms.
> Davis: Ask Muhammad Ali. If he comes, he can't fight two minutes. Shit, he couldn't even whip me.
> Interviewer: Would you fight Muhammad Ali under those conditions, to prove your point?

> Davis: You're goddam right I'd fight him. But he's got to promise to fuck first. If he ain't going to fuck, I ain't going to fight. You give up all your energy when you come. I mean, *you give up all of it*! So, if you're going to fuck before a gig, how are you going to give something when it's time to hit?

What neither Davis nor Ali realizes is that sexual intercourse *without* ejaculation prior to a fight or a gig would improve their performances even more than if they abstained altogether.

Artists and athletes rely on optimum levels of physical and mental vitality in order to perform, which is why they are more sensitive to the loss of semen and vital energy through ejaculation. However, other men suffer just as severely from such loss, albeit they remain largely unconscious of it. For example, the male tendency to fall sound asleep after ejaculation is a prime indicator of complete exhaustion. If orgasm in itself were so exhausting, then women would feel the same effects from it, but it is the physical ejection of semen from the body – not orgasm *per se* – that harms man.

The depressing phenomenon of 'post-coital blues' that follows conventional intercourse does not occur at all when men retain semen. Taoist sex is a barter arrangement between Yin and Yang: the man sacrifices a small measure of short-term pleasure in return for the long-term benefits of health and longevity, while the woman enjoys complete unrestricted sexual pleasure in exchange for a measure of her abundant supplies of life-prolonging essence and energy.

The contrasting nature of male and female orgasm has important implications for two types of sexual activity that have aroused a lot of controversy over the ages and appear to be gaining in popularity today: masturbation and homosexuality. Viewed from the angle of Yin and Yang, the results of these two activities are very different indeed for men and women. For men, masturbation represents an irretrievable and uncompensated loss of Yang semen-essence. While healthy males between the ages of 16 and 21 are veritable 'fountains of semen' for whom masturbation is relatively harmless, by the time they reach 25 or so, all the old shibboleths regarding male masturbation come true: weakness in thighs and knees, numbness in lumbar region, loss of vitality, depression, etc. By the time they reach 30, men should entirely give up this self-defeating habit and start conserving semen exclusively for intercourse with women. Men who continue masturbating habitually into their 30s, 40s and 50s rob themselves of the very essence and energy that fuel their lives and protect their health.

A woman, by contrast, may masturbate to her heart's content without

damaging her stores of essence and energy. In the polygamous households of ancient China, female masturbation and sapphism served important social and psychological functions in the harems of sexually
beleaguered gentlemen. And since women do not reach their peak of
sexual potency until their mid-30s (unlike men, who 'peak out' after 18),
masturbation is likely to become ever more important to women as they
grow older since so many men begin losing their potency just as women
'hit stride' around age 35.

The same point applies to homosexual relations: they are harmless for
women but highly detrimental to men, both physiologically and psychologically. Nature has made Yin passive and yielding, and two passive
forces do not conflict. The Chinese refer to sapphic love as 'polishing
mirrors', a term that reflects the fact that female homosexual practices are
largely limited to the rubbing together of similar parts, rather than actual
penetration of the body. And even when the body is penetrated with a
surrogate phallus, it is done through the orifice intended for that purpose. Like masturbation, sapphism was a common practice in the household harems of wealthy Chinese families, where up to a dozen women
might find themselves completely cut off from male company for months
at a time when the man of the house was off on official business.

Taoist physicians regarded homosexuality among men, on the other
hand, as a dangerous practice – for several reasons. First of all, Yang is by
nature an active, aggressive force, and, when two aggressive forces meet,
a fundamental conflict of energies and intentions results. Male homosexuality requires that one partner yield to the other by adopting the female
role, both physically and psychologically, and when this practice becomes a habit it completely undermines the fundamental role of Yang
in the order of nature. Looking at this situation of Yang conflict at a microscopic scientific level, when the sperm from two different men are
mixed together and observed under magnification, they may clearly be
observed fighting one another in a desperate struggle for supremacy.

Psychology aside, the greatest threat posed to men by homosexual
practices are physiological. Anal penetration, the mutual exchange of
Yang sexual fluids, and frequent uncontrolled ejaculations are the culprits. Ancient Taoist physicians noted a pathological condition called
'Dragon Yang Syndrome' which occurred exclusively among promiscuous male homosexuals. 'Dragon Yang' (lung-yang) is a common
Chinese euphemism for male homosexuality, equivalent to the English
word 'gay'. Symptoms of this ailment included weakness and fatigue,
skin ulcers and boils, low immunity, and impotence.

The foregoing observations on the nature of Yin and Yang make it
clear that man and woman are not created equal. Yin is abundant and

enduring, while Yang is limited and vulnerable, and this is reflected in the fact that throughout the world women tend to outlive men by a factor of five to ten years. The key to redressing this inequity is properly regulated relations between 'fire' and 'water'. As the Taoist alchemist Ko Hung wrote in the fourth century AD:

> Both fire and water can kill, yet both may also bestow life. It depends entirely on whether one knows Tao. If a man knows Tao, then the more he makes love, the better becomes his health. If he is ignorant of Tao, just one woman is sufficient to hasten his journey to the grave.

Lest male readers further hasten their journeys to the grave due to ignorance of Tao, let us now get down to the crux of the matter – the Way of Yin and Yang – a way that shows us how to use sex to pave a path to health and longevity rather than to perdition.

The Way of Yin and Yang

The Way of Yin and Yang is of paramount importance in the Taoist system of health and longevity. It is also one of the most ancient elements of Chinese thought on record. *The Yellow Emperor's Classic of Internal Medicine (Huang Ti Nei Ching)* and the invaluable *Classic of the Plain Girl (Su Nü Ching)*, both of which date from the third – fourth centuries BC, are based on materials handed down through ancient China's Imperial Archives ever since the time of the Yellow Emperor and his various Taoist advisors.

As with the Tao itself, the essential elements in the Tao of Yin and Yang are balance, harmony and the union of opposites:

> For a man to nurture his male powers, he must nourish his Yang essence by absorbing Yin essence. When men and women indulge freely in sex, exchanging their bodily fluids and breathing each other's breath, it is like fire and water meeting in such perfect proportions that neither one defeats the other. Man and woman should ebb and flow in intercourse like the waves and currents of the sea, first one way, then another, but always in harmony with the Great Tide. In this manner, they may continue all night long, constantly nourishing and preserving their precious vital essence, curing all ailments, and promoting long life. Without this basic harmony of Yin and Yang, neither medicines refined from the five minerals, nor the most potent aphrodisiacs, will be of any use. If the vital essences are dried up due to excessive emission or complete neglect, they can never be revived.   [*Su-Nü Ching*]

When sex is performed according to the Way, it becomes an inexhaustible source of energy, like a well that never runs dry, rather than an exhausting ordeal. However, sex can also 'drown' you if you don't know how to stay 'afloat' during intercourse.

Unless you are a highly accomplished adept who has mastered the transmutation of sexual energy into pure spiritual power, celibacy will harm your health as much as reckless indulgence:

> Yellow Emperor: I do not wish to make love any more.
>
> Plain Girl: As human beings, we must not do anything that contradicts nature. Now, your majesty wishes to refrain from sexual intercourse and that is entirely against nature. When Yin and Yang are not in contact, they cannot complement and harmonize each other. We breathe in order to exchange stale old air for fresh new air. When the Jade Stem is not active, it will atrophy. That is why it must be exercised regularly. If a man can learn to control and regulate his ejaculations during sex, he may derive great benefits from this practice. The retention of semen is highly beneficial to man's health.
>
> [*Su Nü Ching*]

Preserving semen lies at the very heart of Taoist bedroom arts, as illustrated in the following line from a commentary on the adept Pien Chang's biography in *Dynastic History of the Later Han*:

> The art of the bedroom consists of suppressing emissions, absorbing the woman's fluids, and making semen return to strengthen the brain, thereby attaining longevity.

Thus, a man must treasure and conserve his semen during intercourse; whenever he does emit it, the loss must be compensated by absorbing the 'essence' of woman's secretions. That is why ejaculations through masturbation or homosexual relations are regarded as being especially harmful to the Yang essence and energy.

Figure 6.1 Male and female exchange Yin and Yan energies through their linked Microcosmic Orbits during properly regulated intercourse. Note how the partners' Microcosmic Orbits intersect through points of contact at the mouth, heart and genitals

By now, male readers must be wondering, 'How can there be pleasure in sex without ejaculation?' This question also occurred to the Yellow Emperor after his advisors encouraged him to start regulating his ejaculations. The Emperor's enquiry on this matter sparked the following exchange between two of his closest counsellors, Peng-Tze and the Rainbow Girl, recorded in *Secrets of the Jade Bedroom*:

> Rainbow Girl: It is generally assumed that a man gains great pleasure from ejaculation. But when he learns the Tao of Yin and Yang, he will ejaculate less and less. Will this not diminish his pleasure as well?
>
> Peng-Tze: Not at all! After ejaculating, a man feels tired, his ears buzz, his eyes get heavy, and he longs for sleep. He is thirsty and his limbs feel weak and stiff. By ejaculating, he enjoys a brief moment of sensation but suffers long hours of weariness as a result. This is no true pleasure!
>
> However, if a man regulates his ejaculations to an absolute minimum and retains his semen, his body will grow strong, his mind will be clear, and his vision and hearing will improve. While the man must occasionally deny himself the fleeting sensation of ejaculation, his love for his woman will greatly increase. *He will feel as if he could never get enough of her.* Is that not the true and lasting pleasure of sex?

The last point is a particularly subtle and significant observation: a man who maintains consistently high levels of testosterone, sperm, semen and other male-essence by practicing ejaculation control will experience an overwhelming enhancement in his love and affection for his woman. He will also gain the capacity to act upon that loving urge over and over again.

Compare this with the adolescent attitude toward sex revealed in the best-selling book *Everything You Ever Wanted to Know about Sex*, written by the self-styled American sex expert David Reuben. He writes:

> In eating, the first bite is tastiest, the first helping the most appetizing. The third helping of strawberry shortcake just doesn't taste as good as the first time around. The third copulation of the evening is more for the record books than the enjoyment of the participants.

Reuben writes from the point of view of a man who has already ejaculated twice and must now force himself to rise to the occasion once more, 'for the record books'. He doesn't even consider the feelings and point of view of the woman, for whom a third round is no effort whatsoever and who, like water slowly simmering over a fire, is still 'hot' after the first two rounds. For a man who knows the Tao of Yin and Yang, there is always room for a 'third helping of strawberry shortcake'.

In Taoist lovemaking, the emphasis lies not on romantic love but rather on correct technique; therefore it's like a football game or cricket match: wanting to win is not enough – both teams have to be 'in shape', in practice, and know the rules of the game. This approach is well illustrated by the traditional Chinese literary analogy of the boudoir as a 'flowery battlefield'. But the Chinese image of sex as battle is not at all the same notion as the Western 'battle between the sexes'. The latter indicates a fundamental conflict of wills and severe competition for sexual supremacy that extends beyond the boudoir, while the Chinese metaphor stresses the practical, tactical aspects of actual intercourse – what the Chinese call 'bedroom strategy'. In the Ming Dynasty erotic novel *Prayer Mat of the Flesh* by Lee Yü, we find an amusing rendition of this martial approach to sexual relations:

> Apart from the number of combatants involved, are there really any differences between battles fought by armies and those fought in bed? In both cases, the commanders' first priority is to survey the terrain and assess the opponent. In sexual encounters, it is the hills and valleys of the woman that first attract the man's attention, while she is most curious about the size and firepower of his weapons. Who will advance and who will retreat? In bed as in war, it is just as important to know yourself as it is to know your opponent.

Unlike battles fought with swords and spears, however, it is women who hold the advantage over men in sexual engagements, and therefore men require the most 'training' to prepare for the 'battle'. Most men, however, fondly regard themselves as 'stronger' than women and therefore consider their five-minute blitzkriegs in bed to be par for the course.

In order to fully satisfy his partner in bed, as well as nurture rather than deplete his essence and energy, a man must learn to prolong the act as long, and resume it as often, as is necessary for his partner to experience complete satisfaction. The Plain Girl calls this method 'contact without leakage'. In *Secrets of the Jade Bedroom*, the Taoist sage Peng-Tze urges men to treasure and preserve their semen as a fundamental source of life:

> In sexual intercourse, semen must be regarded as a most precious substance. By saving it, a man protects his very life. Whenever he does ejaculate, the loss of semen must then be compensated by absorbing the woman's essence.

Foreplay, the Four Attainments, the Five Signs, the Five Desires, the Ten Indications and the Five Virtues

The Yellow Emperor's chief advisors on sexual affairs were all good Taoists, so they did not rely entirely on clever words and philosophical arguments to illustrate the Way. They peppered their dialogues with all sorts of practical guidelines and concrete instructions. They taught the Yellow Emperor how to observe his partner's responses, how to approach the 'flowery battlefield' and how to engage in the 'combat' of sexual intercourse. The Plain Girl and the rest of the Emperor's Taoist retinue introduced their most important practical instructions under the headings of Foreplay, the Four Attainments, the Five Signs, the Five Desires, the Ten Indications and the Five Virtues. These serve as signposts along the winding road to a woman's orgasm, and every man should learn to read them.

Figure 6.2
'Triple Yin Intersection' point on legs
(San-yin-jiao)

Foreplay

Foreplay is a primary preventive measure against the common problems of insufficient female lubrication and insufficient male erection prior to intercourse. The Plain Girl explains that lubrication of the vagina and engorgement of the penis before the two organs meet directly is the first fundamental sign of the interplay of Yin and Yang. Foreplay also primes the body's energy system for the intense stimulation of sexual intercourse. In Taoist parlance, foreplay helps bring the 'water' to a boil while keeping the 'fire' burning slowly.

Foreplay should commence at the body's extremities, not at the genitals. Start by massaging the hands and wrists, feet and ankles, and working your way up the arms and shoulders to the chest and up the legs and thighs to the abdomen and waist. Learn the routes of the major

267

energy meridians and the locations of their most sensitive vital points. Massaging these points is highly stimulating and generates a lot of energy. Under the influence of sexual excitement, this energy travels along the meridian network to the sexual organs. For a woman, deep finger pressure on the point called 'Triple Yin Intersection' (*San-yin-jiao*), (see Figure 6.2) located just behind the shin bone about three inches up from the inner ankle bone is particularly effective in arousing sexual energy. The lower back, spine and inside the surfaces of arms and legs are sensitive erogenous energy zones on both men and women.

The Four Attainments

The Four Attainments refer to the four fundamental conditions that the male organ must attain during foreplay before it is 'qualified' to enter the Jade Gate for intercourse. On this subject, the Mysterious Girl dispenses some of her frankest and most useful advice to men:

> Mysterious Girl: A male who desires intercourse must first pass through four stages of attainment: elongation, swelling, hardness, and heat.
>
> Yellow Emperor: What do these attainments mean?
>
> Mysterious Girl: If the stalk does not attain sufficient elongation, the man's vital energy is too depleted for the act. If he attains elongation but little swelling, this means that his muscular energy is insufficient for the task. If he achieves swelling but not hardness, it means that his joints and tendons are too weak for the act. If the organ gets hard but not hot, then his spirit is insufficient for the act.
>
> In order to prepare properly for sexual intercourse, you must first harmonize your muscles and bones with your energy and your spirit [i.e. harmonize the Three Treasures]. You must also exercise self-discipline, follow the basic principles of Tao, and never waste your semen carelessly.

In a further guideline to male arousal, the Mysterious Girl informs us that 'The feet and toes can influence male sexual potency.' In other words, vigorous massage of a man's feet and toes will assist him in attaining the four conditions of erection by stimulating energy to travel to the associated organs through the meridian network. The liver, which controls and releases the extra supplies of blood required to engorge the penis, is directly stimulated by foot massage, therefore regular stretching, massaging, flexing and acupressure of the feet and toes, when adopted as a daily exercise, help promote and maintain overall male sexual vitality.

The Five Signs

The Yellow Emperor asked, 'How do I know when a woman feels the joys of sex?' Replied the Plain Girl, 'By the Five Signs, Five Desires, and Ten Indications. By observing these changes, you will know exactly how she feels and the appropriate action to take.'

The First Sign is when 'her face reddens'. That means the man should play his organ gently over and around her Mound of Venus. The Second Sign is when 'her nipples harden and beads of sweat appear around her nose'. This signals that she is ready for the man to insert the Jade Stem slowly into the Jade Gate. The Third Sign is 'parched throat, dry lips, and difficulty swallowing,' which indicates that the man should begin agitating more vigorously inside. The Fourth Sign occurs when 'the Jade Gate grows wet and slippery' with lubrication and means that the man should now thrust fully to the hilt and move about deeply inside the Celestial Palace. The Fifth and final Sign is thick viscous fluid dribbling down the inside of the woman's thighs. This means she has experienced her 'high tide' and it is time for the man to stop thrusting and slowly withdraw. By paying close attention to these and other responses in his partner, a man knows the right move to make at the right time.

The Five Desires

The Five Desires reflect the degree to which a woman desires and enjoys sexual intercourse. 'The First Desire is called "intent"'. The intent towards sexual intercourse occurs during initial foreplay and is reflected by short, shallow breathing and a rapid pulse. 'The Second Desire is called "awareness"', and it means that she wishes for the man to touch and stimulate her genitals. It is indicated by flared nostrils and parted lips. The Third Desire occurs when the woman's Yin fluids are brimming over and she approaches her peak of passion. At this point, her entire body shakes and shimmies with excitement, and she clutches the man closely.

The Fourth Desire comes at orgasm and is called 'concentration'. She breaks into a warm sweat that 'dampens the sheets'. The Fifth Desire occurs only if she achieves a state of extreme passion and pleasure beyond the normal orgasm, in which case her body straightens out and grows rigid, her eyes close, and she clamps her thighs tightly together around the man, as if trying to draw him in deeper. She appears as though 'her spirit were floating on clouds and wind'.

By observing the external manifestations of a woman's Five Desires, a man is able to discern her various responses to the maneuvers he makes based on the Five Signs, especially as she approaches orgasm. These signals enable him to amplify, modulate, harmonize and otherwise enhance his tactics to meet her responses and desires.

The Ten Indications

The Ten Indications describe in greater detail the physical maneuvers a woman uses to cleave close to her man during intercourse and indicate to him what she wants him to do. While the Five Signs describe involuntary sexual responses in the aroused female, the Ten Indications are precise voluntary signals indicating what a woman wants her partner to do next.

The First Indication occurs when 'the woman embraces the man with both hands and feet and presses their bodies together'. This indicates that she now wishes for their genitals to make contact and rub together. The Second Indication comes when she arches up on her buttocks – a signal of urgent desire for more direct stimulation at the Jade Gate. The Third Indication happens when she stretches her torso and spreads her thighs wide, indicating that she wants the man to waste no more time making his entry.

When her arms quiver, shoulders shake and 'buttocks move about in joy', this is the Fourth Indication, which signals to the man that she is now feeling deep pleasure. When she wants the man to thrust more vigorously inside the Celestial Palace, she gives him the Fifth Indication by 'raising up both legs, twisting her ankles, and clasping the man's body tightly with her feet'.

The Sixth Indication is a vital turning point en route to her orgasm. She suddenly straightens out her legs and crosses them behind the man's calves, clamping her thighs tightly together in order to grip the man's Jade Stem more firmly inside. This indicates that the mounting itch of sexual ecstasy is growing unbearable inside, that her tide is rapidly rising, and the man must not fail her now. This is soon followed by the Seventh Indication, in which she signals the man to thrust more deeply to the left and right by rocking her hips from side to side. Then, in the Eighth Indication, 'she raises up her entire body and presses it tightly against the man', a clear indication that her orgasm is now within reach.

As she gets closer to it, the Ninth Indication occurs, in which she suddenly straightens out her body full-length again and her limbs grow rigid, indicating that she is now fully immersed in her 'high tide' and that she feels waves of pleasure right down to her hands and feet. The Tenth Indication, like the Fifth Sign, occurs when 'slippery fluids flow from the Jade Gate and her vital-essence has been released'. It is the equivalent of a standing ovation after a command performance, indicating to the man that he performed the act flawlessly, that her orgasm was complete and fully satisfying, and that he may now rest and gradually withdraw his implement from the 'flowery battlefield'.

Women generally reach orgasm more slowly and with more difficulty than men, who tend to rush to the brink of orgasm and ejaculate quickly, like a 'flash in the pan'. However, it's not so much a matter of a woman taking a 'long time' to reach orgasm as it is a problem of a man ejaculating much too quickly. If this tendency towards quick ejaculation is not redressed with correct techniques and enlightened attitudes, it will inevitably lead to disappointment and strife between lovers, for nothing can compensate for the nagging dissatisfaction of a sexually inept partner.

The Plain, Mysterious and Rainbow Girls therefore address their advice mostly to men, who most need to hone their skills as lovers. The Five Signs, Five Desires and Ten Indications are meant to help men navigate their way through the churning sea of bewildering female sexual responses. Note that according to these signals, a woman's sexual responses occur throughout her body, from head to foot, while the Four Attainments of male erection are all confined to a man's genitals. This clearly indicates that a woman's sexual responses are far more subtle and complex than those of a man, and it reflects the spirit of objective scientific observation in which Taoist sexologists conducted their research.

The findings of these ancient adepts agree remarkably with the conclusions of Kinsey as reported in his book *Sexual Behavior in the Human Female*, in the section entitled 'Physiology of Sexual Response and Orgasm'. The reddening of the face, quickening of respiration and pulse, erection of nipples and other responses recorded in Taoist texts all appear in Western scientific jargon in Kinsey's work. The fact that such information has been generally available to Chinese couples for over 2,000 years accounts for the remarkable stability of Chinese families and society through the ages and explains the refreshing absence of the sexual neuroses and pathology that have plagued the Western world ever since the dawn of the Christian era.

The Five Virtues

The five cardinal virtues of Chinese philosophy are Benevolence (*ren*), Justice (*yi*), Courtesy (*lee*), Honesty (*hsin*) and Wisdom (*jir*). When the raw animal passions of sexual attraction are tempered with these human virtues, sexual relations between man and woman become civilized, balanced and harmonious. Benevolence in sex, for example, means approaching intercourse with a spirit of kindness, generosity and self-sacrifice. Sexual justice means that neither partner forces intercourse when the man is not up to the task or the woman simply doesn't feel like it. It is the virtue of appropriate and timely action. Courtesy in sex implies self-restraint on the man's part so that the woman may enjoy her full measure of pleasure. It means mutual respect between man and woman and reverence for the sexual act itself.

The virtue of 'honesty' in sex demands a frank and open attitude regarding sexual relations. It means appraising oneself and one's partner objectively and not trying to hide one's weak points. Sexual 'wisdom' means that you should use your head as well as your hormones in sexual relations. Wisdom in sex means understanding the virtues of self-restraint and careful deliberation in avoiding impulsive, indiscriminate encounters. Partners should know themselves and get to know each other before steering their relationship into bed.

Taoist texts on sex offer a variety of detailed suggestions regarding the ideal number and ideal type of partners a man should have in order to cultivate the Way of Yin and Yang as a road to health and longevity. This aspect of the Way has caused more controversy through the ages than any other – not only between Taoists and non-Taoists, but also among Taoists themselves. Let's see if we can sort out this ancient imbroglio.

In *Secrets of the Jade Bedroom*, Peng-Tze states categorically:

> Those who practice the Tao of Yin and Yang and absorb vital energy in order to cultivate long life cannot succeed with one partner alone.

According to Peng-Tze's view, frequent sex with the same partner depletes the potency of the essence and energy exchanged during the act. This view became even more pronounced during the Sung Dynasty (AD 960–1279), when Chinese society, under the influence of Neo-Confucianism, took another decisively strong turn towards patriarchal, polygamous family structures. In those days, Chinese men of means enjoyed unlimited access to young women, both within and without their households. Health benefits aside, the real purpose of learning to 'service' multiple partners was social: it insured that every woman in a man's household received her fair share of attention from Yang, and this in turn insured peace and harmony in the family.

The early Taoist texts do not stress sexual intercourse with multiple partners as much as they do prolonged, multiple intercourse with the same partner, and this view cleaves closer to the original Tao. Lao Tze, the ultimate authority on Tao, made this point very clearly in the *Tao Teh Ching*:

The Spirit of the Valley is inexhaustible . . .
Draw on it as you will, it never runs dry.

In other words, it is just as beneficial for a man's health to make love with one healthy woman three or four times in an evening as it is for him to make love with three or four different women, and, since the 'water' stays hot once the 'fire' brings it to a boil, it is much easier to perform the former than the latter act.

Depending on individual circumstances, both views are valid. If a man's wife or lover is healthy, vigorous and sexually active, he is unlikely to require outside resources. On the other hand, if she is of delicate constitution and frail health with a weak libido, an adept of Tao would certainly have to practice with other partners from time to time in order to obtain sufficient doses of Yin essence and energy. The same principle applies to a strong, healthy woman with a weak and chronically ailing man who is unable to provide her sufficient doses of Yang essence and energy. Such disparity, and the consequent requirement for 'extracurricular activities', usually becomes more apparent as a couple grows older and the vitality of one lags behind the other.

This aspect of Tao presents problems only for adepts who equate marriage and monogamy. In traditional Oriental societies, both past and present, married men are not expected to remain monogamous, and discreet outside liaisons usually pose no threat to marriage. If domestic and financial circumstances permit a man to make love regularly with several different women, and if this is done according to Tao rather than as reckless self-indulgence, the benefits to his health and happiness are certainly manifold.

Western readers often have trouble accepting traditional Chinese attitudes toward sex due to their own extreme moral biases on the subject, instilled by thousands of years of Judeo-Christian sexual taboos. But the Chinese, even today, find Western attitudes toward sex equally baffling and highly hypocritical. The fact remains, the Chinese view sex as a basic human function similar to eating, sleeping, and so forth, and they cultivate it as an art and a pleasure, as well as an adjunct to health and longevity. And ultimately, the Taoist way of sex enhances both the health and happiness of both partners, regardless of the social and historical background.

Health and happiness in sex are of course important for both man and woman, but the Tao informs us that for a man health is the main focus, while for a woman happiness is the more difficult goal. That's because for a man ejaculation can be extremely debilitating, while for a woman complete physical orgasm is not only harmless but important for her health. In order to achieve this delicate balance between health and happiness in man and woman in sexual intercourse, the Tao offers the one and only 'way:' prolonged intercourse with male retention of semen and complete female orgasm, repeated as often as required or desired. There simply does not exist a similar solution in Western tradition, for in the West sex is regarded as either sacred or profane, not as a legitimate and effective means toward health and longevity.

For single people in Western societies today, multiple partners present relatively little conflict, but married people should not engage openly in extra-marital liaisons unless both husband and wife are followers of Tao and both fully understand the principles and practices involved. For such enlightened couples, occasional bouts with younger, more vigorous partners not only benefit health and vitality, they also reinforce the marriage itself by eliminating the greatest single threat to matrimonial bliss, which is not infidelity but sexual dissatisfaction and boredom. The dire threat to matrimonial health and happiness posed by sexual frustration is well put by Robert Graves, the Western world's great love poet, in the following stanzas from his poem *Call It a Good Marriage*:

> Call it a good marriage –
> For no one ever questioned
> Her warmth, his masculinity,
> Their interlocking views . . .
>
> Though few would still subscribe
> To the monogamic axiom
> That strife below the hip bones
> Need not estrange the heart,
> Call it a good marriage . . .
>
> Call it a good marriage:
> They never fought in public . . .
> Thus the hazards of their love-bed
> Were none of our damned business –
> Till as jurymen we sat on
> Two deaths by suicide.

The same point was made by C.G. Jung, generally acknowledged to be one of the greatest thinkers in Western history. His 52-year marriage to Emma Rauschenbach was, by all accounts, a complete success, despite his many open liaisons with other women, several of whom actually lived in the Jung household. Wrote Jung, 'The prerequisite for a good marriage is the license to be unfaithful.'

Regarding the ideal type of woman for cultivating the Tao of Yin and Yang, Taoist texts all agree that health and vitality are the major relevant factors, that youth is helpful but not absolutely essential, and that seductive beauty is totally irrelevant. In *Secrets of the Jade Bedroom*, Peng-Tze puts it this way:

> Women do not have to have fine looks and seductive beauty.
> The most desirable types are young, amply fleshed, and have
> not yet borne children.

'Young' is of course a relative term, but it generally means under 30. Still, some people are 'old' at 25, while others are still 'young' at 45, depending on their health and vitality. To be 'amply fleshed' is important for a woman's health as well as her libido. According to Dr Barbara Edelstein, author of the *Woman Doctor's Medical Guide for Women*, 'the average 25-year-old woman needs about 20 to 25% body fat to stay healthy'. This is about 10 pounds more than the vogue 'stick figure' look of today permits. The anemic, emaciated specimens flaunted by Western fashion houses and movie moguls as being the embodiment of ideal feminine beauty and allure are in fact undernourished, devitalized females. Such skinny women have little energy to spare for sex, and they usually have great difficulty reaching orgasm due to insufficient supplies of blood.

As for childbirth, pregnancy inevitably drains women of essence and energy, which are transferred to the fetus during gestation. Healthy, vital women will recover most of their strength (eventually) after giving birth, but they will never again be as strong a source of vital essence and energy as a woman who has never borne children. Indeed, women who have had children benefit greatly from intercourse with virile young men who can afford to 'donate' large doses of their vital Yang-essence through unrestrained ejaculations. Healthy mothers also remain perfectly sound sources of vitality for men who have already mastered Tao and are able to retain their semen during intercourse.

Remember, however, that whether your sexual relations are monogamous or polygamous, the primary condition for judging whether a partner is suitable for sex is health, not physical beauty or romantic love. Men and women alike should avoid sexual intercourse with partners suffering from any sort of communicable disease – not just venereal disease but *any* sort of transmitable disease. In Asia, for example, hepatitis B is a far greater killer and debilitator than AIDS, and the primary method of transmission is sexual intercourse. All Taoist masters stress the importance of robust health and vitality as the primary prerequisites in selecting sexual partners. The materials presented in this section are not meant to encourage promiscuity and indiscriminate sex; on the contrary, they are aimed at teaching both men and women how to correctly discriminate between healthy and unhealthy sexual practices and partners.

The famous Ming writer Lee Yü, who was also a renowned womanizer and a practicing Taoist, portrayed the relative attributes of 'useful women' and 'frail beauties' in this humorous passage from his novel *Prayer Mat of the Flesh*:

> Women can be divided into two general categories: those who please the eye and those of practical use. The beauty always possesses the following qualities: slender body, delicacy, and a fine figure. Useful women are well covered with flesh and have strong bodies, they are rarely slender and delicate, always strong and lusty . . .
>
> The thin woman is like a rock, a wooden log under the man's body . . . On the other hand, a useful woman is an extension of the soft bedding, into which he may sink without concern, confident that she will not complain, into whose body he may thrust forever as deeply and fiercely as he wishes. For men of experience, the well-fleshed body is far superior to the frail and slender beauty . . .
>
> To lie on a frail woman is like sleeping on an unsafe bed – it can suddenly collapse beneath you. If one of the pleasures of the sex battle is to completely abandon oneself to unbridled action, how can a man fully commit his resources to the fray when he knows his opponent is too frail to put up a good fight? *A robust plain girl is always preferable to a slender beauty*.

Like all living things on earth, people possess their greatest stores of essence, energy and spirit during the full bloom of youth, a natural fact of life that has nothing whatsoever to do with beauty or morality. All people – male and female alike – begin to lose vitality after the bloom of youth has blown. Taoist sexual regimens aim at slowing down the rate of dissipation and retarding the overall aging process by establishing mutually beneficial sexual relations between man and woman based on medical rather than moral considerations.

The Great Libation of the 'Three Peaks'

Taoist sexual yoga teaches men how to benefit from the 'Great Libation of the Three Peaks'. The Three Peaks refer to the tongue and lips, the two breasts, and the Mound of Venus on a woman's body, while the Great Libation refers to the various secretions that appear at these 'peaks' during sexual excitement. Over 2,000 years ago, the Han Dynasty adept Wu Hsien extolled the virtues of the Great Libation as follows:

> The top peak is called Red Lotus Peak. Its essence is called Jade Spring and it flows from two ducts beneath the woman's tongue. The man should lick this secretion with his tongue and swallow it, for it is extremely beneficial to health.
>
> The central peak is called Twin Peaks. Its essence is called White Snow and it secretes from the woman's nipples. It is white and sweet tasting. Of all three libations, this one is far superior, especially if the woman has never lactated.
>
> The lower peak is called the Dark Gate. Its essence is called Moon Flower and it is locked deep within the Palace of Yin. This fluid is very lubricating. However, the Palace of Yin is almost always closed, and it opens only when the woman is aroused to the point that her face flushes red and her voice becomes a moan. That is when this essence pours forth. At this point, the man should withdraw about one inch and continue thrusting, while at the same time kissing and licking her lips and sucking hard on her nipples.
>
> Such are the Libations of the Three Peaks. He who knows Tao sees this clearly and does not get carried away by passion. Even though such a couple may appear to be absorbed in lust, theirs is no earthly lust, and therefore they derive great benefits from it.

Semen Retention

The importance of the man retaining semen during sexual intercourse is emphasized over and over again in Taoist literature. The basic purpose of this method is to increase as much as possible the quantity of life-giving, age-retarding hormones secreted in a man's body during sexual excitement, while at the same time decreasing as much as possible the loss of semen and its related hormones through ejaculation. Called *huan-jing bu-nau* in Chinese (literally 'return the semen to nourish the brain'), the method has often been ridiculed by Western sceptics who take the term too literally and out of context, rather than making a serious effort to understand it. It does not mean that retained semen literally travels up the spine and into the brain. It means that the essential elements of retained semen are reabsorbed within the man's body, especially in the soft tissues of the prostate and the spongy portion of the urethra, whereby they naturally enter the bloodstream and circulate throughout the body, 'nourishing' all tissues and organs, including the brain. It's a well-known medical fact that semen and cerebrospinal fluids consist of the same basic ingredients, so preserving semen nourishes the brain by making more essential nutrients available to it. Women accomplish this naturally because they retain their sexual secretions during intercourse.

The reabsorption and general circulation of retained semen-essence may be greatly enhanced in both men and women by performing some deep abdominal breathing immediately after withdrawing from intercourse. In men, the deep rhythmic massage of the prostate that occurs during deep breathing facilitates absorption of essential elements from retained semen into the bloodstream, and in women deep breathing serves the same purpose for the secretions retained in the vagina. In both men and women, post-coital deep breathing helps re-establish equilibrium after the intense excitement of sex, and, owing to the heightened sensitivity of the body's energy systems, it greatly enhances the balance and distribution of *chee*. For novice males, this practice also helps relieve the 'full feeling' sometimes felt in the scrotum after voluntary retention of semen.

Tao is a Two-Way Street

As is clear from the foregoing material, most Taoist advice on sex is addressed to men, who need it most. Yang is by nature weaker and more vulnerable to depletion than Yin, and therefore it needs to be carefully nurtured, especially during sexual intercourse. Nevertheless, the Tao is a two-way street, and Chinese history offers us several colorful examples of aggressive women who applied the Tao the other way, 'using Yang to nourish Yin'.

A prime example is the Taoist legend of the Queen Mother of the Western Paradise. Though her story is apocryphal, like most legends it clearly reflects the thought that created it. Chung Ho-tze, a sixth century AD adept whose work appears in *Secrets of the Jade Bedroom*, introduces her as follows:

> Every time she had intercourse with a man, he would immediately fall ill, while she remained young and beautiful, her face so smooth and lustrous that she had no need for rouge or powder.
>
> The Queen Mother had no husband, but she was fond of making love with young virgin boys.

It is said that after she had successfully drained 1,000 virgin boys of their Yang essence and energy, she attained immortality and rose to Heaven, much as the Yellow Emperor did at the age of 111 after a lifetime of disciplined sexual relations with his harem of 1,200 young women. In applying the Tao like this, a woman must make absolutely certain that her partners are healthy, vigorous young men in their sexual prime and that they ejaculate inside her every time.

Then there was the case of the Chinese emperor who was so well versed in Taoist bedroom arts that he insisted all of his concubines be selected from a certain district in Fukien Province renowned for its passionate women. To his chagrin, he soon discovered that even he, the Son of Heaven, was incapable of satisfying all of them. Before long they became morose and listless from a surfeit of Yin and deficiency of Yang. The emperor consulted his Taoist physicians, and they frankly informed him that the best medicine for his lusty entourage of ladies would be a platoon of palace guards. An enlightened and generous man, as well as a trained Taoist, the emperor agreed and promptly dispatched the recommended prescription to the women's quarters. Several days later he paid them a visit, and to his great delight found his ladies radiant and happy, brimming with vitality and good humor. Then he noticed several men slouched unconscious on couches nearby, so utterly exhausted that they looked dead. Sternly he demanded to know who they were and what they were doing in his private seraglio. Replied one of his consorts, 'Oh Dragon Lord, these are the empty bottles from the medicine you prescribed!'

The most famous – and notorious – 'Dragon Lady' in Chinese history was the Empress Wu Tze-tien (AD 624–705). She began her career as a pretty but anonymous chambermaid whose duty it was to stand beside the emperor holding a bowl of freshly perfumed water in which to rinse his fingers after relieving the imperial bladder. On one such occasion, the Son of Heaven commanded her to raise her head, liked what he saw, and without further formalities immediately 'introduced the Ambassador' at her Jade Gate right there on the couch beside the toilet. She soon became his favorite consort, and quickly rose through the ranks of palace ladies.

However, as the emperor aged, his vitality flagged and he soon proved incapable of satisfying her lusty appetites, so she secretly – and wisely, it turned out – seduced the crown prince and became *his* favorite as well. According to the custom at that time, whenever an emperor died, all of his consorts were required to shave their heads and enter Buddhist convents as nuns, a fate that did not appeal to Wu Tze-tien. Therefore, she enticed the crown prince with her charms so exquisitely that, when he in turn ascended the throne and she entered the convent, he thought of her day and night and finally flew in the face of tradition by recalling her from the nunnery to resume her place at his side.

Before long, in time-honored fashion, she connived to have the emperor's two senior wives tortured and killed on trumped-up charges, and she herself became his empress. A few years later, as the emperor lay dying (some historians say owing to sexual exhaustion), she again plotted to have all heirs to the throne summarily killed, including her own adolescent son. The emperor died, and she became the first woman in Chinese history to sit as ruler of 'All under Heaven' on the Dragon Throne.

One of her first official acts as empress was to appoint an Imperial Sex Selector, a woman whose duty it was to 'test' various studs for suitability as consorts for the sexually voracious empress. She began by testing 3,000 men of the Palace Guard, but after only a month of duty, the Selector complained, 'My parts are so tender that I can no longer sit, my mouth is so sore that I can no longer eat, and my body is so painful that I can no longer sleep.' Sympathetic to her pleas, the empress instead appointed one of her best generals to comb the empire for virile young men for her couch, a duty that shamed the general to the marrow. But he knew her temper and dutifully set out on his mission. After many fruitless months, he finally found the right man, whose name was Hsueh Huai-yi, lolling about in a brothel, where he apparently enjoyed great renown for the size and power of his Yang Weapon.

Hsueh Huai-yi was a peddlar of aphrodisiacs and other drugs and by all accounts he was very 'well hung'. The Empress Wu was not disappointed: she consorted with him day and night, sometimes within view of eunuchs and courtiers. By the time she found Hsueh, she was already 45 years old but still 'ravenous as a tiger'. Once, after a particularly satisfying bout, she appeared before her court in full regalia, grabbed hold of Hsueh's mammoth implement and pulled it out for all to see, as she declared, 'This thing that I hold here in my hand gives me greater pleasure than my entire empire!'

However, her pleasure was cut short, for so voracious was her appetite for sex that Hsueh Huai-yi died only two years after entering into her 'service'. Once a strong and virile man, he was completely drained of his vital essence and energy in a manner that serves posterity as a perfect example of what the Tao warns against.

As for the empress, she was just beginning to hit full sexual stride. When Hsueh died, she immediately retired to a mountain palace to mourn him – accompanied by a retinue of 400 swarthy young men and 30 Taoist alchemists, who concocted for her a special elixir composed of tiger's blood and fresh semen milked from her consorts. This elixir worked so well for her that she continued using it until the end of her life at the age of 81.

Empress Wu remained sexually active until her 80th year, long after menopause and long after the romantic novelty of sex had worn off, because she cultivated her essence and energy in the prescribed Taoist manner. She followed Taoist dietary rules, took daily infusions of herbal aphrodisiacs, and practiced the Tao of Yin and Yang throughout her long life. And despite her excesses, she was by all accounts an intelligent and highly capable ruler, maintaining order and advancing imperial rule where her male predecessors had failed. In her rapid rise to power, she cleverly utilized Yin's superiority over Yang and applied Lao Tze's principle of 'getting underneath' in order to get on top. Both as ruler and lover she believed that 'all's fair in love and war', and she was therefore victorious on both fronts.

Lest contemporary readers unfamiliar with Chinese history discount the Empress Wu's story as an eccentric fable (which it is not), let's bring this point into modern focus with a current example from the West. Here is what a 75-year-old American woman has to say about sex in old age, as reported in the *Redbook Report on Female Sexuality*, published in 1975:

> I had no special sexual enjoyment until after menopause. My former husband was as virile at 77 as when we were married 30 years before. My present husband is a wonderful lover. That is the trouble with the young ones, they have not learned the art of lovemaking, which is really the best part of marriage. At 75 we are enjoying a sexual experience that young people of my generation missed out on. People seem to have the mistaken idea that one should cease to have sex because they are in their 60s or older. This is a fallacy.

As long as she keeps her health intact, sex is enjoyable as well as beneficial for a woman for as long as she lives, just as it is for a man. And the longer she remains sexually active, the better are her chances of keeping her health intact and living a long, active life. That is the Tao in a nutshell. Truly, the Tao works all ways and always – man and woman, past and present, East and West.

The Harmony of Yin and Yang

In addition to its medical benefits for both genders, Taoist sexual yoga helps establish harmony between man and woman, enabling them to 'make love, not war'. Nothing is more disruptive to harmonious relations

281

between husband and wife, boyfriend and girlfriend, than the incapacity to provide mutually satisfactory sexual relations.

In a manuscript called *Family Instructions*, written by a wealthy Chinese householder around AD 1550, the importance of the Tao of Yin and Yang in maintaining household harmony is illustrated by an amusing anecdote:

> To the east of our street lives a young and virile man of impressive demeanor. Yet his women quarrel from morning till midnight and pay him no heed. To the west of our street lives an old greybeard who walks with a stoop. Yet his women do their very best to please and serve him obediently. How can this be explained? The answer is that the old man knows the subtle secrets and arts of the bedroom, while the young man is ignorant of them.

Taoists believe that there is far more to sex than the 'wham, bam, thank you M'am' attitude that still prevails today among a remarkably broad segment of the general male population, both East and West. A genuine Taoist tries his best to thoroughly satisfy his sexual partner each and every time, even with prostitutes, who, thanks to the countless ejaculations of their more conventional clients, are well regarded by Taoists as extraordinarily potent sources of vital essence and energy. There are stories in China about Taoist recluses who came down from their misty mountain hermitages once or twice a year to sell the rare medicinal herbs they'd gathered at market-towns, only to take their earnings to the nearest brothel and hire out the entire household of women for the night. One by one they would work their way from girl to girl, continuing tirelessly all night until they had drawn an orgasm or two from each and every one, without ever spilling a single drop of semen themselves.

Taoists advocate living in complete harmony with the great patterns of nature, and they venerate womanhood precisely because women are by nature far closer to the primordial powers of the cosmos than men. There is no place for male chauvinism, practical or philosophical, in Taoist tradition. A man who clearly understands the nature of a woman's sexual superiority has already taken the first step towards utilizing that superior power. All he needs to do now is to practice the proper skills. But a man who denies nature and defies Tao will wilt and perish long before his time, no matter how chauvinistically he preens and prances.

In addition to health and longevity, a thread of spiritual ecstasy also runs through most Taoist sexual literature, an association between sex and the sublime made possible by China's refreshingly frank and pagan approach to sexual relations. In *Prayer Mat of the Flesh*, there appears a quatrain that equates intercourse and prayer and provides the novel's title:

> So toss aside the coarse straw mat
> Of self-denial in this world,
> And for your prayer mat take flesh
> As the place for your devotions.

From the moment of birth, an invisible umbilical cord connects a man to the mysterious place of his creation, and throughout his life he continues to draw health and vitality from that connection, a point echoed in this anonymous poem from the Ming Dynasty:

> We enter this world through the portals
> Of the Jade Gate,
> And once born, we seek forever
> To return.
> This eternal truth
> Holds a message:
> That a man's joy and vigor
> Come from the same place
> As his creation.

Significantly, mystics East and West often describe their spiritual experiences in strikingly sexual terms, while ordinary laymen sometimes describe particularly ecstatic intercourse as a spiritually sublime event. The renowned Catholic mystic St Theresa, for example, said that her spiritual trances felt like an angel plunging a fire-tipped golden dart into her heart. Perhaps this is the origin of the Western association of love with the angel 'Cupid' and his golden heart-darts. Wrote St Theresa: 'There occurs between the soul and God such a sweet love transaction that it is impossible for me to describe what happens,' but the pleasure of this experience 'penetrates to the very marrow of the bone'. If mystics experience spiritual ecstasy in sexual terms, then it stands to reason that lovers who learn how to provide complete and mutual sexual ecstasy may also gain intimations of divine experience.

The Tao Comes Westward

The great Dutch sinologist R. H. van Gulik concludes his pioneering work *Sexual Life in Ancient China* with the following observations:

> A historical survey of Chinese sexual relations, the mainspring
> of life, makes me incline to the belief that it was primarily the

careful balancing of the male and female elements – studied in China as far back as the beginning of our era – that caused the permanence of Chinese race and culture. For it would seem that it was this balance that engendered the intense vital power that, from remote antiquity to the very present, has ever sustained and renewed the Chinese race.

Looking back upon the broad sweep of Chinese history and social development, one cannot help but notice the salient themes of 'health', 'sex', and 'longevity' cropping up time and again through the ages. No other civilization on earth has even come close to the sort of 'national longevity' enjoyed by China for almost 5,000 years, and, not coincidentally, no other civilization has paid such close attention to details of food and sex. Free from the severe sexual pathology and highly resistant to many of the chronic debilitating diseases that plague and sometimes destroy other civilizations, it seems clear that the Chinese possess some valuable secrets about health, sex and longevity from which the rest of the world stands to benefit.

Ironically, the current communist regime in China has all but destroyed knowledge of Tao there, and this could well explain, at least in part, the abysmal stagnation of mainland Chinese society since 1949. Even communist cadres openly admit that 'there's something wrong', that the Chinese people on the mainland lack the traditional drive of their cousins in Taiwan, Hong Kong and Singapore. Read any newspaper, and you'll see reports of troublesome social phenomena in mainland China that very rarely occurred prior to 1949 – problems such as rape, impotence, frigidity, sexual ignorance, marital violence and other manifestations of discord between Yin and Yang.

The highly practical, no-nonsense Taoist Pillow Books, such as the *Classic of the Plain Girl*, which used to be part of every newlywed couple's bedroom, have today been replaced in China by a single, officially sanctioned brochure, blandly entitled 'Information on Sex'. Most recently reprinted in 1980, it contains gems of 'information' such as the following:

- People should not commence intercourse until the age of 25.
- Men should wear loose underpants rather than tight briefs to avoid 'heating the genitals', and this is a good way to suppress sexual drive.
- After marriage, couples may indulge in intercourse once or twice a week for the first few months. Later, as familiarity and age increase, sexual desire declines and one should have intercourse no more than two or three times per month.'

- The best remedy for strong sexual desire is 'abstinence and correct political thinking'.

The Yellow Emperor and his retinue of sage Taoist advisors would no doubt shake their heads in sadness and bewilderment to see their descendants, after 5,000 years of harmony with nature, wandering so far from the Way.

Fortunately, like so many other ancient Oriental ways, the Tao of Yin and Yang seems to be slowly but surely seeping into the Western world, just as modern science and technology from the West are gradually transforming the East. During the mid-1950s, for example, Kinsey's surveys of American sexuality revealed that over 75 per cent of all American men ejaculated within 2 minutes of penetration during intercourse. That's hardly long enough for a woman even to notice a man's presence down there. But in 1975, the *Redbook Report on Female Sexuality*, in which American women candidly discussed their sex lives, indicated that up to 75 per cent of married women in America 'almost always reached orgasm during intercourse' and that most of them require 6–10 minutes of vigorous action to do so. This is a clear sign that American men are beginning to realize the importance of prolonging intercourse, and the reason for this progress is the growing sexual candor of American women. If American men were now to make the extra mental and physical effort required to learn and practice Taoist sexual disciplines, they could increase the average time for intercourse up to 15, 20 or even 30 minutes and provide their partners with one or more orgasms each and every time, much to the benefit of both parties.

As another recent survey of American sexual habits, conducted by Morton Hunt, concludes:

> Prolonging the act is no longer an act of altruism, but something done for the sake of both partners. Nowadays the goal is as much to maximize the enjoyment of the whole act as to reach its peak moment.

This is good news indeed for Western society, for social harmony as a whole begins in the bedroom. As Freud and Jung argued, most forms of crime and other anti-social behavior can be traced back to some form of sexual dysfunction or frustration. Those who learn and practice Tao in the bedroom will thus be making concrete and lasting contributions to the harmony of Yin and Yang on a grand scale, promoting social order and world peace, even as they promote their own health and happiness.

Essence and Energy

One cannot manage the myriad matters
Of Heaven and Earth,
Unless one stores up energy.
Storing energy means absorbing essence,
And absorbing essence doubles one's power.
Doubling one's power, one acquires a strength
That nothing can overcome.

[*Tao Teh Ching*]

Human life begins when a single sperm cell out of the millions contained in a shot of semen penetrates and fertilizes the single ovum floating in female semen-essence during intercourse. Again, the innate superiority of Yin over Yang is clearly reflected here, for it takes millions of sperm cells to fertilize just one egg. That single egg is essential for conception, but over 99.99% of the sperm cells are entirely expendable. In a sort of microcosm of the 'law of the jungle', only the fittest sperm cell wins the race to fertilize the egg, while all the others live and die in vain.

The meeting of sperm and ovum sparks the energy of life and martials it into action by establishing the polarity of Yin and Yang energies within the newly fertilized cell, now called a 'zygote'. This polarity of energy within the zygote is what triggers cellular division.

The fertilized cell divides to form two, and the two divide to form four identical cells. At this point, a crucial parting of the ways occurs among the four fundamental cells of the zygote. Three branch off and start multiplying very rapidly to form specific tissues. One gives birth to the ectoderm, which forms the body's skin and nervous system. Another develops the mesoderm, which includes the skeleton, muscles and circulatory system. The third cell engenders formation of the endoderm, including all the vital organs and glands.

But what about the fourth cell? Basically, it goes into 'hibernation', reproducing itself very slowly and identically. This single cell stores the entire genetic code of the organism for transferral to future generations of the species. When the body's limbs and organs are all fully formed and mature, the descendants of this fourth cell wake up and activate the process of puberty, forming the secondary sexual characteristics of male and female. While the trillions of descendants of the first three cells of the zygote are inevitably destined for annihilation in death – 'ashes to ashes, dust to dust' – a few descendants of the fourth cell – the sexual cell – escape ultimate extinction by contributing sperm or ovum to a new zygote during sexual intercourse. In a very real sense, therefore, this fourth cell achieves a sort of immortality by perpetually passing itself from generation to generation through sexual reproduction. This is one reason that in Oriental philosophies the sex cells are regarded as sacred. In Western civilization, the sacred nature of sex was once similarly acknowledged, as evidenced by the name given to the region of the body that governs sexual reproduction: the sacrum.

Throughout our adult lives, our sexual organs and hormones exert a profound and decisive influence on thought and behavior. They literally 'drive' men and women into each other's arms in order to insure propagation of the species, and this drive is so powerful and compelling that it completely overrides the instinct for safety and personal survival. When 'in love', both men and women will defy death and disregard social conventions in order to be together and 'make love'. 'Love', of course, is a Western euphemism for 'lust', which, despite its negative connotations in the West, is regarded as a natural sign of health and vitality in the East.

Hormones and Health

Chinese physicians pinpoint what they call the 'kidney glands' (*shen-hsien*) as the key regulators of sexual potency, especially in men. These glands, which straddle the tops of both kidneys like hats, are called the 'suprarenal glands' in Western parlance.

The suprarenals, also known as the adrenal cortex, produce a variety of hormones of vital importance to various metabolic processes and biological functions. In both male and female organisms, adrenal hormones include small but physiologically significant amounts of androgens (male hormones) and relatively minute quantities of estrogens (female hormones). These sex hormones, or Yin and Yang 'essences', regulate the secretions of all other sex glands such as the ovaries, testes and prostate, and also influence secretions from the pituitary, pineal and thyroid glands. It is the *balance*, not the *quantity*, of these microscopic elements of Yin and Yang essence that counts. Insufficient secretion of androgens in the male, for example, results in the loss of sexual drive and potency. Excessive androgen secretion in the female can cause such masculizing effects as beard growth and breast shrinkage. Thus, a primary goal of Taoist sexual regimens is the enhancement of male and female hormone secretions in optimum balance.

Belatedly, Western science has also established intimate links between sexual stimulation and hormone production, and between hormone production and health. In 1974, for example, the Max Planck Institute in Munich, West Germany, conducted tests on the physiological effects of mildly erotic films on healthy males aged 21–34. After half an hour of viewing, 75 per cent of the subjects showed marked increases in testosterone levels in their blood, thereby establishing a clear connection between sexual excitement and hormone secretions. Subsequent research revealed that men with high testosterone levels, high sperm count and dense, viscous semen were completely immune to many common communicable diseases and were highly resistant to others, while those with low testosterone and sperm count and thin, watery semen had only partial immunity to disease in general and were highly vulnerable to many specific diseases. It is also well known to Western medical science that women have always enjoyed higher immunity and resistance to disease, recover more quickly from illness, and live longer lives than men.

According to the Taoist view, the ravages of aging are caused by the progressive depletion of hormone production and the dissipation of vital energy. Since essence is the 'root' of the Taoist Trinity, with energy as the 'stem' and spirit as the 'blossom', the entire plant may be nourished simply by cultivating the roots, which consist of blood, bile, enzymes, hormones and other forms of 'essence'. Of all these elements of essence, hormones exert by far the most profound and powerful physiological influences, even in the most minute quantities, and, of all Taoist regimens, disciplined sexual intercourse provides the most direct stimulation to vital hormone production and endocrine balance. While sexual excitement remains one of the most effective means of stimulating vital hormone production in both men and women, women have the additional mechanisms of menstruation and pregnancy to promote production of sexual hormones, even in the absence of sexual intercourse. Men, on the other hand, have no such alternative mechanism, and for them sexual intercourse remains the best way to stimulate hormone production. As a person gets older, it stands to reason that sexual intercourse grows ever more important as a form of preventive therapy against disease and aging. When enhanced secretions from the male 'kidney-glands' are preserved through properly disciplined intercourse without ejaculation, they enter the bloodstream, travel throughout the body, and prevent hair loss, skin wrinkling, poor muscle tone, arthritis, rheumatism, impotence and other disasters associated with aging. For Taoists, the issue of sexual intercourse in old age is not a moral or social one – it's a matter of life and health.

To keep things in perspective, let's again verify this fundamental Taoist viewpoint with some solid medical evidence from Western science. A recent study conducted in America revealed that frequent sexual intercourse considerably relieves the chronic pain of rheumatism in elderly couples by stimulating secretion of cortisone in the adrenal cortex.

According to the Taoist view, the adrenal cortex is the gland most directly influenced by sexual excitement.

On the other hand, according to Western science, excessive coitus inhibits adrenal functions in the male. Since 'coitus' includes ejaculation in Western medical and sexual terminology, we see that the Taoist view that excessive ejaculation ruins the 'kidney-glands' in men is essentially correct.

Absorbing Essence and Storing Energy

In both men and women, sexual secretions contain many pure, potent, biochemically active substances: hormones, enzymes, proteins, vitamins and other elements. When female secretions are released into the warm, moist environment of the vagina during intercourse, they come into direct contact with the sensitive, paper-thin skin of the man's blood-engorged penis. Body heat opens wide the pores of this stretched skin, and the rhythmic rubbing of vagina and penis causes biochemically significant amounts of female 'essence' to be absorbed by the male. In fact, less than a pinhead quantity of an essential hormone suffices to exert profound physiological effects upon the entire endocrine system once it enters the bloodstream. In the sexually excited male, blood courses powerfully through the penis and picks up whatever hormones are absorbed in the vagina by friction and osmosis. Similarly, the spongy tissues of a woman's vagina absorb active elements from her own secretions and from male semen after a man ejaculates inside.

Despite its obvious logic, most Western physicians still deny that such mutual exchange of vital hormones takes place during sexual intercourse, even though they fully acknowledge that 'germs' can be exchanged in this manner. If syphilis, herpes and AIDS can be 'picked up' through contact of sexual organs in diseased people, then why can't hormones and enzymes be exchanged in the same way in healthy people?

Look at it this way. If you crush several cloves of garlic and place them on your thigh or abdomen or anywhere else on the body, cover them with a warm, damp cloth and rub them against the skin, then your breath will soon smell of garlic! Garlic oil, which like hormones is a highly concentrated substance, enters the skin in microscopic quantities and is absorbed by the bloodstream, which carries it to every part of the body, including the lungs. If a tiny drop of garlic 'essence' can permeate the skin, enter the bloodstream and cause 'garlic breath' far from the point of entry, then a drop of sexual essence from male or female semen should be able to do the same thing through the even thinner, moister, warmer surfaces of the vagina and penis, especially if one uses Taoist techniques to prolong direct contact.

For women, frequent intercourse with orgasm is the most efficient method of cultivating sexual essence and energy. For men, frequent intercourse with infrequent ejaculation is the key technique for cultivating sexual essence and energy. Furthermore, retaining semen during intercourse enables a man not only to preserve and reabsorb his own essence, it also enables him to prolong the act sufficiently for his partner to reach full orgasm, thereby releasing her most potent secretions for his benefit. In effect, he 'kills two birds with one stone', preserving his own essence while releasing and absorbing hers.

As noted earlier, a man's sexual responses are largely limited to his penis (the Four Attainments), whereas a woman's occur throughout her body (Five Signs, Ten Indications). The same goes for sexual secretions. A man's essence comes mainly from his sexual organ, but a woman emits essence from all 'Three Peaks': tongue, nipples and vagina. Men who practice Tao benefit from all three 'libations'.

In *Secrets of the Jade Bedroom*, Peng-Tze points out the medicinal benefits of the 'upper libation', but he states clearly that only the saliva secreted 'during intercourse' contains the magic elixir: 'During intercourse, if a man takes in a lot of the woman's saliva, it will purify his stomach like medicinal broth.'

As for the potent therapeutic value of the 'middle libation' secreted from a woman's nipples, Western medical science has recently uncovered evidence that tends to confirm the traditional Taoist view. It has been firmly established that mother's milk contains powerful immunity factors secreted from certain glands in the breasts which protect nursing infants from a wide range of dangerous diseases. It is logical to assume, therefore, that the ducts that produce these immunity factors in a woman's breasts may be stimulated to secrete those factors by a combination of intense sexual excitement and strong, prolonged sucking of the nipples during intercourse, and that these secretions form the 'Great Libation of the Middle Peak'.

Regarding the lower libation, it should be noted that Taoists have always regarded cunnilingus as an excellent way to absorb this elixir, although they advise against fellatio ('blowing the flute') owing to the risk of uncontrolled ejaculation.

That covers cultivation of sexual essence through intercourse. Now let's take a look at the energy situation. According to Tao, a brief burst of explosive energy occurs when a man or woman reaches orgasm. Western science has already established that, at the point of sexual orgasm, human brain wave patterns alter radically, literally putting the person into an 'altered state of consciousness'. Profound physiological and electrical changes occur throughout the system during orgasm, and a burst of energy is indeed emitted. Partners may absorb one another's burst of sexual energy at the moment of orgasm by following three basic guidelines:

- Keep your head nuzzled under your partner's ear when he or she ejaculates in order to avoid inhaling the 'muddy breath' exhaled at that moment. Owing to the intense 'fire' that occurs in the lower abdomen during orgasm, this burst of breath is regarded as a sort of waste product.
- Hug your partner very tightly and maintain maximum surface contact between your skins. At orgasm, the entire body radiates energy from its surface contact.
- Press and rub the pubic regions closely together. The biggest burst of sexual energy during orgasm naturally occurs in the region of the 'Sea of Energy' (*chee-hai*), located below the navel.

Now let's take a look at the various possibilities for exchanging essence and energy between Yin and Yang during intercourse. If the man ejaculates before the woman reaches orgasm, she gains the benefits of both his semen-essence and his energy, while he loses both and gains neither of hers. If the couple ejaculates at the same moment, the woman again gains the man's essence and energy, but the man gains only her burst of energy, because he loses his erection before it has had a chance to absorb the essential secretions of her orgasm. If the man controls himself long enough for the woman to reach orgasm then suppresses his own ejaculation, he absorbs both his own and her essence as well as her energy, while she still derives the benefits of reabsorbing a measure of her own sexual secretions. The fourth and final alternative is for the man to permit himself an ejaculation (when his emission schedule calls for it) after his partner has reached orgasm, but only after he has spent some time 'dragging the Yin essence in through the Yang peak'. In this case, both partners absorb each other's sexual essence and energy in a perfectly balanced coition.

For a man who has thoroughly mastered the techniques of ejaculation control, there are additional steps he may take to facilitate absorption of female secretions and to further stimulate reabsorption of his own semen-essence. The first method is to 'thrust inward fiercely but draw outward slowly, thereby dragging the Yin essence in through the skin of the Yang peak'. Swelling and contracting the penis deep inside the vagina by deliberately flexing the muscles of the penile shaft is another highly recommended technique for promoting absorption of Yin essence during intercourse. After the woman has experienced one or more orgasms and is thoroughly satisfied, the man should start thrusting again deeply and rhythmically. When pressure to ejaculate mounts, he should stop and 'return the semen' to the prostate, using the methods introduced in the next chapter. When his semen is back under control and his heart once again calm, he may repeat this process again, three to five times. The prolonged friction between Jade Gate and Jade Stem facilitates absorption of Yin essence, while the excitement of repeatedly approaching the brink of ejaculation greatly increases the man's own internal sexual secretions. Such serial retentions also redirect the man's unexploded sexual energy inward and upward. This can often be felt coursing up along the spine as 'goose bumps', or as heat waves at various points in the body.

Men should not attempt this method of 'pumping up' extra essence and energy by repeatedly 'playing with the fire' of ejaculation until they have first mastered semen retention and established their own ideal ejaculation frequencies. Otherwise, they risk the loss of even more essence and energy than normal owing to enhanced secretions of seminal fluids. Note also that this method should not be employed when a man is due for an emission because it primes the prostate with extra semen and thus increases the loss due to ejaculation. It should be done only when semen is to be retained. The old adage 'practice makes perfect' applies to this and all the other methods used in the Tao of Yin and Yang, and these practices must be mastered step by step.

To borrow another adage, 'to the victor go the spoils'. A sexually active man who is unwilling to hone his sexual skills and correctly adjust his attitudes in preparation for the 'flowery battlefield' of sexual intercourse will, sooner than later, deplete his sexual potency, dissipate his vital energy, lose his immunity and foreshorten his life. Such men become as expendable to the species – and as useless to women – as drones driven from the beehive.

CHAPTER 7:

—————————— ◐ ——————————

Ejaculation Control

A man may attain health and longevity if he practices an ejaculation frequency of twice monthly, or 24 times in a year. If at the same time he pays careful attention to proper diet and exercise, he will live a long and healthy life.

[Sun Ssu-mo]

As Dr Sun points out, diet, exercise and sexual discipline form the three pillars of Taoist health and longevity regimens. The principles of Tao apply equally to men and women. In both men and women, semen-essence is the fuel that drives sexuality. It is the source not only of physical capacity for sex but also of sexual interest and emotional affection for the opposite gender. However, since women do not 'leak' when they ejaculate, orgasm does not rob them of sexual drive and interest after the 'first act'. Therefore, the practices required to achieve the harmony of Yin and Yang must be cultivated primarily by men. This chapter is thus addressed mainly to men, although the information contained herein should also be studied and understood by women who consort with Taoist men or who wish to convert their men into Taoists.

Western medicine claims that men naturally replenish their semen supply soon after ejaculation and that the male's capacity for producing semen is virtually limitless. This is a highly misleading generalization. Simply compare ejaculation with blood donation, and you'll see the fallacy. After donating a pint of blood, you feel weak and tired for a day or two, until the lost pint is replenished. Blood clinics advise donors not to give blood more than a few times each year in order to avoid chronic fatigue, low resistance and excessive strain on the circulatory system.

According to Chinese physicians, the same point applies to semen, except that the loss of semen is even harder to replace than blood. The body must invest a lot of essence and energy to fully replenish semen supplies and re-establish proper hormone balance after a man ejaculates.

When ejaculation frequency exceeds the capacity of the body to *fully* replenish semen, men experience chronic fatigue, low resistance, irritability and other symptoms of essence and energy deficiency. They also lose all sexual interest in their partners, who may well be ready for more action. True, teenaged boys and young men in their early 20s replenish semen faster than they could possibly expend it, but the notion that this capacity continues indefinitely into adulthood is patently false. It is women, not men, whose sexual potency is 'inexhaustible'. Celibacy, however, is not the answer either, for that deprives men of the therapeutic benefits of sexual stimulation. The answer is ejaculation control. Frequent intercourse with infrequent ejaculation maintains a man's *interest* in the act as well as his capacity to continue indefinitely until his partner is fully satisfied.

Men who ejaculate once or more on a daily basis may eventually 'lose their minds', since 20 per cent of male semen is composed of cerebrospinal fluid. Frequent ejaculation thus causes a chronic drain of the vital fluids that the brain and spine require to function properly. The resulting deficiency of cerebrospinal fluid can cause such increasingly common conditions as premature senility, inability to concentrate, chronic depression, loss of sexual drive and a host of other related symptoms.

Furthermore, recent medical evidence indicates that with each and every ejaculation men suffer a significant loss of zinc, a rare but vital trace element. Frequent ejaculation thus results in a chronic, critical deficiency of zinc, symptoms of which include loss of memory, mental confusion, paranoia and hypersensitivity to sunlight. These facts seem to verify the 'old wives tale' that excessive male masturbation addles the mind, weakens the spine and leads to blindness.

Regulating Ejaculation Frequency

All schools of Taoism agree that retention of semen and proper regulation of its emission are indispensable skills for male adepts of the Way. In their writings, the adepts of ancient China each left us their own personal guidelines for determining emission frequency. By combining their various suggestions with your own individual requirements and practical experience, you may readily determine an emission schedule that suits your personal needs.

Let's start with some plain talk from our old friend and sexual mentor, the Plain Girl. Confused by the concepts of 'sparing vital essence' and 'regulating leakage', the Yellow Emperor addressed his doubts to the Plain Girl and got this reply:

Some men are strong, some are weak, some men are old and others are in their prime. Each should live according to his own vitality and not try to force the joys of sex. Forcing joy is harmful. Thus, a robust male of 20 may ejaculate twice daily, but an emaciated one should do so no more than once daily.

A 30-year-old male may ejaculate once a day, but only once every two days if he's an inferior specimen. A flourishing man of 40 may emit semen once every three days, but if he's weak he may do so only once every four days.

A robust man of 50 may ejaculate once every five days, but only once every ten days if he is weak. A 60-year-old man in good health may emit once every ten days, or once every 20 days if his health is poor.

At 70, a robust man emit once a month, but a weak one should no longer emit semen at all.

The Tang Dynasty physician Lee Tung-hsüan, in *Mysterious Master of the Cave*, used frequency of intercourse rather than day-intervals as his recommended measure for regulating emission:

When having sexual intercourse with women, a man should emit semen only two or three times in ten.

Master Liu Ching, a Han Dynasty adept credited in dynastic archives with achieving a lifespan of over 300 years, preferred to regulate his emissions according to the cosmic cycles of seasonal change:

In spring, a man may permit himself to ejaculate once every three days, but in summer and autumn he should limit his ejaculations to twice a month. During the cold of winter, a man should preserve his semen and avoid ejaculation altogether. The Way of Heaven is to accumulate Yang essence in winter. A man who follows this guideline will live a long and healthy life. One ejaculation in cold winter is one hundred times more harmful than an ejaculation in the spring.

The most practical advice of all on the subject of ejaculation control comes from the centenarian physician Sun Ssu-mo, the Tang Dynasty adept who outlived three emperors by practicing what he preached. His general yardstick, quoted at the head of this chapter, was twice a month, or 24 times per year. His own personal regimen, however, was only one emission per 100 copulations. Dr Sun lived to the age of 101.

According to Sun Ssu-mo a man should 'become acquainted' with Tao by the age of 30 and 'acquire a thorough working knowledge' of it by 40:

Before the age of 40, most men are still full of vigorous passion. But as soon as they reach their 40th birthday, they suddenly notice their potency declining. Just at that very point of declining potency the myriad ailments will descend upon him like a swarm of bees. If this situation continues unchecked, he will soon find himself beyond cure.

Dr Sun repeatedly warned his male patients of the dangers involved in excessive ejaculation. He compared the situation to that of a sputtering oil-lamp: just before the fuel is spent and the lamp is about to extinguish, the flame suddenly flares up brightly, then dies:

Each and every time a man restrains himself and retains his semen it is like adding new oil to a lamp that is about to extinguish. But if a man fails to control himself and ejaculates every time he lies down with a woman, it is like removing oil from a lamp that is already nearly burnt out.

As Sun Ssu-mo sums up so well, 'If a man squanders his semen, he will soon die. For a man, this is the most important point to remember about sex.'

On the other hand, like the Plain Girl, Dr Sun also advises against complete abstinence:

If a man has no intercourse with woman, his mind will grow restless and he will yearn for female company . . . Forcibly suppressing the natural urge to emit semen at certain intervals is not only difficult for a man but will actually make it easier to lose semen. He will lose it during sleep through nocturnal emissions [i.e. 'wet dreams'] . . . One emission of semen in this manner is equivalent to the loss suffered by one hundred emissions during normal sexual intercourse.

Sun Ssu-mo's advice to men on regulating ejaculation frequency can be summarized as follows:

- By the age of 30, a man begins to lose vitality and should stop squandering his semen recklessly. It is time to give up the habit of masturbation and to become acquainted with the Tao of Yin and Yang.
- By the age of 40, a man has reached the critical turning point in his life. If he wishes to prevent the rapid downhill slide into the grave which undisciplined sexual relations cause at this stage in life, he must now start practicing ejaculation control as a habit.

296

- By the age of 50, his ejaculation frequency should be no more than once every 20 days.
- By the age of 60, most men should completely curtail ejaculation (but not intercourse). Exceptionally healthy men with strong libidos, however, may continue emitting semen about once a month, or, better yet, once in every 100 coitions.
- By the age of 70, if a man is still hale and hearty, he may continue using Dr Sun's ideal measure of once in every 100 indefinitely.
- Practicing ejaculation control is just as important for strong, healthy males as it is for the weak and elderly. Those who start this regimen early in life avoid the worst ravages of old age, retard the loss of vital energy and live longer lives than those who wait until middle age to begin.
- For most men, complete abstention from ejaculation is just as harmful as excessive emission. It creates a deep yearning for sex that disrupts the harmony of essence, energy and spirit, and ultimately leads to the even greater loss of sexual essence and energy through the uncontrollable, intense ejaculations caused by 'wet dreams'.

In order to determine your own ideal emission schedule, you must first master the methods of semen retention introduced below, then follow the guidelines already given in a trial-and-error appraisal of your own vitality. An ejaculation should leave a man feeling as light and refreshed as a woman feels after orgasm – not exhausted, empty and uninterested in further sex. Such an ejaculation may be experienced only when semen supply is what the Chinese call 'full' and 'flourishing'. If an ejaculation leaves you tired and depressed, you should increase the interval between emissions.

You may also help minimize the loss of essence and energy due to semen emission by learning to 'come lightly' when you choose to ejaculate. Instead of thrusting to a frenzy just prior to ejaculation, approach the brink slowly and gently and savour the exquisite sensation of release, then deliberately 'squeeze off' the urogenital canal with a deep contraction of the anus and penile shaft *before* the ejaculation is over. This will conserve about 20–30 per cent of your semen while still providing the desired ejaculatory release. Immediately after emission, rhythmically contract the entire urogenital diaphragm for a minute or two by practicing anal sphincter locks. This tightens up the pelvic floor, which becomes loose and flaccid after ejaculation, and thereby prevents post-coital loss of *chee* through the perineum, anus and urogenital canal. This exercise is highly beneficial for women as well, because it prevents loss of *chee* through the vagina and encourages sexual energy to move up the spinal channels to the brain.

Since few men will be induced to adopt such a disciplined and unconventional approach to sexual relations unless thoroughly convinced by personal experience of its necessity and efficacy, here are a few simple experiments any man may perform to establish the truth of Tao in sex. Try engaging in a vigorous bout of intercourse about half an hour before participating in an athletic event or stage performance – once with ejaculation and once without – and compare your resulting performances. You'll be amazed by the difference. Or try intercourse with and without ejaculation late at night and compare the amount of sleep you need and how you feel upon arising the next morning. An even more stark comparison is the difference in vitality felt throughout the day after having sexual intercourse first thing in the morning, with and without ejaculation.

Try experimenting with other factors as well, such as weather, mood and physical condition. You will most certainly notice a profound difference in how you feel after intercourse with and without ejaculation on a freezing cold day in mid-winter, when, as Peng-Tze points out, 'one ejaculation is one hundred times more harmful than one in spring'. Men who sharply reduce their emission frequencies during the winter season without reducing intercourse suffer far less from colds, influenza, chills, the winter 'blues' and other symptoms related to cold weather. And when you're feeling in 'low spirits' to start with, an ejaculation will only drag you deeper into depression, while a prolonged bout without emission of semen is an excellent way to 'pick up your spirits' again. The same goes for physical condition: when a man is ailing, the loss of semen only makes his condition worse by robbing him of his greatest source of resistance just when he needs it most. Disciplined intercourse, on the other hand, is an excellent palliative for many chronic ailments, especially those influenced by hormone levels. Miles Davis and Mohammad Ali came to these conclusions in precisely this manner – by trial and error – and so can you.

Every man must establish his own ideal emission rate as an overall guideline, but he must also consider the unique circumstances of each occasion before deciding whether it is appropriate to ejaculate or not. The calendar may well tell you that it is time to treat yourself to an ejaculation, but if you happen to be drunk at the time, or gorged with food, or ill, then you'd best forgo that brief spasm of pleasure and keep your batteries fully charged. In the Taoist text entitled *Essentials for Nurturing Life*, we find the following warning:

> Ejaculation is strictly forbidden when a man is drunk or gorged
> with food. Such emissions injure a man a hundred times more

than under normal conditions and may cause dizziness and ugly
sores.

Mastering the Methods of 'Contact without Leakage'

As in all Taoist health regimens, ejaculation control involves all Three
Treasures – essence (body), energy (breath) and spirit (mind) – in a
coordinated effort towards a single goal. 'Spirit directs energy, energy
commands essence', states the *Yellow Emperor's Classic*. This means that
the adept may use his mind to control his breath, breath to control blood,
and blood to control semen, because 'when blood stops, semen stops'.
Note how ejaculation is always preceded by a rapid acceleration of the
heart, and you'll realize the importance of keeping your pulse normal
during intercourse.

Since breathing controls heartbeat, the first and foremost exercise for
developing ejaculation control is deep, rhythmic abdominal breathing
performed in the same manner as during breathing exercises. It is not
necessary to apply the abdominal and neck locks with every breath
during intercourse, but the anal lock should be applied frequently. Each
application of the anal lock serves to keep the semen from pouring forth.
The moment you lose track of your breathing, your heart immediately
accelerates, pushing you ever closer to the brink of emission.

Of course, it takes a few years of practice for men to master complete
voluntary control over body, breath and mind during sex. In the meantime, there are a few clever tricks devised by the ancient adepts to assist
fellow Taoists in regaining control over their semen when they feel they
are on the verge of losing it during intercourse. The most important of
these methods are breath retention and 'locking up' the entire sacral
region with strong contractions of the urogenital diaphragm. The Taoist
physician Lee Tung-hsüan discusses these methods in *Mysterious Master
of the Cave*:

> When a man feels on the verge of ejaculation, he should always
> restrain himself, at least until the woman has reached orgasm.
> He should draw the Jade Stem out shallowly and play it between
> the Lute Strings [frenulum of clitoris] and Wheat Buds [labia
> minor] . . . He should close his eyes, concentrate his mind, press
> his tongue against the roof of his mouth, arch his spine, and
> stretch out his neck. He should then open his nostrils wide, close
> his mouth, and take in a very deep breath. If he does this in time,

he will not ejaculate. Instead, the semen will return and ascend naturally by itself. In this manner, a man may completely regulate his ejaculations.

In the section entitled 'Healthy Sex Life' in *Precious Recipies*, Sun Ssu-mo provides us with a few further embellishments of these methods. He suggests opening the eyes wide and gnashing the teeth because these are tried-and-true Taoist methods for drawing vital-energy upwards to the head and away from the sexual organs, especially when combined with deep breathing. In addition to constricting the anal sphincter, he also suggests the method of pressing a vital point called 'Confluence of Yin', which is located midway between the anus and the scrotum. Pressure here tends to suppress ejaculation.

The Han Dynasty adept Wu Hsien considered 'locking the gate' to be the most effective of all methods for controlling ejaculation: 'if you tighten the lower part of your bowels to shut off the flow of energy there, semen will stop moving naturally.' The sort of contraction he suggests begins with the same basic anal lock used in breathing exercises, but it is further extended along the entire length of the perineum all the way to the urogenital tract. This method quite literally 'blocks' the outward flow of semen. Until you master this method, however, you may substitute digital pressure at the 'Confluence of Yin'. As the *Classic of Immortality* states, 'Take the index and middle fingers of the left hand and press them at the point midway between anus and scrotum. If this is done with sufficient pressure and combined with deep, slow breathing and gnashing of the teeth, then the semen will not be lost.'

Taoist techniques of thrusting and withdrawing during intercourse also aim to prolong the act by delaying or preventing ejaculation. In frontal intercourse, for example, the man is advised to make the major point of friction occur between the women's clitoral region and the top side of the base of his penis – not between the glans of the penis and the inner vaginal walls. When thrusting in this manner, the man should move his shaft vertically up and down against the Lute Strings and Wheat Buds rather than thrusting the entire length of it deeply in and out the vagina. This sort of thrust is called a 'shallow thrust' in Taoist parlance, while deep vaginal thrusts are called 'deep thrusts' (see Figure 7.1). Shallow thrusting permits a man to deliver strong, direct stimulation to a woman's most sensitive zone – the clitoris – using the least sensitive section of his penis, while keeping his own most sensitive spot – the tip of the penis – relatively immobile deep inside her. Taoist pillow books make frequent reference to various thrusting patterns such as 'three shallow, one deep', 'six shallow, two deep', and so forth, but the one

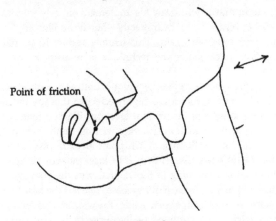

Figure 7.1a **Deep thrust**

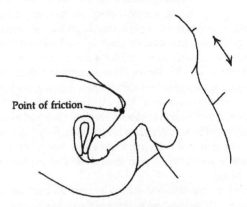

Figure 7.1b **Shallow thrust**

recommended most often by the ancient adepts is 'nine shallow, one deep'. In addition to providing a rhythmic counterpoint to shallow thrusts by giving the woman a sudden change of pace, deep thrusts are very effective in 'pumping' the penis back up to full tumescence whenever a man loses part of his erection in applying techniques of ejaculation control. Deep thrusts also provide direct stimulation to a woman's sensitive 'G-spot'.

If, owing to poor timing or insufficient attention, deep breathing, 'locking the gate', acupressure on the Confluence of Yin and other methods all fail to rein in a man's mounting ejaculatory pressure, his last resort is to temporarily withdraw his implement entirely from the 'flowery battlefield', returning to the fray only when he and his implement are cool, calm and collected again. This usually results in partial loss of erection, which necessitates the technique of re-entry known as 'soft entry'.

'Soft entry' is a most excellent technique, both as a method of re-entry during ejaculation control and as highly effective therapy for men who suffer from impotence or insufficient erection. When a man withdraws entirely to prevent ejaculation, he may wish to apply the anal lock or acupressure to the Confluence of Yin point as extra precautions while waiting for the urge to subside. Even if he loses most of his erection, the natural lubrication remaining in the vagina, plus the cooperation of an understanding partner, make it quite easy to reinsert the Jade Stem inside the Jade Gate. As soon as it's back inside, the warmth and wetness of the vagina plus a deep thrust or two usually suffice to fully recover the 'Four Attainments' of length, swelling, heat and hardness. The Plain Girl assures us that by practicing this method often, the male implement will grow 'as hard as iron and as hot as a torch, enabling a man to overcome all oncomers and to win one hundred victories in one hundred battles'.

In cultivating ejaculation control, a man's mental attitude is just as important as his physical skills. He should realize, for example, that love and sincere intentions do not in themselves make him a good lover and that he must, by his very nature as a male, learn and practice methods of self-control during intercourse. He should shift his attention away from his own sensations and focus instead on his partner's Five Signs and Ten Indications, on her skin and hair, her sounds and scents. And, as Sun Ssu-mo summarizes succinctly, 'A man should think about how the act will benefit his health'.

If a man permits his mind to wander too far from the business at hand during intercourse, or if he indulges too long in the exquisite sensations of a mounting ejaculation, he will soon lose control and the whole show will be over before he even realizes it. In one of her most charming and *apropos* analogies, the Plain Girl illustrates the dangers of male carelessness during intercourse as follows:

> Making love to a woman is like riding a galloping horse with a frayed rein, and as dangerous as walking along the edge of a deep pit full of sharp spikes.

A brief lapse in attention can suddenly send a man careening uncontrollably into the pit of ejaculation, effectively ending the 'ride' for both partners. When 'riding a woman' (*yü-nü*), a man must be as attentive to technique as if he were galloping through the woods on a wild stallion.

Over 2,000 years ago, the Han Dynasty adept Wu Hsien recorded some very succinct and sage advice regarding ejaculation control, addressed specifically to beginners on the Way. We'll conclude this section on mastering the methods of 'contact without leakage' by quoting his guidelines in full:

- The beginner should avoid getting overly excited or too passionate. While it is true that one derives the greatest pleasure when one loves one's partner, when first learning and practicing ejaculation control, one should try to remain indifferent in order to maintain one's composure.
- The beginner should begin with a woman who is not too attractive and whose Jade Gate is not too tight. If she is not extremely beautiful, he will not lose his head, and if she's not to tight, he will not ejaculate quickly owing to excessive excitement.
- The beginner must thrust gently and slowly, then pause to recompose himself before resuming a few moments later. If he feels overly excited, he should stop thrusting immediately and withdraw his Jade Stem so that only one inch remains inside the Jade Gate. After he has calmed down, he may resume thrusting.
- The beginner should first try thrusting sets of three shallow and one deep, then five shallow and one deep, and finally nine shallow and one deep.
- The beginner should learn the method of withdrawing hard and re-entering soft.
- In order to satisfy his partner, the beginner should learn to be kind and gentle so that she may reach orgasm more quickly.
- The beginner must avoid impatience in learning how to control ejaculation.

The last point is perhaps the most important of all for ultimate success. It takes most beginners many months of diligent practice just to master the basic methods of breathing and 'locking the gate', and it takes most men even longer than that to overcome the habitually ingrained attitude that sexual intercourse is incomplete and unsatisfactory without ejaculation. Only through prolonged and patient practice of the methods discussed above will a man finally come to realize the folly of his former ways and the profound truth and power of the one and only Way.

Novices will also be happy to learn that regardless of how strong their urge to ejaculate may be, if they can 'hold on' until the woman has reached orgasm, that urge will quickly diminish, and, if she has two or three orgasms, it will diminish even more. That's because the male's Yang polarity is balanced by absorption of woman's Yin energy at the point of her orgasm. He can also balance his polarity by pouring his semen into her, but then he ends up with a net loss of essence and energy. In balancing his excess Yang polarity ('horniness') by retaining semen and absorbing his partner's burst of Yin energy, he ends up with a net gain and no loss.

Learning How to 'Lock the Gate'

When teaching tennis, tennis pros tell their students that 'it's all in the wrist', but it takes many months of practice before beginners learn to adapt their wrists to the game. The same principle applies to ejaculation control: it's like learning a new sport, and in this case the anatomical focus of activity is the sacral region.

The rhythmic contraction and relaxation of the anal sphincter introduced as a long-life exercise in Chapter 4 can be practiced any time, anywhere, in any position. Be sure to contract both the external and internal sphincters and to hold the contraction for several seconds before relaxing it.

When utilizing the anal lock for ejaculation control, you should apply it strongly as your lungs fill up, hold it tightly while you briefly retain the breath, but *do not* release it during exhalation, as you would in ordinary breathing exercises. Hold it locked tightly through two or three complete breathing cycles, or for as long as necessary to regain composure and control. Only then should you release it, slowly and gently. Remember that this exercise also benefits women by toning up the entire urogenital diaphragm and drawing sexual energy upward.

The muscles that control the anal sphincters may be further contracted to exert control over the prostate, the ureter and the entire penile shaft. When properly applied, you can feel this extended contraction lift the entire pelvic floor upwards as it closes off the urogenital canal.

This enhanced anal, prostate and penile lock, combined with breath retention, is the key that 'locks the gate', a key that every man may forge for himself by daily practice of a single, simple exercise that is as easy to remember and perform as going to the toilet. Here's how it's done: while urinating, a few seconds before the flow of urine stops, sharply lock the anus and contract the penile shaft to 'squeeze off' the ureter and halt the flow, as if you were 'holding it' while looking for a toilet. After a second or two, relax the contraction, let the flow of urine resume, then immediately 'squeeze it off'' again. Each squeeze will cause a strong spurt of residual urine as the ureter is contracted. Repeat this three to five times, or until no more urine spurts out when you squeeze, then hold the last contraction for 5–10 seconds while you tuck yourself back in and zip up.

You can further enhance the effects of this exercise by standing up on your toes while doing it.

If a man performs this exercise habitually every time he urinates, he will automatically be practicing the correct method of 'locking the gate' during intercourse – several times a day, every day. In addition to promoting complete voluntary control over ejaculation, this exercise benefits the rectum and the colon, massages the prostate and stimulates the lower terminals of the parasympathetic nervous system, which regulates digestive processes and balances the endocrine system. Only a Taoist could take such a mundane daily function as urination and turn it into an effective exercise for cultivating essence and energy!

The Orgasmic Upward Draw for Women

Men must learn ejaculation control in order to prevent depletion of essence and energy during sexual intercourse. While women need not worry about essence and energy loss through ejaculation, they do experience significant loss of vital energy as a result of menstruation and the gradual slackening of vaginal muscles. To reduce such losses, women may practice what Mantak and Mannewan Chia call the 'Orgasmic Upward Draw'.

The key muscle in this exercise is the pubococcygeal muscle, also called the 'Love Muscle', which controls the labia, vagina and other parts of the female sexual organ. Before even attempting the Orgasmic Upward Draw, women should spend a few months tightening and toning the Love Muscle by practicing deep contractions of the anus and perineum and extending the contraction all the way through the vagina. This exercise alone will eventually reduce menstrual bleeding, prevent loss of *chee* through the vagina, stimulate secretions in the sacral glands, and help open the lower channels of the Microcosmic Orbit.

The Orgasmic Upward Draw is the technique by which women may direct the energy of orgasm inward and upward through the spinal energy channels, so that the sexual energy spreads to all parts of the body and into all the vital organs via the meridian network. Not only does this conserve energy and tonify the organs, it results in a total body orgasm that only women are capable of experiencing.

To cultivate the Orgasmic Upward Draw, first practice alone and unaroused, as follows. Sit on the edge of a stool or chair and perform a few minutes of Bellows breathing. Then inhale slowly and deeply, retain the breath, and lock up the entire body by clenching feet and fists, contracting anus, perineum and vagina, and applying neck and abdominal locks as well. Press tongue to palate, tilt sacrum forward to straighten sway in lower spine, and roll eyes up towards top of head. Then slowly exhale through the nostrils as you gently release all locks and relax all muscles and visualize energy moving up the spine. After practicing this exercise for a few weeks, try it in a state of self-arousal, applying the locks and retention when you are about 95 per cent towards the brink of orgasm.

When you start feeling heat gathering in the vagina and perineum and energy tingling up your spine during this exercise, then you are ready to practice it during sexual intercourse with a man. During actual intercourse, the most important thing is to start applying the Orgasmic Upward Draw *before* actual orgasmic contractions of the vagina commence, but *after* the energy of orgasm has already been aroused inside. Just prior to orgasm, lock the gates, tighten the muscles, inhale deeply and retain the breath. Then tuck the pelvis forward to straighten the spine and perform six to nine deep contractions of the pubococcygeal muscle. When properly performed after long practice, this will cause orgasmic contractions to reverse the flow of sexual energy during orgasm, sending it coursing up the spinal channels instead of out through the vagina, and filling the entire body with the ecstatic sensation of orgasm.

Taoist Birth Control

In the Taoist system, birth control and eugenics are two sides of the same coin. Whether the goal be conception or prevention, the key is control, and in both cases human nature and Mother Nature are harmonized toward the desired goal without going against the grain of Tao.

In the Western world, eugenics has become a thing of the past. According to figures released by US government health authorities in December 1985, babies born in America today run a significantly higher risk than *ever before* of being born with cardiovascular dysfunctions, severe respiratory ailments, malformations of vital organs, and other defects acquired during gestation in the womb, and *not* due to hereditary factors. The report concludes by saying the cause of this disturbing phenomenon is 'unknown'.

The 'unknown' factor of course is eugenics, which means properly nurturing and protecting a potential new life from its origins as separate sperm and ovum, through the stages of conception and gestation, all the way to birth and beyond. In ancient China, young brides and grooms were fed all sorts of nourishing foods and potent tonic herbs to 'strengthen their essence' and 'nurture their energy' prior to conception. The quality of both the man's and the woman's reproductive plasma was regarded as the key factor in the conception and development of a healthy fetus. To conceive a new life while drunk or undernourished or ill was 'inconceivable'.

After conception, women in ancient China followed a rigorous regimen of eugenic care. Special diets were devised to benefit the bones, blood and other vital elements of both the mother and the developing child. Women were advised to avoid physical strain and, even more importantly, emotional stress. Extreme emotions such as anger or grief have powerful disruptive effects on a pregnant woman's energy system, and these ill effects are transferred directly to the fetus. Pregnant women are always encouraged to look at beautiful objects and listen to lovely sounds in order to harmonize their spirits, which, through the triple network of essence/energy/spirit, calm the fetus. Today, it is common in the Western world to see women in advanced stages of pregnancy smoking cigarettes, drinking coffee and cocktails, eating 'junk food', driving in heavy traffic, and doing other things that quite literally 'pollute' their developing infants. Small wonder that congenital birth defects are on the rise in the West, despite the 'wonders of modern medicine'.

Looking at the other side of the coin, we find revealed the safest, most natural and least distracting method of birth control ever conceived by man. That method is male ejaculation control scheduled according to the female fertility cycle.

A woman is relatively 'safe' from conception during the seven days prior to and immediately following the first day of menstruation. If as an extra margin of safety we reduce that to five days, we then have an 11-day period each month during which pregnancy cannot occur. During that period, a couple may make love any time, any place and as often as they wish, with or without male ejaculation, without worrying about unwanted pregnancies. This is the traditional 'rhythm method'.

Many Western physicians contest the 'safety' of this method by pointing out that more than once pregnancy has occurred during this period. If pregnancy occurs during the five days before or after a woman's menstruation commences, it's a clear indication that her entire system is way off balance and not functioning normally – a common condition these days. Such women should first restore their health and recover their natural body rhythms before using this method of birth control. Remember, we've been talking about sex between two healthy partners, so, if you're not healthy, go back to the chapters on health to restore yourself, then apply the Tao of Sex. If a woman ovulates 'on time', she will not get pregnant during the 'safe period' recommended here.

During the remaining 17–20 days, during which the woman is vulnerable to conception, the couple may continue making love any time, any place and to their hearts' content, without fear of unwanted pregnancy, as long as the man has mastered ejaculation control. Indeed, using ejaculation control to prevent conception during the 'unsafe' period of a woman's menstrual cycle is a powerful incentive to master the method. If after a week or so of retention the man feels the need to emit semen, he may use a condom for a 'therapeutic' ejaculation, or else the woman may help relieve his 'full' and 'flourishing' condition by other means.

As an added margin of safety, women may determine their exact day of ovulation by taking their own temperatures with an ultra-sensitive thermometer for about a week or two between menstrual periods. Any good gynecologist can show you the method. If a woman's health is 'full' and 'flourishing' but her day of ovulation occurs other than in the middle of her menstrual cycle, then simply time the 'safe period' around the day of ovulation rather than the day of menstruation by avoiding male ejaculation during the 9–10 days before and after the day of ovulation.

The Taoist way frees both man and woman from the clumsy and cumbersome technology of modern birth control. Women need no longer disrupt the delicate balance of their hormonal systems with the synthetic hormones and other dangerous chemicals contained in commercial birth control pills. Couples need no longer pause at the crucial moment of entry to wrestle with clumsy mechanical devices. Taoist birth control lets you have your cake and eat it *twice*: it permits you to enjoy as much sex as you want as often as you wish each and every day, while at the same time controlling conception *and* promoting health and longevity.

Health and birth control aside, the Taoist way also puts romance back into sexual intercourse. Couples who practice Tao may make love spontaneously whenever and wherever the urge strikes, without breaking the mood and romantic emotions of the moment.

Summary Remarks

Despite its novelty in light of conventional sexuality, ejaculation control is really as natural as breathing and flexing muscles. What is most difficult for most conventional men to master is the mentality of ejaculation control. As semen gathers and the exquisite sensations associated with a mounting ejaculation flood the body, men tend to lose their mental resolve and abandon their physical discipline. A nagging little voice bleats inside their heads, tempting them with rhetorical arguments, 'Go ahead! Why not? To hell with Tao! Life is short!' Men who heed this devilish voice too often will indeed discover that 'life is short'.

Beginners often complain that retaining semen during intercourse is 'impossible', or that it leaves them with that full feeling in the scrotum known as 'lover's balls', or that their partners don't 'cooperate' enough. When first attempting semen retention, post-coital pressure in the testicles is perfectly natural and no cause for alarm. It is caused by a very fundamental change in physical habit and a complete reorganization of the ejaculatory apparatus. It is no different than the bloated or jittery feelings you get in your stomach whenever you make a major, permanent change in dietary habits. After the body grows accustomed to the mechanics and biochemistry of the new routine, all uncomfortable side-effects disappear entirely. In the meantime, you can relieve that 'full feeling' with a few minutes of post-coital deep breathing and by gently massaging the region between anus and scrotum.

In order to help smooth the way for beginners on the path to ejaculation control, the author offers the following five fundamental guidelines, which should help any determined man adopt the Way of Yin and Yang in his own sexual life:

1. First and foremost, enlist your wife or lover as a partner in Tao. A man cannot master ejaculation control with strangers. He needs a woman who is fully familiar with him and with the principles and practices involved. An understanding and patient partner serves a novice male as the Plain Girl served the Yellow Emperor, guaranteeing complete cooperation and a carefree relationship. Once a man has mastered the methods, he may apply them with any partner.

2. Start out by practicing ejaculation control during the daytime and promising yourself the treat of an ejaculation later on that day or night. This makes it a lot easier to ignore the advice of that bleating voice as ejaculation approaches, for you may look forward to an emission during a second round later.

3. Once you have learned to suppress ejaculation during daytime intercourse, try skipping the bribe of a later ejaculation, and start experimenting objectively with your physiological and psychological responses to intercourse without ejaculation. Take note of your physical vitality and mental alertness after sex without emission, take pride in your newfound self-control, and take pleasure in your partner's ever-growing satisfaction with your sexual skills.

4. When you have finally mastered both the methods and the mentality of ejaculation control, make it a permanent habit by adopting it as a form of birth control.

5. Taking into account all the relevant factors discussed above, such as age, season, physical condition, etc., follow your own instincts and

personal experience in determining your own ideal ejaculation frequency. Every five or six years, decrease the frequency of emission according to the same factors, without decreasing your frequency of intercourse. This will automatically adjust your sexual habits to suit the requirements of advancing age and guarantees sufficient stores of essence and energy to replenish the depletions associated with aging.

With diligent practice, some men can even learn to approach the very brink of ejaculation and enjoy all the exquisite sensations associated with it, without spilling a drop of semen. These sensations are similar to the series of 'mini-orgasms' women sometimes experience en route to the 'big bang' at the end. As *The Redbook Report of Female Sexuality* reports, 'Males can reach a climax without ejaculating, and this is true for adults as well as for young boys who are not yet physiologically mature.'

The Redbook report cites the case of a young man who claimed that he frequently experienced 'multiple orgasms'. He was wired up to all sorts of sensitive electronic equipment that recorded his vital signs and sexual responses during prolonged intercourse in the laboratory. According to the report, 'Their machines recorded all the signs of sequential orgasms: increased respiration and heart rate, muscular tension, urethral and anal contractions, and the altered states of consciousness that accompany orgasm.' Another man, aged 49, was tested in a similar manner, and he 'decided to see how far he could go and how much control he could muster over the number of pre-ejaculatory orgasms. He got to 25 before going over the final cliff.'

Such cases – and indeed the entire Tao of Yin and Yang – shatter many commonly held myths regarding male sexuality, especially the ingrained assumption that male ejaculation is the inevitable conclusion of intercourse. It proves conclusively that men who learn to control their own sexual apparatus and instincts may become as potent and tireless lovers as any woman. It shows that men too may experience sequential 'mini-orgasms' without actual ejaculation, and it dispels the notion that birth control is primarily a female responsibility. It also clearly exposes the male instinct to ejaculate fast and frequently as a 'little death', a primordial suicidal impulse designed to sacrifice the individual for the higher goal of propagating the species.

Having shattered all those myths, the Tao proceeds to show men how to control and regulate their primal procreative urges in such a way that they benefit the health and longevity, and prolong the pleasure, of both partners. As Peng Tze notes, 'He will feel as if he could never get enough of her. Is this not the true and lasting pleasure of sex?'

CHAPTER 8:

———————— ◐ ————————

Taoist Bedroom Arts

> The arts of the bedroom constitute the climax of human emotions and encompass the totality of Tao. Therefore, the ancient sages regulated man's external pleasures in order to control his inner passions, and they made detailed rules governing sexual intercourse. If a man regulates his sexual pleasure, he will feel at peace and attain longevity. If, however, a man abandons himself to sexual pleasure without regard for the rules set forth in the ancient texts, he will soon fall ill and gravely injure his life.
>
> [*Dynastic History of Later Han*]

These rules have been handed down from generation to generation in China in an unbroken tradition spanning 5,000 years. Proceeding from the fundamental Chinese premise formulated in the third century BC by the philosopher Ko Tze that 'food and sex are life's most natural appetites', the ancient sages researched every aspect of the culinary as well as the sexual arts and developed practical techniques by which men and women could derive both health and pleasure from these natural appetites. They referred to this field of inquiry as *fang-shu* ('bedroom arts'), *fang-shir* ('bedroom affairs'), or simply *fang-nei* ('within the bedroom').

The results of their sexual research were recorded in illustrated texts aptly called 'pillow books', copies of which formed part of every bride and groom's wedding trousseau from the third century BC until the communist regime banned them in 1949. Unlike the *Kamasutra* of India and the rash of self-styled 'Joy of Sex' guides published for mass consumption in the West, Chinese pillow books focus as much on how to make sexual relations benefit health and promote longevity as they do on how to make the act mutually pleasurable. Indeed, the idea of harnessing sexual energy to promote health and prolong life remains one of the most unique and valuable contributions of traditional Chinese culture to the mainstream of human civilization. Unfortunately, when Westerners first 'discovered' China about 500 years ago, prudery and prejudice prevented any serious study of China's ancient Taoist bedroom arts; otherwise they would probably be as popular throughout the world today as Chinese food and culinary arts.

In traditional Chinese households, bedrooms usually contained several volumes of erotically illustrated pillow books for reference both before and during intercourse. They were called 'pillow books' precisely because they were propped up on a pillow for easy reference during the act. The role of pillow books in the sex life of traditional China is well illustrated in the following excerpt by the Han poet Cheng Heng (AD 78–139), translated here by R. H. van Gulik:

> I have swept clean the pillow and bedmat,
> And have fitted the burner with rare incense.
> Let us now lock the double door with the golden lock,
> And light the lamp to fill our room with brilliance.
> I shed my robes and remove my paint and powder,
> And roll out the picture scroll by the pillow.
> The Plain Girl I shall take as my instructress,
> So that we may practice all the variegated postures,
> Those that an ordinary husband has but rarely seen,
> Such as taught by Tien-Lao to the Yellow Emperor.

This poem is a goldmine of information about sexual life in ancient China. The first line starts by mentioning the importance of hygiene, while the second reflects the Chinese custom of enhancing ambiance by sweetening the air and blankets with rare incense. The desire for privacy, the preference for making love by lamplight rather than groping in the dark, the role of pillow books, the reverence for the Plain Girl as sexual mentor, and the emphasis on 'practicing all the variegated postures' are all mentioned. These guidelines were followed by the general populace, not just by Taoist adepts, for even the most conservative Confucian bureaucrats turned to Tao when they entered the boudoir. Despite the conservatism and conformity the Chinese display in public, they have always enjoyed remarkably rich and ribald sex lives in the privacy of the bedroom.

Compare the poem above with the following excerpt from the *Redbook Report on Female Sexuality*, published in 1975. As above, it is the woman who speaks for the couple, and it is she who acts as host in the boudoir. Married to the same man for 31 years, she reports:

> We usually have intercourse with all the trimmings from four to
> five 'settings' a week – and always on Sunday. By 'settings', I

mean we rarely have intercourse only one time. We learned before marriage that you do not need to have an orgasm each time to enjoy it, that you can prolong the sessions and sensations with practice.

This enlightened American couple discovered the basic principles of the Way all by themselves, which no doubt accounts for the longevity and obvious joy of their marriage. Thanks to the growing self-awareness and sexual candor of Western women, Western men are now beginning to appreciate the virtues of prolonged multiple intercourse without ejaculation, and the Tao of Yin and Yang is now beginning to rise on Western horizons.

One of the most imaginative and aesthetically pleasing aspects of Taoist bedroom arts is the poetic terminology used to denote various sexual organs and activities. Unlike Western sexual jargon, which is either coldly clinical (penis, vagina, clitoris, etc.) or lewdly colloquial (cock, cunt, fuck, etc.), Chinese erotic terms conjure up all sorts of romantic and guilt-free images in the minds of the participants, and this imagery greatly enhances the ambiance of sexual intercourse. It also enabled Chinese poets and writers to discuss sexual relations at great length without offending conservative readers or breaking established literary conventions. For example, take 'clouds and rain', which is the Chinese poetic term for sexual intercourse. 'Clouds' symbolizes the gathering storm of female essence, while 'rain' refers to the ejaculation of male semen. Hence, Chinese writers could use these terms to describe sexual intercourse in detail without offending anyone, with such creative metaphors as 'the clouds gathered but the rain never came', 'after the rain fell, the clouds dispersed', 'light drizzles' 'sudden downpours', and so forth.

Western readers with a taste for florid imagery and an aesthetic attitude toward sex may well wish to adopt the English equivalents of these terms when discussing sex with their paramours. Listed below, in alphabetical order of their technical meanings, are some of the most charming Chinese terms from the *Jade Bedroom*:

Technical meaning	Literal translation
cervix	Inner Gate
clitoris	Jade Terrace
	Precious Pearl
	Seed
	Yin Bean
clitoris (frenulum of)	Lute Strings
clitoris (prepuce of)	Divine Field

Technical meaning	Literal translation
cunnilingus	Sipping the Vast Spring
fellatio	Blowing the Flute
intercourse	Clouds and Rain
	Firing the Cannon
	Friendly Relations
homosexual sex (female)	Rubbing Mirrors
homosexual sex (male)	Splitting the Peach
	Dragon Yang Relations
labia minor	Wheat Buds
	Red Pearls
Mound of Venus (mons veneris)	Sedge Hill
orgasm (female)	High Tide
	Tide of Yin
orgasm (male ejaculation)	Lose Essence
	Leak
	Surrender
	Die
penis	Jade Stem
	Jade Implement
	Yang Peak
	Yang Weapon
	Turtle Head
	The Ambassador
penis (erect)	Arisen
	Angry
penis (limp)	Dead
urethral orifice (female)	Vast Spring
urethral orifice (male)	Gate of Life and Death
vagina (orifice)	Jade Gate
	Jade Door
	Cinnabar Cave
	Child Gate
	One Square Inch
vagina (lower vestibule)	Little Stream
vagina (middle)	Deep Valley
	Hidden Place
	Path of Yin
vagina (upper)	Celestial Palace
	Valley of Solitude
vulva (upper)	Golden Gulley
vulva (lower)	Jade Vein

Technical meaning
uterus

Literal translation
Child Palace
North Pole
Vermillion Chamber

It is abundantly clear from the above sampling of terms that Chinese poets, like Taoist physicians, paid far closer attention to the details of female anatomy than to male, and that the focal point of their attentions was always that mysterious, magical 'one square inch' portal known so fondly as the 'Jade Gate'. Taoist bedroom arts aim at prolonging as long as possible the 'Ambassador's' visit to the 'Celestial Palace' by teaching the man proper protocol and endowing him with the correct 'credentials' as a master lover.

Most men are far too obsessed by the size and shape of their penis and pay far too little attention to the skills required to wield the Jade Stem properly. Let's listen in on a dialogue between the Yellow Emperor and the ever-candid Plain Girl regarding the primacy of skill above size in wielding the Yang Weapon:

Yellow Emperor: Do the differences in size and shape of a man's implement affect the pleasure a woman feels during intercourse?

Plain Girl: Such differences are merely external. The true pleasure of sex is internal, and it can only be achieved by harmonizing Yin and Yang in the Ultimate.

Yellow Emperor: What variations are there between long and short, hard and soft implements?

Plain Girl: A long implement that gets only half hard is not as effective as a short one that grows hard as iron. A short, hard implement that is wielded roughly and without due consideration for the woman's feelings is not nearly as desirable as one used with expertise and careful attention to the woman's responses. As with everything else under Heaven, one should strive for the Golden Mean in achieving the harmony of Yin and Yang.

The very best accessory to a happy, healthy sex life is the Tao itself!

The Thrust of the Matter

In order for a man to make the right moves at the right time during intercourse, he must first learn to observe and interpret his partner's and his own vital signs and respond accordingly. Rather than thrash about wildly in the dark, he should keep his attention focused on the Five Signs and the Ten Indications of his partner's responses and adjust the depth, pace and angle of his thrusts according to her signals. He must remain as alert and attentive as a master chef at the stove, as careful as a man galloping on a horse with a frayed rein. By learning to read the roadsigns along the winding route to a woman's orgasm, a man may easily master the art of timely response to the heavy traffic on the way.

When foreplay has lubricated the woman with sexual secretions and fully endowed the man with the Four Attainments of erection, the time is ripe to 'introduce the Ambassador' at the Jade Gate and 'present his credentials' in the Celestial Palace. Protocol demands that this be done slowly and respectfully. Having established a firm foothold inside, the man should begin with slow shallow thrusts, pressing the base of the penis tightly against the Mound of Venus and rubbing it against the clitoris, rather than sliding in and out. By minimizing friction of the man's sensitive glans and maximizing stimulation of the woman's sensitive clitoris, the divergent demands of Yin and Yang are harmonized.

As intercourse progresses, the art of the bedroom calls for the man to meet the woman's various responses with the appropriate sort of thrust. In *Mysterious Master of the Cave,* the Tang physician Lee Tung-hsüan explains the art of timely thrusting:

> Deep and shallow, slow and swift, straight and slanting thrusts are not at all the same. Each has its own unique effects and characteristics. A slow thrust should resemble the movement of a fish caught on a hook, while a swift thrust should be like the flight of birds against the wind . . . One should apply each style at the appropriate time and not cling stubbornly to just one style due to laziness or personal convenience

Taoist pillow books put great emphasis on the style and number of thrusts delivered by the man during intercourse. They frequently mention 'one thousand thrusts' as the correct measure for fully satisfying a woman. To the uninitiated, this may sound like a sexual version of the New York Marathon. In practice, a thousand thrusts take about half an hour of intercourse – not at all long for a Taoist lover. Compare this to the puny measure of male potency suggested by American author David Reuben in *Everything You Ever Wanted to Know about Sex*:

> A reasonable yardstick for male potency is the ability to continue intercourse for 5–10 minutes. During that time a normally potent male will deliver from 50 to 100 pelvic thrusts.

Once again, Reubin writes exclusively from the point of view of a sexually beleagured male with no reference whatsoever to the female angle. His 'yardstick' of 50–100 thrusts and the timetable of 5–10 minutes would barely suffice a healthy woman to reach the Second Sign and Third Indication of pleasure, and they certainly do not define the standards for a 'normally potent' Taoist.

Taoist texts suggest a variety of different thrusting styles, and they invariably describe these with poetic metaphors that in themselves enhance the aesthetics of the act. Lee Tung-hsüan listed a number of these thrusting styles in *Mysterious Master of the Cave*:

- Press the root of the Jade Stem tightly against the mound above the Jade Gate, shuttle up and down, and saw at the Gate as if cutting open an oyster to reach the Precious Pearl inside.
- Thrust deeply into the Jade Gate, then slowly withdraw the Jade Stem up against the Golden Gulley, as if slicing through stone in search of precious jade.
- Use the Jade Stem to thrust vigorously in the region of the Jade Terrace, as if using an iron pestle to grind medicine in a mortar.
- Jab the Jade Stem back and forth with short, slow thrusts inside the Celestial Palace like a farmer tilling the field to sow his seeds.
- Grind the Jade Stem and the Jade Gate heavily together, like two avalanches meeting midway.
- Use the Jade Stem to strike out to the left and right, like a brave warrior trying to break through enemy ranks.
- Move the Jade Stem up and down, like a wild stallion bucking through a stream.
- Make deep and shallow thrusts in quick succession. like a huge stone sinking into the sea.
- Push the Jade Stem in slowly, like a snake crawling into a hole to hide.
- Thrust the Jade Stem swiftly, like a frightened mouse running into a hole to hide.
- Rise up high, then plunge in low, like a big sailboat braving stormy seas.

By practicing the various styles of thrusting, couples soon learn which sorts of thrusts suit them best under various conditions. The Tao offers 'different strokes for different folks', depending on physique, feelings and personal preferences. And since Taoist intercourse lasts much longer than the conventional variety touted by Reuben as 'normal', different strokes prevent the monotony of a single repetitive maneuver and provide intercourse with the spice of variety.

The Plain Girl and other Taoist sages seem to favor the thrusting sequence of nine shallow/one deep, especially for beginners. This involves nine consecutive 'bump and grind' type thrusts with friction focused between the root of the man's penis and the woman's Mound of Venus, followed by a long, slow withdrawal to the Wheat Buds and a swift, vigorous 'deep thrust' back up to the Celestial Palace. Note that a 'shallow thrust' is delivered from a position of deep penetration and a 'deep thrust' requires a withdrawal to more shallow depths. In certain positions, especially rear entry, a man with a long and fully erect implement can actually 'knock' at the 'Inner Gate' (cervix) with the 'Turtle's Head' (glans of the penis), but this must be done very gently and only after the vagina is fully lubricated.

The moment of greatest vigilance for a man is when the woman reaches the final stages of the Five Signs and Ten Indications and starts pressing herself urgently against him in the final countdown to her orgasm. If a man is not careful, her growing agitation and pelvic thrusting will overstimulate the Turtle's Head and cause him to ejaculate, taking the wind from his sails just as the woman is ready to race across the finish line. This can be extremely frustrating for both partners and, if it becomes the rule rather than the exception, it can easily ruin a relationship. It is at this stage of intercourse that a man will most appreciate the virtues of deep penetration with 'shallow thrusting', which transfers the point of friction from the sensitive glans to the root of the penis, where it excites him least but stimulates her most. This style of thrusting, combined with deep breathing and anal sphincter locks, enables a man to meet and match indefinitely even the most urgent thrusts a woman makes on the verge of orgasm, without the risk of premature ejaculation.

Adopting Different Positions

Like yoga and calisthenics, adopting different positons during sexual intercourse stimulates different parts of the body, exercises different muscles and joints, and provides different health benefits. Different positions may also be adopted to suit different physiques and moods, such as putting a heavily overweight partner underneath or allowing the most energetic partner to get on top. In prolonged Taoist intercourse, adopting different positions provides a refreshing change of pace and different angles for viewing your partner's body. Variety is the spice of life, and switching positions 'midstream' is almost as exciting as switching partners.

Taoist pillow books distinguish four fundamental positions for man and woman during intercourse, with dozens of variations of each. The

Figure 8.1 A couple engaged in a sexual position called 'Mule in the Springtime', one of the classic Thirty Styles recommended by Taoist masters

Plain Girl advised the Yellow Emperor to practice the four fundamental postures each and every time he made love, as follows:

1. *Man on top.* This is the classic 'missionary' position in which the man lies on top of the woman or kneels between her thighs. In this posture, he commands the action. It is best suited for slender, active men and strong, voluptuous women who reach orgasm with relative ease.

2. *Woman on top.* The woman straddles the man's thighs as he lies on his back and sits down on his implement. In this position, the woman controls the action, and for many women this is the easiest position for reaching orgasm in intercourse. For men it holds the salutary advantage of making gravity work in favor of, rather than against, ejaculation control. It is best suited for overweight men who tend to ejaculate quickly and for slender, active women who require a lot of physical stimulation to reach orgasm.

3. *Side by side, face to face.* Man and woman lie on their sides facing each other and adopt various positions of entry from that angle. This style is least tiring for both partners, but it requires a bit of agility and close

319

coordination. It is best suited for the later stages of prolonged sessions between partners who are familiar with one another's bodies and responses.

4. *Man behind woman.* The man kneels behind the woman, who crouches in front of him on her knees, or lies on top of her as she lies on her stomach, or lies on his side behind her. In this postion, the Jade Stem enters the Jade Gate from behind and below the Full Moon (buttocks). This angle provides the deepest possible penetration of the Celestial Palace and makes the Jade Gate feel tighter than in other postures. Though it provides relatively little direct stimulation to the woman's clitoris, the deeper penetration is highly stimulating to the vagina, especially the sensitive point known in Western parlance as the 'G-spot'. These positions stimulate the male more than other postures do, and are thus best suited for men who have completely mastered ejaculation control, and for women who enjoy deep and vigorous penetration. Anal intercourse, however, is strongly discouraged – not for moral but for medical reasons. The rectum is the body's cesspool, a source of virulent germs and dangerous toxins, not a source of essence and energy.

From these four basic postures Taoist adepts devised a variety of inventive positions for intercourse, and these constitute an important aspect of the bedroom arts. These positions are introduced in Taoist texts as the 'Nine Ways' and the 'Thirty Styles'. Since the latter are an elaboration of

Figure 8.2 **A variation of one of the Thirty Styles, called 'Mandarin Ducks',**
with the man approaching the woman from behind.
This is an excellent position for those who like to watch the action down below

Figure 8.3 Couple embraced in the position known as 'Silkworm Spinning', one of the Thirty Styles and a variation of 'Dragon Turning'. The ancient Chinese were very fond of making love outdoors

the former, we will discuss only the Nine Ways here. This should be more than enough to inspire couples embarking on the Way.

In the *Classic of the Mysterious Girl*, we find the following dialogue between the Yellow Emperor and his second Taoist sex counsellor, the Mysterious Girl:

> Yellow Emperor: I have heard about the Nine Ways, but I have no idea how to practice them. I want you to explain these to me in order to reveal their purpose. I shall carefully guard these secrets and practice their methods.
>
> Mysterious Girl: The first of the Nine Ways is called 'Dragon Turning'. Let the woman lie on her back and let the man lie on top of her between her thighs. He should tickle her Seed with the Jade Stem, then enter the Jade Gate from above, using the method of eight shallow/two deep thrusts. He should roll his hips from side to side to stimulate the upper rim of the Jade Gate. Supporting his weight on elbows and knees, the man appears as a dragon turning in the sky.
>
> The second way is called 'Tiger Stalking'. Have the woman kneel in a crawling position, face down and buttocks up, while the man kneels behind her, grasps her hips, and

inserts the Jade Stem deeply inside her. He starts by thrusting vigorously until the Yin fluids flow freely, then he slows down to a more comfortable pace. In this position, which is the way animals mate, the man resembles a tiger on the prowl, ready to pounce on his prey. The woman's vagina is tight, and the man enjoys a clear view of her soft shoulders, curved back, and round buttocks. When she emits the Tide of Yin, it is time to withdraw and rest.

The third way is called 'Monkey Leaping'. The woman lies on her back and raises both legs and buttocks straight up into the air. The man kneels before the exposed Jade Gate, supports her legs on his shoulders, and inserts the Jade Stem deeply inside.

Figure 8.4 **A variation of one of the Nine Ways, known as 'Monkey Leaping'.** The gentle rythmn of the boat bobbing on the water enhances the couple's pleasure

This may also be performed with the woman lying on the edge of the bed so that the man may stand on the floor rather than kneel on the bed.

The fourth way is called 'Cicadas Mating'. Let the woman lie flat on her stomach with her legs extended, while the man kneels behind her to insert the Jade Stem. He then lies down on top of her and supports his weight with his hands. She should raise up her buttocks so that he may rub the Red Pearl with thrusts of six deep/one shallow and nine deep/one shallow. Deeply agitated within, the Jade Gate opens up and her emissions flow forth. When the woman rejoices, the man withdraws.

This position is most suitable for women whose vaginas are located further back than others. The man must be sure to support his weight in order not to interfere with the woman's breathing, or else adopt the side-by-side version of this position, which puts weight on neither partner.

The fifth way is called 'Turtle Mounting.' Have the woman lie on her back and bend her knees up until they touch her breasts. While pushing back her feet so that her legs remain well bent against her breast, the man enters and pierces deeply inside. Using deep and shallow thrusts, he causes the Jade Stem to rub against her Seed. Feeling pleasure, the woman's body shakes and shimmies. When her Tide of Yin begins to flow, the man should thrust vigorously to the very deepest extremity, being careful however not to injure the woman. If a man performs this without losing his semen, his vitality will increase a hundredfold.

The sixth way is called 'Phoenix Fluttering'. Let the woman lie flat on her back and raise her legs up slightly off the bed, crooking them so that the man may crawl between her thighs and insert the Jade Stem deeply inside, supporting his weight on hands and knees. Hard and hot he enters, carrying out thrusting sequences of eight shallow/one deep and three shallow/one deep. When her buttocks suddenly press tightly together, the Jade Gate opens wide and her Yin secretions naturally flow forth.

The seventh way is called 'Rabbit Licking Its Fur'. The man lies flat on his back with his legs fully extended, while the woman straddles him from above with her head facing his feet and slightly bent forward. The man then inserts the Jade Stem from below and stabs at her Lute Strings. The woman grows ecstatic and her vital essence flows inside her like a stream. In this position, the woman resembles a rabbit licking clean its fur.

The eighth way is called 'Fish with Scales Conjoined'. The man lies flat on his back with legs extended, while the woman straddles him from above, facing his head. He calmly inserts the Jade Stem from below but enters only slightly, stopping to move it about there like a child sucking at it mother's breast, until the woman in her excitement suddenly sinks it in to the hilt. Let the woman move about and strive for pleasure by herself and prolong this for as long as possible.

Figure 8.5 A creative alfresco variation of the position known as 'Fish with Scales Conjoined'

For most women, this is the most comfortable, flexible, and stimulating of all positions for intercourse, and for men it's the easiest one in which to maintain ejaculation control. It also frees a man's hands to roam about and caress the woman's body, exposes her undulating torso to full view, and permits him to suck in the Great Libation of the Middle Peak locked inside her breasts.

The ninth way is called 'Cranes Crossing Necks'. The man sits upright on his knees, and the woman straddles his thighs, kneeling down on top of him with her legs splayed open. She embraces him with her arms around his neck while he inserts the Jade Stem from below, striking at the Wheat Buds and searching for the Seed. The man embraces the woman holding her around the buttocks, thereby assisting her upward movements. The woman feels great pleasure, and when her essence flows forth, the man ceases thrusting.

This position is very exciting for both partners and provides intense stimulation of the woman's sensitive clitoral region. However, the man's knees must be fully flexible, his thighs strong, and his back firm in order to maintain this position during intercourse.

The Nine Ways introduced above should suffice to inspire imaginative couples to contrive further variations of their own, uniquely suited to their own personal preferences and physiques. Remember too that the various different styles of thrusting may all be used in each of the various positions, providing even greater variety of response.

Artful Accessories

Just as any serious gourmet sooner or later discovers that the Chinese are the world's most inventive cooks, so connoisseurs of erotica eventually realize that the Chinese also rank among the world's most inventive lovers. For a society that firmly believes that 'food and sex are life's most natural appetites', such cultural priorities are not surprising.

In addition to illustrated pillow books, Chinese boudoirs usually contained a complete armory of artful sex accessories, often fashioned from precious materials by highly skilled craftsmen. Not only were Chinese artisans skillful in the production of such implements, Chinese lovers were unabashed in their use. When a Chinese gentleman of the late Ming Dynasty went out with friends to enjoy an evening of wine and

Figure 8.6 **Two love birds in the garden commune in the position called 'Cranes Crossing Necks'**, with Mother Nature as their boudoir

women, he always carried with him some gifts of silk and perfume to help seduce potential paramours, perhaps a 'pocket edition' of his favorite pillow book, and a pouch full of 'sex weapons' to meet every possible contingency. In the erotic Ming novel *Golden Lotus*, we find the hero Hsi Men-ching arriving for an amorous tryst fully armed for the 'flowery battlefield':

> Miss Joy invited him into the bedroom where she had arranged a sumptuous banquet. The table was laden with a variety of chicken and duck dishes, as well as meats and other savory delicacies. As he sat down to the feast, he loosened his clothes and she poured him a cup of wine. They ate and drank for a while without much talk, but by the end of the meal the wine had considerably relaxed their mood. They moved their chairs together and embraced, then she placed her tiny feet on his lap and let him touch them. With this signal, they both stood up and undressed one another, and he carried her over to the bed.
>
> She had carefully prepared the bed. She had placed a double down-quilt underneath so that they could roll about in comfort, and she had dusted the blankets with fragrant powder. A painting of the Green Dragon and White Tiger sporting together hung above their heads, and little bells hung from the bedposts. Miss Joy was delighted to notice that her careful preparations were immediately appreciated, for she could clearly see that he was already fully aroused.
>
> 'I'll be with you in a minute,' he said, pulling out a pouch of embroidered silk.
>
> He opened the pouch and carefully set the following implements along the edge of the quilt:
>
> A Silver Passion-clip
> A Cap of Eternal Desire
> A Sulphur Lust-ring
> Medicinal Passion-ribbons
> A Jade Dragon-ring
> Lust Ointment
> Burmese Love-bell
>
> 'Well, what do you think of my battle implements?' He asked.
>
> Struck speechless by the sight, she lay back on the pillows without a reply, fearful yet full of anticipation. Her mouth fell open and her breathing accelerated. Her arms felt weak, but

327

already her knees were rising up from the bed. After attaching the Silver Passion-clip to the Jade Stem, he anointed it well with Lust Ointment, then moved in between her thighs. He tested the position with a brief foray against the Jade Gate, then withdrew and added a Sulphur Lust-ring as well as a yellow and a blue Medicinal Passion-ribbon. His implement thus reinforced, he made resolute entry into the Pleasure Chamber, and she immediately cried out in pain and joy, as if a sword were driving ever deeper into her.

This is a fairly typical scene from the *Golden Lotus*, which, despite its erotic slant, remains one of the most accurate portrayals of life in traditional Chinese society ever recorded. Note how the 'combatants' first fortify themselves with food and drink prior to 'battle', and how the hero first tests his position at the Jade Gate to determine what sort of armaments he requires. Let's take a closer look at some of these 'weapons':

Burmese Love-bell: This is a hollow sphere of pure silver with a small silver pellet sealed inside. Inserted inside the vagina prior to intercourse, it plays a constant refrain of 'Jingle Bells' as the couple make love. The vibrations also enhance the woman's sensations inside.

Sulphur Lust-ring: A ring composed of sulphur compound, it fits around the base of the penis during intercourse. When the sulphur comes into contact with the woman's wet parts, it activates and stimulates them and causes the Wheat Buds to contract, making the Jade Gate tighter.

Medicinal Passion-ribbons: These are long silk ribbons dusted with stimulating medicinal powders. When a man feels his erection flagging during prolonged intercourse, he winds a ribbon or two around the root of his penis. Pressure from the ribbons constricts the veins and prevents the outflow of blood, while the powders stimulate the Jade Stem back into action.

Lust Ointment: An ointment containing powerful tropical drugs extracted from plants and minerals, it is applied directly to the penis and vagina to stimulate and arouse them when foreplay has failed to fully do the trick.

Dragon Ring: Perhaps the most useful of all Chinese sex accessories, this should be part of every 'Dragon Lover's' arsenal (see Figure 8.7). Carved from ivory or jade, the ring fits snugly around the base of the penis. A ribbon may be run through the hole in the bottom and under the scrotum, then tied around the

Figure 8.7 'Dragon Ring'

waist to hold the ring firmly in place. When the man contracts the anal spincter and perineum, causing the penis to swell, the ring exerts pressure on the veins, preventing loss of erection, and on the urogenital tract, preventing loss of semen. The bump protruding from the top rim directly massages the woman's clitoris with every loving thrust of the Jade Stem. Show this illustration to any good ivory or jade carver in the Far East, and he will immediately recognize its function and carve a masterpiece for you. Note that the inner diameter from top to bottom is exactly 44 mm.

Owing to the prevalence of sapphism and masturbation among neglected women in the large polygamous households of ancient China, it is not surprising to find that purveyors of sex aids carried a few items exclusively for use by women. The most popular female accessories were single or double dildos, usually corrugated and highly polished, and 'Jade Terrace Polishers', which were instruments designed to massage the clitoris. For reasons unexplained in Chinese erotic lore, dildos were euphemistically called 'Mr Kuo', which is a common Chinese surname. Perhaps Mr Kuo was a highly talented craftsman or an itinerant peddler of erotic wares, whose products were dear to the women of wealthy households.

The double dildo was used simultaneously by two women, each of whom could control its 'thrusting' by tugging on attached ribbons. The single dildo was used for masturbation and had an ingenious, energy-saving design: it was tied to the ankle with ribbons so that a woman could effortlessly arouse the Tide of Yin with leisurely flicks of her foot. So popular was 'Mr Kuo' among Chinese women that Chinese medical records refer to a common female complaint called 'Coxcomb Clitoris', an inflammation of the clitoris caused by excessive friction with sex aids.

Sex Therapy

Just as the culinary arts play medical as well as epicurean roles in Chinese culture, and the martial arts are used for combat as well as physical therapy, so the Chinese bedroom arts may be adapted for sexual therapy as well as pleasure. When abuse of the pleasure principle leads to debility, impotence and low resistance, it is time to turn the Jade Bedroom into your own private sex clinic. Writes Dr Lee Tung-hsüan in *Secrets of the Jade Bedroom*:

> Reckless indulgence in extreme passions inevitably brings on serious illness. This is most evident in sexual intercourse. Since one falls ill this way, one may also get cured this way. This is similar to sobering up by drinking some wine.

Before discussing the details of Chinese sex therapy, it is important to establish the correct Taoist perspective on these subjects, a perspective that must embrace all Three Treasures of life – essence, energy and spirit. Western sex therapy, like Western philosophy, is dualistic: it attacks the problem from *either* an exclusively psychological angle *or* a purely physiological approach. The Chinese way covers both angles and is based on the intimate interplay of body, breath and mind, and approaches sexual dysfunction as a critical imbalance among the three.

According to the Taoist view, sexual excitement begins in the mind, which in turn arouses sexual energy, quickens the breath and accelerates the heartbeat, which in turn stimulates hormone secretions, increases body heat, circulates blood, and other physiological manifestations of sexual arousal. Unless the mind is properly primed for action by initial awareness and spontaneous thoughts of sex, neither energy nor essence can be fully mustered for the act.

By far the most common sexual dysfunction today is male impotence. This may result from a variety of factors, but most cases are due to the intense anxiety that results from approaching intercourse in the wrong mood or with the wrong attitude. The essential role of the 'right mood' for harmonious sexual relations is discussed in detail by the Yellow Emperor and the Plain Girl:

> Plain Girl: The way to create the right mood is to induce the Five

Right Intentions of man and be guided by the Five Signs and Ten Indications of woman.

Yellow Emperor: And what are the Five Right Intentions of man?

Plain girl: First, he should remain relaxed and calm, which induces the intention of 'Unpretentiousness'. Second, since he intends to bestow pleasure to another with his Yang implement, he must induce the mood of 'Generosity'. Third, by correct breathing, the various cavities in his body expand, inducing the intention of mustering his full 'Capacity'. Fourth, he must maintain a mood of complete 'Serenity'. The Fifth Right Intention of man, however, is the only legitimate excuse for the retreat of the Jade Stem from the Jade Gate. That intention is 'Loyalty' to his own desire for solitude. If a man desires solitude, then nothing should interfere with his loyalty to such a noble mood.

In this passage, the Plain girl presages the findings of Kinsey and Masters and Johnson regarding male impotence. They determined that the single greatest cause of impotence in men today is fear of failure in bed, a fear that exists solely in the mind, is maintained by the mind and can only be overcome by the mind. Fear and anxiety are powerful emotions that cause very real physiological repercussions, such as dry mouth, cold sweat, cold hands and feet, and contraction of sexual organs. These physiological repercussions inhibit sexual arousal and erection in men. The resulting failure to respond physically further fuels the fear, which further inhibits response, in a vicious circle that can last a lifetime.

Chinese physicians also deal with cases of impotence caused by physiological problems, in which case the right intentions and proper mood are not sufficient to effect a cure. If the inability to achieve and maintain erection does not stem from the realm of the mind, then it must lie within the realm of energy and essence. Failure to achieve all Four Attainments of male erection (elongation, swelling, hardness and heat) are most commonly caused by poor circulation, low vitality, shallow breathing, bad diet, pollution of the body, and other physiological factors. In such cases, men are advised to cultivate the skill of 'soft entry' (along with strict continence of semen) as physical therapy for restoring circulation to the sexual organs, tonifying the muscles, tendons, sphincters and other parts that control the sexual organs, and generating energy in the deficient vital parts.

As mentioned earlier, the essential requirements for practicing soft entry are a cooperative and understanding partner, sufficient female lubrication and a serene approach by the male. In addition, the man may use his thumb and index finger to form a 'Dragon Ring' around the base of his penis as he slowly maneuvers it into the Jade Gate. By squeezing the base, he forces blood into the shaft and glans, making them swell up to facilitate soft entry. He should maintain this finger pressure until he is well within the Jade Gate, where the warmth and wetness of the vagina will soon begin to produce a natural erection. Not only is soft entry an effective palliative for most forms of physiological impotence, if performed successfully a few times it greatly bolsters the sexual self-confidence of otherwise healthy men who suffer needlessly from impotence caused by fear of failure. However, neither soft entry nor anything else will work if a man is exceedingly exhausted, under-nourished, toxic or ill. In such cases, a man must first restore his overall health and vitality through diet, exercise and herbal medicine, before approaching the symptomatic problem of sexual impotence.

Ailments due to sexual excess may be cured by sexual discipline, and as usual it is the man who suffers most from such problems. Indeed, as the Empress Wu's example proves, women may actually thrive on sexual excess owing to their natural retention of sexual secretions. In her discourse with the Yellow Emperor, the Plain Girl listed 'Seven Ills' that may strike men who abuse their sexual drive, including impotence, nocturnal emissions, anemia, energy deficiency and hormone exhaustion.

The Plain Girl goes on to explain that the best cure for all Seven Ills is frequent serial intercourse with the same woman without *any* emission of semen whatsoever, several times daily, for 10 days in a row. She suggests favoring the female-superior positions for intercourse, which permits the man to rest passively below and make gravity work in favor of ejaculation

Figure 8.8 Taoist physicians often recommend controlled sexual intercourse as therapy for male sexual depletion. In this case, the woman always lies on top and controls all movement, while the man rests quietly below and focuses on breath and energy control. Absolute male continence of semen throughout the therapy is essential for successful results

control. The best time of day for therapeutic sexual intercourse is between midnight and dawn, when cosmic Yang energy prevails in the atmosphere and food in the stomach is completely digested. When combined with diet, breathing and herbal aphrodisiacs, this prescription truly works wonders for impotence, premature ejaculation and other forms of male sexual dysfunction, but it's easier said than done. Unless the man maintains strict continence of semen throughout the 10-day program, he will end up even more exhausted, disordered, blocked and stagnant than when he started.

In a nutshell, Chinese sex therapy 'is similar to sobering up by drinking some wine'. Excessive loss of semen as a result of frequent intercourse with ejaculation is the prime cause of impotence in men, and frequent intercourse with no ejaculation is its prime cure. This makes good medical sense because nothing in the world stimulates secretion of vital hormones as effectively as sexual excitement.

With the above medical perspectives in mind, we are now ready to explore the fertile field of Chinese aphrodisiacs.

The Legend of the Goat

Long ago, in a remote mountain province of southern China, there lived a goatherd with a very 'horny' herd of goats. His billygoats, it seemed, simply 'couldn't get enough' of their ewes, mounting them and rutting repeatedly in remarkably brief spans of time. The curious goatherd soon noticed a pattern: whenever his billygoats nibbled from a certain patch of weeds, their promiscuous proclivities peaked for hours thereafter. Before long, Chinese herbalists learned what goats had always known: that the plant *aceranthus sagittatum*, a nondescript weed that grows in the wild, is one of the most potent male aphrodisiacs on earth. Logically, they named the new medicinal herb *Yin-Yang-huo* – 'Horny Goat Weed'.

The subject of aphrodisiacs is cloaked in fantasy and misunderstanding, so let's start by defining our terms. Webster's Dictionary defines an aphrodisiac as 'something which excites sexual desire'. That could mean a drug as well as a dirty movie. The Plain Girl is more precise: she defines an aphrodisiac as 'a potion or a practice that increases sexual potency in males'. Clearly, it is the male who most needs his sexual potency bolstered by external means, not the female. And, as the Plain Girl points out, for some men certain practices are more effective than even the most powerful potions in arousing male potency – practices such as switching positions, intercourse with unusual partners, 'bondage', and so forth. As one astute adept points out in *Secrets of the Jade Bedroom*, 'There is no greater aphrodisiac for a man than variety in women.'

Herbal aphrodisiacs, like all herbal medicines, each have their own specific 'natural affinities' (*gui-jing*) for certain organs and glands in the body. In the case of aphrodisiac potions, herbalists select ingredients with known affinities for the sexual organs, blood and vital glands, especially the sexually all-important suprarenal glands. The herbs tonify these tissues, stimulate secretions from glands and promote circulation to the minute capillaries of the sexual organs. The net result is an overall stimulation of vitality (energy) and hormones (essence); the enhanced sexual potency that follows is largely a *side-effect* of this general tonification of essence and energy.

Take, for example, Horny Goat Weed. The essential active element in this remarkable herb has natural affinities for the suprarenal glands and for the circulatory system. Recent studies have shown that sperm count and semen density increase substantially in men during the first few hours after ingestion of this herb. Besides stimulating hormone production in the suprarenal glands, which in turn stimulates other related glands, this drug has a salutory effect on circulation of blood. When it enters blood vessels, especially the finer capillaries, its presence there causes them to dilate, thereby greatly enhancing circulation in tissues fed mainly by small capillaries, such as a man's penis. It also facilitates delivery of the extra hormones secreted into the bloodstream by the same drug. And, since it expands blood vessels, it causes a proportional decrease in blood pressure, making the herb safe for those who need it most.

Like all herbal therapy, aphrodisiacs must be taken over an extended period of time in order to have the desired effects. Since they employ no synthetic chemicals or other artificial ingredients, they must work naturally with the body's circulatory and endocrine systems, and this takes time. Count on two or three months of daily doses for noticeable enhancement of sexual potency to become apparent.

Aphrodisiacs are strong medicine, and if your stomach is weak or not working properly, you're just wasting money on these herbs because they will pass right through your system. The liver and circulatory system must also be functioning properly to derive full benefits from aphrodisiac herbs. That means you must be careful about diet while taking them, especially avoiding food combinations that inhibit digestion. A daily regimen of breathing and exercise should also be maintained to promote optimum circulation.

Most important of all, aphrodisiacs must be utilized in accordance with Taoist sexual disciplines. Since aphrodisiac prescriptions tonify sexual tissues and increase secretions of sexual hormones, they enhance a man's voluntary control over his sexual apparatus. However, they also make retention of semen and regulation of ejaculation even more vital for a man because they increase the amount of semen lost per ejaculation. On the other hand, when semen is retained under the influence of aphrodisiacs, the amount of essence reabsorbed internally is greater than under normal conditions.

There are, of course, certain powerful aphrodisiac drugs that fulfill all the fond fantasies men harbor about these potions. They are based largely on mineral extracts, including such toxic ingredients as cinnabar, mercury and arsenic, and they do indeed produce 'instant erections' by irritating the urogenital tract and the prostate gland. They are dangerous concoctions long since discredited within the mainstream of Taoist practice, although certain irresponsible renegades still dabble with and dispense them. No such formulas are given here.

As a final warning against such concoctions, consider the fate of Hsi Men-ching, the lecherous hero of the Ming erotic novel *Golden Lotus*, who obtained a powerful aphrodisiac pill from a wandering Taoist alchemist, along with the express warning never to take more than one a day and only to use them while his health was good and his vitality 'flourishing'. Returning home drunk late one night after cavorting all evening with a courtesan at a wine-house, our hero is confronted by Golden Lotus, his angry, sexually voracious Number 6 wife. Dragging him to bed and demanding her due satisfaction, she finds him too drunk and depleted to respond, so she takes out his pouch and pops three aphrodisiac bombs down his throat. Lo and behold, his Yang Implement began to swell and stood straight up, so she eagerly straddled him in the position 'Fish with Scales Conjoined' and sank the Jade Stem in to the hilt. After her third orgasm, he exploded with a powerful ejaculation that, to her amazement, continued unabated. Disengaging herself, she found the Jade Stem spewing semen like a fountain, and when the semen ran dry, blood spurted out in its place, followed by water, and finally by feeble spasms of cold air which drained his very life away. That's why the male ejaculatory duct at the root of the penis is called the Gate of Life and Death, and, though the incident above is fictitious, its message is deadly serious.

Cupid's Cornucopia

If you try the 7-day fast recommended in Chapter 2, you will no doubt notice a marked decline in sexual drive that continues until you resume eating again. In fact, however, what you are experiencing is a rare return to *normal* libido. What we call a 'normal' diet today is chock full of seasonings and other ingredients with aphrodisiac properties, and these provide the libido an artificial boost that is sorely missed when withdrawn.

Take, for example, chocolate, which has become a culinary passion throughout the world in recent years. Why are so many people addicted to a food that ruins the complexion, constipates the colon, makes you fat, gives you headaches, and inflates the budget? Because it contains large amounts of a chemical called phenylethylalamine, a substance produced in the brain when a person is 'in love'. *Cosmopolitan* magazine recently proclaimed chocolate to be one of the top ten aphrodisiacs available in the world today, and at the court of Louis XV it was taken frequently as a sexual stimulant. Yet today, people munch several chocolate bars a day without even knowing why.

Garlic and pepper are common cooking ingredients in most kitchens, East and West, but they are also listed in the Chinese pharmacopeia as potent aphrodisiac foods. Garlic contains aliin, which is a stimulant, and pepper contains myrystin, an even stronger sexual exciter. If you eat a lot of garlic and pepper every day, simply try eliminating both from your diet for a week or two, then observe the results for yourself when you enter the Jade Bedroom without these boosters in your system.

Oysters, long touted in the West as an aphrodisiac, are similarly listed in Chinese medicine. The Chinese say, however, that they must be eaten fresh and raw to have the desired effects. Raw oysters contain a number of active enzymes and hormones, as well as a lot of zinc, a vital trace element that plays a major role in prostate function, which in turn plays a pivotal role in male sexual potency.

And, speaking of the prostate, Chinese men (as well as Turks, Bulgarians and gypsies) have for centuries chewed the humble, inexpensive pumpkin seed as a daily snack to preserve their sexual potency and enhance production of prostatic hormones. Two or three ounces of pumpkin seeds per day will do more than anything else in the world to protect a man's prostate gland from cancer and maintain its functional integrity into advanced age. Raw pumpkin seeds should be part of every Taoist adept's daily diet.

Here again Western medical science agrees with Chinese practice. Dr Marsh Morrison, in his report entitled *Disease Dominating Foods*, attributes the efficacy of pumpkin seeds in promoting prostate function to their rich supplies of unsaturated fatty acids, generous quantities of organic iron and 30 per cent content of the purest, most assimilable protein. All of these substances are vital for prostate function, and Western medicine has established that certain highly purified amino acids, such as those contained in pumpkin seeds, effectively reduce swelling and dysfunction of enlarged prostate glands. Other examples of common foods with aphrodisiac properties, such as cinnamon, nutmeg, saffron and so forth, are listed in Appendix III of Chapter 1 (pages 93–126).

The most potent Chinese aphrodisiacs – other than the dangerous mineral-based compounds alluded to earlier – are derived from medicinal plants and certain animal parts. Sexually tonifying herbs include Chinese wolfberry, Korean ginseng, angelica root, foxglove, cinnamon and licorice. Aphrodisiac ingredients derived from animals include deer horn, red-spotted lizards, sea horses, dried genitalia of male seals and sea lions, tortoise shell, chrysalis of silk worms and dried human placentas. The reason that these latter items are such potent male aphrodisiacs is not, as commonly assumed by sceptics, due to superstitious association of these parts and shapes with the male phallus. The reason is that they are densely packed with vital proteins such as albumins, gelatins and various amino acids that directly stimulate the prostate and enhance semen production. They also contain enzymes, hormones and minerals of vital importance to male potency, including collagen, keratin, lysine, arginine, androsterone, calcium and many others.

Among the dozens of items recommended by Chinese physicians for bolstering male potency, deer horn has always been regarded as the most efficacious. Not just any deer will do. The Chinese attribute the most 'horny' qualities to the Sika deer (cervus sika), a breed that thrives in northeast China. Here's what the great Tang physician Sun Ssu-mo has to say about deer horn in Precious Recipes:

> There is nothing better than deer horn to make a man robust and youthful, to make him tireless in bed, to prevent deterioration of his vitality, and to preserve his facial complexion.

The horns of young deer still covered in velvet have the most potent aphrodisiac properties. Since the horns of young deer are still growing, they are laced through and through with the potent male hormones that control development of male traits, and these hormones are harvested along with the horns. Around the turn of the century, Russian physicians performed some experiments on mice in which they fed Sika horn extract to males. They noted a marked enhancement of sexual potency in those fed with the extract, resulting in a great increase in the frequency and duration of copulation.

Aphrodisiac potions abound in Chinese medical texts and literature. Surely one of the most exotic male aphrodisiacs in the entire Chinese pharmocopeia – and one that is still utilized today by wealthy, well-connected Chinese gentlemen in Taiwan and Hong Kong – employs the Great Libation of the Lower Peak, i.e. the vaginal secretions of young girls, preferably virgins. The man carefully selects and purchases some plump, perfectly formed jujubes (zizyphus jujuba), also known as 'Chinese Dates', which in themselves have aphrodisiac properties. He then arranges with the parents of young girls – for a very stiff fee – to have the jujubes inserted into their vaginas for a specified period of time, after which he returns to take delivery of the now fortified jujubes. Rendered soft and porous by body heat, the jujubes absorb the girl's vaginal secretions – her very 'essence' – which are in turn absorbed by the man when he eats them. Here again we see that there is no end to the inventiveness of the Chinese people when it comes to matters of food and sex, health and longevity.

So dear were aphrodisiac potions to Chinese men that they even wrote verse in praise of their virtues. Here's how the author of the *Golden Lotus* described the special aphrodisiac pill obtained by the hero:

> Swallow this aphrodisiac,
> And wintry nights become springtime mornings.
> Like a hurricane in the boudoir,
> You will sweep away all oncomers.
> Be there two or twelve, five or fifty women,
> Not a single one will be left unsatisfied.
> Yet ever stronger will grow your response,
> With glands nourished and testicles unflagging,
> The Jade Stem rigid and the appetite keen . . .
> If what I claim seems incredible,
> Try feeding this pill to the oldest tomcat.
> Within three days he will rut without pause,
> Within four days he'll chase after dogs and rabbits too.
> His fur will turn from white to black
> And finally he'll keel over dead
> From neglecting to empty his bowels.
> So remember the fate of this cat,
> And don't neglect your bowels
> Due to your passion,
> Nor forget about the icy winds of winter,
> Nor ignore the depleting heat of summer . . .

Florid and fanciful as it may be, this poem does not neglect to advise users of aphrodisiacs to use them sparingly and warns them not to overlook their general health as a result of excessive passion. It also reflects the ambition of men in ancient China to become formidable 'Dragon Lovers' – not so that they could ejaculate more often, but so that they could satisfy 'two or twelve, five or fifty women' sufficiently to release the life-prolonging essence contained in the 'Tide of Yin'.

Springtime in a Bottle

Having clearly established the importance of using Chinese aphrodisiacs strictly within the context of Taoist sexual disciplines, the author is now pleased to present the reader a single effective patent formula that shifts the libido into high gear prior to intercourse, while at the same time serving as a long-term tonic for promoting health and preserving sexual vitality. The recipe is for what the Chinese call 'Medicine Wine' (*yao-jiou*), more aptly known as 'Spring Wine'.

Spring Wine is made by steeping potent medicinal herbs in strong alcoholic spirits for up to a full year, during which time the essential active elements are extracted from the herbs by the spirits. This is one of the most ancient methods on record for preparing Chinese herbal prescriptions, for Chinese physicians discovered long ago that alcohol not only extracts, absorbs and preserves the active ingredients in herbs, but also facilitates their rapid assimilation from stomach to bloodstream, and catalyzes their metabolism in the tissues to which they travel. So fundamental is alcohol to Chinese medicine that the defining element in the written ideogram used to form the words 'medical' and 'doctor' is the symbol for 'wine'.

The formula presented here is based on the personal prescription of the Taoist adept Yang Sen, a retired general from mainland China who lived and practiced Tao in Taipei until his death at age 98 in 1976. His formula represents the 'essence' of many decades of practical experience. The author's own experience with this potion is reflected in a few further refinements to Yang's original formula.

A few pointers must be kept in mind when using this potion. It is most effectively assimilated, circulated and metabolized when taken on an empty stomach. Note that the prescription is a great 'appetizer' for either food or sex and tends to make one hungry for both. Taken as a 'cocktail' just before dinner, it serves as a strong stimulant to the appetite. Taken about half an hour before bed, it perks up the libido, stimulates glandular secretions, enhances blood circulation and flushes the organs with heat and energy. While most formulas for Spring Wine are geared exclusively to male requirements, this one benefits women as well. However, neither men nor women should expect thunder and lightning after downing a shot – just a warm, steady surge of vital energy, a sense of physical well-being and a visceral urge for food and contact with the opposite sex.

Spring Wine is most beneficial to the body as a general tonic during cold winter weather. You may take up to 2 or 3 ounces a day to stoke up your internal 'furnace' in winter. During spring and autumn and on mild summer days, about 1½ ounces is the correct measure. On extremely hot and humid days, you should refrain from taking this tonic, because under such conditions the drugs heat up the vital organs at a time when they are trying to expel excess environmental heat. Since the ingredients have strong affinities for the kidneys and suprarenal glands, you'll note a significant increase in volume and frequency of urination after taking it. Many users also report sleeping less and awakening more refreshed than usual after taking Spring Wine.

Never use this or any other potent tonic when you are feeling ill, physically exhausted or emotionally upset. Under such conditions, they will merely give you a brief lift, then hurl you down again with a vengeance. The body and its energy system must be well balanced and in good working order to handle these tonics, extract their potent essence and make 'wintry nights become springtime mornings'. Otherwise, they'll simply overload your system, put a strain on your vital organs and pass through you without bestowing much benefit.

To make Spring Wine at home, obtain the medicinal ingredients listed opposite from a reputable Chinese herbal pharmacy. If you live anywhere near New York, Chicago, San Francisco, Los Angeles, London or Paris, or any other urban center with a sizable 'Chinatown', you'll have no trouble locating a genuine Chinese herb shop. Otherwise your best bet is to have someone purchase the ingredients for you in Hong Kong, where the best Chinese herbs from the mainland are all abundantly available at reasonable prices.

Place all ingredients in a large glass or ceramic vat of 8–10 liter capacity. Pour in 6 liters of brandy, rum or vodka. The most palatable blend seems to be half brandy, half rum. Seal the vat very well and set it aside to steep for three to six months. Give it a few shakes occasionally to help blend the ingredients.

After three to six months (the longer, the stronger), pour out about half the brew and strain it into clean bottles through a funnel lined with several layers of cheesecloth or gauze. Add 3 more liters of fresh alcohol to the remaining brew, re-seal the vat, and set to steep for another three to six months, for a total yield of nine bottles. After the final straining, dump all the solid ingredients into a large collander, set it over a big bowl, and place a heavy rock or other weight on top to squeeze out residual liquor from the herbs. This is the most potent portion.

Sweeten each bottle of Spring Wine with several lumps of crystal rock sugar or 1–2 tablespoons of honey or 1–2 tablespoons of pure fructose syrup, and shake well. Rock sugar gives the potion a slightly viscous texture like liqueur. The sweetners also facilitate rapid metabolism of the herbal extracts contained in the liquor. The strained liquor may look cloudy at first, but after being set aside for a few hours the sediment will all settle to the bottom, leaving a transparent, richly amber potion. It may be stored indefinitely in well-sealed liquor bottles.

Cheers!

Latin botanical name	Common name	Chinese name	Quantity
Cervus sika	Deerhorn shavings	鹿茸	60 grams
Cervus sika	Deerhorn resin	鹿膠	60 grams
Equus asinus chinensis	Resin made from the hides of wild black donkeys	阿膠	60 grams
Clemmys chinensis	Resin made from tortoise shells	龜膠	60 grams
Aceranthus sagittatum	Horny Goat Weed	淫羊藿	60 grams
Rehmannia glutinosa	Rehmannia rhizome	熟地黄	60 grams
Astragalus haongtchy	Astragalus root	黄耆	30 grams
Angelica polymorpha	Angelica root	當歸	25 grams
Eucommia ulmoides	Eucommia bark	杜仲	25 grams
Lycium chinense	Chinese wolfberry	枸杞子	25 grams
Ligustrum japonicum	Japanese wax-privet seeds	女貞子	25 grams
Cynomorium coccineum	Cynomorium stems	鎖陽	25 grams
Homo sapien	Dried human placenta	胎盤	25 grams
Panax ginseng (best grade)	Korean ginseng root	人參	15 grams
Rubus coreanus	Raspberry seeds	覆盆子	15 grams
Hippocampus coronatus	Sea horse	海馬	2 each
Phrynosoma cornuta	Red-spotted lizard	蛤蚧	2 each (1 male 1 female)

PART III

The Tao of Longevity

長壽之道

CHAPTER 9:

———————— ◐ ————————

Historical Perspectives on Longevity

> Yellow Emperor: I have heard that men of old antiquity lived
> over 200 years, and that men of middle antiquity lived up to 120
> years. But today men often die before the age of 30. These days,
> so few men are relaxed and at ease with themselves, and so
> many suffer from diseases. What is the reason for this?
> Plain Girl: The reason men die so young today is that they do not
> know the secrets of Tao.
>
> [*Classic of the Plain Girl*]

The Yellow Emperor's lament has a remarkably modern ring, even
though he was speaking 5,000 years ago, at the dawn of Chinese civilization. It seems quite clear by now that the culprit is civilization, which
splits the primordial unity between men and Tao and isolates him from
his roots in nature. If civilization is the cause of poor health and short life,
then it stands to reason that nature is the cure.

The drastic decline in human health and longevity as a result of
civilization is a worldwide phenomenon today. Indeed, the more 'advanced' a society becomes, the shorter grow the lives of its members.

Taoists regard 100 years to be the normal natural lifespan for
humans, and 150 years to be a 'long life'. Advanced adepts of the higher
disciplines have been known to live well over 200 years. If we take nature
as a measure for man and apply the scientific method of analogy, we
discover the logic of the Taoist view. If the current average human
lifespan of 60–70 years were 'normal', that would make mankind the
biggest 'baby' on earth, as far as the ratio of infancy and childhood to total
lifespan is concerned. By the age of 15, when the human body is mature,
people today have already used up 20–25 per cent of their lifespans. On
the other hand, if we calculate human lifespan according to the average
ratio of infancy to longevity in such species as dogs, cats and chimpanzees, we come up with the Taoist standard of 100–150 years.

Taoist adepts rarely reveal their numerical age in years, for they regard this statistic as irrelevant. Instead of counting birthdays, Taoists measure their lives by counting breaths, heartbeats and (for males) ejaculations. They know that when a person's allotted number of heartbeats and breaths expires, his life ends, and therefore they strive to *slow down* the pace of life in order to prolong its span. Those who try to squeeze as much activity as possible into every waking minute will never even come close to the normal human lifespan of 100 years.

Some Enlightening Examples of Longevity

Longevity has always been the first and foremost wish of Chinese people in this life, and their history records numerous instructive examples of individuals who achieved it. References to longevity in China start at the very beginning of Chinese history with the Yellow Emperor, who is said to have lived to the age of 111 after learning the bedroom arts from the Plain Girl. His five immediate successors to the Dragon Throne are said to have lived to the ages of 98, 105, 117, 99 and 100 years respectively. Then of course there is Lao Tze who rode off into the mountains at the advanced age of 160–200 years, according to legend.

Moving into the realm of historical record, we find the great Han Dynasty Taoist physician Hua To, who was executed on trumped up charges by the despot Tsao-tsao just short of his 100th birthday. Hua To attributed his health and longevity primarily to the rhythmic *dao-yin* calisthenics and deep-breathing exercises that he practiced and prescribed so enthusiastically. About a century after Hua To's time, later Han Dynasty annals record the case of an adept named Leng Shou-kang, who lived over 150 years, and another adept named Wu Tzu-tu, who lived to the age of 205. In his case, the enhancement of essence and energy that results from the practice of the Tao of Yin and Yang was cited as his main source of health and longevity.

Moving along to the Tang Dynasty, we meet the greatest Taoist physician of them all, Sun Ssu-mo (AD 581–682), who left us so much valuable advice in his book *Precious Recipes*. Dr Sun stressed the prime importance of taking preventive measures against disease and degeneration early in life:

When a man is young, he usually does not understand Tao. Even if he hears or reads about it, he is unlikely to fully believe or practice it. When he grows old and vulnerable, then he suddenly realizes the significance of Tao, but by then it is often too late, because he is usually too sick by then to benefit from it.

Dr Sun advised a balanced program of nutrition, regular exercise and carefully disciplined sexual intercourse.

Chia Ming was already 100 years old when he presented his book on health, longevity and diet to the founding emperor of the Ming Dynasty in 1368, and he lived another six years after that. His main advice was to scrupulously avoid mixing foods and drinks whose fundamental pharmodynamic natures conflict in the stomach, injure the vital organs and inhibit vital functions. Then, in 1594, we hear from the 'Greybeard of 95 years', who in his memoirs extolls the virtues of sexual intercourse without male ejaculation for promoting health and longevity:

> Though I am now advanced in years, I'm still not tired of sex,
> and I can still satisfy several women in one night.

Such cases of longevity in China continued to appear on record right down to the twentieth century, and even today there are Taoist adepts who, oblivious to an incredulous world, continue to cultivate the Way and attain normal human lifespans exceeding 100 years. In his book *Taoism: The Road to Immortality*, John Blofeld quotes an article that appeared in China's leading newspaper *Ta Kung Pao* in 1939:

> A gentleman of Wan Hsien, Szechuan province, born in the last year of Chien Lung's reign (1796), worked during the final years of the following reign as secretary to the military authorities in charge of the Yangtse River Region. After retirement, he went off to Tibet in search of medicinal plants, disappearing for so long that he was given up for lost. However, in the autumn of 1931, at the age of 135, he returned to his native district where many aged residents recognised him as someone they had known when still very young. Despite his grizzled hair, he looked no more than 50 and had scarcely changed at all.

The mainstays of his longevity program were the rare life-prolonging herbs he gathered in the mountains of Szechuan and Tibet, which required him to spend most of his time outdoors in the strong sunlight and potent *chee*-charged air of high mountains. He is a perfect example of the incisive etymology behind the Chinese ideogram *hsien*, which means 'immortal' and consists of the symbols for 'man' and 'mountain'.

Two living adepts of Tao who have yet to reach their full terms of longevity are Jolan Chang, and the Grand Master of Hua-Shan, tutor to the adept Kuan Saihung. Jolan Chang has adopted Sun Ssu-mo's own personal measure of one ejaculation per 100 coitions. He also practices Taoist nutrition, breathing, exercise and other longevity arts. Now well into his 70s, he writes, 'Often on a Sunday, I make love two or three times in the morning and then go cycling for nearly the whole day, about 20–30 miles, and then make love again before going to sleep'. Lawrence Durrell wrote a charming portrait of this Taoist in his book *A Smile in the Mind's Eye*, published in 1980.

The Wandering Taoist is one of the most detailed and authentic accounts of the training of a traditional Taoist adept ever recorded in English. At the end of the book, author Deng Ming-dao, who has become a disciple of Master Kuan, recounts his first inquiry regarding Kuan's own teacher, the Grand Master of Hua-Shan:

> 'He must be very old,' I said, trying to keep the subject going.
> Mr. Kuan was quiet, reluctant to discuss the matter.
> 'He is,' Mr. Kuan said after a moment of decision. 'He has long white hair and beard and is now 142 years old. He spends his time in meditation.'
> '142! Is that possible?'
> 'Of course. He's a Taoist.'

One of the most remarkable cases of longevity to spill over into the twentieth century is that of the Chinese herbalist and Taoist adept Lee Ching-yuen, who maintained his youthful vigor, sexual potency and perfect health throughout a long, active life. Lee died in 1933, shortly after marrying his 24th wife, and it remains a matter of historical record in China that he was born in 1677, during the early years of the Ching Dynasty. That made him 256 years old when he died, for those who wish to count the years. Lee died with all his own teeth and hair, and those who knew him say that he looked about 50 when he was already over 200.

Lee Ching-yuen left clear-cut guidelines for those who wish to follow his footsteps and emulate his example. He followed three primary rules in his regimen:

1. Never hurry through life. Take it slowly, take it easy, and take your time. He instructed his students to always keep a quiet heart, sit as calmly as a tortoise, walk as sprightly as a bird, and sleep as soundly as a dog.
2. Avoid extreme emotions of all kinds, especially as you grow older. Nothing drains energy from the body as rapidly, nor disrupts the functional harmony of vital organs as completely, as strong outbursts of emotion.
3. Observe a daily physical regimen of exercise and breathing. The duration and intensity of your regimen are not nearly as important as its daily regularity.

In addition, he gave three specific guidelines regarding diet:

1. Do not overeat on hot summer nights. It causes stagnation of blood and energy.
2. Eat extra quantities of nourishing foods on cold winter mornings. It provides the extra essence and energy the body needs to compensate for having to keep warm in cold weather.
3. Adopt a primarily vegetarian diet, supplemented by life-prolonging medicinal herbs.

The herbs Lee recommended most highly were ginseng, whose properties have already been covered in detail, and a little-known herb called *Hydrocotyle Asiatica minor*, a humble member of the pennywort family which grows wild in the tropical marshes of Asia. At the time, most of the Western medical scientists to whom Lee's case came to attention derided his claims to longevity and scoffed at the simple weed he recommended, but an enlightened handful of scientists took him at his word and investigated. The French biochemist Jules Lepine found a potent alkaloid in the leaves and seeds of this plant which has powerful rejuvenating effects on the nerves, brain cells and endocrine system. Professor Menier of the Académie Scientifique near Paris confirmed Lepine's findings in separate studies. In India, the famous guru Nanddo Narian informed his followers that this very same herb contains a vital ingredient that is missing in the general human diet, an ingredient without which it is very difficult to control the rapid decay that leads to premature death. When he gave this teaching, Guru Narian was already 107 years old and in better health than most of his students.

A man who knew Lee Ching-yuen personally, became his disciple and followed his teachings till the end of his days, was the Chinese general Yang Sen, who moved to Taiwan during the Nationalist exodus from the mainland in 1949. Since Lee was a herbalist by profession, Yang naturally learned a lot about life-prolonging supplements from the great master. In addition to the uses of ginseng and pennywort, Lee taught Yang how to prepare the famous Chinese herbal elixir known as 'Spring Wine', Yang's personal formula for which is presented as a special gift to the reader in Chapter 8.

Yang practiced breathing exercises, soft-style Chinese martial arts and the Tao of Yin and Yang. He celebrated all his birthdays in Taiwan by leading a marathon hike up to the 4,000 meter summit of Jade Mountain, the highest peak in Northeast Asia. Because of the rigors of this trek, usually only young people participated, but Yang Sen made it a point of pride to reach the peak first each and every time. Other Taoists in Taiwan attribute his 'early' demise at the age of 98 to the severe pollution of air, water and food in metropolitan Taipei, where Yang had to live after 1949 owing to his many official duties. Had he remained ensconced in the misty mountains of western China, he would no doubt still be alive and practicing Tao.

Many modern Taoists agree that living full time in big polluted cities these days makes it practically impossible to reach the century mark, regardless how faithfully one follows traditional Taoist health regimens. Adepts of yesteryear did not have to contend with sulphur, lead, carbon monoxide and the other highly toxic elements that fill city airs throughout the world today. For example, about 60 *tons* of airborne dust and other particles fall on each and every square mile of New York City *per month*, and New York is not as polluted as many other cities around the world. Nor did pre-twentieth century adepts have to worry about their water being poisoned by industrial wastes, then further toxified by chemical 'purifiers' such as chlorine. The vegetables and fruits they ate were not impregnated with poisonous pesticides and artificial chemical fertilizers. Taoist purification programs do in fact rid the body of accumulated toxins and their pernicious chronic side-effects, but in the big cities of today no amount of practice can keep ahead of the constant toxification of bodily tissues. Under such conditions the body must muster all its essence and energy just to keep clean, which doesn't leave much power over for practicing the internal alchemy of longevity.

Today, Taoist health and longevity regimens can work for you two ways. If you are bound and determined to live and pursue a career in a large city, these regimens will serve you very well as daily preventive care against disease and decay and will help keep your tissue and bloodstream relatively detoxified. As a direct result of adopting these programs, you will live a healthier, happier, fuller life till the very end of your days, although your lifespan will probably not be much longer than the national average.

The other alternative is to go 'all the Way' and live in an environment commensurate with Mother Nature's ways and in complete harmony with Tao. This does not mean you have to retire forever to a mountain cave or enter a remote monastery in Asia. All it means is that, in order to benefit fully from these regimens and maximize your chances of living beyond the century mark, you must live in an environment that does not do constant, unrelenting and permanent damage to your organs, glands, blood, brain and energy systems. Such environments may be found in small towns and suburbs as well as in the mountains and countryside. At the very least, those who wish to cultivate longevity and maintain perfect health must live in an environment with access to clean air, pure water and wholesome, unadulterated food. In addition to environmental purity, such locations also provide the personal privacy, silence and peace of mind that adepts require to cultivate Tao in earnest.

The Tao will work for you either way. The choice is yours.

Comparative World Lifespans Today

Having had a look at how extraordinarily long dedicated adepts of Tao can live, let's take a look at the average lifespans of ordinary people around the world today. According to the 1985 edition of *World Health Statistics Annual*, published by the World Health Organization in Geneva, the current world leaders in longevity for both men and women are Japan, Switzerland and Iceland, with the United States trailing seventh in both categories (see Table 9.1). These figures are based on life expectancy from the day of birth, and therefore do not necessarily reflect better health in adulthood.

Table 9.1 *Comparative world lifespans, 1985*

World rank	Average male lifespan		Average female lifespan	
1	Japan	74.8	Switzerland	80.8
2	Switzerland	73.8	Japan	80.7
3	Iceland	73.4	Iceland	80.6
4	Israel	73.1	Netherlands	79.8
5	Netherlands	73.0	Norway	79.8
6	West Germany	71.3	Australia	79.0
7	United States	70.9	United States	78.4

Japan's top ranking is at least partly due to the fact that Japan currently enjoys the world's lowest infant mortality rate of only 6–8 deaths per 1,000 births. The significance of this figure in calculating overall longevity becomes obvious when you compare the Japanese statistic with the average of 100 deaths per 1,000 births in most of Africa and much of southern Asia.

Still, Japanese lifestyles have certain advantages for longevity. First and foremost is diet. Most of the protein in the Japanese diet comes from fresh raw fish (*sashimi* and *sushi*) and soy bean products. Both sources are virtually fat-free and very rich in a broad range of vital amino acids. Raw fish retains its full complement of active enzymes, which greatly facilitates the digestion and metabolism of the proteins it contains. It is most interesting to note that the ancient Chinese ideogram that the early Japanese people borrowed to denote the term '*sushi*' is none other than *shou*, which means 'longevity'. The Japanese are also very fond of fresh fruits and vegetables. The advantages of the Japanese diet are further reflected in the fact that Japan enjoys the world's lowest rate of death due to coronary heart disease – 47 deaths per 100,000 population.

351

Japanese people also spend a lot more of their leisure time outdoors than Western people do, thereby exposing their lungs and skin to fresh air and their eyes to beneficial ultraviolet radiation from the sun. Japanese homes are generally not centrally heated or air-conditioned, which insures plentiful supplies of vitalizing negative ions, even indoors. The Japanese, having been tutored by ancient Chinese culture, fully understand and accept the importance of *chee*, and today they compensate for its lack in large office buildings, hotels and high-rise apartments by installing negative ion generators to revitalize indoor air. Not only does this practice enhance the energy of indoor air, it also helps purify indoor air of pollutants carried in from outdoors, because negative ions act like mini-magnets to trap and neutralize the big positive ions of pollution. Beyond all the above, Japanese people are avid practitioners of traditional Chinese martial arts, breathing therapy, soft-style calisthenics, acupuncture and herbal medicine, and other health and longevity regimens learned from China about 1,400 years ago.

Until his death at age 120 in February 1986, Shigechio Izumi of Japan was listed in the *Guinness Book of World Records* as the oldest living person on earth. Some of his habits are instructive for adepts of longevity. He attributed his longevity primarily to three factors: a daily regimen of walking and working in his garden; a mainstay diet of fresh vegetables grown in his own garden; and a glass or two of *shochu* (a potent liquor distilled from sugar cane) every day at sunset.

Switzerland's high rank in world longevity may be attributed to several factors. Perhaps most important is altitude. The air at higher altitudes, especially in regions with abundant wind, water and vegetation, is by far the richest in the life-giving negative ion energy of *chee*. Usually such alpine airs are also completely free of atmospheric pollution. Another factor is hygiene: everything in Switzerland from food and water to personal hygiene and public sanitation is kept meticulously pure and clean. Like the Japanese, the Swiss are fond of spending as much leisure time outdoors as possible – summer, autumn, winter and spring – and at those altitudes not only is atmospheric *chee* stronger but so is ultraviolet energy from the sun.

The Soviet Union was not listed in the WHO rankings because accurate statistics from that country are not available. But it is a well-known fact that some of the world's most long-lived people reside within Soviet borders. The most famous are the Hunzas, a tribe in Soviet Turkestan whose members routinely live beyond the age of 100. In addition to lots of fresh vegetables and whole grains, with relatively little meat and dairy products, the Hunzas' mainstay diet includes apricot kernels, which provide the world's richest source of vitamin B17, popularly known as 'laetrile'. This nutrient, banned in the USA because of claims by holistic healers that it can help prevent and cure cancer, is almost entirely missing from Western diets.

Another factor that would influence longevity behind the Iron Curtain is Soviet medical practice. For example, it remains standard procedure in all Soviet hospitals to administer thorough colonics to all patients as soon as they enter the hospital. Until the body is detoxified of the poisons that cause so many chronic ailments, it is pointless to attempt any cure, a fact that is lost on most American physicians. Soviet medical science is also very keen on natural healing systems such as fasting, the 'grape cure', mineral and mud baths, massage, herbs, and so forth. Along with France, the Soviet Union leads the Western world in serious scientific research on the subject of *chee* and its role in human health and longevity.

The situation in America, by contrast, is well documented, and the picture is not so rosy. Despite its claim to be the world's leader in science and technology, the USA ranks only seventh in longevity and about 90th in the overall health of its adult population. It is obvious therefore that science and technology do not hold the keys to health and longevity. If anything, they seem to impair one's chances of living a long, healthy life. In 1900, the United States Public Health Service ranked America as the healthiest place to live of all 93 civilized countries in the world. By 1920, using the same standards, America dropped to second place. By 1978, the last year the US Public Health Service dared to reveal these figures to the public, America had dropped to 79th place!

Yet health 'authorities' throughout the world claim that 'medical progress' has extended human lifespans by 20–30 years since the turn of the twentieth century. Statistics tell us that a person born in America in 1850 could expect to live 38.3 years, *from the moment of birth*. By 1950, a baby born in America had a life expectancy of 68 years from the moment of birth. However, this great leap forward in human lifespan is largely a myth whose benefits are restricted entirely to the first year of life. In 1900, 29 babies out of 100 in America died within the first year of life owing to nature's system of natural selection and 'survival of the fittest'. By 1950, only 5 out of 100 perished in their first year of life. This is of course a wonderful development, but the lifespan of the child who survives infancy and childhood today has improved very little during the past half-century once the child reaches the age of 15. A 40-year-old man in 1950 could expect to live only five years longer than a 40-year-old man in 1850, and this slight improvement is due primarily to emergency life-saving measures, not to better health. A 50-year-old man in 1950 could expect to live only three years longer than a 50-year-old man in 1850, and for 60-year-old men the improvement was a mere 1.7 years. In other words, medical science increased the lifespan of 60-year-old people by less than two years in over a century. Dr Norman Joliffe, in an article published in the 15 September 1955 issue of the *New York State Medical Journal*, writes:

> Although in America the life expectancy at birth is near the best of any civilized country in the world – at the age of 40 life expectancy in America is near the bottom.

What's more, even infants and children no longer enjoy the benefits of 'medical progress' in America: since 1960, the infant mortality rate in the United States has been on the rise again, while cancer has replaced accidents as the biggest killer of American children under 15.

Dr Jean Mayer, nutrition advisor to President Nixon during his reign, reveals the real story about American lifespans. Dr Mayer's studies showed that the USA now ranks 37th in the world for the life expectancy of a 20-year-old man and 22nd for a woman of the same age. This means that the average American college student today cannot expect to live as long or healthy a life as a typical peasant or beggar of the same age in many of the world's so-called 'backward' countries. It is truly ironic that America makes such a big deal of providing 'foreign aid' to many nations where people enjoy longer, healthier lives than donors in America.

The fact of the matter is that a man or woman who made it to the age of 50, 60 or 70 fifty to a hundred years ago had no significantly shorter life expectancy than men or women of the same age today. Furthermore, they enjoyed far better health and vitality than their peers today, who now suffer unprecendented incidence of arthritis, rheumatism, constipation, premature senility and other chronic degenerative conditions. What's the point of living to the age of 80 if the last 20 years are spent confined to a wheelchair, bed or nursing home?

It is important that readers of this book, in order to fully appreciate the Taoist approach to health and longevity, realize that, if they are over 20 years old and living in any industrialized Western country, their chances of living even a foreshortened lifespan of 60–70 years are only slightly better than a person of similar age at the turn of the century. And, without the benefits of a rigorous, regular program of personal health and purification to compensate for ever-growing environmental pollution, your chances of reaching that age with sufficient health and vitality to enjoy it are practically nil.

Today, men and women can no longer rely on public health institutions to protect their health and prolong their lives, for worldwide trends in public health and longevity are clearly on the decline and continue to plunge downward at alarming rates. Instead, you must rely entirely on your self and on Tao, which are, in the long run, the only two things in life you can really be sure of.

The reason that America has one of the highest ratios of doctors to population in the world is not because America is so advanced but because Americans are so sick. The American medical establishment continues to stubbornly reject the validity of any and all alternative health care systems, despite overwhelming evidence that American medicine is losing the battle against chronic disease, rapid degeneration and premature death. But mention the therapeutic benefits and remarkable efficacy of fasting, colonics, breathing and sunlight to your typical American doctor, and he will give you a stern lecture about the dangers of such 'superstitious' practices.

Fundamental Factors in Longevity

Based on our surveys of individual examples of longevity as well as worldwide trends, we can now cull the most vital factors involved in determining human lifespans.

Climate and geography

A 1982 study of longevity in China revealed that of the 3,765 centenarians discovered there, about two-thirds live in remote mountainous regions, far from urban and industrial centers. Tibet, one of the poorest, harshest environments in the world, had an unusually high ratio of centenarians. The mountain-dwelling Swiss, despite their dairy-rich diets, rank second in world longevity. A related factor seems to be climate itself; cooler, drier climates seem to benefit human health and longevity more than hot, humid ones. We may therefore conclude that high altitudes, pure air and cool climates rank among the strongest promoters of human health and longevity.

Diet and nutrition

The 1982 survey of centenarians in China reports that 'They enjoy eating beans and green vegetables, and their calories are mainly obtained from carbohydrates'. Low-fat, low-protein, high-fiber, vegetable-based diets are without doubt major factors in longevity. The diets followed in traditional Taoist hermitages in ancient China were precisely of this sort, and the long-lived Japanese consume a diet of fresh raw fish unadulterated by cooking, supplemented with abundant fresh vegetables and soy bean products.

It seems clear by now that an occasional nip from the bottle also promotes longevity. A 97-year-old woman in Fengyuan, Taiwan, claims that her sound health and long life are due primarily to her daily consumption of one bottle of rice wine, taken in three portions with each meal. Western doctors also agree that moderate daily doses of liquor significantly reduce the risk of heart attacks and strokes in the elderly.

Exercise and breathing

All healthy centenarians list a regular daily regimen of physical exercise as an absolutely indispensable factor in their longevity. In addition to calisthenics, Taoists cite deep breathing as the most important element in their daily exercise regimens.

Pollution and purification

Purification of the body has always been an absolute prerequisite for embarking on the higher spiritual paths of Taoism. People who habitually pollute themselves with indiscriminate eating habits, excessive smoking and drinking, drugs, exposure to polluted air, and so forth are doomed to foreshortened lifespans plagued by chronic disease and discomfort, *unless* they implement strict compensating purification programs.

In this age of clogged colons and chronic constipation, purifying the bloodstream of pollutants picked up from toxic wastes in the digestive tract may be the single most important factor in maintaining good health and promoting long life.

Sex

First of all, it helps to be a woman: 70.5 per cent of the centenarians surveyed in China in 1982, and 80.1 per cent of those in Japan in 1979, were women. With the glaring exception of India, where traditional Hindu society treats women so poorly that their initial genetic advantage of being born female is negated, women throughout the world live five–ten years longer than men. The basic reason for this is women's superior endocrine systems, their superior sexual power and their superior harmony with the rhythms of nature. Men may also extend their lifespans through the cultivation of sexual energy by learning to retain semen during intercourse. This technique not only conserves male vitality, it gives a man the skill and stamina required to help a woman reach the 'high tide' of orgasm, which in turn further bolsters a man's vitality.

In addition to actual intercourse, men may learn other equally important lessons from female sexuality. For example, among the basic secrets of female power is to yield rather than fight, to express rather than suppress emotions, to be patient and tolerant rather than proud and prejudiced, to be flexible rather than rigid, soft rather than hard, more like water than fire.

Life-prolonging supplements

There is no question that, when properly used, certain varieties of herbal and nutritional supplements can significantly prolong life. Most of these supplements work by releasing essence and energy that specifically stimulate vital organs and glands and enhance circulation. However, life-prolonging supplements are only effective when applied within the context of a well-balanced, comprehensive program of health and longevity, including diet and nutrition, exercise and breathing, purification and sexual discipline.

Knowledge and practice of Tao

This would seem to be an obvious factor, but it's more subtle than it seems. Many people gain knowledge of Tao without ever putting it into practice, which is as pointless as going through four years of medical school without ever practicing medicine. 'An ounce of practice is worth a ton of theory'. On the other hand, practicing nutrition or breathing or sexual yoga without clearly understanding the underlying principles that bind them all together is just as pointless as theory without practice. It's sad to think how many people have 'tried' diet *or* exercise *or* heliotherapy *or* whatever happens to be the current health fad and come away from it so bitterly disappointed with lack of results that they subsequently reject the entire field of natural health therapy, returning with renewed passion to their old, conventional, self-destructive habits. In Tao, there are no half-way measures: it's 'all the Way' or nothing.

Unlike so many other things in life, Tao is 'easier done than said', not 'easier said than done'. Indeed, in the very first line of the *Tao Teh Ching* Lao Tze warned us, 'The way which can be spoken is not the real Way'. It is those who *practice* Tao, not those who brag about it, who attain longevity. Lao Tze makes a remark in the *Tao Teh Ching* that speaks on behalf of all accomplished adepts pestered by pointless inquiries from curious dilettantes:

> Those who know do not speak:
> Those who speak do not know.

A man who lives to the age of 150 years does not need to argue in order to prove the validity of the Way of Longevity: his very existence proves the point. As long as the adept never wavers from the Way, his actions will always be correct and his entire life will form a clear reflection of Tao.

Unfortunately, once having found the Way, many people find it so disarmingly pure and simple that they quickly lose interest in it. Cruising along the great highway to health and longevity, which is public and open to all travelers, they are constantly tempted to take the well-advertised by-ways to instant gratification and short-lived pleasures, promising themselves to 'get back on the road again' soon. These exits off the main highway of Tao often turn out to be the traveler's final resting place, for every time he leaves the Way he wastes precious fuel and precious time that could be better spent reaching his ultimate destination. Every time you lose the Way it's harder to muster the energy and discipline to find your way back. Lao Tze was well aware of the problem, and made the point succinctly in the *Tao Teh Ching*:

> Anyone with the least scrap of sense,
> Once he has embarked on the great highway,
> Has nothing to fear as long as he avoids turnings,
> For great highways are safe and easy.
> But men love by-ways.
>
> So long as things are in order at court,
> They let their fields run to weed
> And their granaries stand empty.
> They wear fancy patterns and embroideries,
> Carry weapons and gorge themselves with food and drink,
> Acquiring more possessions than they can use.
> These are the riotous ways of larceny;
> They are not the Great Highway.

CHAPTER 10:

————————— ◉ —————————

The Tao of Nurturing Life

Men of high antiquity knew Tao and patterned their lives on the harmony of Yin and Yang, living in complete accordance with the rhythms of nature. They observed moderation in food and drink, regularity in their daily lives, and they did not recklessly over-strain themselves. Consequently they lived long lives. But people today are different. Their daily lives are irregular, they eat and drink indiscriminantly without knowing what to avoid, and they do not observe moderation. They give themselves over to dissipation, indulge freely in richly flavored foods, ignore the Golden Mean, and are perpetually dissatisfied with what they have. Consequently most men today are ruined before the age of 50.

[Hu Szu-hui]

This passage comes from a medical treatise on the arts of nurturing life written by the court physician Hu Szu-hui and presented to the reigning emperor of China in the year 1330. Its message applies even more to the human condition today than it did then.

Self-pollution has been the biggest bane of human health and longevity ever since civilization seduced man into divorcing himself from his happy marriage with nature. Indiscriminate eating habits, irregular lifestyles and immoderate sexual indulgence go hand in hand with the so-called 'good life' espoused by popular culture throughout the civilized world today. The problem is further aggravated by the pernicious pollution of air, water, food and light by modern commerce and industry. Subtler forms of environmental pollution take their toll as well: noise, crime, stress and myriad messages of misinformation from mass media.

Let's take a look at just one major pollutant that pervades the environments of all modern industrialized countries today – carbon monoxide (CO), the primary poison emitted in automobile and industrial exhaust.

CO has an affinity for human hemoglobin that is *240 times* stronger than that of oxygen. Hemoglobin is the substance in blood designed by nature to carry oxygen from the lungs to the rest of the body. Therefore with every breath of CO-polluted air you take, greedy carbon monoxide molecules 'elbow aside' the beneficial oxygen molecules in the race to attach themselves to the hemoglobin in the blood. This leads to a state of chronic oxygen-deficiency in the blood and in the organs, especially the brain. Unless compensated with rigorous regimens of self-purification, this condition inevitably leads to disease, degeneration and premature death.

Even sunlight is no longer exempt from the ravages of industrial pollution. Over the past 50 years, atmospheric pollution has reduced the overall intensity of solar energy reaching the earth by 10 per cent and has shrunk the amount of life-supporting ultraviolent radiation by 26 per cent, robbing the endocrine system of the ultraviolet energy it requires to function properly.

In the final analysis, though, most of modern man's internal pollution is self-induced. Until he learns to 'clean up his own act' inside, it is not only impossible but also pointless to deal with external factors. The two most severe and common forms of self-pollution today are bad dietary habits and smoking. That makes the lungs and the colon the two most abused organs in the human species. It's interesting to note that, in traditional Chinese medicine, the lungs and the colon are linked as a Yin/Yang pair, which means that any damage to one also has a depressing effect on the other. Both are anatomical extensions of the body's external surface, and thus they form the body's most direct contact with the environmental factors of food and air.

The condition of the typical human colon today is downright shocking, and all one needs to do to be sufficiently 'shocked' into remedial regimens is to fast for one week and watch the festering, impacted wastes that come out. As 94-year-old V. E. Irons states:

> A toxic colon has everything in the world to do with premature aging . . . Poisons from a toxic colon will travel to every part of the body, such as the heart, the brain, the kidneys, and the liver, and age those organs prematurely. It is the toxic filth in our systems which kills us. That is why people age so rapidly today – they are actually rotting and decaying from the inside out.

Pollution and Purification

Anyone who takes a close, unbiased look at what has happened to health and longevity in America since the turn of the twentieth century cannot help but wonder whether 'modern life' is really worth the price. In his *Report on the Health of the Nation*, published in March 1956, Dr Coda Martin revealed the following facts about health in America. Out of 1,000 apparently healthy American businessmen studied, whose average age was 48, only 13 per cent were found to be in sound health and free of debilitating physical defects; 41 per cent suffered from serious diseases that they had not been aware of; while 11 per cent had diseases they were aware of. In other words, over half the sample populace was suffering from severe ailments that they *took for granted* as a 'normal' condition of life.

That's not all. Sixty per cent of the sample complained of chronic, debilitating fatigue, which in Chinese diagnosis is the first and foremost symptom of energy deficiency and imbalance. Recall as well that a more recent US health survey revealed that 49 per cent of all Americans suffer chronic stomach pain, constipation and other gastro-intestinal distress. Dr Martin's report painted an equally grim picture of childhood health in America: 60 per cent of American children aged 6–16 failed a simple physical fitness test, compared with only 9 per cent failure rate for European children of the same age performing the same test. And fully 75 per cent of American teenagers aged 13–19 showed clear signs of serious malnutrition, despite their obesity, pimples, acne and other symptoms of overeating.

This whole mess is a direct result of self-pollution, which in turn comes from a complete lack of respect for body and nature, which in turn grows from ignorance and indifference towards the real facts of life. Of all the myriad species on earth, only the human species feels itself exempt from the laws of nature and therefore breaks those laws with impunity daily. In the long run, however, nature strikes back, breaking her lawbreakers with a vengeance that inevitably surprises them. There is no medicine in the world that can 'cure' the myriad ailments caused by self-induced pollution. Nor can any medicine – natural or synthetic – impart therapeutic benefits to a body polluted with poisons and clogged with festering toxic wastes.

Fortunately, those individuals with sufficient motivation, insight and discipline to take their lives and bodies into their own hands and take full responsibility for their own health and longevity will find a ready and willing ally in the ancient Taoist system of self-cultivation called *yang-sheng-dao*, the 'Tao of Nurturing Life'. It comprises a complete, self-contained system of health and longevity that works on all three levels of existence – essence, energy and spirit. *Yang-sheng-dao* is as relevant today as it was 3,000 years ago and its potential benefits for those who cultivate it are greater today than ever before. *Yang-sheng-dao* includes many different disciplines, but the essential principle is to combat the debilitating, deathly effects of environmental poisons and self-pollution with the rejuvenating, death-defying antidote of personal hygiene and self-purification.

Self-purification of the body is fundamental to all schools of Taoism. Its importance is based on the view that from the very moment of birth we begin to pollute the pristine condition of our body, breath and mind. The purpose of regular regimens of self-cleansing is simply to stay a few steps ahead of the inexorable process of pollution and decay. 'Aging' is not a matter of time alone; it is the *rate* at which we permit our bodies to decay over a period of time. Some people 'age ten years' in a matter of only one year, while others 'don't look a day over 40' at the age of 70. Today, with the natural environment polluted beyond precedence, self-purification has become more important than ever for human health and longevity.

In order to commence the serious business of self-purification, man must first learn to reintegrate himself with nature. The Tao teaches us how to make friends with our bodies and how to re-establish our primordial unity with nature by showing us how to manipulate and master the cosmic formula known to ancient alchemists as the 'Unity of the Triple Equation', i.e. the interplay of essence, energy and spirit. It is important, therefore, for Western people to develop a healthy respect for their bodies prior to embarking on Eastern programs of self-purification and self-cultivation. Without that basic respect, it is difficult to muster the motivation for such self-discipline.

Self-purification must be done by yourself: it cannot be done for you by others. The foregoing chapters have already introduced in detail the various Taoist regimens for self-purification, so let's just briefly review them below, according to daily, weekly and annual programs.

On a **daily** basis, breathing and diet are the front-line defenses against pollution. Daily deep-breathing exercises to purify lungs and blood are especially important for those who smoke and live in big polluted cities. Among the breathing exercises presented, the Bellows is by far the most effective purifier of lungs and blood. Two or three minutes of Bellows breathing performed two or three times a day effectively eliminates residual smoke, dust and other particles from the lungs and thoroughly purges the bloodstream of carbon dioxide, carbon monoxide, carbolic acid and other metabolic wastes. The Bellows should always be followed up with at least a few minutes of deep diaphragmic breathing to restore normal O_2/CO_2 balance in the blood and recharge the lungs and bloodstream with *chee*. Smokers who cannot kick the habit may, in addition to practicing the Bellows, reduce the damage of smoking by restricting the habit to the waning Yin hours of the day (noon till midnight), when atmospheric energy is weak anyway. By abstaining during the waxing Yang hours (midnight till noon) they give their lungs and blood a chance to benefit from the potent *chee* that permeates the atmosphere during those hours.

Diet is the other pillar of daily defense against self-pollution. Even the most wholesome natural foods become nutritionally useless and digestively toxic when consumed indiscriminately without regard for the trophological laws of nature. Therefore, proper food combining is by far the most important dietary rule to follow. In selecting individual items, go for those known to have purifying benefits for the various vital organs, such as fresh raw fruits and vegetables.

It's also a good idea to keep your tongue clean. The tongue is a major absorber of pure *chee* from food and drink, which the tongue detects as 'flavor' and extracts by prolonged contact during ensalivation and mastication of food in the mouth. Ever wonder what happens to the 'flavor' of food chewed for a long time? It is the most volatile element in food, and it can only be absorbed in the mouth. Those who bolt down their food in half-chewed lumps miss not only the flavor but also the purest form of its energy. Many people miss this flavor and energy even if they do chew well, because their overall dietary habits and internal pollution leave a perpetual sticky film on their tongues.

To remove this film from your tongue, simply take an ordinary teaspoon and scrape the tongue's surface from back to front, with the edge of the spoon held against the tongue. You'll find a foamy white or yellow residue in the spoon, which is invisible when spread out over the tongue. This residue clogs the taste buds and leaves a constant sour taste in the mouth. Scrape the tongue clean each time you brush your teeth, and you will not only enhance your tongue's ability to absorb *chee* from food and drink, but you'll also enhance its capacity to savor flavors.

On a **weekly** basis, there are a number of measures you can take to keep self-purification ahead of self-pollution. The neti nasal douche should be done at least once a week. It's also a good idea to take a dose or two of psyllium seed powder once or twice a week to furnish fibrous bulk and serve as an intestinal broom, especially if you don't eat at least 50 per cent raw food in your daily diet. Fasting one day a week is an excellent way to purify the system. You could make it a pure water fast, or an orange juice fast, or a carrot juice fast, or whatever appeals most to your system. If you own a Colema Board, this weekly one-day fast may be greatly enhanced by taking a colonic irrigation or two that day.

On an **annual** basis, there is nothing in the world more important or more effective in this age of pernicious pollution than to go on a seven-day fast, preferably combined with daily colonic irrigations. *Everybody* should do this, *anybody* can, and *nobody* who lives a conventional modern lifestyle can ever hope to achieve optimum health and longevity unless he or she does this. Seven-day fasts cleanse not only the colon and entire alimentary canal, but also the entire body and all of its vital organs, glands and tissues, right down to the individual cellular level. There exists no better way on earth to effect such a thorough purification of the body and such a complete rejuvenation of spirit and vitality.

The Way is there for all to see: all it takes is the will to follow it.

Cultivating the Three Treasures

All three levels of existence – body, breath and mind – are involved in the *yang-sheng* system. People are born in complete harmony with Tao, and during early infancy their Three Treasures are well integrated with nature. Babies eat when hungry, sleep when tired, cry when upset, and smile when happy – all according to internal signals rather than arbitrary schedules. However, as children grow older and learn the artificial habits of civilization, they begin to favor their mental whims at the expense of their bodily needs and gradually lose awareness of their energy systems.

Traditionally, the Taoist arts of nurturing life are divided into two broad avenues: *nei-dan* ('Internal Elixir') and *wai-dan* ('External Elixir'). The Internal Elixir approach focuses primarily on internal energy, and involves deep breathing, sexual disciplines and meditation. The External Elixir method deals mainly with essence, and includes such disciplines as diet and nutrition, physical exercise and life-prolonging herbal supplements. What confounds Westerners is the role of energy and the mind within the biological and physical functions of the body.

External Elixir Approach

We have already discussed diet and physical exercise in detail. The third branch of the external approach is a program of life-prolonging herbal supplements. 'With guidance in the use of herbs', wrote Ko Hung, 'you may achieve longevity, but still you will have to die'.

Life-prolonging supplements only work within the context of a complete, well-rounded Taoist program of nurturing life; otherwise, you'll just be wasting time and money on these products. Before commencing such a program, you must first detoxify your entire system and purify your bloodstream with a seven-day fast, then wash away the foul toxins excreted through the skin.

Furthermore, in order for such supplements to work, your stomach and all other digestive organs must be functioning perfectly, otherwise they cannot extract and utilize the potent elements contained in these supplements. This is an aspect that Western physicians routinely overlook when prescribing strong drugs of all sorts. You must carefully control your diet in order to avoid elements that interfere with the action of the supplements and to favor elements that enhance them. For example, when taking tonic potions such as Spring Wine, you should avoid tea, coffee and other beverages containing caffeine, which neutralizes the therapeutic effects of the potion. When taking herbs for gastric disorders, one must cut beans and seafood from the diet. When taking prescriptions to correct kidney problems, delete chili, alcohol and caffeine, all of which irritate the urogenital canal. You must also regulate your sex life so that you don't dissipate all the extra energy acquired, and you must maintain a daily breathing regimen to help convert essence to energy and circulate it evenly throughout the system.

Last but not least, you must give herbal supplements a fair chance to do their work. Remember, they are natural products, not synthetics, and they require regular measured doses applied over an extended period of time, within a complete regimen of self-purification and overall health care.

Ginseng remains the all-time favorite life-prolonging supplement among Taoist adepts of health and longevity. Lee Ching-yuen, who as a rule ate nothing that grows below the ground, made two exceptions to this dietary rule: ginseng and garlic. Both have already been discussed in detail in previous chapters.

Lee Ching-yuen also recommended a humble weed of the pennywort family as an excellent longevity supplement, and the efficacy of that herb has been confirmed by French medical scientists. Another life-prolonging herb employed for millennia by Taoist recluses is the mysterious 'magic mushroom' known as *ling-jir* (*Porio cocos*), a subterranean fungus that grows near the roots of certain varieties of conifer. Recent research in Taiwan has shown this fungus to be highly effective in reducing and eliminating cancerous tumors in rats and other laboratory animals. The herb is calming, nutritive and detoxifying and is frequently used by elderly Chinese to ward off the symptoms of aging.

In the Western world, where natural medicinal herbs are not generally available for systematic use, by far the best life-prolonging supplements available are the freshly extracted juices of fresh raw fruits and fresh raw vegetables. There are many ways in which raw fruit and vegetable juices promote longevity. First of all, they are chock full of living enzymes, the only nutritional element capable of carrying the vital spark of life (*chee*) into the human system. By providing you with this energy, they save your own vital stores for use in prolonging life. People who live on primarily cooked-food diets waste an enormous amount of energy every day digesting and eliminating stagnant piles of 'dead' food in their systems.

Raw fruit and vegetable juices are the very best source of organic vitamins and minerals, as well as free-floating amino acids, all of which the body requires to replenish dead and damaged cells. By taking them in the form of juice, these elements are available for use within minutes of entering the stomach, rather than the hours required for their digestion in bulk form. These juices also effectively neutralize excessive acidity in the stomach and eliminate the condition known as 'acidosis' in the blood, both of which are caused by eating too many refined sugars and starches, too much animal protein, too much cooked food. Thus, they keep the pH levels in the blood in optimum balance, and proper pH balance (i.e. Yin/Yang balance in blood) is absolutely essential for maintaining natural resistance and immunity and promoting longevity of the whole body and all its parts.

But don't exclude bulk raw fruits and vegetables from the diet. They provide the fibrous bulk the bowels require to keep clean. They sweep through the alimentary canal like a broom, dragging all sorts of toxic debris out with the feces. Once this fiber is cooked, it no longer acts like a broom: cooked fiber loses its texture and becomes more like a wet mop, pushing loose debris out before it but also leaving a lot of slime in its wake.

Internal Elixir Approach

Taoists, of course, take the External Elixir regimens of diet and herbs for granted as the 'normal' way to live. They therefore pay most careful attention to cultivating the subtler but more potent Internal Elixirs.

First and foremost among them is deep abdominal breathing and internal energy control. Deep breathing provides two major benefits simultaneously: up in the nasal passages, head and lungs, deep breathing extracts vital negative ion energy from the air and propels it into the human energy system; down in the abdomen, deep rhythmic breathing gives the vital organs and glands a thorough therapeutic massage, regulates the heartbeat and gives a tremendous boost to blood circulation. All schools of Taoism, Buddhism and Hinduism, without exception, stress the prime importance of correct breathing for health and longevity as well as for spiritual progress, but in the Western world the benefits of proper breathing are virtually unknown.

Sexual intercourse with retention of semen is a uniquely Taoist method of cultivating the Internal Elixir of health and longevity. In tantric Buddhism, sexual intercourse without ejaculation is also practiced by some sects as a highly esoteric and powerful spiritual discipline, but only by very advanced adepts. In Taoist tradition, disciplined sexual relations as a means of cultivating health and longevity are practiced by ordinary men and women in all walks of life, and all that is really required for success on this path is practice. Here too, however, the big point to remember is that, like all the other arts of nurturing life, sexual discipline must be practiced within the overall context of a complete Taoist program of health and longevity and in complete accordance with the spirit of Tao. As Peng Tze put it:

> Unless a man knows the Tao of Yin and Yang, regardless how well he eats and drinks, he will not live to a great age . . . But man has long neglected to cultivate the harmony of Yin and Yang, and therefore his health and vitality are in decline. If only he would apply the Tao of Yin and Yang, he could avoid these ills, recover his health, and embark on the road to longevity.

In a nutshell, cultivating the Three Treasures to promote health and longevity boils down to three basic daily regimens, each of which is governed by two simple rules. If you observe these regimens daily and faithfully follow their rules, you should have no trouble achieving good health and living a long life with your vitality intact:

Diet

• *Rule 1*. Forget everything you ever learned about calories, cholesterol and portion control in food, and remember instead one simple guideline when selecting items of food to eat: favor the fresh over the stale; choose enzyme-active over enzyme-dead food; select more raw and less cooked foods. To benefit fully from raw foods, they must comprise at least 50 per cent of your diet.

• *Rule 2*. Having selected ingredients for a meal according to Rule 1, combine and consume them according to the natural laws of trophology – the science of food combining.

Exercise and breathing

• *Rule 1*. Observe a regular regimen of physical exercise and deep breathing *daily*, at least once a day. Twice a day is preferable, but once a day is indispensable.

• *Rule 2*. Do it *right*. Perform each exercise as correctly as possible each and every time you practice. If time is limited, it is far more beneficial to do one or two exercises correctly and fully, than trying to rush through half a dozen carelessly. Many of the best benefits derived from breathing and physical exercise are invisible and unnoticed during the performance, but cumulative in their long-term therapeutic effects. Slipshod practice negates these benefits.

Sex

• *Rule 1.* Stop treating sex as a toy or a drug, and start regarding it as a powerful method for cultivating and exchanging vital essence and energy. Men should establish a healthy, well-regulated regimen of ejaculation control specifically suited to their age, physical condition, diet and the season, and women should support men in this effort.

• *Rule 2.* Having established a regimen, stick to it! Men have an especially strong tendency to disregard their own established regimens 'under the influence' of sexual passion, particularly when feeling strong and healthy, so women should encourage them to observe their regimens.

The Highway to Health and Longevity

The regimens of self-purification and the pointers on cultivating the Three Treasures outlined above form the framework for the *yang-sheng* system of nurturing life, but *yang-sheng* goes much deeper than the daily disciplines of diet, exercise and sexual relations. *Yang-sheng* is a whole enlightened attitude towards self and nature that can lead to a whole way of life.

For example, emotional control is every bit as important in the Tao of Nurturing Life as ejaculation control and breath control, especially as one grows older. This point cannot be overemphasized, but it is often overlooked. Emotions are pure energy, and emotional 'outbursts' are a pure waste of vitality. When carefully controlled and balanced, emotional expression of internal feelings is a healthy habit, just like any form of energy balance is healthy. But when feelings are repressed and twisted up inside under stress, then permitted to explode in uncontrolled outbursts, enormous amounts of vital energy are lost and specific organs related to specific emotions are severely impaired. All strong emotions cause fundamental biochemical changes in the blood, and the by-products of these reactions can be highly toxic. Anger and fear, for example, cause excessive secretions of adrenalin. When this adrenalin is not utilized for the purpose for which it was intended, i.e. for 'fight or flight', it quickly breaks down to form two toxic by-products, which play havoc with metabolism and other vital functions and pollute the blood-stream.

The most dangerous emotion from the point of view of health is uncontrolled anger, which does untold damage to the liver. The Chinese term for 'get angry' is *sheng-chee*, literally 'to generate energy', a term that clearly identifies emotion with energy. Anger generates and wastes enormous stores of vital energy, as is evident from the fact that temper tantrums always leave people feeling physically depleted and mentally depressed the moment the outburst of energy is spent.

The following passage from an old text entitled *Record of The West Mountain Assembly*, translated by John Blofeld, emphasizes the central importance of emotional equilibrium:

> Sorrow and melancholy are harmful. Ready anger is harmful. Excessive affection for loved ones is harmful. Forever engaging in field sports is harmful. Spending time on idle gossip and pleasantries is harmful. Drinking copiously and eating oneself into a state of lethargy are harmful. Rushing about until one gasps for breath, doing something with such zeal that serenity is lost, allowing resentment to get out of hand, laughing until tears come to the eyes – all these failures to balance the Yin and Yang are harmful. Those who permit such harm to accumulate throughout the years die young.

Closely related to emotional restraint is the idea of abstention from greed, vice and other activities that distract the mind and disrupt the natural harmony of the Three Treasures. Abstention from the basic vice of wretched excess is an absolute prerequisite, though not a guarantee, of longevity. Abstension and moderation, like detoxification of the bodily tissues, pave the way for other regimens to perform their tasks. As Ko Hung put it, 'One must be moderate in everything'.

Worrying about success in cultivating the Way is also regarded as a form of emotional excess that forms an obstacle to success. Worry is a pointless waste of energy that accomplishes absolutely nothing and only obscures your real goals. Worry reflects indecision, lack of confidence and fear of failure, and it completely disrupts the harmony of body, breath and mind. That's evident from the fact that any kind of worry causes rapid, shallow breathing and freezes the diaphragm into immobility. Yet worry is one of the most difficult emotions to control, especially in this modern age of chronic stress, perpetual dissatisfaction with one's lot and spiritual uncertainty. The point is: either do something or don't, but don't constantly worry about the results. Instead of worrying about money, marriage, fame, success and so forth, the adept of Tao either takes decisive action to obtain them, or else gives them up entirely and turns his attention to more important matters.

On the subject of restraint and moderation as keys to health and longevity, an ancient Taoist maxim sums it up well: 'Those who strive for longevity should maintain the "Four Empties".' The Four Empties form an excellent general guideline for avoiding wretched excess in our daily lives and maintaining mental serenity:

- 'Empty Mind'. Try to keep your mind free of pointless discursive thought, idle fantasy and needless worry, for these are a constant drain on vitality and a form of 'mental self-pollution'. Don't dwell on the past or worry about the future, for these are merely mental excuses for not facing the present and dealing directly with present realities. Try to 'be here now' at all times. The mind, like the body, requires rest, but unlike the body it does not always find the rest it needs in sleep. Keeping your mind free of mental clutter is the best rest you can give it, which is why daily meditation practice is so beneficial to health and longevity. Indeed, 'empty mind' is the very goal of Taoist meditation.

- 'Empty Stomach'. Eat when you're hungry but stop before you're full. One of the quickest paths to the sickbed and the grave is paved by chronically overstuffed stomachs. Gluttony pollutes the entire digestive tract with the toxic by-products of putrefaction and fermentation, and these toxins seep into the bloodstream to pollute the entire body. Eat moderately, and eat in accordance with the two basic rules of diet cited above. If you're not really feeling hungry at a scheduled mealtime, do yourself and your body a tremendous favor and skip that meal entirely.

- 'Empty Kitchen'. If possible, keep only enough food in your kitchen to last two or three days. Large stores of fresh foods kept for longer than three days get stale, spoil, attract rats and roaches, and lose their vitality. The canned, processed, preserved and frozen foods that keep indefinitely will only degrade the overall quality of your entire diet with 'empty calories' and clog your colon with foul, mucus-encrusted toxic wastes. Keeping an 'empty kitchen' motivates you to shop more frequently for fresh foods, to pay more attention to what you eat and how you combine different foods, and to eat less.

- 'Empty Room'. Avoid excessive clutter and noise in your private living quarters, especially the bedroom and the room where you exercise and meditate. Under conditions of constant distraction it is difficult if not impossible to keep body, breath and mind in harmony. The best decorations for private rooms are living plants, which enhance the quality of air in the room and whose appearance brings nature indoors.

Modern man and woman must learn to forego fashion, convenience and modern conventions in order to re-establish their long lost contacts with nature. This does not mean you must entirely give up wearing fashionable clothes, or going to the disco, or eating rich pastries from time to time, but it does mean you must put all these things into proper perspective and re-order your priorities. In order to recover their natural legacy of health, vitality and longevity, modern man and woman must break down the mental barriers that divide their minds from their bodies and their bodies from nature.

China has been civilized much longer than any other nation on earth, and therefore Chinese adepts of Tao have had a lot more time to ponder the problems that civilization poses for human health and longevity. One of the most beneficial popular customs that grew from this concern with longevity is called *deng-gao*, 'ascending to high places'. Throughout the world today, Chinese people still make a point of hiking up high mountains at least once, and often several times, a year to recharge their batteries with the pure and potent *chee* that rises to the top of geographical formations, just as cream rises to the top of milk. In America and Europe, where mountains are plentiful and lie within ready access of most major cities and where people have more leisure time than anywhere else in the world, 'ascending to high places' several times a year is one Taoist longevity regimen that should not be too difficult to follow.

In the final analysis, the most important requirement for nurturing life is knowledge and practice of Tao, with knowledge providing the introduction but practice playing the major role. The inner self, when properly viewed, provides an accurate reflection of Tao, a complete microcosm of the universe. As Lao Tze wrote:

To understand others is to have knowledge;
To understand oneself is to be enlightened.
To conquer others requires strength;
To conquer oneself is even harder.

We can either be our own worst enemies or our own best friends, depending entirely on our *attitude* toward our selves and our *approach* to nature. To *know* this, however, is never enough; one must *act* on the knowledge, *practice* the theory and *conquer* rather than coddle one's own self-destructive habits.

There's one more point to make here. Though the Tao is identical with nature and therefore as obvious as the morning sun, not everyone is able to perceive and practice it. In order to perceive and practice Tao, one must have the *capacity* to do so. Though capacity to perceive and practice Tao may indeed be cultivated, in most cases one's initial reaction to Tao upon hearing about it determines whether or not one will ultimately muster the motivation and discipline to practice it. Lao Tze anticipated this discrepancy among his future readers in the following passage from the *Tao Teh Ching*:

> When a man of high capacity hears Tao,
> He does his best to put it into practice.
> When a man of middling capacity hears Tao,
> He is of two minds about it.
> When a man of low capacity hears Tao,
> He laughs out loud at it.

In the long run, it's the man of high capacity who does his best to put Tao into practice who enjoys the last laugh, for it is he who survives to savor his full measure of health and longevity and muse over the graves of former friends and fellows.

CHAPTER 11:

— ☯ —

'Sitting Still Doing Nothing'

Let the Void be your cauldron; let Nature be your furnace; for your primary ingredient, take stillness; for your reagent, use quietude; for mercury, take your vital essence; for lead, use your vital energy; for water, use restraint; for fire, take meditation.

[*Union of the Triple Equation*]

The alchemical terminology in which the ancient masters couched their teachings has caused all sorts of confusion, as well as downright skepticism, among Western translators and readers. The fact of the matter is that there exists no words to accurately describe what happens during the 'internal alchemy' of deep meditation, which opens up realms of consciousness that lie far beyond the grasp of words and rational thought. Therefore, external alchemy provides a convenient analogy for the manner in which the 'Triple Equation' of essence, energy and spirit unite to form the Golden Elixir of immortality during deep meditation. As Master Chao Pi-chen writes in *Taoist Yoga*:

The generative force changes into vitality when the body is still; vitality changes into spirit when the heart is unstirred; and spirit returns to nothingness because of immutable thought.

There are three basic stages in the internal alchemy of Taoist meditation. Each stage is associated with one of the three vital-energy centers known as the 'Elixir Fields' (*dan-tien*). Master Chao Pi-chen describes these in *Taoist Yoga*:

The lower Elixir Field under the navel is where generative force [essence] is sublimated into vitality [energy]; the middle Elixir Field in the solar plexus is where vitality is sublimated into spirit; and the upper Elixir Field in the brain is where spirit is sublimated for its flight into space.

The first stage of meditation – transmuting essence into energy – may be practiced alone by ordinary adepts without the supervision of a master meditator. At this stage, attention should be focused on the lower Elixir Field during meditation, and the adept should use his breath for a bellows and his mind as a spark to light the fire of internal alchemy there. The second stage, in which energy is transmuted into spirit, requires personal instruction from qualified teachers for complete success, although dedicated practitioners of the first stage may occasionally experience glimpses of the second stage spontaneously. The final stage is achieved by only a handful of the most advanced adepts, after many years of prolonged practice in complete seclusion from the 'dusty world of man'. Such adepts are known as *shen-hsien* ('Immortal Spirits') because they have already developed indestructible spirit-bodies (also called 'diamond bodies'). For them, it is only a matter of time before they discard the flesh like a worn-out robe, enter their shining spirit-bodies for the last time, and soar off to the stars on wings of pure energy.

'Meditation' is a poor English translation for what the Chinese simply call 'sitting still doing nothing' (*ching-jing wu-wei*). The real point of sitting still and doing nothing is to empty the mind entirely of all conceptual thought, and let the spirit abide in emptiness, silence and stillness. Only in that state will the spirit awaken fully and seek its long-lost unity with the Void of pure Tao.

An apt analogy for meditation is tuning a radio receiver to pick up certain radio waves that are on the air all the time but cannot be 'heard' by the ear alone. They can, however, be measured and transmuted into audible sound by running them through a properly tuned and powered radio receiver and amplifier. The human organism also exists on two levels at once: the physical body exists on the level of 'essence' and may be perceived by normal consciousness, while the astral or spirit-body exists on the level of pure energy and can be perceived only by transcendant consciousness. The meditator does not create or 'imagine' what he experiences in meditation any more than a radio receiver creates the music it transmits.

By nature, energy and matter are identical, indivisible, interchangeable. Einstein proved this to the satisfaction of Western science with his famous formula $E=mc^2$. It is man's *mind* that builds conceptual barriers between the realm of pure spirit and energy and the physical phenomenal world. By withdrawing his mind from the external senses of perception (the 'Five Thieves' of meditation), the adept restores the primordial identity of energy and matter, body and mind. Obviously, this identity can only be experienced, not described in words, for it requires an 'altered state of mind' that lies beyond the realm of rational thought and linear logic. 'The way which can be spoken is not the real Way.'

Taoists and Buddhists alike believe that every human is born with a 'precious pearl of original spirit' deep inside the core of his or her being. This precious pearl is a mirror that reflects the entire universe. (As Chao Pi-chen writes, 'When the mind is stilled, the spirit radiates a brilliance that illuminates all the great mysteries of the universe'.) As a child grows older and becomes socialized, this shining pearl gets buried ever deeper in the mental morass of education, obscured by passion and desire, dulled by the dust of illusion, and drowned in the murky waters of discursive thought. It is our most precious possession and our most uniquely human attribute, but owing to our infatuation with the external physical world and its passing phenomena most people go through life without ever realizing its existence, though everyone gets a glimpse of it at the moment of death.

The purpose of meditation is to peel away the layers of illusion, passion and conceptual thought so that the precious pearl of original spirit can fill our consciousness with the lustrous light of cosmic insight. The precious pearl of original spirit is our *one and only* immortal link to the universe. It is the immortal spiritual seed that is released from the flesh at death and replanted in the womb when new life is conceived. It is also the seed of the 'Immortal Spirit', which the most advanced adepts cultivate in their quest for spiritual immortality. By sprouting this seed and cultivating an indestructible spirit-body, such adepts escape the endless cycle of death and reincarnation and soar free forever in the cosmos, with their consciousness intact.

Regardless whether your ultimate goal is to roam forever among the stars or simply to enhance your health and prolong your life on this earth, here and now, the methods of Taoist meditation will greatly accelerate your progress.

The Eight Stages of Internal Alchemy

In practicing the internal alchemy of spiritual enlightenment through meditation, the adept progresses through eight stages of development.

(1) Conservation of essence

'When the oil is used up, the lamp goes out,' says an old Taoist adage, which means 'When semen is exhausted, life ends.' Therefore, the first step on the road to physical longevity as well as spiritual immortality is to conserve semen either through strict celibacy or else through 'dual cultivation', which means sexual intercourse without ejaculation.

(2) Restoration of essence

Semen is conserved and collected in order to restore it to its original state of purity and potency. This is an especially important stage for adepts who previously spent a lifetime squandering their semen in reckless sexual indulgence. Semen is restored through the External Elixirs of diet, herbs and exercise, in alliance with the Internal Elixirs of breathing, meditation and sexual restraint.

(3) Transmutation of essence

Transmutation of essence into energy can occur only after conservation and restoration of semen-essence is complete. Until then, essence is insufficiently pure and potent for transmutation into energy. This transmutation stage requires the perfect stillness of body, breath and mind that can be achieved only through meditation. Breathing plays a vital role at this stage, acting as a gentle bellows to fan the inner fires of internal alchemy.

(4) Nourishing energy

Having learned to transmute essence into energy, the adept is now ready to 'nourish energy', which means accumulating sufficient stores of pure vitality from both external and internal sources in order to completely restore his *yuan-chee*, or 'original vitality'. Man is animated by the same cosmic energy that permeates the entire universe and everything in it, and he may enhance and renew his own individual stores of this energy by learning how to draw upon the great cosmic 'battery' with breath and mind during deep meditation. This stage is indispensable for success in subsequent stages of spiritual cultivation, because those stages require tremendous amounts of energy.

(5) Transmutation of energy

This stage raises the centre of attention from the lower Elixir Field below the navel up to the middle Elixir Field in the solar plexus, where the heat from the fires of essence-to-energy transmutation below rises up to catalyze the transmutation of energy into spirit in the higher centers. At this stage the adept enters the nebulous realm of pure spirit, a realm so fantastic that it makes the alchemy of essence and energy seem like mere child's play. The transmutation of energy into pure spirit involves the opening of certain subtle energy channels that connect the lower and middle Elixir Fields directly with the energy centers located in the brain.

Adepts must learn how to drive their vital-energy into these channels, collect and concentrate it there, then draw it up into the energy centers in the head, where transmutation into pure spirit occurs.

(6) Nourishing spirit

The *Yellow Emperor's Classic* states, 'Nourishing the spirit is the highest task'. Spirit is the divine spark of cosmic radiance planted in all human souls at conception, and it forms the shining light of human consciousness. By nourishing spirit, the adept expands his consciousness and strengthens his direct spiritual bonds with the cosmic powers of Tao. Adepts who reach this stage are those whose ultimate goal is immortality via the indestructible 'diamond body' of pure spirit, which serves as a vehicle for carrying consciousness beyond death. Their sole purpose in cultivating physical health and longevity is to give themselves sufficient time and energy to complete the final stages of internal alchemy required to forge indestructible spirit-bodies.

(7) Transmutation of spirit

An ancient adept known as the 'Master of Celestial Mystery' wrote, 'When the spirit of knowing ceases, then great wisdom is born.' Ordinary human spirit abides within the restricted realm of ordinary knowledge and is bound by words, facts and fancy. True cosmic wisdom transcends all arbitrary human knowledge with direct, overwhelming awareness of Tao. This awareness and wisdom can be achieved only by transmuting ordinary spirit into cosmic spirit, a long and difficult process in which the adept gradually peels away layer upon layer of illusion and sheds ordinary knowledge until he uncovers the precious pearl of original spirit.

This precious pearl of original spirit is the hidden treasure that all adepts of advanced meditation seek within themselves. The moment they find it, ordinary spirit transmutes and merges with it in a spontaneous reaction variously translated into English as 'enlightenment', 'transcendance', or 'liberation'. In Chinese, it's called *wu-dao* – 'to realize the Way' – and it may occur at any time, any place, not just during meditation. There are stories of adepts who first saw the Way in a flash of brilliant insight while chopping wood, working in the garden or squatting down to defecate. Such adepts, having completed Stage 6, live in a perpetual state of stillness and nothingness, regardless of what their physical bodies are doing.

(8) Transmutation of pure cosmic spirit into Void

Taoists refer to this stage as 'return to the Source'. Since an adept who has already achieved pure cosmic spirit has no ego, no personal identity and no mundane desires to bind him to life on earth, he may at the time of his own choosing abandon his material body and leap into the great cosmic Void from where his precious pearl of original spirit came. In so doing, he gains spiritual immortality, although he may also choose to be reborn in this world at the time of his own choosing, if he so desires. Prior to death, such adepts practice for the final leap into space by projecting their spirit-bodies beyond their physical bodies during deep meditation, so that they will be fearless and fully prepared when the final moment arrives.

Everyone has the choice of how to spend his or her life. We may choose to dissipate the Three Treasures of essence, energy and spirit in a brief lifetime of riotous sensual self-indulgence, but then we must face early death and complete personal extinction thereafter. We may also choose a more moderate lifestyle and cultivate the Three Treasures in such a manner that we enjoy a long and healthy life on this earth, leaving the 'afterlife' and the 'next life' up to fate. Or we may gird our loins, steel our minds and discipline our lives for the ultimate goal of forging an inde-structible spirit-body that can carry our consciousness intact into the Void after our physical bodies die.

Western religions promise eternal salvation and spiritual immortality to anyone in exchange for a few simple vows, unquestioning faith, prayer and the observation of rituals. But Taoism and Buddhism teach that individual men and women must *earn* their own salvation and spiritual immortality by their own intensive efforts in this life, just as ordinary men and women must ultimately earn physical health and longevity by their own individual efforts. Cultivating spiritual immortality requires a life-time of hard work, self-discipline and a little luck, with no iron-clad guarantee of achieving the desired results, which is why so few people choose to devote their lives to this path.

This book is concerned primarily with the path of physical health and corporeal longevity, a path that anyone with sufficient discipline and determination can follow by his or her own volition and power. The path to spiritual immortality requires not only a long lifetime of difficult practice, but also the personal guidance of an enlightened master who has already reached that state. Such masters are difficult to find, and it is even more difficult to be accepted as their students. Nevertheless, after intro-ducing a few basic meditation techniques of great practical benefit to ordinary adepts of health and longevity, we will conclude this book on an appropriately cosmic note by taking a brief look at what the 'cosmic astronauts' of Tao experience in their quest for spiritual immortality.

Meditation for Health and Longevity

Even if you're not interested in cultivating spiritual immortality, basic meditation still holds great potential benefits for those who seek health and longevity in this life. 'Sitting still doing nothing' is the one and only way to give your mind a complete rest. During sleep, the body rests and recovers vitality, but the mind wanders off into dreamland, a journey so exciting that it leaves some people tossing and turning all night. Intense dreams and nightmares can be so mentally exhausting that you awaken less rested than before you went to sleep. Even while resting at ease in a chair with eyes closed, the mind roams far and wide, fills with pointless conjectures and vibrates with cerebral static.

Only after you have commenced a regular program of meditation will you begin to appreciate how difficult it is to calm the spirit, silence the incessant internal dialogue that constantly clutters consciousness and tranquilize the 'playful monkey' of mind. However, 30–40 minutes of deep uninterrupted meditation can leave the brain feeling more refreshed than several hours of sleep, make the spirit as clear and bright as a cloudless dawn, and render the churning ocean of mind as serene and placid as an alpine lake on a windless day. Only a clear and placid mind can serve as an inner mirror to reflect the eternal truths of Tao. There is nothing mysterious or magical about such meditation. It is as precise, practical and effective an exercise for the mind as push-ups are for the body and breathing is for energy.

One of the major goals and benefits of meditation for health and longevity is the equanimity it imparts to the spirit. Through meditation one gradually comes to realize that most of the worries that plague us are merely mental illusions of our own creation, with no basis in reality whatsoever, and that most mental stress is the direct result of mental vulnerability, just as physical disease is the result of physical vulnerability.

Meditation provides perspectives on life that are impossible to find elsewhere because meditation creates a *state of mind* in which things are perceived differently from ordinary consciousness. One of those perceptions is the insight that nothing in the world is absolutely good or absolutely bad, completely right or completely wrong. For example, an ordinary person might be totally devastated to wake up one morning and find that he'd been fired from his job. He might even commit suicide. The meditator, however, rather than succumb to stress, would simply smile and take it all in his stride, realizing that this apparently 'bad' event may in fact free him for a 'good' opportunity down the road a way, such as a more interesting job.

The Tao's most basic lesson is that the only permanent thing in life is impermanence, yet we consistently behave as though our blessings as well as our problems were permanent. Meditation teaches the lessons of impermanence and relativity and shows us how to flow with rather than fight the currents of constant change.

Meditation balances energy and harmonizes the Three Treasures under the leadership of spirit. Every time you meditate, you practice putting your mind in charge of body and breath, rather than permitting body and breath to call the shots, as in normal activity. This practice eventually spills over into ordinary activities. For example, you'll find it easier to control your diet and men will find it easier to control ejaculation after commencing the practice of meditation. Regular meditation accustoms body and breath to taking orders from mind and therefore reverses the constant drain on spirit caused by undisciplined loss of essence and energy.

Meditation also puts time into perspective. Most people say, 'I don't have time to meditate – I'm too busy.' These are the same people who spend 2–3 hours in a bar drinking cocktails after work or 5–6 hours watching television every night. Hours spent in this manner fly by like the wind, leaving the mind benumbed with useless fragments of information, distorted images of life and the impression that there really is 'no time to spare'. A mere half an hour of meditation can easily be fitted into even the busiest schedule, and its results inevitably merit the small investment in time. Depending on how successfully the meditator withdraws his mind from conventional consciousness and frees it for a while from its self-imposed morass of mental clutter and arbitrary values, 30 minutes of meditation can seem like 3 hours or 3 minutes.

Meditation is excellent therapy for anyone who suffers from high blood pressure, hypertension, premature ejaculation, indigestion, anxiety and other chronic conditions caused by stress and consequent imbalance in vital functions. Sitting still doing nothing slows down and deepens the pulse of all vital biorhythms, especially those of the heart and respiratory system, which in turn regulate all the others. Meditation gives the Three Treasures and all the vital organs a daily 'tune-up', enhancing their functional harmony and balancing their energies. During meditation, the body and mind relax sufficiently for the vital-energy channels to open up and conduct *chee* to every nook and cranny, every cell and tissue in the body, restoring the organism's overall vitality.

Ladies and gentlemen concerned about their physical appearance might be interested to know that regular meditation makes your face more beautiful. More muscles come into play cracking a smile or furrowing the brow than in throwing a baseball or tossing a chef's salad. In normal consciousness, facial muscles are constantly twitching and flexing, stretching and contracting, in an exhausting, fitful dance that mirrors the restlessness of the mind and the intensity of conflicting emotions. Even in sleep, the face twitches constantly as the mind gets involved in dreams and subconscious thought. Eventually, deep lines and furrows are etched permanently on to the face. Meditation gives the facial muscles a chance to rest and recuperate. As your mind relaxes, you can actually feel your face getting softer, as if it were melting. This feeling is most obvious around the eyes, on the forehead and in the jaw muscles. This complete facial relaxation smoothes out deep lines in the skin and helps iron away the wrinkles around the tensest facial muscles. In order to enhance the rejuvenation of facial muscles during meditation, you should practice a few minutes of the face-stretching and eye-rolling exercises prior to commencing meditation. A few months of such practice will show definite results.

When learning how to 'sit still and do nothing', beginners should bear in mind a few basic practical pointers. The three major points of attention are body, breath and mind, i.e. the Three Treasures of essence, energy and spirit. An ancient text on internal alchemy states: 'Shut off the three external treasures of hearing, sight and speech in order to cultivate the three internal treasures of essence, energy and spirit.' Specific points of attention for practicing meditation include the following:

- The body must be kept perfectly still, stable and balanced. If the full or half lotus is difficult or painful for you, try crossing your legs naturally, or sitting on a firm, low stool (see Figure 3.5, page 159).
- The most important point of posture is to maintain an erect spinal column from the tip of the coccyx to the top of the head. Don't lean forward or back, left or right. Pretend there is a string attached to the crown of your head, pulling it and your entire spine straight upward.
- The back of the neck should be stretched up in a straight line with the spine, with the throat slightly compressed in front to partially constrict the carotid arteries. This will cause head, but not neck, to tilt slightly downward.
- Eyes should be half-lidded – neither fully open nor tightly shut – and aimed unfocused at the floor a foot or two in front of your lap. Closed eyes permit fantasy to arise more readily in the mind, while wide open eyes are easily distracted by external objects.

• Keep the tongue placed firmly against the roof of the mouth, behind the upper teeth. This stimulates secretion of beneficial saliva below the tongue and serves as a bridge for the energy to flow from the end of the Channel of Control in the palate to the top of the Channel of Function in the throat.

• Keep the shoulders slightly rounded and completely relaxed. Rounding the shoulders keeps the rib-cage and thorax relaxed. Avoid the tendency to hunch the shoulders and contract the neck, for this causes muscular tension, which interferes with circulation of blood and energy.

• Don't let the gut hang out in front like a 'pot belly'. Keep the abdominal wall slightly contracted, without excessive effort or tension. The anal sphincter and urogenital diaphragm should also be slightly contracted, without exerting much effort. The point is to keep abdomen, anus and genital orifice slightly contracted to prevent escape of vital-energy. This promotes internal circulation of *chee*.

• Many meditation masters recommend doing the various face-rubs outlined in the long-life exercises in Chapter 4 as a preliminary to meditation. Rub palms together to charge them with *chee*, then use index and middle fingers to rub circles around the eyes and ears and to rub up and down along the sides of the nose. This helps relax the face, which in turn relaxes the mind, and it polarizes the upper terminals of the energy channels to facilitate the rise of *chee* up the spinal channels into the head during meditation.

• Begin your meditation session with a few gentle Bellows breaths to expel stale air from the lungs, followed by a few deep deliberate breaths to warm up your energy channels. Then switch over to the more natural, relaxed Scholar's Breath and try to keep your breathing as smooth, soft, and silent as possible, but without expending deliberate effort on it. Keep your mind focused on your breath.

• Turn your hearing inward to focus on the sounds of breathing and heartbeat. Even when the breath has grown so fine that it is inaudible, continue to focus hearing on it rather than external sounds. You might wish to use ear-plugs at first.

• Do not attempt to 'force' stray thoughts from your mind: the forced mental attempt to empty the mind is a thought and a distraction in itself. Instead, let discursive thoughts and idle fantasies pass through your mind like a freight train, without focusing attention on any of the individual 'cars'. If you simply ignore the stream of thoughts and words, they will eventually get weaker and weaker and grind to a halt for lack of attention. This can take anywhere from 5 minutes to half an hour, depending on how well you control the 'playful monkey' of mind. The 'internal dialogue' must cease entirely before you begin to benefit from meditation. Be patient but firm, relaxed but vigilant, in learning to 'let go' of your mental dialogue. Remember, there is nothing 'to do' in meditation; instead, the point is to 'do nothing', both physically and mentally, and then just relax completely and let whatever happens in your mind happen.

With the above points in mind, let's sit through a session of meditation together. Select a quiet, well-ventilated room where you will not be disturbed. Loosen belt and collar, remove glasses and jewellery, and adopt a comfortable sitting position on a thick, firm cushion. Put a phone book under the cushion for extra elevation if necessary.

Begin by clearing the lungs with a few Bellows breaths and some deep diaphragmic breathing. Stretch the facial muscles and twist the neck back and forth, roll the eyes around in both directions, get the legs comfortably folded. All this preparation takes about 5 minutes.

Now shift into the gentle Scholar's Breath, breathing smoothly and effortlessly through the nose, leave the eyes half-lidded and unfocused, and get the spine in line. Focus attention fully on the breath, paying closest attention to the exhalation stage, which should be slower and longer than inhalation. Don't worry about depth of breath or retention. Let the freight train of thoughts and images clatter by unnoticed as you concentrate attention on the breath.

Those who find it difficult to shift attention away from the 'internal dialogue' and focus on the breath may employ the following method. Mentally count your inhalations, one after the other, from 'one' through 'ten' then start over counting the exhalations from 'one' to 'ten', then back to the inhalations, and so forth. Whenever you lose count, start over at 'one'. This sounds easy, but it's remarkably difficult to go through even two complete counts of ten without losing track. The 'penalty' of having to start over each time you lose track eventually induces your mind to *really* start paying attention to the breath, at which point the internal dialogue simply fades away. After counting three or four sets of inhalations and exhalations alternately, your mind should be sufficiently calm to simply drop the counting and sink silently into the void of 'empty mind'. Maintain that state of mental equilibrium for as long as possible, or until the end of your meditation session, whichever comes first.

As you practice and progress in meditation, you will grow accustomed to ordering your mind to 'shut up' and telling your body to 'sit still', and they will gradually learn to obey. Regular practice decreases the time required to enter the state of 'empty mind' each time you meditate. The longer and the deeper you remain in the silence and equilibrium of 'empty mind', the greater the benefits you derive from your meditation.

After you have fully mastered this first stage of meditation, which usually takes at least five or six months of regular practice, you are ready to start exploring your internal energy systems and experimenting with the Microcosmic Orbit.

The Microcosmic Orbit

The first sign of success in meditation is a feeling of warmth in the region of the navel, or lower 'Elixir Field'. This is the seat of vitality where energy gathers naturally when the body is still and the mind is calm, and when the breath is deep, slow and rhythmic. Other related signs of success are chills or 'goose bumps' running up the spine, tingling sensations in the feet, hands and/or genitals, and waves of warmth flowing like water across the surface of the body. These signs indicate that vital-energy has begun to concentrate and circulate within the body's two most important energy channels, which together form what is known as the Microcosmic Orbit (*hsiao jou-tien*). This is explained as follows by Master Chao Pi-chen in *Taoist Yoga*:

> To transmute the generative force consists of raising it in the Governing Channel from the base of the spine up to the back of the head and into the brain, then lowering it in the Channel of Function to the cavity behind the palate, the throat, the solar plexus, and then to the *dan-tien* under the navel. This is microcosmic orbiting.

Study carefully the Microcosmic Orbit as depicted in Figure 11.1 and memorize the various vital-energy terminals along the way. The Governing Channel (*du-mo*) belongs to Yang and commences at the perineum point (*hui-yin*) midway between anus and scrotum, rises up through the coccyx to the Gate of Life (*ming-men*) directly opposite the navel, then moves up to the Spinal Center (*ji-jung*) opposite the solar plexus, on up to the Extreme Yang (*ji-yang*) point between the shoulder blades, then up into the Great Hammer (*da-chui*) point where the thoracic and cervical vertebrae meet. From there it enters the base of the skull at the Wind Mansion (*feng-fu*) point, moves on up to the crown of the head at the Myriad Confluence (*bai-hui*) point, down between the eyes to the point associated with the pituitary gland and called the Sealed Chamber (*yin-tang*) or 'Third Eye', and finally down to the cavity behind the palate (*yin-jiao*), where it stops. From there it connects with its Yin opposite, the Channel of Function (*ren-mo*), also known as Channel of Conception, which runs down the front of the body.

The Channel of Function receives the energy coming down from the

Governing Channel at a point just below the tongue called the Fluid Collector (*cheng-jiang*). In order to make this vital-energy connection, the tongue must be pressed up against the palate to form a bridge so that the energy may cross the gap between upper and lower jaw. From the tongue the energy drops down to the Pearl Jade (*hsuan-ji*) point at the base of the throat, down to the Central Stage (*shan-jung*) point at the heart, on down to the Central Bay (*chung-wan*) in the solar plexus, onward to the Spirit Shrine (*shen-chueh*) at the navel, into the Sea of Energy (*chee-hai*) below the navel, and finally back down to the Confluence of Yin (*hui-yin*) midway between anus and scrotum, where the energy links up again with the Governing Channel.

At first, simply try to focus your mind internally on these two powerful energy channels and their major staging points. Look for any signs of warmth, chills, tingling or 'opening' along the Microcosmic Orbit, and if you find any, then focus attention on it. Once you have developed a 'feel' for these channels and terminal points, you may eventually progress to the stage of 'using mind to move energy' rather than simply following energy with mind. However, this must be done without excessive mental effort, which tends to tire the spirit and block the breath. Just try to keep the mind as light and empty as possible, while leisurely exploring the inner channels for energy, and above all don't worry about 'results'. It requires many words to describe this in writing, but in actual practice it all occurs spontaneously, non-verbally and totally intuitively. Patience and prolonged practice are the only keys that can open the gates of the Microcosmic Orbit.

Proper manipulation of the eyes and tongue can facilitate opening of the Microcosmic Orbit. The tongue is the bridge that conducts energy across the chasm from palate to throat. There are three positions: directly behind the teeth, mid-palate, and all the way back to the soft rear section of the roof of the mouth. The last position is particularly good for energy circulation. During love-making, partners may intersect their Microcosmic Orbits by touching tongues, and if the man retains his semen they may intercirculate their energies internally. This completes the circuit of 'dual cultivation', causing Yin and Yang energies from man and woman to flow from one partner into the other and back again, with their linked genitals forming the lower terminals and linked tongues the upper terminals of their enhanced Microcosmic Orbits (see Figure 6.1).

As for the eyes, the *Elixir Classic* states, 'Spirit is aroused by rolling the eyes and energy is aroused by breathing.' You may assist the mind in guiding energy by slowly rolling the eyes up in a clockwise direction until they reach '12 o'clock' position, then crossing the eyes and bringing them back down to the inside corners, then rolling them up again in the opposite direction, crossing and bringing them down again, then back up clockwise, etc. As you roll the eyes upward, imagine energy rising up the spinal channel, and as you cross and lower them, visualize energy dropping down from palate to throat to solar plexus to navel.

By coordinating eyes and breath during meditation, spirit and energy are harmonized and the mind gradually gains control over the flow of energy through the Microcosmic Orbit. Master Chao Pi-chen advises the adept to roll eyes up and raise energy during inhalation. However, Master Chao's method involves the breath known as 'reverse abdominal breathing' and should only be cultivated after you have made solid progress in both basic breathing and basic meditation. Many masters recommend drawing energy from the sacrum up the spinal channel and into the head during the exhalation stage, then dropping it down from head to abdomen during inhalation. For beginners, this approach is probably the easier method. The fundamental principle of breath and energy control in deep breathing is, 'During inhalation, energy descends; during exhalation, energy rises.'

The ultimate purpose of circulating energy in the Microcosmic Orbit is to sublimate sexual energy from the loins into spiritual vitality in the head, then drop this enhanced vitality down into the energy center below the navel for storage as pure vitality. Sexual energy is by far the most powerful and pervasive form of *chee* in the human system, male and female. Sexual potency is absolutely indispensable to spiritual progress, for sexual energy is the key to making all breakthroughs on the spiritual path. A sexually weak or impotent person stands no hope whatsoever of reaching the higher stages of spiritual development, because he simply cannot muster sufficient energy. He or she must *first* fully restore his or her sexual vitality through detoxification, proper nutrition, breathing and exercise, and well-regulated sexual intercourse, then use this enhanced sexual potency as a bottomless battery of power to propel the spirit to ever-higher realms of experience on the wings of pure vitality.

Adepts of the Microcosmic Orbit and other advanced practices generally opt for a vegetarian diet in order to avoid the distracting aphrodisiac side-effects of such foods as meat and fish. They also avoid excessively stimulating seasonings for the same reason. Master Chao Pi-chen advises practitioners to 'abstain from the Five Pungent Roots, which are aphrodisiac and increase production of generative fluid'. These roots are garlic, leeks and the three varieties of onion. On the other hand, if you are sexually weak or impotent, it's a good idea to start out by including aphrodisiac herbs and foods in your diet in order to build up sufficient semen and sexual hormones to generate the vitality required for successful meditation. However, it is equally important for such adepts to

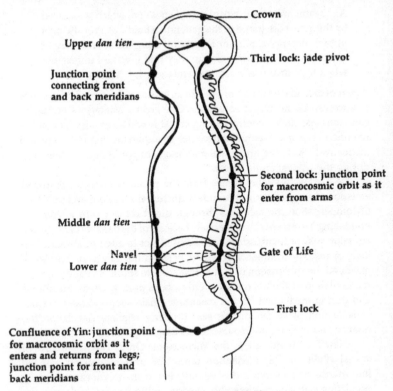

Figure 11.1 **The Microcosmic Orbit**

conserve rather than expend their newfound sources of sexual essence and energy. If they build up their semen and hormones only to indulge in reckless ejaculations, they will end up more impotent than ever. Ordinary people simply let the generative force gradually drain away through excessive ejaculation, nocturnal emissions, sexual fantasies, weak genitals, 'leaky' anal sphincters, etc., until the 'lamp runs out of oil and the light goes out'. Opening the Microcosmic Orbit prevents such loss of vitality through the lower orifices and thereby replaces the process of gradual depletion with the process of gradual accretion.

Regarding nocturnal emissions in men, recall that Sun Ssu-mo and other Taoist physicians stated categorically that nocturnal emissions are by far the greatest threat to male sexual potency and overall physical vitality. Master Chao Pi-chen makes an interesting point regarding 'wet dreams' in *Taoist Yoga*:

All dreams are unreal except that of emission, which is followed by the actual discharge of the generative fluid . . . Worldly men in their dreams acquire or lose many things such as money or objects but when they wake up they find it was all unreal; but when they dream of nocturnal emission, it is always real.

A year of careful cultivation of *chee* can all go down the drain with a series of uncontrolled nocturnal emissions. One great advantage of practicing conscious ejaculation control during actual sexual intercourse is that the retention response eventually becomes so automatic that the adept will instinctively 'lock' the urogenital diaphragm to prevent ejaculation even during the wildest erotic dream.

The danger to vitality comes from the prolonged and uncontrolled emission of semen during involuntary nocturnal emissions and from lack of compensation for such loss through direct contact with a woman's nourishing Yin essence. It is precisely because of the dangers of nocturnal emission that ordinary adepts are advised not to attempt absolute celibacy or absolute continence of semen, at least until they have completely mastered the sublimation of sexual essence into spiritual vitality through manipulation of the Microcosmic Orbit, both during sexual intercourse and during meditation. In the meantime, male adepts should practice conservation of semen during sex, properly regulate ejaculation frequency and prolong intercourse for as long as possible.

A few final words about the Microcosmic Orbit. The importance of sexual vitality in this meditation cannot be overemphasized, nor the importance of preserving this vitality. For men, this means carefully regulating ejaculation, preferably staying within Sun Ssu-mo's measure of two emissions per month, or 24 per year. For women, it means maintaining sufficiently good health to feel sexually vibrant. Men generally cannot awaken the Microcosmic Orbit unless they have at least two or three weeks of semen stored up, and it's virtually impossible within the first few days after an ejaculation. On the other hand, the first few hours after prolonged sexual intercourse without ejaculation is an excellent time to sit still, do nothing and explore the Microcosmic Orbit.

Once you have opened the Microcosmic Orbit, you can practice circulating energy through it any time, any place, under any conditions, simply by using mind and breath in combination. When both partners in a sexual relationship have opened their channels, sexual intercourse takes on dimensions of energy and ecstasy previously unimagined and beyond reach. Such lovers can cause the hot Yang and cool Yin energies to meet and mingle and pass them back and forth via the linked tongues and linked genitals. It takes many years of practice with a loving and understanding partner to reach such heights of alchemy and ecstasy, but the rewards are well worth the effort. Such practice makes long-term mono-gamous relationships far more interesting and satisfying, not to mention far more healthy and life-prolonging, than conventional sexual relations, which not only grow boring over the years but also drain the male of his vital life-force as well as his interest in his partner. But remember, patience and practice are the keys to success, and in the meantime you should focus on the journey, not the goal.

The Macrocosmic Orbit

The Macrocosmic Orbit is the energy circuit formed by the Eight Myste-rious Channels, the two most important of which form the Microcosmic Orbit. Advanced adepts are able to consciously send their energy cours-ing through all eight channels, which completely revitalizes the entire system.

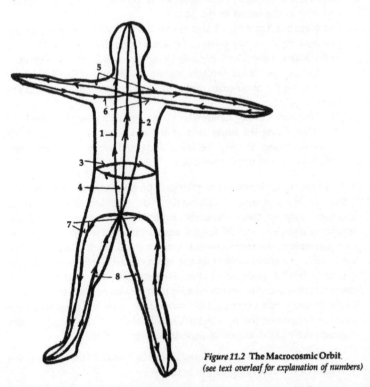

Figure 11.2 **The Macrocosmic Orbit.**
(see text overleaf for explanation of numbers)

The eight channels of the Macrocosmic Orbit run as follows (see Figure 11.2):

1. The Channel of Control or Governing Channel (*du-mo*) rises from the *hui-yin* point midway between anus and scrotum, through the coccyx, and up the spine into the head.
2. The Channel of Function or Conception (*ren-mo*) descends from the cavity behind the palate, down through the throat and heart, to the solar plexus and navel centers, and back to the *hui-yin* point at the perineum.
3. The Belt Channel (*dai-mo*) circles the abdomen from the navel, forming a 'belt'.
4. The Thrusting Channel (*chung-mo*) rises from the perineum point at the root of the genitals up to the heart, then on up to the *bai-hui* point at the crown of the skull.
5. The Positive Yang Arm Channels (*yang-yu*) run from the shoulder blades down the outer sides of the arms, through the middle fingers, and stop in the center of the palms.
6. The Negative Yin Arm Channels (*yin-yu*) run from the center of the palms along the inner sides of the arms to reach the chest.
7. The Positive Yang Leg Channels (*yang-jiao*) run from the perineum point at the root of the genitals, midway between anus and scrotum, down along the outer sides of the legs and ankles to the center of the soles.
8. The Negative Yin Leg Channels (*yin-jiao*) run up from the centers of the soles, along the inner side of the ankles and legs, back to the perineum point midway between anus and scrotum, where they connect with the upper meridians.

The Macrocosmic Orbit is the next stage of progress after the Microcosmic Orbit has been opened. Occasionally, you may feel energy stirring spontaneously in these channels, especially during standing deep-breathing exercises and prolonged sexual intercourse without ejaculation. Generally, however, it takes a long time and much diligent practice for an ordinary adept to open up the Macrocosmic Orbit without special guidance from a qualified teacher. Nevertheless, for those spiritually dedicated and naturally endowed adepts who manage to stir the channels of the Macrocosmic Orbit by their own efforts, here is a deep-breathing exercise recommended by Master Chao Pi-chen for circulating energy through the eight channels of the Macrocosmic Orbit:

- Breathe in to drive the energy along the spinal column through the region of the coccyx up to the brain.

- Breathe out to lower the energy from the throat to the abdomen and return it to the genital region.
- Breathe in to raise the energy from the genital region to the lower abdomen and to the navel, where the Belt Channel starts from both sides of the navel to form a belt. Here the energy divides into two to reach the small of the back, then travels up to the shoulders, where it stops.
- Breathe out to let the energy flow from the shoulders down into the channels along the outer arms to the outer sides of both wrists, to the middle fingers, before reaching the centers of both palms, where it stops.
- Breathe in to lift the energy from the centers of both palms into the channels along the inner sides of the arms up to the chest, where it stops.
- Breathe out to drive the energy down to the Belt Channel, where its two branches reunite below the navel before returning to the genital region.
- Breathe in to lift the energy from the genital region into the Thrusting Channel and raise it up to within 2 inches of the heart. It should not rise above the heart.
- Breathe out to send it from the heart back down to the pubic region, where it divides into two to descend into the two channels on the outer sides of the legs to the toes of the feet, before reaching the center of the soles, where it stops.
- Breathe in to raise the energy from the soles of the feet into the channels on the inner sides of the legs, up to the pubic region and on up to the lower abdomen, where it stops.
- Breathe out to send the energy from the lower abdomen back down into the genital region, where it stops.

Shen-hsien: The 'Cosmic Astronauts'

Shen-hsien ('Immortal Spirits') are truly the 'cosmic astronauts' of Taoism. While ordinary adepts focus on promoting physical health and prolonging corporeal life, Immortal Spirits take a giant step forward and focus on forging indestructible spirit-bodies for their final journey into the cosmos after death. For such advanced and adventurous adepts, meditation paves a highway to the stars. The goal of this fantastic 'flight into space' is spiritual reunion with the vibrant, all-embracing Void of Tao, known as tai-hsü, 'Supreme Void'. This emptiness is not the deep, dark, lifeless vacuum of outer space; it is a bright and shining emptiness, pregnant with the purity of self-existing energy, clear as crystal, luminous as a cloudless dawn. It is still and silent, empty and undifferentiated, the Ultimate Source of everything.

The raw material for forging an adamantine spirit-body is the Golden Elixir (*jin-dan*). As we have seen, this elixir is refined by the transmutation of sexual essence and cosmic energy into pure vitality, which is stored in the lower Elixir Field. While there is no means of measuring this inner elixir during life, it does leave a marvelously mysterious sign of its existence in the cremated ashes of the greatest adepts.

It has been observed and recorded throughout the Orient ever since the death and cremation of Sakyamuni Buddha over 2,500 years ago that the ashes left behind when the bodies of great meditators are cremated contain dozens, and sometimes hundreds or even thousands, of tiny, luminous, indestructible nuggets, called *ssu-lee-dze* ('relic seeds') in Chinese. These little nuggets cannot be broken with hammers or cut with knives. They range in size from a sesame seed to a sunflower seed, are somewhat opaque and glow in various colors. They have baffled skeptics and delighted followers of Tao and Dharma for centuries.

Typically, for lack of a better explanation, Western investigators of this phenomenon discount these nuggets as 'kidney stones'. This is ludicrous, for kidney stones are easily pulverized with a hammer, being nothing more than crystallized inorganic minerals. And if that were indeed the case, the highly accomplished Buddhist monk who died during the early 1950s in Taiwan and whose ashes yielded well over 10,000 nuggets would have had to have kidneys the size of flour sacks. In 1985, a famous Buddhist nun died in Taiwan, and her ashes contained over 2,500 'relic seeds'. These nuggets have *never* been found in the ashes of ordinary people, or in the remains of ordinary adepts, but *only* in the ashes of a handful of the most highly accomplished adepts of the highest spiritual disciplines. Buddhists and Taoists, who share similar meditive methods at the highest levels, explain that these nuggets are formed when the fires of cremation act upon the gross remains of the Golden Elixir which these meditators collect in their lower abdominal energy centers during a lifetime of practice.

The adept of immortal spirit cultivates the Golden Elixir in order to form the 'Immortal Fetus'. The Immortal Fetus is conceived in the adept's 'womb' through the union of spirit (based in the heart) and vitality (based in the lower navel center). This union of spirit and vitality is compared with the cosmic intercourse of Yin and Yang. It is also regarded as a sort of 'internal copulation' of positive Yang and negative Yin energies ('fire' and 'water'), giving birth to the Immortal Fetus in the 'womb' of the solar plexus and navel regions.

The Immortal Fetus is similar in nature to an ordinary fetus. Prior to actual birth, the spirit and vitality of a human fetus in the womb are indivisible. It is only when the umbilical cord is cut and the infant draws his first external breath of air through the lungs that the spirit becomes separated from the source of its own vitality. In other words, the 'fire' of spirit soars upwards to the brain, where it fuels the mind and drives all mental functions, while the 'water' of vitality flows downward to form and fill the sexual organs and energy centers, from where it ultimately drains away through conventional sexual activity after puberty. The adept of Immortal Spirit reverses this process by restoring the primal unity of spirit and vitality through internal alchemy.

Taoist masters refer to an 'Original Cavity of Spirit' located in the very center of the brain, directly between and behind the eyes. This spot, also known as the 'Gateway to Heaven and Earth' and the 'Third Eye', lies precisely in the central brain cavity where the mysterious pineal gland and the all-important pituitary gland are located. Recall that the pituitary is connected directly to the powerful optic nerve, which explains some of the fantastic 'visions' experienced when adepts stimulate this master gland by driving energy into the Original Cavity of Spirit. The basic technique of Taoist meditation is to drive sexual energy up from the genitals and through the sacrum, transmute it into vital energy in the spinal channels, then draw it further up into the head to fill the Original Cavity of Spirit, where the energy is transmuted into pure spiritual vitality.

An old Taoist maxim informs us,

> Without the body, Tao cannot be attained,
> With the body, Truth can never be realized.

What this means is that the highest goal of spiritual immortality can only be reached through the living vehicle of the human body and its powerful vitality. But once the adept has arrived at this goal, he may only realize the ultimate truth by abandoning the body for his final spiritual 'flight into space'. A good analogy here is a chicken embryo growing inside its eggshell. If the shell breaks before incubation is complete, there is no life; similarly, if an adept's body 'breaks' and dies before he has completed 'incubation' of his spirit-body, he loses his chance of spiritual immortality after death. When the inner embryo in a chicken egg is fully developed, however, it *must* crack open the shell and discard it in order to live. Similarly, once the adept has fully developed his spirit-body, he *must* abandon the flesh sooner or later in order to let his spirit roam freely in the cosmos. This exit occurs through an actual crack that develops in the sutures on the crown of the skull in such adepts. Only newborn babies and the most advanced adepts have such loose sutures in their skulls.

Prior to death, *shen-hsien* adepts must thoroughly master the highly subtle art of fusing consciousness to their spirit-bodies and projecting them beyond the flesh into space. Taoist health and longevity regimens can enable the tree of the adept's physical body to last for as long as several centuries, but unless the adept uses this time to practice the internal alchemy of spiritual immortality, the golden leaves of his spirit will fade into extinction soon after falling from the tree of life.

The adept of the Golden Elixir of immortality therefore 'rehearses' for his final act of freedom by actually simulating death in meditative trance. He transfers his awareness to his spirit-body, then projects it out into space through an aperture in the crown of the skull which develops as a result of opening the top psychic energy center of the Central Channel. Without such regular rehearsal, his spirit might get 'stage fright' at the crucial moment of death. Such fear would cause his spirit to recoil from the vibrant intensity of the Void, lose its memory and return to one of the cyclic realms of existence for rebirth, like ordinary mortal souls. These rehearsals for death are what is known in Western parlance as 'astral flight'. Masters advise adepts who succeed in conceiving the Immortal Fetus to project and 'exercise' their spirit-bodies once a week for three years in order to 'train' and strengthen them. Like a child, the spirit-body needs time to gradually grow familiar with the worlds around it – the physical, spiritual and other worlds to which only pure spirit has complete access.

Decades of strict discipline and solitary practice profoundly alter the bodies and minds of these 'cosmic astronauts'. The most advanced recluses actually can live on 'wind and dew', i.e. nothing but air and water, for they can derive vitality from these two sources alone. In deepest meditation, their breathing virtually stops altogether, for they are able to absorb cosmic energy directly through the head and skin.

Opening the Central Channel

The actual avenue of egress by which the adept projects his mature spirit-body upward and outward into the void is the Central Channel, which also provides the final boost of energy. The next step on the difficult path chosen by Immortal Spirits is therefore to open up the powerful Central Channel and awaken the eight psychic energy centers that form a sort of cosmic totem-pole from perineum to crown. These energy centers correspond precisely to the 'chakras' of Hindu and Buddhist Kundalini yoga (see Figure 11.3). This highly advanced discipline is called *ling-hsiou* ('Cultivating Spirit') in Chinese and described as follows in *The Wandering Taoist*:

> One of the highest meditations that Saihung learned, the *ling-hsiou* meditation, opened the psychic centers. The body centers, situated in a straight line from the base of the body to the top of the head, had specific healing and spiritual powers. Meditation aimed at bringing the life-force straight up through each of the centers to the crown. Paralleling the Indian Kundalini meditation, the Taoists opened each of the centers until, at the very top, they reached what the Hindus called Samadhi, the Buddhists called Nirvana, and the Taoists called Stillness. Saihung began to practice the attainment of that Immortal Spirit.

The first center, located midway between anus and scrotum is the perineum (*hui-yin*), a sexual center that draws raw energy like a magnet from the adept's own genitals in the case of celibacy, from his partner in the case of 'dual cultivation', and from the earth itself. The next three centers – the sacral, genital and navel centers – are all involved in the

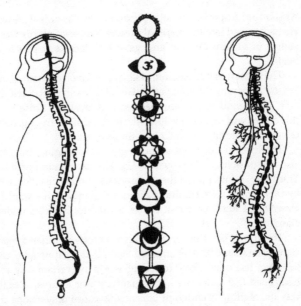

Figure 11.3 **The Central Channel**
Left: Power Points on the Central Channel in Taoist System
Centre: 'Chakras' (power points) on Central Channel in Hindu Kundalini Yoga
Right: Corresponding nerve centers (plexus) in Western physiology

refinement of sexual essence and energy, in sexual reproduction and in storage of vitality. According to Saihung's master in *The Wandering Taoist*, opening these four lower centers entails great dangers for all but the most disciplined adepts:

> The Grand Master warned him that feelings of physical and sexual power would become so strong that he might be reluctant to go on. He said that many adepts remained at these centers, cultivating massive strength and sexuality for all sorts of deviant purposes. When Saihung opened the centers, he found it was true. Deep sexual cravings and the realization that he could develop the power of an almost unbeatable martial artist tempted him and strained his discipline.

These lower centers are the source of the great power used in 'Black Magic' and other sorcery.

The solar plexus center and those above it bring the adept into the calmer realm of spiritual energy. Again, let's follow Saihung's experience as recounted in *The Wandering Taoist*:

> As soon as he opened the solar plexus center, his ordeal ceased. He had passed into the spiritual centers. The solar plexus was a source of vitality for him and gave him increased power to heal . . .
>
> The heart was compassion, skill, appreciation of beauty, and artistry. Opening it developed artistic ability and supported the arts. The Grand Master emphasized that creativity arose from this center and that people like Mist in the Grove, an unusually talented musician, naturally had theirs open.
>
> The throat center, not surprisingly, aided singing, but was also responsible for clairvoyance. Used in combination with the Third Eye, it interpreted the perceptions of other realities seen by that center. Often Saihung did not understand his spiritual experiences until the throat center poured forth verbal understanding.
>
> The upper *dan-tien*, or Third Eye, perceived other dimensions. The Grand Master stressed again that most people, and Saihung, had only agreed to see the world in a certain way and had called that 'existence'. In actuality, it was not real. Reality was the shifting of different illusions, because dimensions co-existed. Using the Third Eye, Saihung could pierce through the illusory world for the meaning behind it . . .
>
> Now he entered his final center. He was on the threshold of a

level that was at once a culmination of many arduous years and the foundation for higher states: the crown center. The thousand-petal lotus bloomed. His senses dropped away. There was no external reality, no internal reality. He felt nothing, thought nothing. He merged completely with voidness.

Death and Immortality

In order to truly understand the nature of life, the nature of the human condition and the meaning of 'immortality,' we must first understand the nature of death, for *death is life's only certainty*. Most people fear and loathe death, and therefore they go through life as though death does not exist and life continues forever. Taoists and Buddhists shatter this common illusion by viewing life as a dream and death as an awakening.

In *Taoism: Road to Immortality*, John Blofeld describes Immortal Spirits, as follows:

> An immortal is one who, by employing to the full all his endowments of body and mind, by shedding passion and eradicating all but the simplest and most harmless desires, has attained to free, spontaneous existence – a being so nearly perfect that his body is but a husk or receptacle of pure spirit. Death, when it comes, will be for him no more than the casting off of a worn robe. He has won to eternal life and is ready to plunge back into the limitless ocean of pure being.

Taoists and Buddhists generally agree that death occurs in four specific stages for all human beings, adepts and ordinary souls alike. The crucial difference is how the spirit reacts to the process of death. First, one loses all sensory contact with the physical world and sinks into a milky white fog that completely engulfs one's awareness. Next occurs a glowing redness that similarly overwhelms the dying person's consciousness. In the third stage, everything turns pitch black, darker than night, so completely and utterly black that even the advanced adept temporarily loses consciousness. At this point the ordinary soul totally blanks out and believes it's all over. But there comes a fourth stage, known in Tibetan parlance as 'the clear light of death', a blinding light that bursts from the absolute blackness of the third stage as suddenly and sharply as a flashbulb. This is the crucial moment that distinguishes the Immortal Spirit from the ordinary layman.

The spirit of the ordinary layman cringes and recoils with fear at this all-embracing light, for never before has it experienced such overwhelm-

ing, awesome, penetrating power. Adepts who experience it in meditation prior to death describe this light as brighter than a hundred suns,
clearer than the clearest crystal, luminous and vibrant beyond imagination. Unprepared for death in the first place, then further frightened by
this sudden explosion of piercing luminosity, the ordinary spirit turns
away and falls into unconsciousness for a few days, after which it
awakens to find itself wandering back on earth, seeking out its former
haunts, thinking it's still alive. It returns to its home only to be ignored by
former friends and family, who are not aware that the spirit of the
deceased is calling to them from 'the other side'. Only after repeated
frustration in trying to communicate with the living does the deceased
spirit finally come to realize that it has died, and the shock of this
realization once again causes it to faint into black oblivion.

Buddhists calculate the hiatus between death and rebirth to last an
average of 49 days, although it can last for many years or just a few days,
depending on the spirit's level of accomplishment and other circumstances at death. During this time the spirit gradually loses personal
memories from its recent sojourn on earth and drifts ever closer to its next
incarnation as a human, animal, ghost, demon, god or whatever its
behavior in former lives merits.

Tibetan Buddhists call the state of limbo between lives the 'bardo'
and the process of merit that determines rebirth is 'karma'. This wheel of
reincarnation turns endlessly, literally 'recycling' the spiritual seeds of
deceased beings over and over, until the individual spirit finally takes
advantage of a human lifetime to cultivate full spiritual realization and
seek its freedom once and for all in the eternity of the cosmic Void, never
to be reborn again in the gross material world.

Immortal Spirits, on the other hand, do not cringe with fear when
facing the clear light of death, for they have already experienced it many
times in their meditations. Thus they seize this precious moment to make
a death-defying leap that transfers their consciousness from the dying
flesh to the indestructible adamantine spirit-body that they have been so
carefully cultivating for this moment. The spirit-body then exits through
the adept's crown and carries the adept's consciousness away on the
wings of his own energy, which, owing to the adept's lifetime of practice,
does not scatter and dissipate at death but instead enters the spirit-body
along with consciousness. The important point here is the spirit's reaction
to the clear light of death. That light itself is like a huge magnet: fear repels
one from it while familiarity attracts. It is the light itself that furnishes the
final boost of power the adept requires to separate spirit from flesh with
consciousness intact. That opportunity comes only once in a lifetime – at
the final stage of the death process. There are no 'second chances', which

is why *shen-hsien* adepts practice so diligently for this moment.

Actually, even the state of spiritual 'immortality' to which *shen-hsien* aspire is limited to several hundred thousand or a few million years at most. During this time, the adept's spirit continues to cultivate itself for ultimate reunion with the Supreme Source of all creation – the Tao itself. This is truly the final step, the end of the line. The spirit merges completely with the vibrant emptiness of the cosmos and, in so doing, consciousness expands like a cloud of rising steam to embrace the entire universe.

What's it like to roam the universe as a 'cosmic astronaut'? Perhaps the best description ever rendered in English is that of Saihung's first celestial journey in *The Wandering Taoist*, a journey that required him to spend several years of intensive daily meditation in complete seclusion deep inside a subterranean cave:

> The Big Dipper came to him. He called it. He willed it.
>
> He entered it, and it lifted him past the highest clouds, through the sleek canopy of the azure sky into blackness. All was dark save the scatter of stars. The universe was night, but day exploded and burned in its folds.
>
> He hung there floating. It was soundless. He had projected the stars into himself and now he himself was projected like a star. He was a body in space. Like a plant. A meteor. A sun.
>
> But there was a deeper state. He still was a body. Why was it here, but not over there?
>
> His body expanded in a silent explosion. His perfect mechanism unwound and shot itself in a thousand directions. The body was gone, but an intention still lingered. A memory, distant and shimmering – a strange streak of individualism still floating in space.
>
> The streak dissipated. Beyond stars, planets, and dimensions, beyond any kaleidoscope of reality, piercing infinite layers. Gone. There was only Nothingness.

Those who wish to join the Taoist 'Space program' and become 'cosmic astronauts' will have to find and apprentice themselves for life to an experienced master of meditation. But be forewarned: it is very difficult to qualify for such training, and the training itself is even more difficult. Perfect health, complete control over one's sexuality and longevity are bare minimum requirements, for without these basic accomplishments human beings lack sufficient energy and time to cultivate the Golden Elixir and conceive the Immortal Fetus within themselves.

Whether you aspire to go 'all the Way' for spiritual immortality or settle for the more modest goal of prolonging your corporeal life in this world, you must first embark on the same path of health and longevity outlined in this book. Once you have mastered the basic Taoist disciplines of harmonizing the Three Treasures and balancing Yin and Yang through diet and herbs, breathing and exercise, sex and meditation, you are already 'on the Way'. How far you travel along that path is entirely up to you, for it is no exaggeration to say, 'The sky's the limit.'

Bon voyage!

Additional Recommended Reading

The following books are recommended to the reader for additional general background and specific information on the various topics covered in this book. This list is a partial bibliography of the major English-language materials used in researching *The Tao of Health, Sex and Longevity*. Periodicals such as technical journals, scientific reports, newspaper and magazine articles are not listed here, but most of those are cited by name and date within the text.

Original materials in Chinese used in research are not listed below, for they are of no use to the general reader of English and they are not available in the Western world.

Taoism in Chinese History

Blofeld, John, *Taoism: The Road to Immortality*, Shambhala, Boulder, 1978.

Blofeld, John, *Taoist Mystery and Magic*, Shambhala, Boulder, 1982.

Deng, Ming-dao, *The Wandering Taoist*, Harper & Row, San Francisco, 1983.

Lin, Yutang, *The Wisdom of China*, Modern Library, New York, 1963.

Needham, Joseph, *Science and Civilization in China* (Vol. II), Cambridge University Press, Cambridge, 1954.

Waley, Arthur, *The Travels of an Alchemist*, Broadway Travelers, London, 1931.

Waley, Arthur, *The Way and Its Power: A Study of the Tao Teh Ching and Its Place in Chinese Thought*, Grove Press, New York, 1958.

Welch, Holmes, *Taoism: The Parting of the Way*, Beacon Press, Boston, 1957.

Wilhelm, Richard and Cary Baynes, *The I Ching, or Book of Changes*, Princeton University Press, Princeton, 1966.

Wu, K. C., *The Chinese Heritage*, Crown Publishers, New York, 1982.

Diet and Nutrition

Abramowski, O. L. M., *Fruitarian Healing System*, Essence of Health Publishing Co., Durban, South Africa, 1976.

Bieler, Henry G. (MD), *Food is Your Best Medicine*, Ballantine Books, New York, 1982.

Bragg, Paul, *Vegetarian Gourmet Health Recipes*, Health Science, Santa Barbara, 1985.

Ehret, Arnold, *Mucusless Diet Healing System*, Ehret Publishing, Beaumont CA, 1922.

Gregory, Dick, *Dick Gregory's Natural Diet for Folks Who Eat: Cookin' With Mother Nature*, Harper & Row, New York 1973.

Hunter, Beatrice, *Consumer Beware*, Simon & Schuster, New York, 1971.

Lust, John (MD), *Raw Juice Therapy*, Thorson's Publishers, Wellingborough, England, 1974.

Null, Gary, *Food Combining Handbook*, Pyramid Publications, New York, 1973.

Shelton, Herbert M. (MD), *Food Combining Made Easy*, Dr Shelton's Health School, San Antonio, 1976 (31st printing).

Szekely, Edmund, *Treasury of Raw Foods*, Academy Books, San Diego, 1973.

Tilden, J. H. (MD), *Food: Its Influences as a Factor in Disease and Health*, Keats Publishing, New Canaan, 1976.

Walker, N. W., *Diet and Salad*, O'Sullivan Woodside & Co., Phoenix, 1985 (23rd printing since 1940).

Walker, N. W., *Fresh Vegetable and Fruit Juices*, O'Sullivan Woodside & Co., Phoenix, 1985 (23rd printing since 1936).

Watson, George (MD), *Nutrition and Your Mind*, Bantam Books, New York, 1972.

Fasting and Excretion

Bragg, Paul, *The Miracle of Fasting*, Health Science, Santa Barbara, 1985 (34th printing).

Brandt, Johanna, *The Grape Cure*, Lust Enterprises, Sini CA, 1967.

Ehret, Arnold, *Rational Fasting*, Lust Enterprises, Sini CA, 1971.

Shelton, Herbert (MD), *Fasting Can Save Your Life*, Natural Hygiene Press, Chicago, 1964.

Walker, N. W., *Colon Health: The Key to a Vibrant Life*, O'Sullivan Woodside & Co., Phoenix, 1979 (15th printing).

Breathing and Exercise

Cheng Man-ching and Robert Smith, *Tai-Chi*, Charles Tuttle Co, Rutland VT, 1966.

Reid, Daniel P., *Chi Gung: Harnessing the Power of the Universe*, Simon & Schuster, London, 1998.

Da Liu, *Taoist Health Exercise Book*, Quick Fox, New York, 1974.

Iyengar, B. K. S., *Light on Yoga*, Schocken Books, New York, 1977.

Lysebeth, Andre van, *Pranayama: The Yoga of Breathing*, Unwin Paperbacks, London, 1979.

Lysebeth, Andre van, *Yoga Self-Taught*, Unwin Paperbacks, London, 1971.

Nakamura, Takashi, *Oriental Breathing Therapy*, Japan Publications, Tokyo, 1981.

Reid, Howard and Michael Croucher, *The Way of the Warrior: The Paradox of the Martial Arts*, Century Publishing, London, 1983.

Chinese Medicine and Therapy

A Barefoot Doctor's Manual (Contemporary Chinese Paramedical Manual), Running Press, Philadelphia, 1977.

Blate, Michael, *The Natural Healer's Acupressure Handbook*, Falkynor Books, Pembroke Pines FL, 1976.

Hsu, H. Y. and C. S. Hsu, *Commonly Used Chinese Herb Formulas with Illustrations*, Oriental Healing Arts Institute, Los Angeles, 1980.

Keys, John, D., *Chinese Herbs*, Charles Tuttle Co., Tokyo, 1976.

Kisaki, Kuniyoshi (MD), *Miracle Korean Ginseng*, Korean Ginseng Research Institute, Korea, 1980.

Mann, Felix (MD), *Acupuncture: The Ancient Chinese Art of Healing*, Heinemann, London, 1971.

Mann, Felix (MD), *Acupuncture: Cure of Many Diseases*, Heinemann, London, 1971.

Mann, Felix (MD), *The Meridians of Acupuncture*, Heinemann, London, 1974.

Needham, Joseph, and G. D. Lu, *Celestial Lancets: A History and Rationale of Acupuncture and Moxa*, Cambridge University Press, Cambridge, 1980.

Ott, John N., *Health and Light*, Pocket Books, New York, 1976.

Palos, Stephan, *The Chinese Art of Healing*, McGraw Hill, New York, 1971.

Read, Bernard E., *Chinese Materia Medica: Animal Drugs* (1931), reprinted by Southern Materials Center, Taipei, 1976.

Read, Bernerd E., *Chinese Materia Medica: Insect Drugs* (1941), *Dragon and Snake Drugs* (1934), *Fish Drugs* (1939), reprinted by Southern Materials Center, Taipei, 1977 (three volumes in one).

Reid, Daniel P., *Guarding the Three Treasures: The Chinese Way of Health*, Simon & Schuster, London, 1993.

Reid, Daniel P., *Handbook of Chinese Healing Herbs*, Shambhala Publications, Boston, 1995.

Stuart, G. A., *Chinese Materia Medica: The Vegetable Kingdom*, American Presbyterian Press, Shanghai, 1911; reprinted by Southern Materials Center, Taipei, 1976.

Veith, Ilza, *The Yellow Emperor's Classic of Internal Medicine*, University of California Press, Berkeley, 1966; reprinted by Southern Materials Center, Taipei, 1977.

Wong, C. M. and L. T. Wu, *History of Chinese Medicine*, National Quarantine Service, Shanghai, 1936; reprinted by Southern Materials Center, Taipei 1977.

Sex

Bieler, Henry (MD), *Dr. Bieler's Natural Way to Sexual Health*, Bantam Books, New York, 1972.

Chang, Jolan, *The Tao of Love and Sex*, Dutton, New York, 1983.

Chang, Jolan, *The Tao of the Loving Couple*, Dutton, New York, 1983

Gulik, R. H. van, *Sexual Life in Ancient China*, E. J. Brill, Leiden, 1974.

Ishihara, Akira and Howard Levy, *The Tao of Sex*, Shibundo, Japan, 1968.

Tavris, Carol and Susan Sadd, *The Redbook Report on Female Sexuality*, Dell, New York, 1978.

Wile, Douglas, *Art of the Bedchamber: The Chinese Sexual Yoga Classics, Including Women's Solo Meditation Texts*, N.Y. University Press, Albany, 1992.

Meditation

Blofeld, John, *Gateway to Wisdom*, Shambhala, Boulder, 1980.

Blofeld, John, *The Tantric Mysticism of Tibet; A Practical Guide*, Prajna Press. Boulder, 1982.

Gyatso, Geshe Kelsang, *Clear Light of Bliss*, Wisdom Publications, London, 1982.

Kongtrul, Jamgon, *The Torch of Certainty*, Shambhala, Boulder, 1977.

Luk, Charles, *Taoist Yoga*, Samuel Wiser, New York, 1970.

Steiner, Rudolf, *A Road to Self Knowledge and The Threshold of the Spiritual World*, Rudolf Steiner Press, London, 1975.

Trungpa, Chogyam, *Cutting Through Spiritual Materialism*, Shambhala, Boulder, 1973.

Trungpa, Chogyam, *Journey Without Goal*, Shambhala, Boston, 1985.

Trungpa, Chogyam, *Meditation in Action*, Shambhala, Boulder, 1972.

Index